The Landscape

Photography Book

Scott Kelby

Author of the top-selling digital photography book ever—*The Digital Photography Book*, part 1

The Landscape Photography Book Team

MANAGING EDITOR
Kim Doty

COPY EDITOR
Cindy Snyder

ART DIRECTOR
Jessica Maldonado

PHOTOGRAPHY
Scott Kelby

PRODUCTION PHOTOS
Scott Kelby
Erik Kuna
Jason Stevens
Dave Williams

PUBLISHED BY

Rocky Nook
1010 B Street, Suite 350
San Rafael, CA 94901

Composed in Univers and Myriad Pro by KelbyOne.

Trademarks
All terms mentioned in this book that are known to be trademarks or service marks have been appropriately capitalized. Rocky Nook cannot attest to the accuracy of this information. Use of a term in the book should not be regarded as affecting the validity of any trademark or service mark.

Photoshop and Lightroom are registered trademarks of Adobe Systems Incorporated.

Warning and Disclaimer
This book is designed to provide information about landscape photography. Every effort has been made to make this book as complete and as accurate as possible, but no warranty of fitness is implied.

The information is provided on an as-is basis. The author and Rocky Nook shall have neither the liability nor responsibility to any person or entity with respect to any loss or damages arising from the information contained in this book or from the use of the discs, videos, or programs that may accompany it.

ISBN-13: 978-1-68198-432-2

10 9 8 7 6 5 4

Printed and bound in Korea
Distributed in the UK and Europe by Publishers Group UK
Distributed in the U.S. and all other territories by Publishers Group West

Library of Congress Control Number: 2018952211

www.kelbyone.com
www.rockynook.com

*This book is dedicated to my dear friend, colleague,
and renowned landscape photographer, Moose Peterson.*

*I've learned so much from him over the years, and
a lot of that made it into this book. Moose was so kind
and patient with me back when I started in landscape
photography that I wanted to create a book that would
honor his legacy of sharing what he has learned with others.*

*I also wanted to dedicate this book to Moose
because he also reminded me what a true friend is.
A few years ago, when it really started raining on me,
Moose was right there holding an umbrella, and that
is something my family and I will never forget.*

Acknowledgments

Although only one name appears on the spine of this book, it takes a team of dedicated and talented people to pull a project like this together. I'm not only delighted to be working with them, but I also get the honor and privilege of thanking them here.

To my amazing wife Kalebra: You continue to reinforce what everybody always tells me— I'm the luckiest guy in the world. I love you with all my heart!

To my son Jordan: I just can't believe my "little boy" is graduating from college. It all happened so fast, but I'm so thrilled for you, and for the many adventures, the fun, love, and laughter your future holds. If there's a dad more proud of his son than I am, I've yet to meet him. #rolltide!

To my beautiful daughter Kira: You are a little clone of your mom, and that's the best compliment I could ever give you. I love your sense of humor, your constant dancing, the hilarious faces you make, and I particularly love when you and I grab lunch or dinner together. I'm so lucky to be your dad.

To my big brother Jeff: Your boundless generosity, kindness, positive attitude, and humility have been an inspiration to me my entire life, and I'm just so honored to be your brother.

To my editor Kim Doty: I feel incredibly fortunate to have you as my editor on these books. In fact, I can't imagine doing them without you. You truly are a joy to work with.

To my book designer Jessica Maldonado: I love the way you design, and all the clever little things you add to everything you do. Our book team struck gold when we found you!

To my dear friend and business partner Jean A. Kendra: Thanks for putting up with me all these years, and for your support for all my crazy ideas. It really means a lot.

To Erik Kuna: Thanks for traveling all over with me to help get the extra shots I needed for this book. Your friendship, ideas, and counsel have made this book much better than it would have been.

To Jeanne Jilleba: Thank you for constantly putting my wheels back on the track. I'm very grateful to have your help, your talent, and your immeasurable patience every day.

To Cindy Snyder: Thank you so much for working on my books and catching tons of little things others would have missed.

To Ted Waitt, my fantastic "Editor for life" at Rocky Nook: Where you go, I will follow, plus I can't part with you until I at least get dinner at Tony's again. #whodat!

To my publisher Scott Cowlin: I'm so delighted I still get to work with you, and for your open mind and vision. Here's to doing new things with old friends.

To my mentors John Graden, Jack Lee, Dave Gales, Judy Farmer, and Douglas Poole: Thank you for your wisdom and whip-cracking—they have helped me immeasurably.

Most importantly, I want to thank God, and His Son Jesus Christ, for leading me to the woman of my dreams, for blessing us with such amazing children, for allowing me to make a living doing something I truly love, for always being there when I need Him, for blessing me with a wonderful, fulfilling, and happy life, and such a warm, loving family to share it with.

About the Author

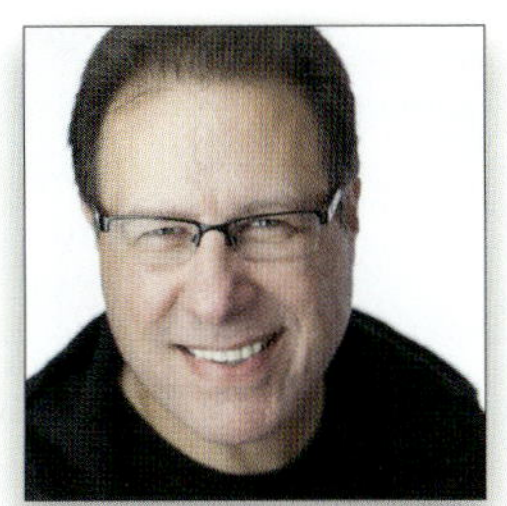

Scott Kelby

Scott is President and CEO of KelbyOne, an online educational community for learning Lightroom, Photoshop, and photography. He is Editor, Publisher, and co-founder of *Photoshop User* magazine; Editor of *Lightroom Magazine*; host of *The Grid*, the influential, live, weekly talk show for photographers; and is founder of the annual Scott Kelby's Worldwide Photo Walk.®

Scott is a photographer, designer, and award-winning author of more than 90 books, including *Light It, Shoot It, Retouch It*; *The Adobe Photoshop Book for Digital Photographers*; *Photoshop for Lightroom Users*; *How Do I Do That In Lightroom?*; *The Flash Book*; and his landmark, *The Digital Photography Book* series. The first book in this series, *The Digital Photography Book*, part 1, has become the #1 top-selling book ever on digital photography.

His books have been translated into dozens of different languages, including Chinese, Russian, Spanish, Korean, Polish, Taiwanese, French, German, Italian, Japanese, Hebrew, Dutch, Swedish, Turkish, and Portuguese, among many others. He is a recipient of the prestigious ASP International Award, presented annually by the American Society of Photographers for "…contributions in a special or significant way to the ideals of Professional Photography as an art and a science," and the HIPA award, presented for his contributions to photography education worldwide.

Scott is Conference Technical Chair for the annual Photoshop World Conference and a frequent speaker at conferences and trade shows around the world. He is featured in a series of on-line learning courses at KelbyOne.com and has been training Photoshop users and photographers since 1993.

For more information on Scott, visit him at:

His daily Lightroom blog: **lightroomkillertips.com**

His personal blog: **scottkelby.com**

Twitter: **@scottkelby**

Facebook: **facebook.com/skelby**

Instagram: **@scottkelby**

Contents

Contents

Chapter 03   **045**

BEFORE YOUR SHOOT

The Art of Prepping for Success

Chapter 04   **059**

COMPOSITION

Framing Is Everything!

Contents

Chapter 05   **081**

HDR & PANOS

Ummm, It's How to Make HDRs and Panos

Chapter 06   **103**

LONG EXPOSURES

The Art of Showing Movement

Contents

Chapter 07   **121**

STARRY SKIES & THE MILKY WAY
Shooting the Heavens

Chapter 08   **145**

POST-PROCESSING
Take Your Images from Flat to Fantastic!

Contents

Chapter 09   **177**

EVEN MORE TIPS

Really, There's More? Yes, More!

Contents

Chapter 10   **197**

LANDSCAPE RECIPES

How to Cook Up Some Tasty Looks

If You Skip These Two Pages,…

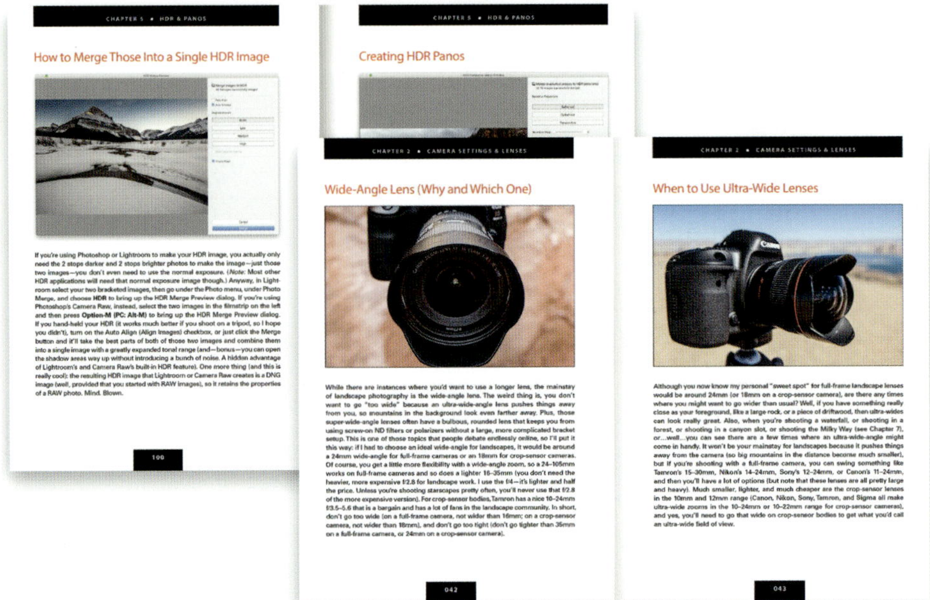

(1) Okay, that headline is a total scam, but it's so important that you read these five things before you read this book that I had to make certain you did, in fact, read them. That's why I wrote a headline that I knew would get your attention, and since you're reading this, it must have worked, so we're off to a great start. Now, what kind of stuff would be so important that if you missed it, it would be bad? Well, if you skipped this, you wouldn't know that there's a special webpage with some videos I created for you that will help you big time. Here's the link to that webpage: **kelbyone.com/books /landscape**. Here are the four other riveting things (stop snickering):

(2) How this book works: Basically, it's you and me together on a shoot, and I'm giving you the same tips, the same advice, and sharing the same techniques I've learned over the years from some of the top working pros. When I'm with a friend, I skip all the technical stuff. For example, if you turned to me and said, "Hey Scott, where am I supposed to focus in this scene?" I wouldn't give you a lecture about hyperfocal distance or depth-of-field zones for acceptable sharpness. I'd say, "Aim your focus point about 1/3 of the way into your image." I'd tell you short and right to the point, so that's pretty much what I do throughout this book.

(3) You don't have to read this book in order. This is a jump-in-anywhere book, so if there's a particular area of landscape photography you want to read first, you can just jump to that chapter and dive right in, no sweat. If you're brand new to all of this, then it would probably be helpful to start up front, because later chapters build on earlier chapters, but you don't have to read it in order.

You Might Damage Your Camera, or Something Worse

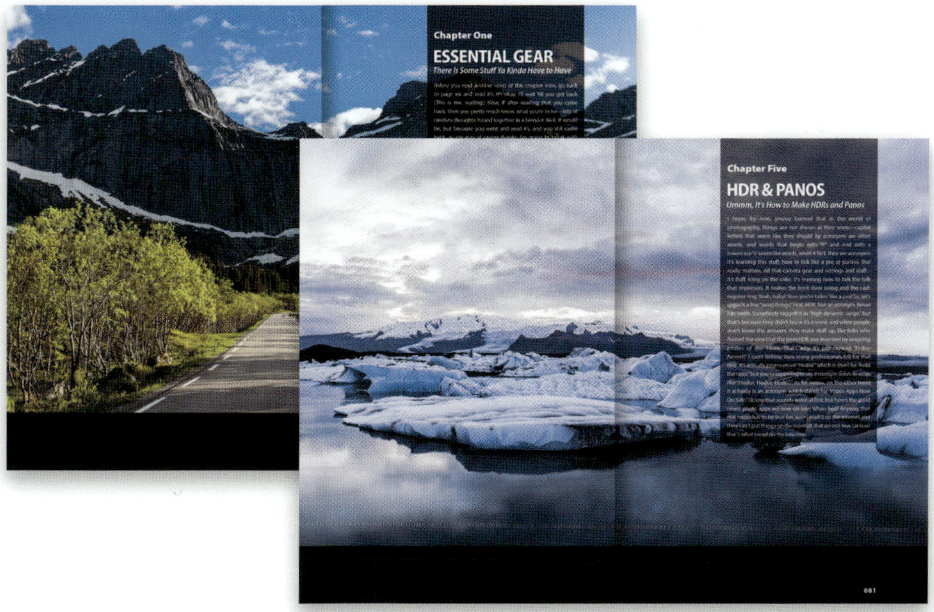

(4) If you're shooting with a Sony, or Olympus, or a Fuji digital camera, don't let it throw you that a Canon or Nikon camera is often pictured. Most of the techniques in this book apply to any DSLR or mirrorless camera, and even many of the point-and-shoot digital cameras, as well. Heck, a bunch will even help if you only shoot with your smartphone's camera. So, don't let brands, makes, or models throw you off—this is about the bigger picture of landscape photography.

(5) Should you read the intro page to each chapter? I have a tradition in all my books that either delights my readers, or sends them into fits of anger. It's how I write the introduction to each chapter. In a normal book, these brief intros would give you some important insight into the coming chapter. But, mine…um…well… don't. These quirky, rambling intros have little, if anything, to do with what's actually in the chapter. They're designed to simply be a mental break between chapters, and a lot of folks really love them (so much so, that we actually published a whole book of nothing but chapter intros from my various books. I am not making this up), however, some "serious type" folks hate them with the passion of a thousand burning suns. Luckily, I've delegated the "crazy stuff" to just those few intro pages—the rest of the book is just straight-to-the-point stuff. But, I had to warn you just in case you're a Mr. Grumpypants, and if that sounds like you, I'm begging you, please just skip the chapter intros altogether. Okay, thanks for taking the time to read these two pages, and now you're ready to launch into this puppy and make the very most of it. Turn the page and let's get to work!

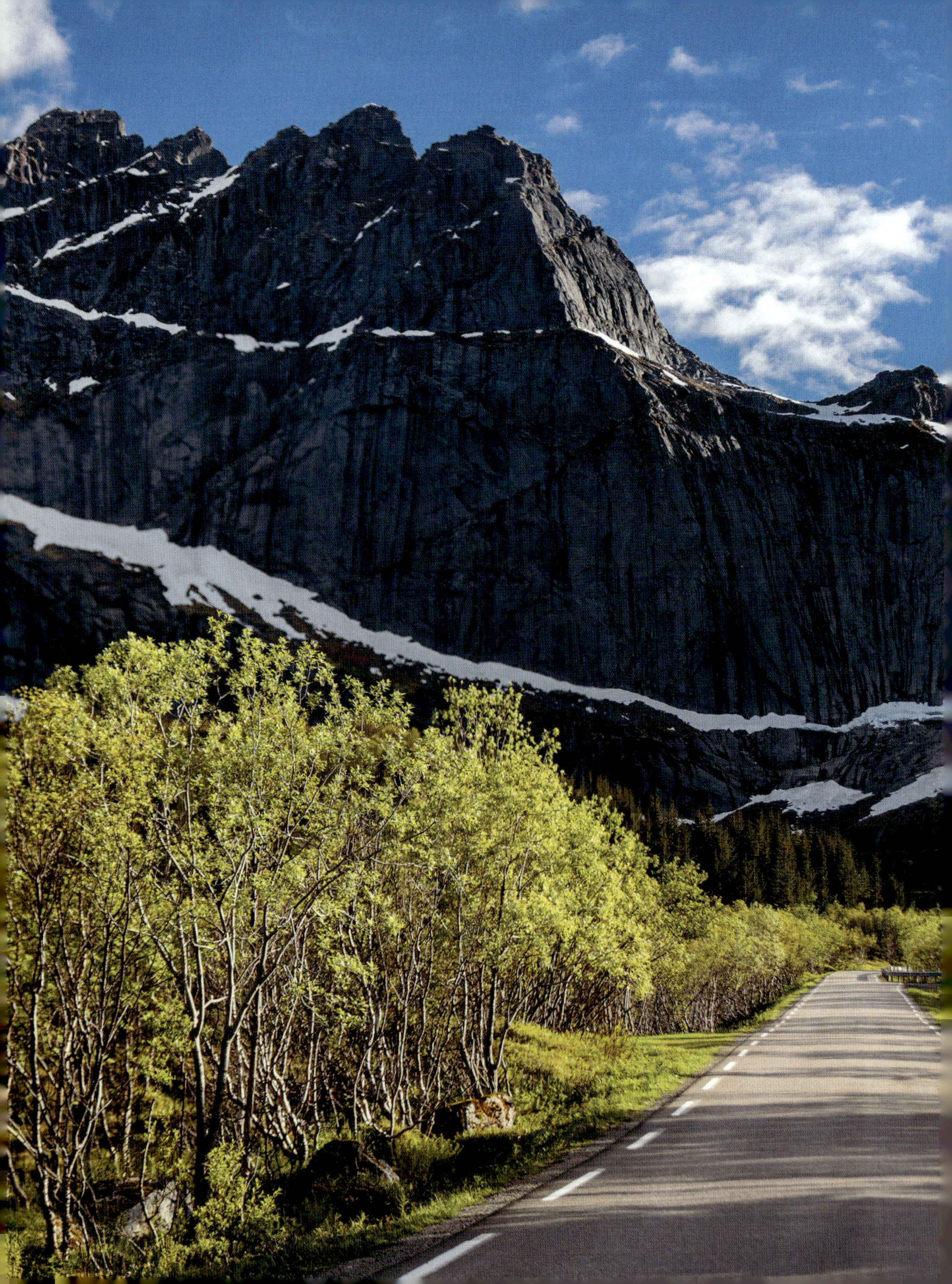

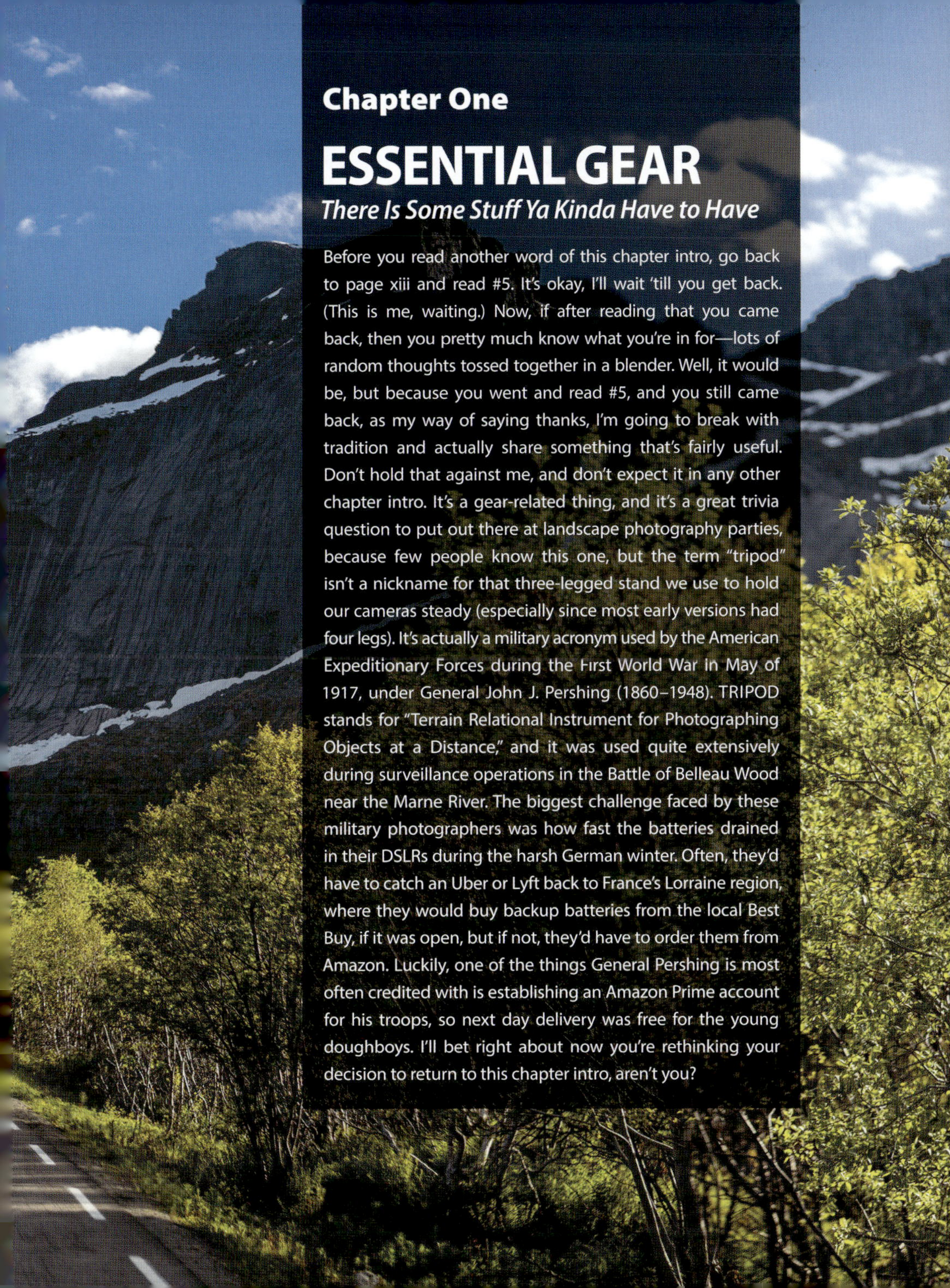

Chapter One

ESSENTIAL GEAR
There Is Some Stuff Ya Kinda Have to Have

Before you read another word of this chapter intro, go back to page xiii and read #5. It's okay, I'll wait 'till you get back. (This is me, waiting.) Now, if after reading that you came back, then you pretty much know what you're in for—lots of random thoughts tossed together in a blender. Well, it would be, but because you went and read #5, and you still came back, as my way of saying thanks, I'm going to break with tradition and actually share something that's fairly useful. Don't hold that against me, and don't expect it in any other chapter intro. It's a gear-related thing, and it's a great trivia question to put out there at landscape photography parties, because few people know this one, but the term "tripod" isn't a nickname for that three-legged stand we use to hold our cameras steady (especially since most early versions had four legs). It's actually a military acronym used by the American Expeditionary Forces during the First World War in May of 1917, under General John J. Pershing (1860–1948). TRIPOD stands for "Terrain Relational Instrument for Photographing Objects at a Distance," and it was used quite extensively during surveillance operations in the Battle of Belleau Wood near the Marne River. The biggest challenge faced by these military photographers was how fast the batteries drained in their DSLRs during the harsh German winter. Often, they'd have to catch an Uber or Lyft back to France's Lorraine region, where they would buy backup batteries from the local Best Buy, if it was open, but if not, they'd have to order them from Amazon. Luckily, one of the things General Pershing is most often credited with is establishing an Amazon Prime account for his troops, so next day delivery was free for the young doughboys. I'll bet right about now you're rethinking your decision to return to this chapter intro, aren't you?

You're Going to Need a Sturdy Tripod

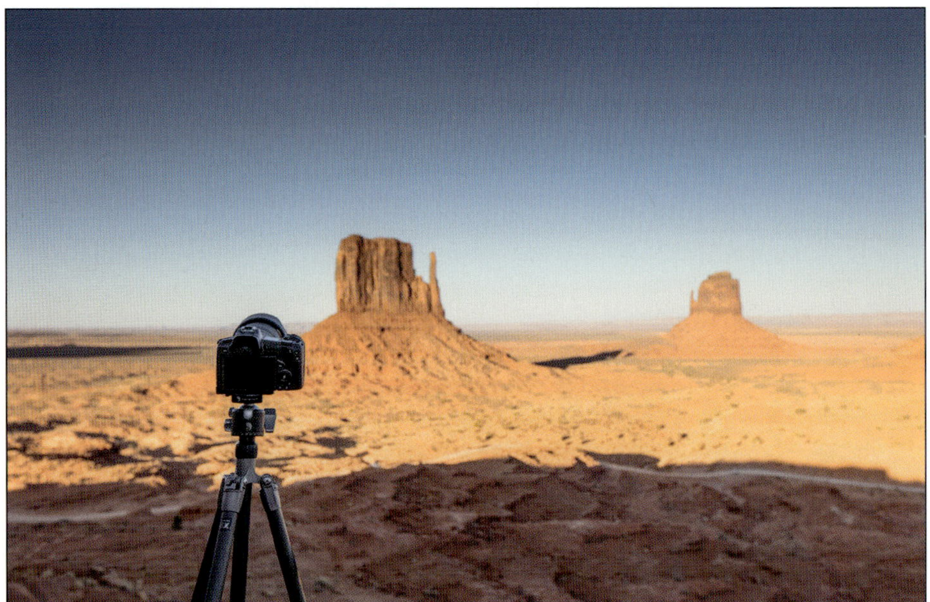

You're going to be shooting in low-light conditions a lot, and your shutter is often going to be open for seconds at a time, so you're going to need a sturdy tripod to keep your camera absolutely still the entire time that shutter is open—it can't move even a tiny bit. Now, the key word here is "sturdy." If you're shooting travel, or architecture, or people, or pretty much anything other than landscapes, you can get away with one of those light, compact, travel tripods, no problem. But, with landscape photography, you'll sometimes wind up shooting in windy, rainy, or just unpredictable weather conditions (some of the best landscape shots are made in rotten conditions), and you don't want to take a chance of your gear literally blowing over. I saw it happen at a workshop I was a teaching—a student's entire camera rig and tripod not only blew over, but it tumbled down the side of a rocky hill. You'll never forget the sound a tripod and camera make as they careen off the rocks while plummeting down the side of a hill. Sad thing was you'd never dream it was windy enough for that to happen, and it wouldn't have if they'd just had a nice, sturdy tripod. A buddy of mine once said, "There are two types of tripods: (1) those lightweight, easy-to-carry ones, and (2) a good one." Don't learn this lesson the hard way—get a good tripod. You'll have it for many years, and it'll serve you well (say that last line with a *Game of Thrones* accent—it'll help you feel more noble when spending the extra money).

Avoid Using the Center Column

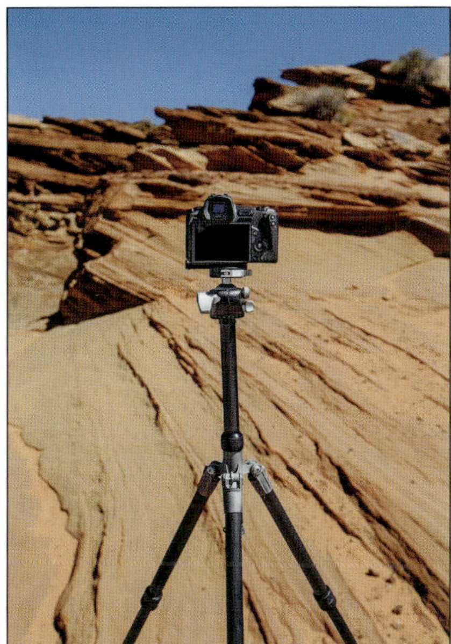 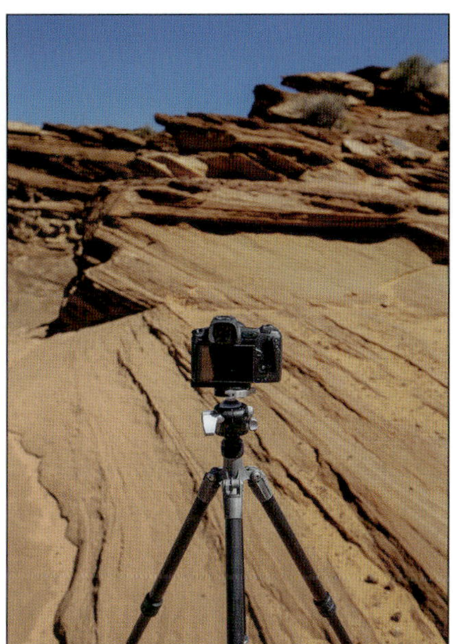

Many tripods these days, especially the compact ones, have a center column that you can extend upward to get your camera high enough to get it comfortably to your eye (as seen here on the left). It's okay to buy a tripod with a center column, just don't ever use it. The code name for that center column in certain camera circles is "the blur maker." That's because it reduces the stability of your camera big time (when your camera is up on that center column, if it gets even a bit windy, you'll actually be able to see your camera moving while you're standing there). To keep from being tempted, buy the right tripod—one that is tall enough that when you extend the legs, it's at your eye height. That way, you won't need that flimsy center column at all.

Extending Your Tripod's Legs

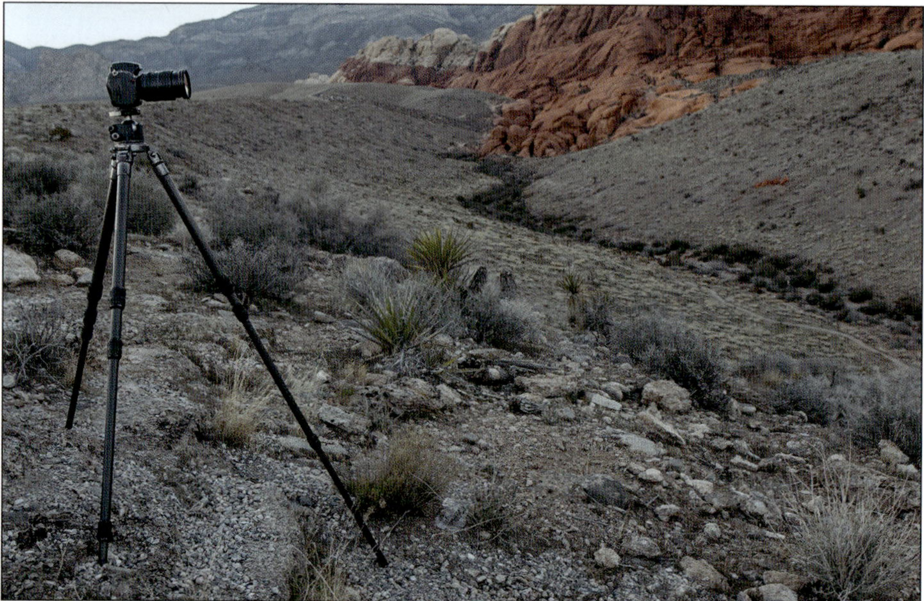

When we're using a tripod (which is often), our goal is always maximum stability, and if it gets even the least bit windy, we want to make sure we're using the thickest, sturdiest legs our tripod has. That might mean that in kinda windy situations, we don't extend those little, thin legs at the bottom of our tripod at all, so we're only using the thicker, sturdier legs. This means that your tripod won't be up quite as high, and depending on which make and model you have, you might have to bend over a little to take your shot. But, at least your tripod will be sturdier and less likely to move or tip. That's why we always extend our tripod legs from the top first, and then work our way down, and we only extend those really thin legs on the bottom if it's not windy at all. One more tip while you're here: the basic rule when setting up your tripod is to put the single leg in front of your lens (since that's where most of the weight will be, and you don't want your tripod tipping over). However, if you're putting your tripod on any kind of an incline at all, you'll want to position it so there's the least chance of it tipping over. So, in that case, put the single leg on the side where it's most likely to do so. For example, if you're shooting up at an angle, the tripod rig is angling back toward you, so you'd put the single leg toward you to act as a brace.

Hanging Weight for Sturdiness

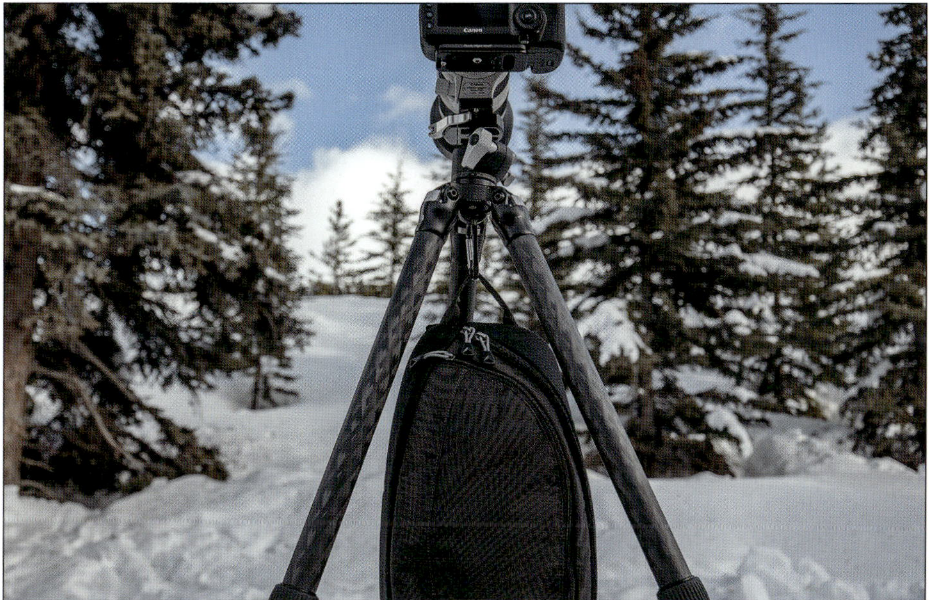

If you're out there shooting and it gets really windy, you're going to want some extra stability, and that's why many tripods have a hook at the bottom of the center column. That hook is for hanging extra weight, which not only helps keep your tripod stable, it helps keep it from blowing over (once you've seen a few tripods with cameras on them go crashing over, it changes how seriously you take this "adding weight" idea). Rather than taking a sandbag with you (by the way, when you buy a sandbag they, generally, don't come with sand inside, so it's easier to take a sandbag with you than you'd think—they just fold right up and slide into the outer pocket of your camera bag. You add the sand on-site, since sand is pretty ubiquitous), a lot of photographers just hang their camera bags from that center pole. So far, I haven't seen one tip over with a camera bag hanging from it, but think of it this way: if you put a sandbag on it, and it tips over, the last thing you'll be worrying about is the sandbag.

How to Splay the Legs

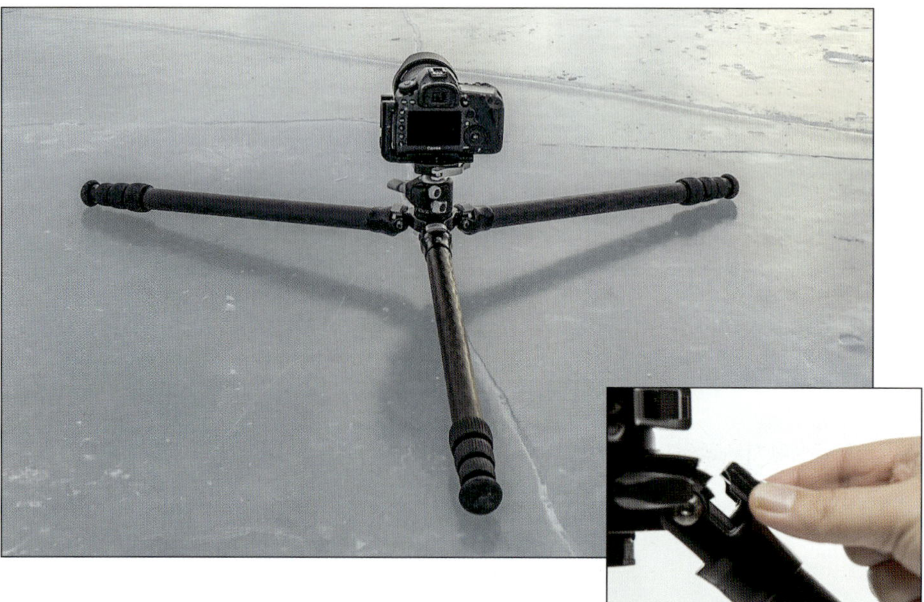

There will be times when you need to get really low, or you're on the rocks of a stream, or need to have a large foreground element in front of you (maybe you're shooting with an ultra-wide-angle lens). In those situations, to get really low, you'll need to splay your tripod's legs out wide. Each tripod is a bit different in how it does this, but the basic idea is that when you normally extend your tripod's legs and pull them out horizontally, they snap into place, kind of at a 45° angle. Splaying the legs lets you go well beyond that default snap-to position. If you look right at the top of each leg, up near where the leg attaches to the center plate (where you attach your ballhead), you'll see a little lever (as seen in the inset above). Pull that lever (or use the release, again, depending on your tripod's make and model), and now you can extend the legs horizontally, beyond that default snap-to stop, to where you can almost make the legs flat. If you look on the release itself, it usually has two or three notches on it, so you can splay the legs out kinda low or really low (like you see here, where my tripod is splayed out on the ice). Being able to use a low perspective like this is important for landscape photography, and it's why so many tripods these days have this splaying feature built right in.

Get Really Low Using a Platypod

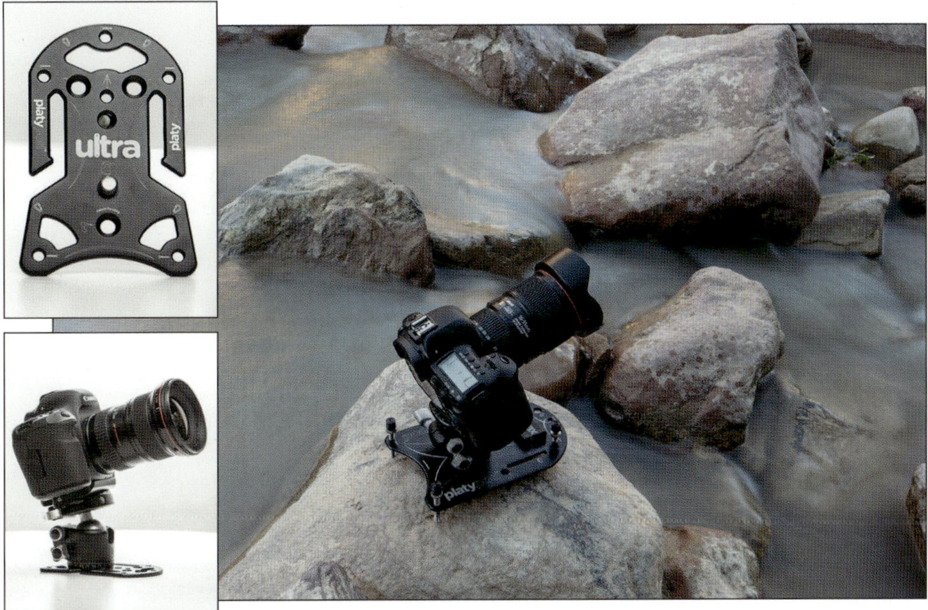

This is a thin, super-sturdy, lightweight (3.2 oz) plate you attach your ballhead and camera to instead of using a tripod. This has been, hands down, one of my favorite all-around camera accessories for the past few years, and I've become somewhat of an accidental evangelist for it, telling everybody all about it because it's so awesome. I use a Platypod (instead of a tripod) when I either: (a) want to get really low to the ground without having to mess with splaying out my tripod legs; (b) need to shoot someplace where tripods are impractical or not allowed; or (c) want to put my camera someplace a tripod won't fit, or might be dangerous (might tip over). I literally keep it in my shirt or jacket pocket. It's made of commercial-grade aircraft aluminum, and it's so strong you won't believe it—I put everything from my camera with my biggest wide-angle lens, to my 70–200mm (using the foot plate mounted on the lens's tripod collar) on it, and it works like a boss! It comes with four screw-in, metal, spiked feet, so it can grip onto rocks or wood, and it has a strap that lets you attach it directly to railings (great at waterfalls or bridges over streams). You will love this accessory on a level that makes you an evangelist, too. It's $59 for the Playpod Ultra, or $99 for its much larger, heavier big brother, the Platypod Max, for folks using really long lenses or those with tip-over anxiety.

You'll Want a Ballhead

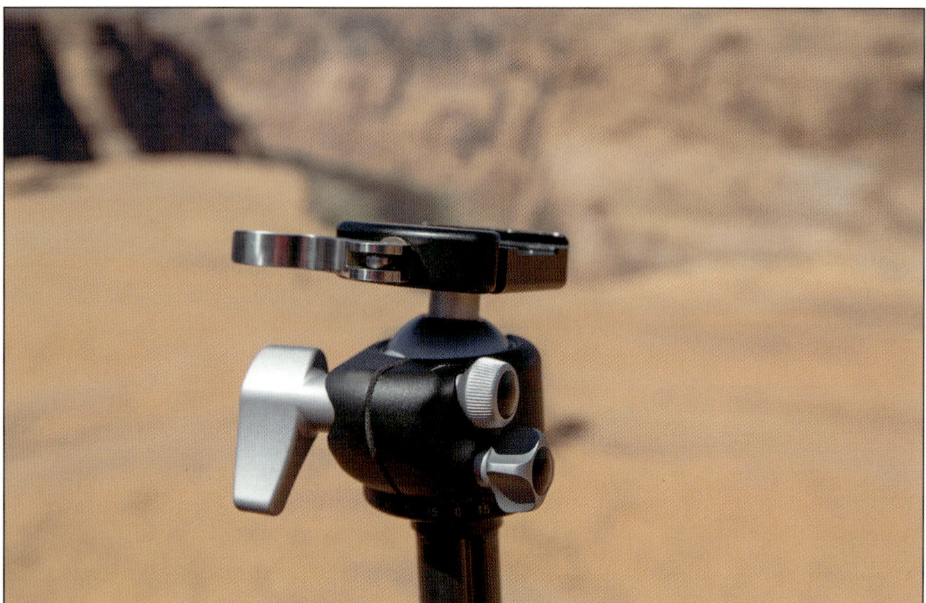

Over the years, I've used every contraption you can think of to mount my camera on top of a tripod—everything from pistol grips to gimbals to pan-and-tilt heads. But, for landscape photography (and about everything else, as well), there's nothing easier to use, or more precise, than a ballhead. They come in all shapes, sizes, and prices. I have a number of different ballheads I've collected over the years, and they range from a Neewer brand ballhead (for around $24) to my beloved Really Right Stuff BH-40, which is one beautifully crafted piece of machinery (considered by many, yours truly included, to be the greatest ballhead ever created). It's not cheap (around $380), but I've had it for more than 10 years, so at $38 a year to use the very best, it's a bargain. Another one I really like is the Oben BE-117, and it's a deal for around $85. There are a lot of great ones out there, and once you use one, you'll never want to use anything else. So easy to use, so precise—just a pleasure.

You'll Need a Cable Release

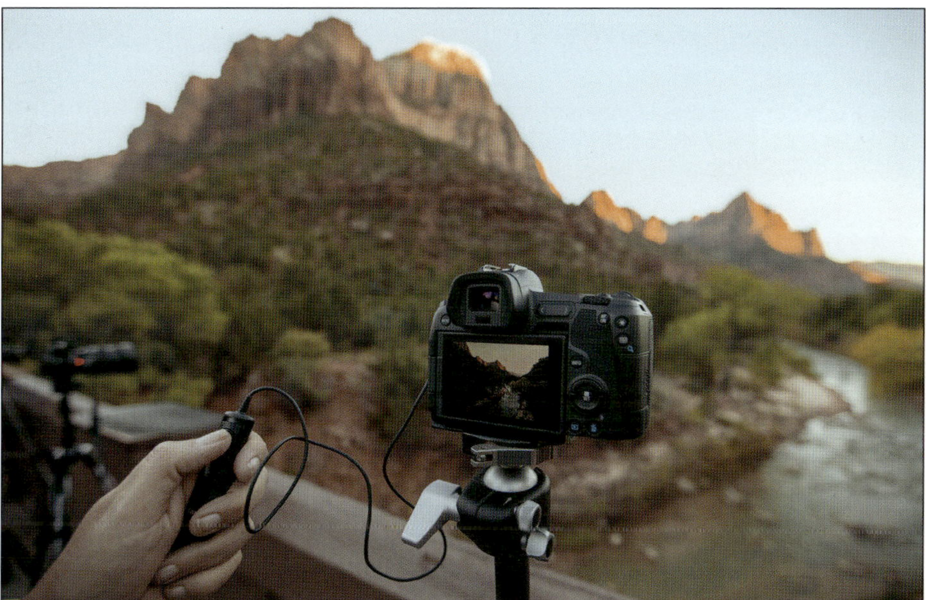

After you've gone through all the expense and trouble of getting a good, solid, sturdy tripod to keep your camera absolutely positively still, you're not going to go and mess all that up by pressing the shutter button on your camera, right? Because if you do press the shutter button with your finger, it will invariably shake the camera just enough to keep you from having a really tack-sharp shot. I know, I know… you're probably thinking, "I'll be really gentle when I press it," which is great because then it will shake less when you press it, but it's still gonna shake. So, why not get a cable release? You plug a thin cable into the small socket on the side or front of your camera that was designed just for this purpose, and then when you press the shutter button on the end of this cable, it takes the shot without you moving the camera whatsoever. Now, you can either go that route, or for most cameras these days, you can get an inexpensive wireless remote that will fire the shutter for you. You can get these as inexpensively as around $14 (that is, unless you have a really expensive camera, in which case, the camera manufacturers figure you must have a lot of money, so they make you pay a whole lot more for a shutter release that does the exact same thing as the $14 one. I know, it stinks). Anyway, the day you buy your tripod, go ahead and get some sort of a cable release/wireless trigger, too. This is pretty essential.

Get Your Horizon Line Straight, Method 1

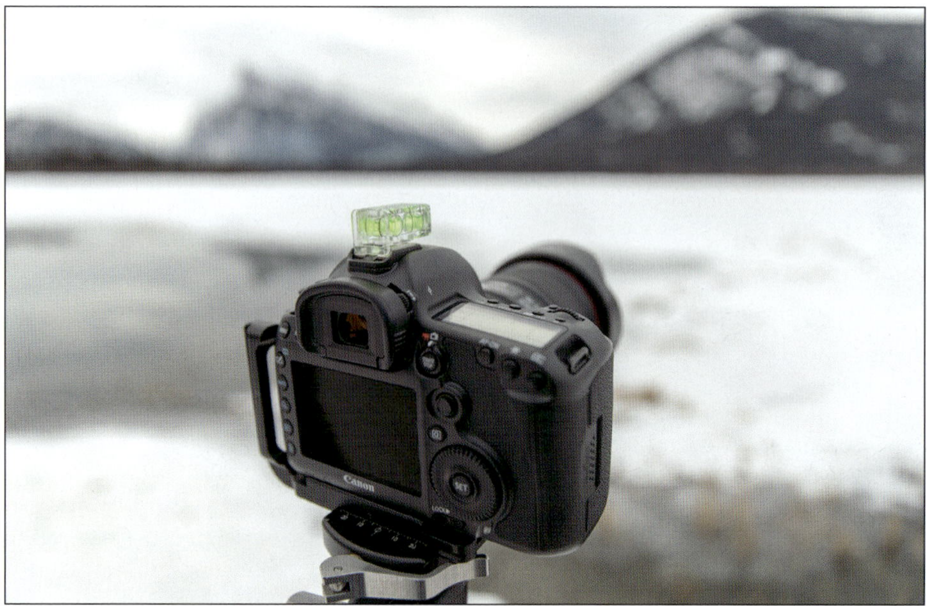

Having a crooked horizon line is one of the "Seven Deadly Sins of Landscape Photography," and yes, you can fix it later in Lightroom or Photoshop (or wherever), but that requires you to rotate your photo, and then you have to crop away those white gaps that are created in the corners. So, basically, you're recomposing your image after the fact, and not because there's a better image within the image you took—you're doing it because you messed up when you took the shot. Why not just get it right in the first place, and then you don't have to fix it later? One way to do that is to buy an inexpensive bubble level. This slides right into the flash hot shoe on the top of your camera (as seen here), and it gives you the type of bubble level you'd find in a traditional hardware store level. You can use this to make sure your camera is perfectly straight when you take the shot, saving you untold toil and trouble later in post (that's short for post-processing, which is long for doing something in Lightroom or Photoshop).

Get Your Horizon Line Straight, Method 2

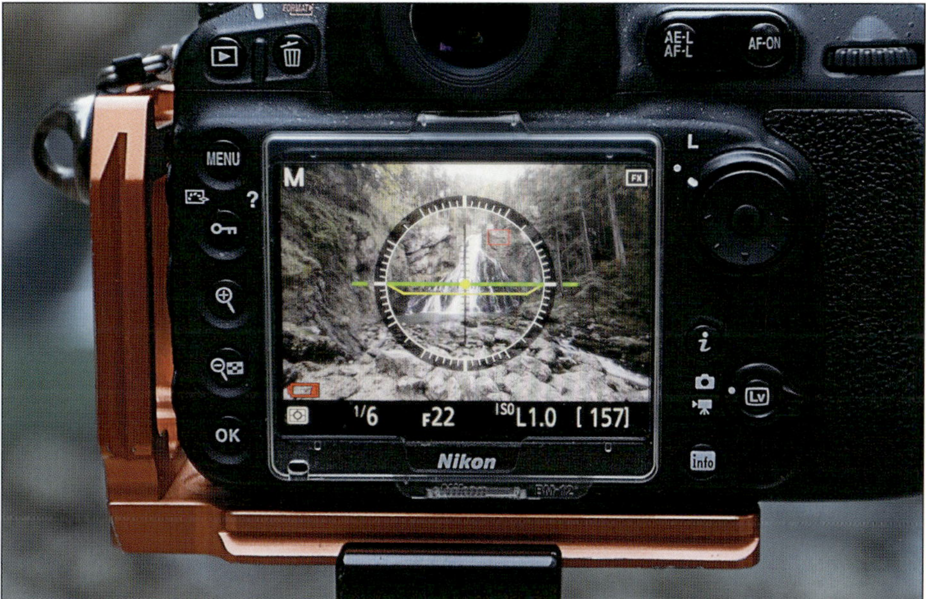

If you bought your camera in the last couple years or so, there's a better-than-good chance you have some kind of digital camera level built right in. They tend to look a lot like the aviation-style artificial horizons pilots use to keep their wings straight while flying—so the passengers in back aren't screaming in panic the entire flight as their drinks slide off their tray tables. That's probably more information than you needed, but anyway, in many cases, they're built in (check the PDF of your camera manual to see if you have one), because having a straight horizon line matters.

The Awesomeness of a Quick Release Plate and an L-Bracket

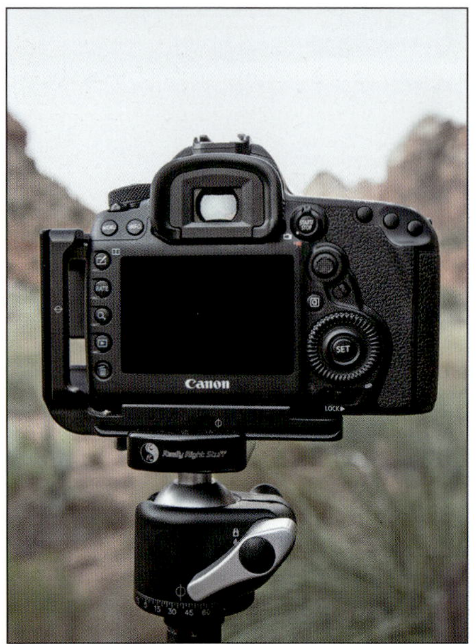 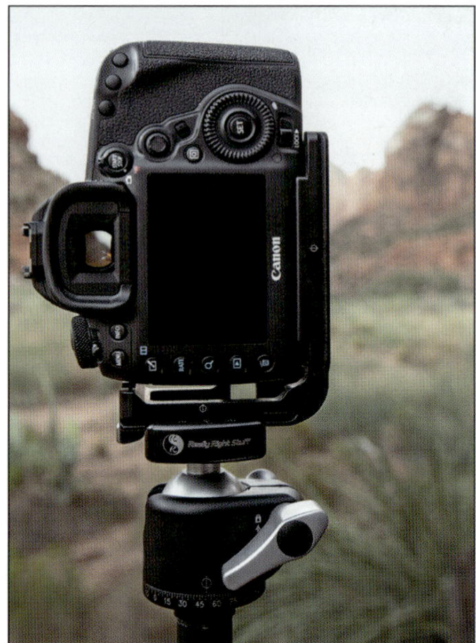

This is one of those accessories that, as a landscape photographer in particular, once you use one, you'll wonder how you lived without it. In short, while shooting on a tripod, it lets you change from shooting with your camera wide (horizontal) to tall (vertical) in all of about four seconds. First, you release the small lever (or knob) on the quick release plate, which sits on top of your ballhead, to release your camera. Then, you turn your camera vertically, and the L-bracket that is attached to your camera (it just screws right into the tripod hole on the bottom of your camera) lets you set your camera down vertically on the quick release plate. Snap down the quick release lever, and you're back to shooting. The reason it's called an "L" bracket is that it forms the shape of an "L," with the short side of the "L" being on the side of your camera (with a properly sized hole, so you can get to your slots for plugging things in, like cable releases and mics and such), and the long end goes on the bottom of your camera. You will super-dig this setup, and you'll see tons of landscape photographers using an L-bracket/quick release system when you're out shooting (in fact, if you don't have one, somebody will probably walk over and ask: "Why aren't you using an L-bracket?"). Britain's 3 Legged Thing makes a nice, inexpensive universal L-bracket for around $50 that works great. However, if you want the crème de la crème of L-brackets, Really Right Stuff makes custom-fitted ones for your camera make and model in the $180 to $200 range. These do cost more, but you get to use the French phrase "crème de la crème" when describing it to others, so….

In Every Landscape Photographer's Bag: A Circular Polarizer

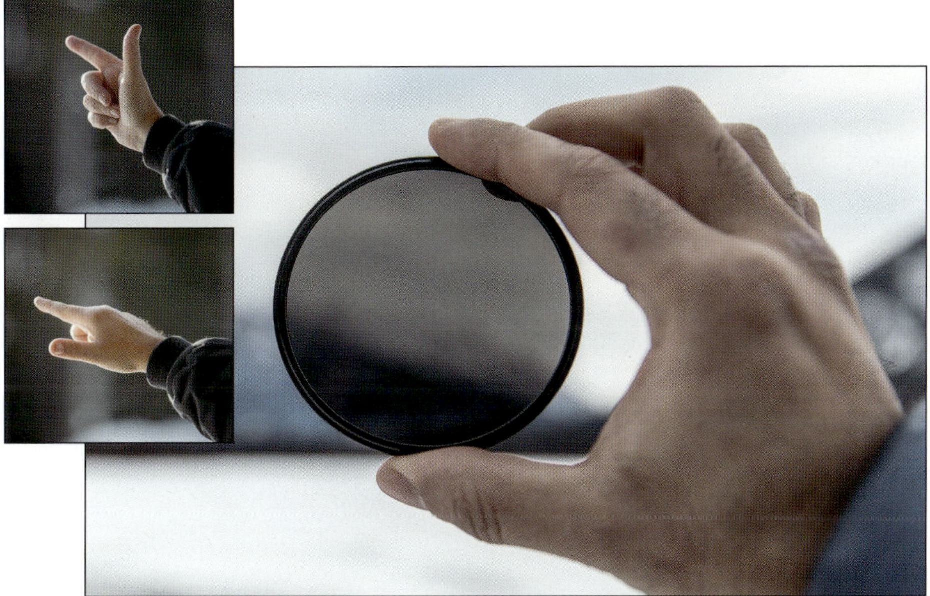

You'll need one of these filters for two reasons. The first is to cut through reflections. This is actually its main job—to cut through reflections in water and streams and such, and it does a terrific job (kind of like putting on a pair of sunglasses—they cut the glare big time). The second is to make a washed-out sky look darker and more blue. That's when the circular part comes in handy, because you can rotate it to choose how much polarization you want, especially helpful when shooting the sky or reducing reflections in water (you don't always want to remove all the reflections in water, so this lets you see a preview as you rotate—just stop rotating when it looks good to you). If you're shooting the sky, you'll get the best results when you're shooting at a 90° angle to the sun. Otherwise, you won't get nearly as much effect from the filter. There's an old trick that helps you determine exactly where the filter will make the most difference: Take your hand, position it like you're making a pretend gun (like you did when you were a kid, or when you were posing for the cover of a *Charlie's Angels* movie poster), then point your fake gun at the sun, turn your hand sideways (either to the left or right), and your thumb will be aiming at the best spot for you to shoot from for maximum effect from your polarizing filter. By the way, while this has nothing to do with landscapes, I also use a polarizing filter to cut the reflection in car windows when I'm doing automotive shoots, and you can't believe the difference it makes.

You'll Need a Graduated ND Filter

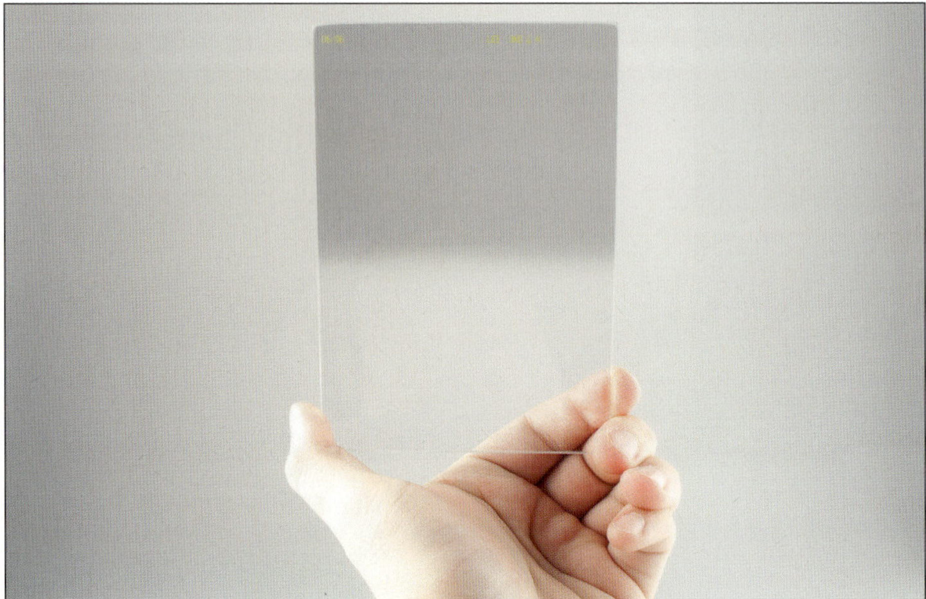

There are two ND (neutral density) filters that are mainstays with landscape photographers and this one, the neutral density gradient filter (simply called an "ND Grad" in landscape circles), is probably the most important of the two because it helps you overcome a sensor weakness. When you're shooting landscapes, particularly during the day, because of the limited range of light that our cameras' sensors can capture, your camera will either properly expose for the foreground, or for the sky, but it doesn't have enough range to do both at once. So, you're going to have to either make the foreground look right (making the sky washed out), or make the sky look right (but then your foreground winds up way too dark). The general rule is to meter (aim the center focus point in your viewfinder) so the foreground is properly exposed. But, to even things out, we put an ND Grad, which is dark gray at the top and gradually goes down to transparent about halfway down, in front of our lenses. This darkens the sky, and by the time the gradient gets down to the foreground in the frame, it's transparent, so it doesn't make your foreground darker, as well. If you look at the filter itself, it looks like a clear piece of glass (or Plexiglass), with a gradient over the top half. You want to line up the bottom of the gradient with the horizon line (this is a big limitation of using a round ND Grad—you can't change the position of the bottom of the gradient, so you have to change your composition instead, which is not awesome). Also, you can order ND Grads that have a soft transition along the horizon to the transparent or a hard-edged transition (I always go with a soft ND Grad myself—it's more forgiving on placement).

And, You'll Probably Want an ND Filter

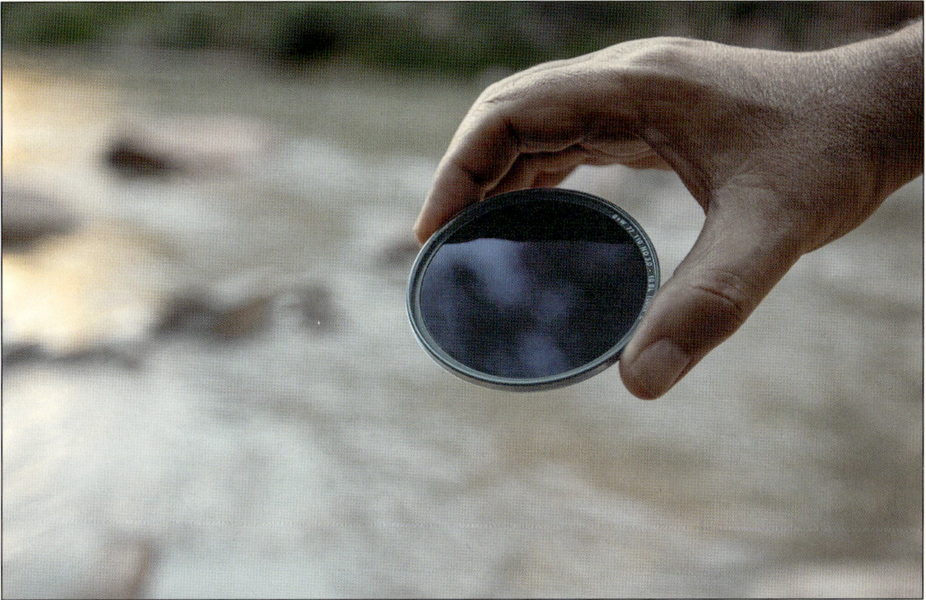

If you want to get silky smooth waterfalls and streams, and smooth streaky clouds above your epic landscapes (provided, of course, that the clouds are moving at a relatively quick pace), then you want the other of the two neutral density filters, simply called an "ND filter." ND filters are dark, so they force your shutter to stay open longer than it normally would in bright shooting conditions, so things that are moving in your image (like water going over a waterfall) get that silky smooth look (there's more on how to use these in Chapter 6). By the way, with ND filters, the entire surface of the filter is darkened from edge to edge, and there are different types of ND filters (and different amounts of darkness, which we'll also discuss in Chapter 6). One type is the square glass or plastic filter that slides down into a bracket that's mounted in front of your lens, and then there are circular ND filters (as seen here), which screw right onto the front of your lens like traditional filters. While I'm a big fan of the square type for ND Grad filters (because, as I mentioned on the previous page, they allow you to align the bottom of the gradient with the horizon line), I prefer the circular ND filters because there's less fuss—you just screw it right onto the end of your lens, whereas the square ones require you to put on a bracket first, then carefully slide the square into its slot, and the whole process just takes twice as long, and has more parts. Performance-wise, they both work the same—they make your camera think it's darker outside than it really is, forcing your shutter to stay open longer.

Seeing Your LCD in Bright Daylight

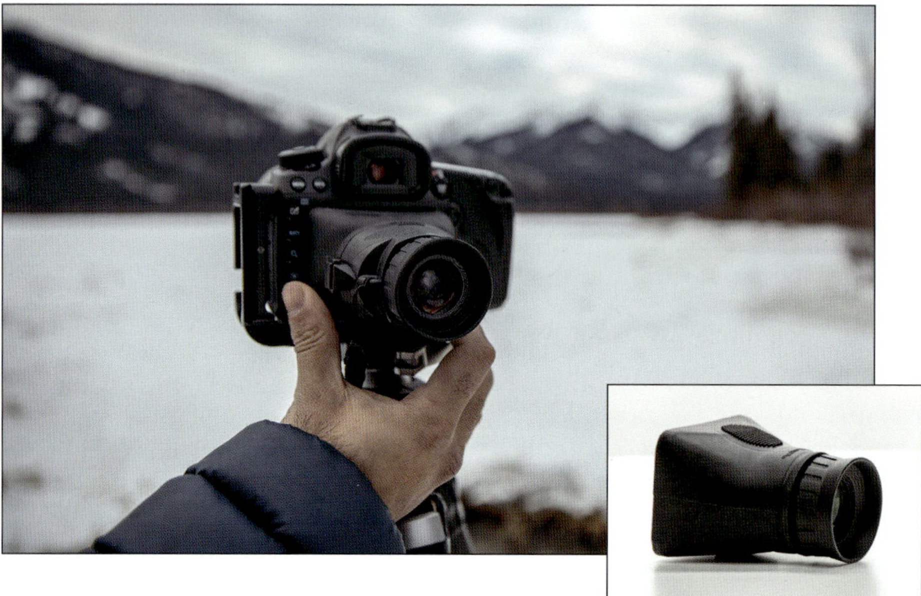

If you're out shooting during the day, and you've ever tried to see your images on the LCD screen on the back of your camera, you already know that unless it's a really cloudy day, you can barely make out anything—the bright sun washes out that tiny 3" LCD screen, and you can't tell if your shots are in focus or composed right or, in some cases, if the camera even fired. That's why I always carry a Hoodman HoodLoupe. It doesn't magnify your screen, but it does cover the LCD and darken the area around it to such an extent that it looks like you're looking at your screen in the dead of night (even though it's crazy bright outside). It's incredibly helpful, and anytime I'm out shooting and another photographer comes over and asks if it's any good, I just hand it to them and tell them to take a look. They put it over their LCD screen and, while they're still looking through it, they all say the same thing, "Man, I gotta get one of these."

You'll Need a Small, Powerful Flashlight

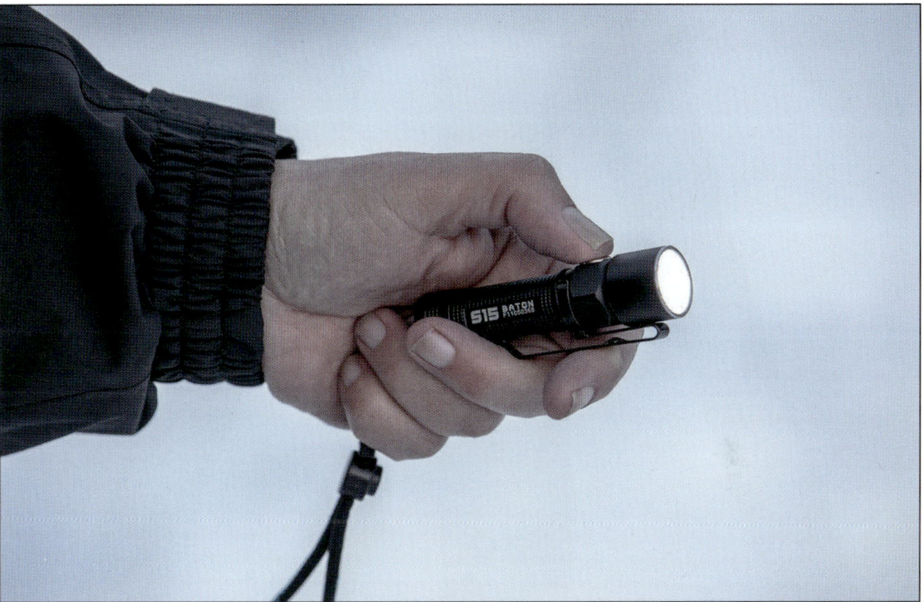

You'll be shooting in low-light situations a lot, often before dawn when it's really dark outside. So, you'll want to have some sort of small LED flashlight to help you make your way around in the dark when you're getting to your shooting location. You'll also need this: (a) for seeing inside your dark camera bag while it's still dark out, or getting dark; (b) for light painting subjects at night (see pages 119 and 142 for more on light painting); (c) for signaling to other photographers when you're shooting at night or before dawn; and (d) to light the scene if you want to do a behind-the-scenes video with your cellphone or camera for social media.

The Greatest Stuff on Earth: Gaffer's Tape

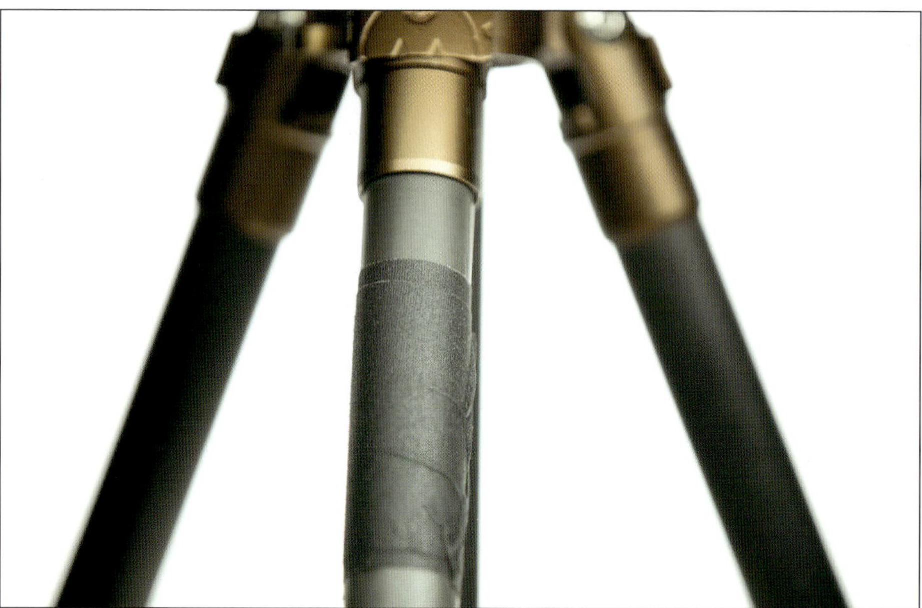

This is another one of those things every photographer needs in their camera bag. Gaffer's tape comes from Hollywood, where it's used to strongly, but temporarily, tape things down—like taping something to a painted wall or wallpaper or a table, where you know you'll need to remove it without taking off the paint or paper or damaging anything, and without leaving a sticky residue or messing anything up. That's gaffer's tape, and it's a landscape photographer's best friend. You'll wind up using it in a dozen different ways when you're out shooting, and you can use it without worrying about messing up your gear. I keep some wrapped around the leg of my tripod, so if I need some when I'm out shooting, I just unroll a little bit, tear off what I need, and go back to shooting. Plus, the great thing about it is it's one of the few thing in photography that's pretty cheap. A whole roll of it (black, 2 inches wide by 12 yards long) from B&H photo is around $6. Heck, buy two and give a roll to a friend. They'll thank you again and again over the next year or so.

A Good, Cheap Lens Cloth

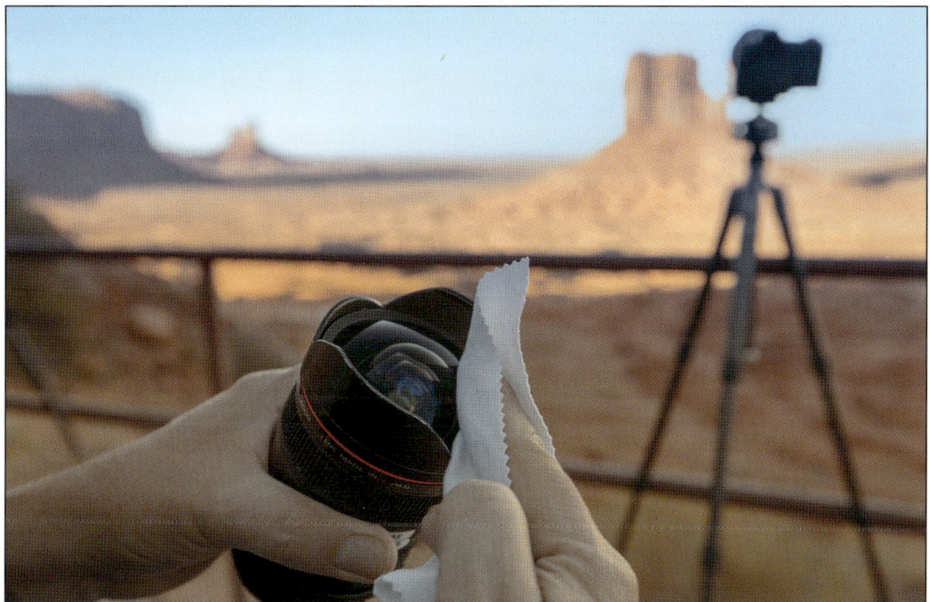

Before you start shooting, you should always give your lenses a quick cleaning with a microfiber cleaning cloth. Some folks like to do it when they pack their gear at the end of a shoot (so it's always ready for the next shoot), and some folks do it once the lens is attached to their camera, right before they start to shoot. It doesn't matter when you do it, just that you actually remember to do it before you start shooting. Here's why this is so important: if you open a shot in Lightroom or Photoshop and you notice there's a speck or spot or fingerprint on it from the outside of your lens, it's not just on that one shot—it's on *all* the shots you took with that lens, and depending on where that smudge or spot is, it can kill an entire shoot. A couple of little circular swipes around the face of your lens with a cheap lens cloth (a lens cloth isn't something you need to spend a lot on), and you sidestep a bunch of problems after your shoot (take it from someone who has paid the price for not cleaning their lens before a shoot—you'll regret it). I like the MagicFiber micro-fiber cleaning cloths—you can get six of 'em for around $10. They work like…aw, you know.

Which Type of Memory Card to Use

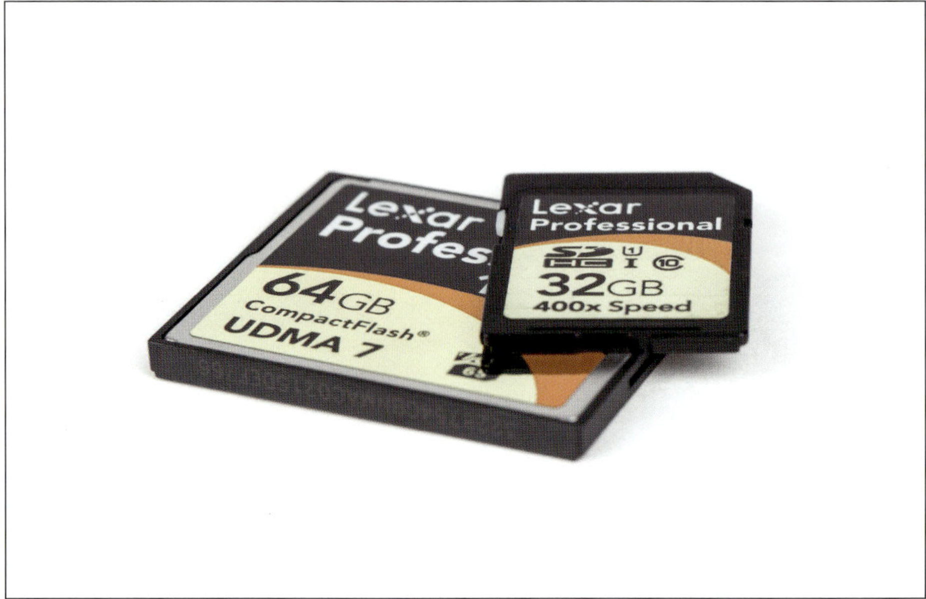

Great news here: you don't need to buy super-fast, super-expensive memory cards for shooting landscapes. The super-high-speed cards are for people who need to shoot a lot of shots in a series and need to quickly clear the buffer in their camera for the next round of shots. So, for example, they're ideal for sports photographers or air show photographers or people who will be tearing off a ton of high-speed continuous shots. Since we're just popping off a shot here or there in landscape photography, we don't need the speed, and we don't need to spend the money to get the speed. You can get good 32GB cards for around $9.99 each that will work fine for landscape photography, and since they're so cheap, you can buy more cards (which would serve you better than buying one really fast card). I have been using Lexar brand memory cards for years now (I'm one of their Lexar Elite Photographers, which means…which means…I remember them telling me it was good and an honor and stuff), and I've had great luck with them. I have some speedy cards and some slower cards, and ya know, they all store my photos just fine. Don't overspend on your cards—it's one of the few things we don't have to spend a bunch on.

A Drive for Backing Up in the Field

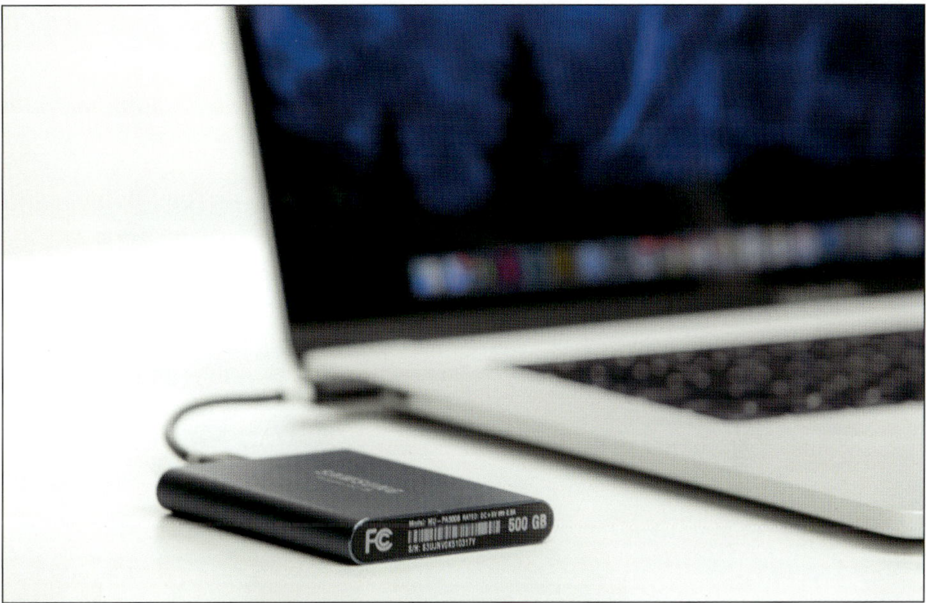

When you're done shooting out on location, you're going to need to back up your images (my own rule is: I have to have at least two complete backups before I ever erase a memory card), and I have two great solutions for you, depending on whether you're traveling with a laptop or just using an iPad or your phone for viewing your images. When traveling with my laptop (I always take mine on shooting trips—I'm too impatient to wait until I get home), I use a Samsung 500GB T5 Portable SS drive. It's so crazy small and lightweight; it's a little bigger than a pack of matches, only weighs 1.8 ounces, it's fast as blazes, and it's only around $115. After my shoot, I connect this to my laptop and back up all my images from the day (and, yes, I do this every night, no matter how tired I am, which is not always easy). If you're not bringing a laptop, then I have another great solution: the WD 250GB My Passport Wireless SSD external portable drive. It has a built-in SD card reader and you don't need a computer—you just pop your SD card in, press one button, and it backs up your images. Also, it does a smart backup the next time you put your card in, only backing up new shots you've taken since the last shoot. Better yet, it has its own built-in closed Wi-Fi network, so once your images are on the drive, you can use its app to view the images on the drive right on your phone or tablet wirelessly, and you can even transfer selected images to your phone or tablet to edit them. How cool is that?! It's around $199.

Extra Batteries (Especially in Cold Weather)

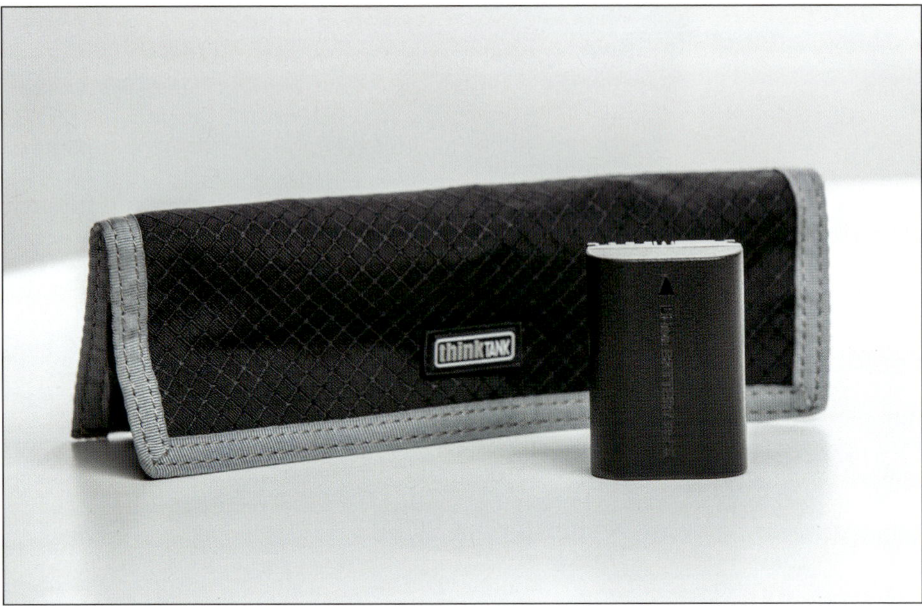

There is nothing worse than ending a shoot just when the light is getting really good because your battery is dead, and you don't have a backup. You need at least two, if not three, backup batteries (at least three if you're shooting a mirrorless body), and if you often shoot in cold weather, your batteries won't last nearly as long, so you might even need a fourth. However, I have good news: these days you don't have to buy your spare batteries from the camera manufacturer. If you've priced replacement batteries from the manufacturers, you've already found out that they are crazy expensive—especially when there are so many good alternatives out there for a whole lot less. For example, instead of spending $64+ for a single battery, I've been buying PowerExtra batteries for my make and model of camera for $11 a battery, and honestly, I haven't noticed a difference in performance whatsoever (and I'm not alone. The photographer who turned me on to these said the same thing). I can buy five of these PowerExtra brand batteries for less than the cost of one battery from my camera's manufacturer (I carry five with me—four in a simply designed Think Tank Photo DSLR Battery Holder [it's around $18] and the fifth one in my camera).

A Good Backpack (but Not a Big One)

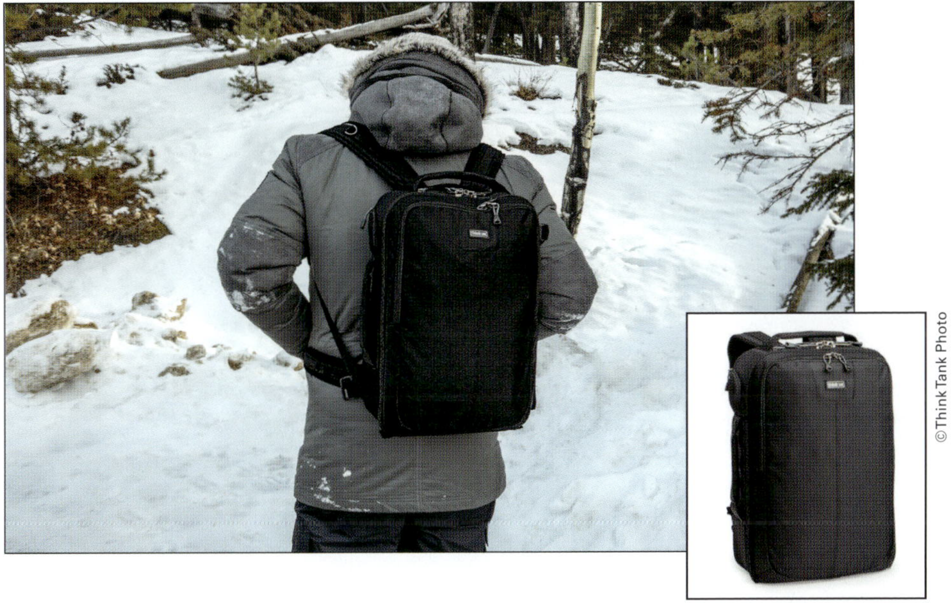

If you buy a big backpack to take out shooting on location, you'll fill it. You'll just keep packing stuff into it until it's so heavy to carry you won't want to carry it out with you past the first day or so. You'll wind up leaving it in the trunk of your car in the parking lot, which stinks because once you're out on location, you'll remember you need "that thing" that's back in your backpack in the trunk. I've seen this scenario play out so many times. So, yes, a backpack is ideal for shooting landscapes on location, but even if you usually shoot within 200 feet or so from your car, I still would recommend getting one that's just big enough to hold your landscape gear, but still small enough that you can't overfill it. What do we put in this backpack? Two bodies if you're going someplace remote (where you wouldn't easily be able to get your camera repaired if it broke or got damaged), a wide-angle zoom lens (I would pack my 16–35mm f/4), a long lens (my 70–200mm), and then just some filters, a cable release, a Platypod, a Hoodman HoodLoupe, extra batteries, memory card holder, cleaning cloth, and a battery charger (if you have access to power). On the side, I can attached my tripod. I use a ThinkTank Photo Airport Essentials backpack and it holds all that stuff easily, without me having to carry a huge bag filled with extra gear I won't really need out there. Plus, it's small enough that it fits in most smaller regional jets, and it adheres to the smaller international carry-on sizes. If I just want to take one bag on board, it'll even hold my laptop and my iPad, but then it defeats the purpose of going light once you're on location (unless, once you get to your hotel, you leave the laptop and iPad locked in the hotel room safe).

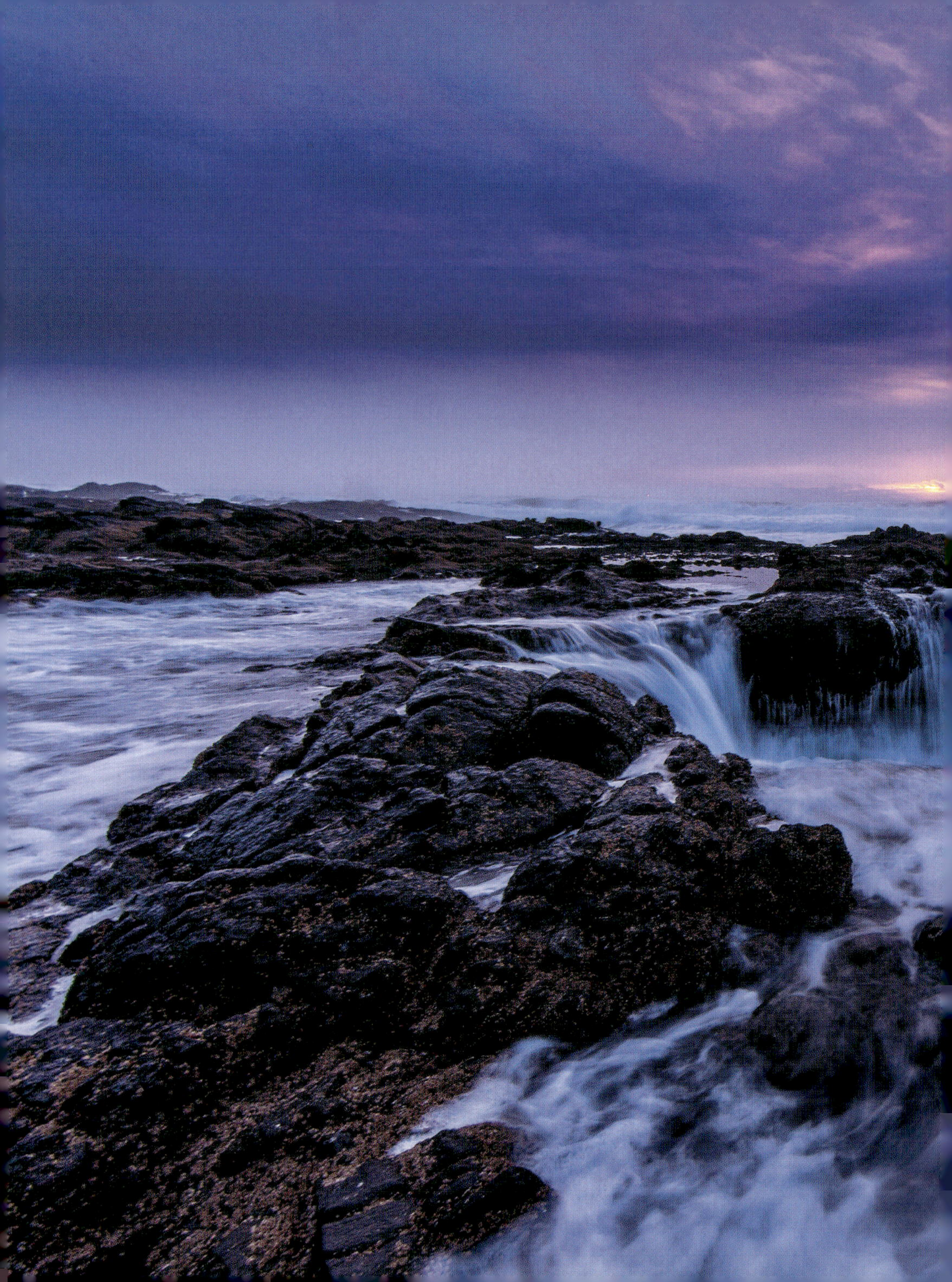

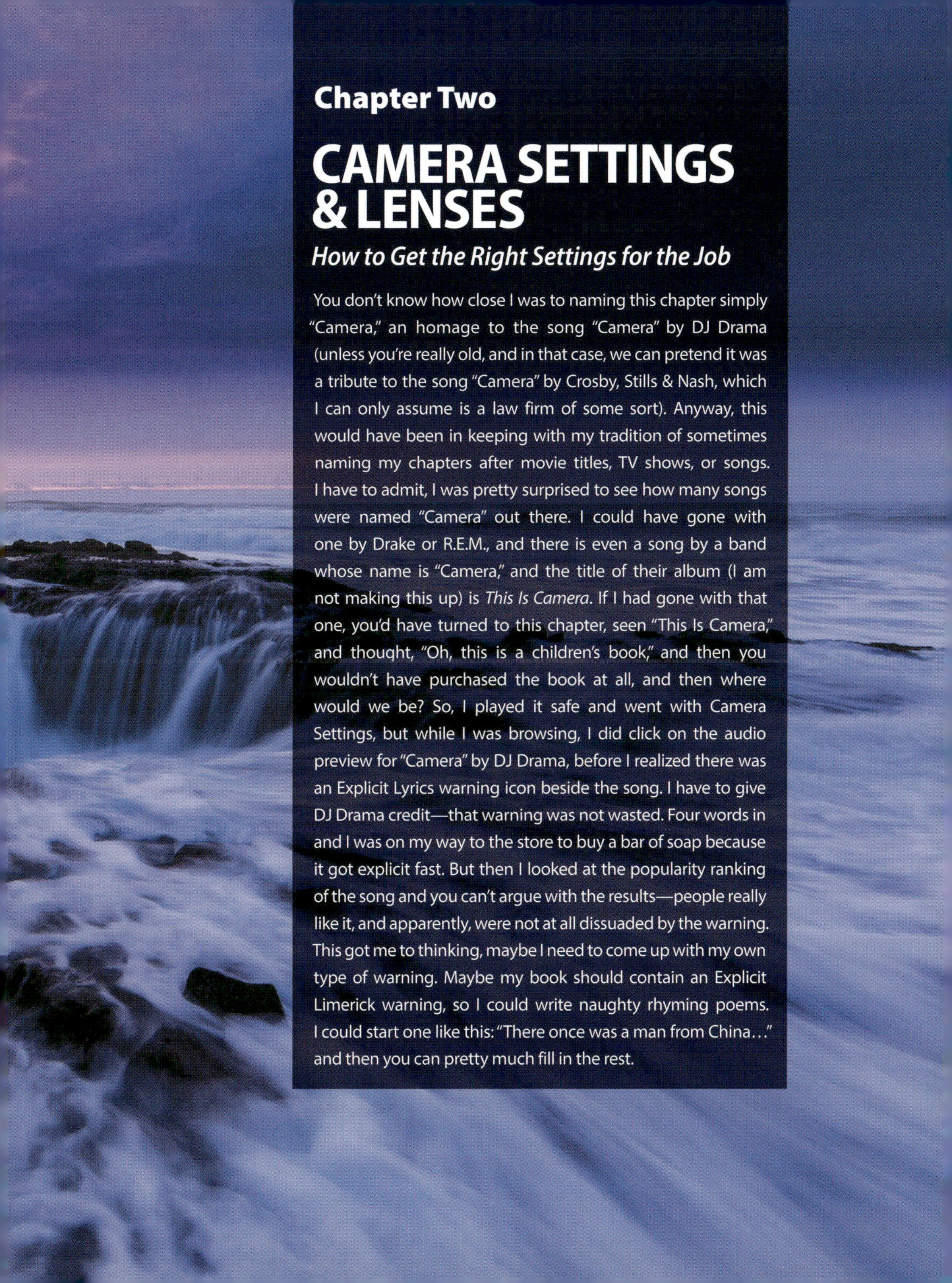

Chapter Two

CAMERA SETTINGS & LENSES

How to Get the Right Settings for the Job

You don't know how close I was to naming this chapter simply "Camera," an homage to the song "Camera" by DJ Drama (unless you're really old, and in that case, we can pretend it was a tribute to the song "Camera" by Crosby, Stills & Nash, which I can only assume is a law firm of some sort). Anyway, this would have been in keeping with my tradition of sometimes naming my chapters after movie titles, TV shows, or songs. I have to admit, I was pretty surprised to see how many songs were named "Camera" out there. I could have gone with one by Drake or R.E.M., and there is even a song by a band whose name is "Camera," and the title of their album (I am not making this up) is *This Is Camera*. If I had gone with that one, you'd have turned to this chapter, seen "This Is Camera," and thought, "Oh, this is a children's book," and then you wouldn't have purchased the book at all, and then where would we be? So, I played it safe and went with Camera Settings, but while I was browsing, I did click on the audio preview for "Camera" by DJ Drama, before I realized there was an Explicit Lyrics warning icon beside the song. I have to give DJ Drama credit—that warning was not wasted. Four words in and I was on my way to the store to buy a bar of soap because it got explicit fast. But then I looked at the popularity ranking of the song and you can't argue with the results—people really like it, and apparently, were not at all dissuaded by the warning. This got me to thinking, maybe I need to come up with my own type of warning. Maybe my book should contain an Explicit Limerick warning, so I could write naughty rhyming poems. I could start one like this: "There once was a man from China…" and then you can pretty much fill in the rest.

Set Your Camera at Its Lowest Native ISO

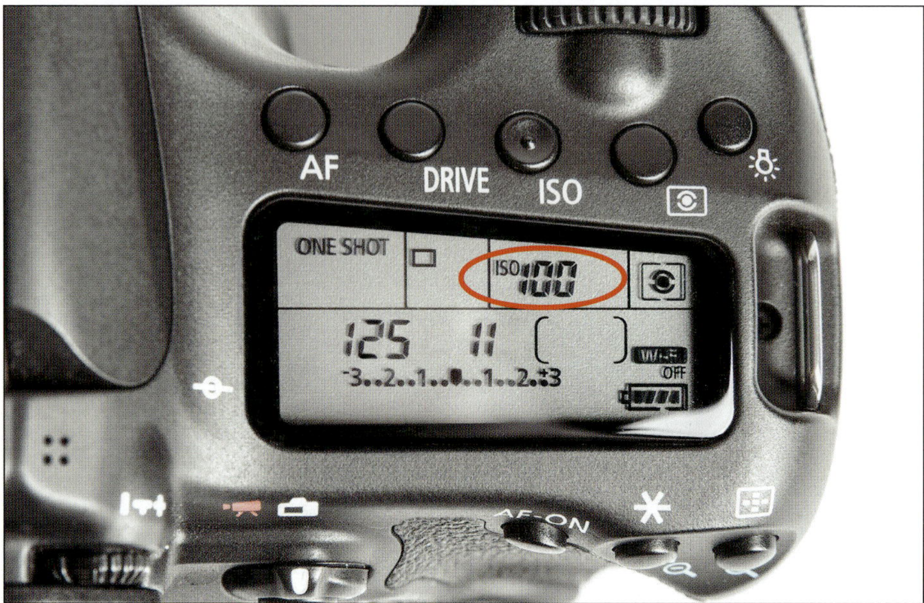

If you're going to be making gorgeously sharp, crisp landscape images, you're usually going to be shooting on a tripod (or at least, hopefully, you'll be shooting on a tripod), and if you're shooting on a tripod, you need to be at your lowest, cleanest native ISO, which for most cameras these days is 100 ISO. Yes, you'll find a camera make/model here and there where its cleanest native ISO is 50 or even 200, but as a general rule, it's 100 ISO (if you're not sure what your cleanest native ISO is, check the PDF of your user's manual). Now, what if you're hand-holding instead of using a tripod? Don't hand-hold. Not if you want that legendary sharpness you're after, and if you're shooting at the right time of day, when the light is beautiful and the shadows are soft, you absolutely need to be on a tripod. Now, what about that instance where it's a big, bright, beautiful mid-day sky, and while the light or shadows aren't awesome, it's still worth shooting? What then? In that case, you'd use 100 ISO. What? Sure! If it's super-bright outside, your shutter speed will be crazy fast (probably over 1/2000 of a second), and you'll still get a really sharp shot with that fast a shutter speed. Not tripod sharp, but ya know, still pretty darn sharp.

Shoot in Aperture Priority Mode

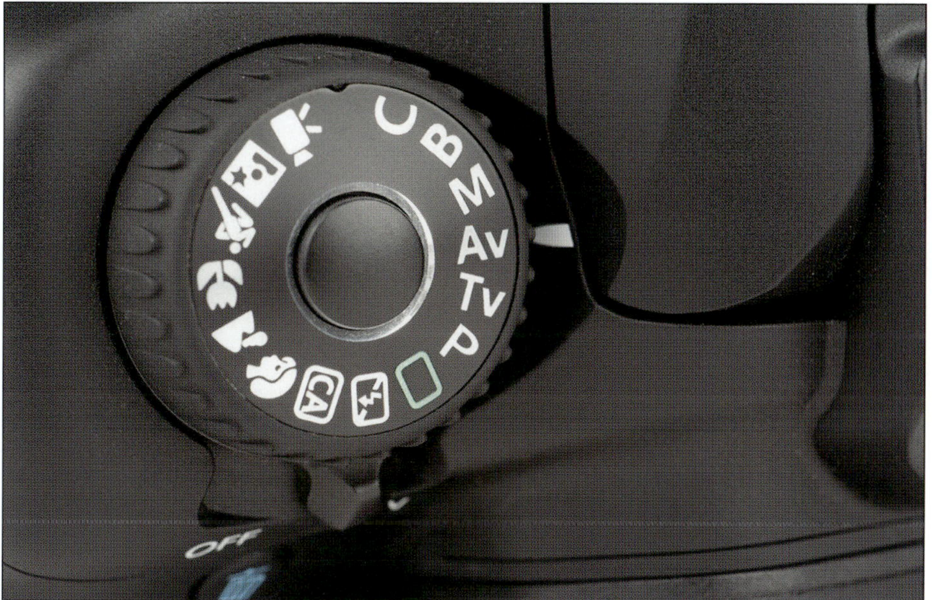

If you've been shooting in manual mode for years, and you love it, just skip this page, but for everybody else, especially somebody fairly new to landscape photography, I recommend shooting in aperture priority mode (it's AV or A on the mode dial of most cameras). What this means is that you choose the f-stop and the camera automatically chooses what it thinks the proper shutter speed is for the scene you're currently aiming at. It's simple (you only have one decision to make, especially since your ISO has already been decided—set it at 100 ISO on a tripod).

Which Aperture (F-Stop) to Use

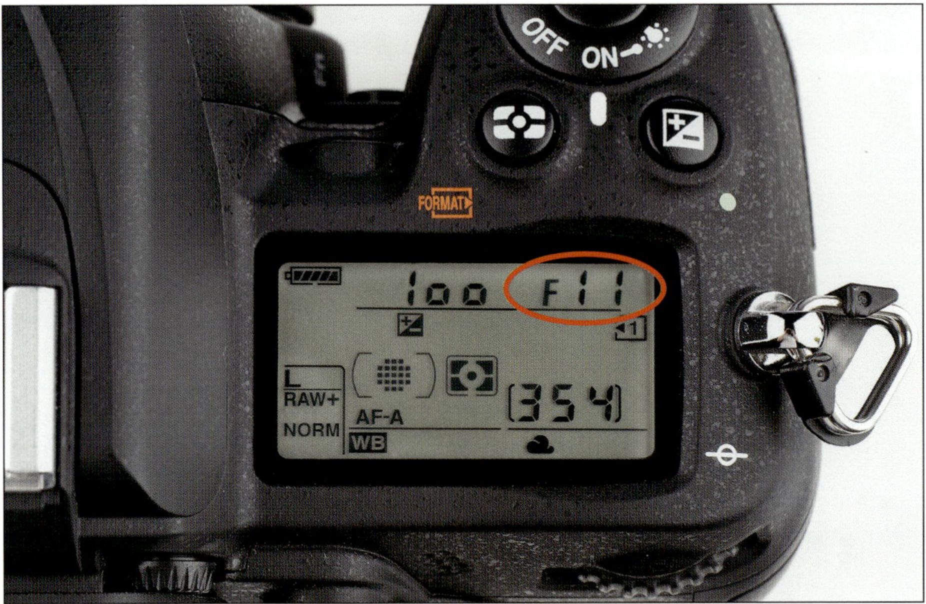

With landscape images, you're generally going to want everything in focus in your frame, from front to back, so you'll want to use an f-stop that's designed to keep everything in focus. This is easier than it sounds. When I want everything in focus, I pretty much always use f/11. Most pros I know use either f/11 or f/16, but those aren't the only f-stops that will keep everything in focus, as f/8 works nicely as well, but f/11 is my favorite. So, for me, it's an easy choice. Would you notice a real sharpness difference between f/8 and f/11 (or even f/16)? With the naked eye, and without greatly magnifying the image, I doubt it. As long as you don't go above f/16, you should be okay. Now, if you want to get technical (nerd alert), an f-stop like f/22, with its smaller lens opening, would theoretically create a sharper image. However, due to an optical lens issue called "lens diffraction," super-small f-stops, like f/22 or f/32, are actually softer and less sharp than regular ol' everyday f-stops, like f/8 or f/11. That's why I recommend avoiding those super-high-numbered f-stops and just sticking with something tried and true—like f/11. One last thing: each lens has an f-stop that is its sharpest, and the old adage was that a lens's sharpest f-stop is found 2 or 3 stops above its widest f-stop (so, if your lens's widest f-stop was f/4, its sharpest f-stop would be around f/8 or f/11. If its widest f-stop was f/2.8, then its sharpest would be around f/8). The only problem is that doesn't always work. It does for some lenses, but not for others. So, without running a series of boring and somewhat cumbersome lens tests, it's pretty safe to say your lens's sharpest f-stop is probably going to be one of those "middle of the road" f-stops, like f/8 or f/11.

What Shutter Speed to Use

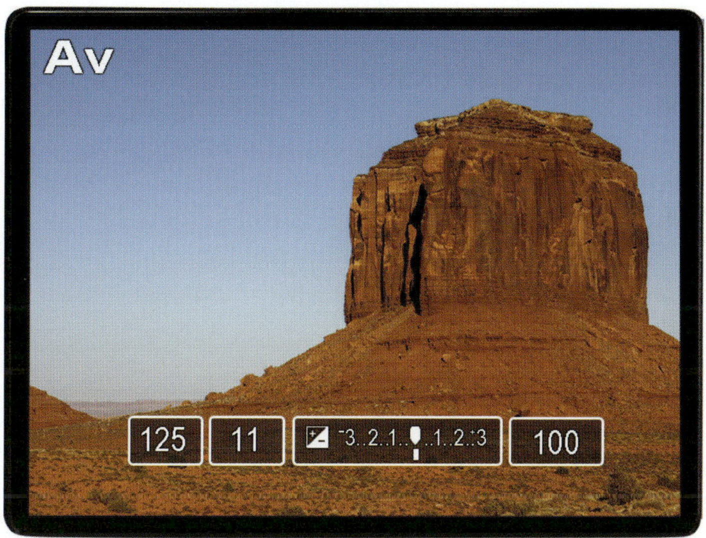

Good news: if you're following my advice and shooting in aperture priority mode, you can take this off your worry list, because your camera will set the shutter speed automatically. You choose your f-stop (f/11) and your camera will do its best to choose the right shutter speed for whatever you're aiming at to make a proper exposure.

Shoot in RAW (Wider Dynamic Range)

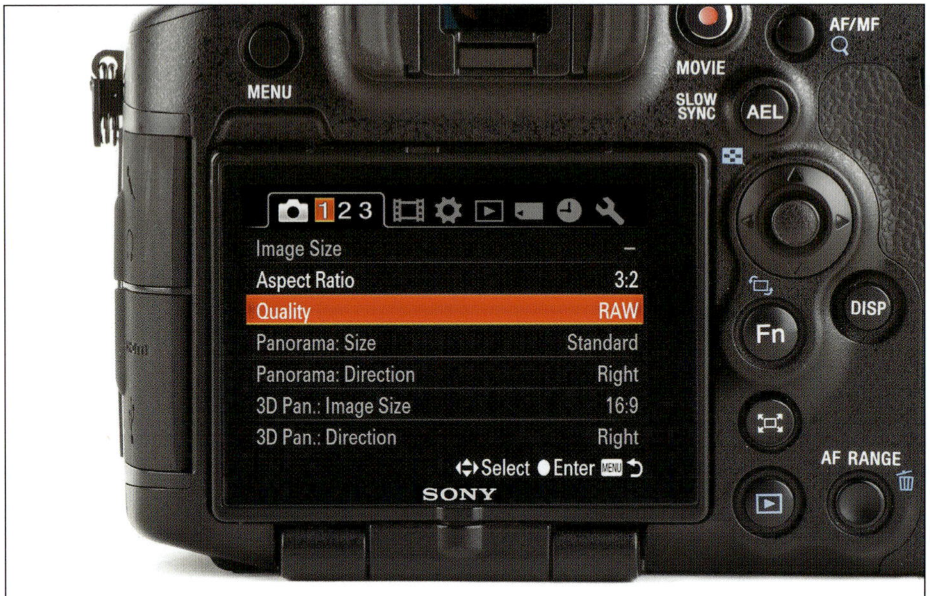

There are a bunch of advantages to shooting in RAW format, particularly for landscape images where we're often capturing a wide dynamic range. The RAW format captures a wider range than JPEG and gives you the highest quality initial image coming out of the camera. Also, RAW files are much more forgiving if you made mistakes (especially when it comes to things like white balance) and you get extra post-processing features (like choosing your own RAW profiles) that you don't get with JPEG images. Plus, if you need to fix serious problems in post-processing, or if you want to really throw a bunch of Photoshop or Lightroom at an image (letting the artist in you run wild), then you'll be happy you shot in RAW, since it shows the least signs of damage from pushing all those pixels around. You'll get smoother gradations in skies with less banding (where you see a visible line where one shade of blue ends and the next one starts), the results look better if you have to recover clipped highlights (see page 152), and it's just a better quality, more robust format all the way around. Those are some of the reasons pro landscape shooters around the world shoot in RAW. So, in short, for the best results from your landscape images, shoot in RAW. I guess I could have just said that.

Right Now, Go Turn On Your Highlight Warning

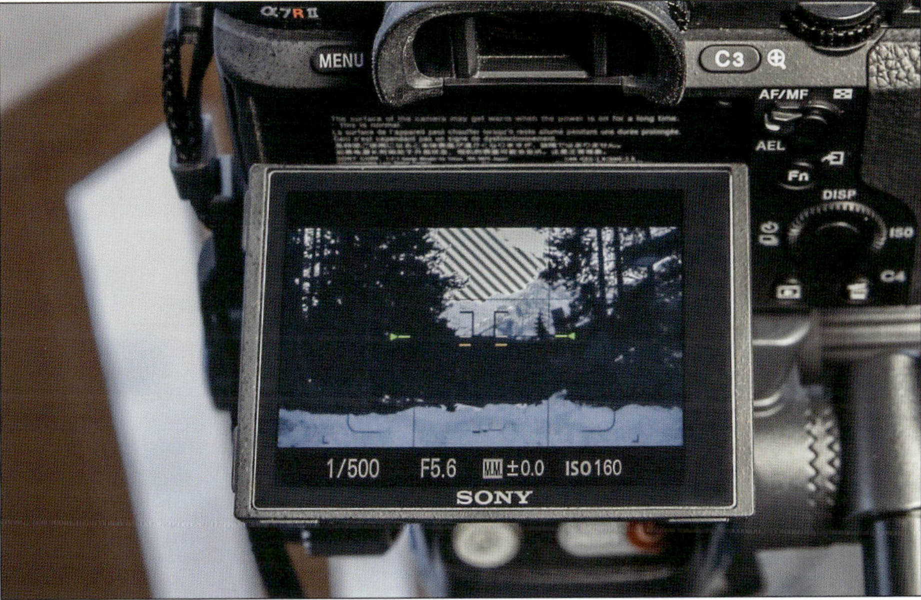

Probably the worst thing we could do to our image in-camera would be to let the brightest part of it get so bright that it actually damages the photo. This is called either "blowing out the highlights" or "clipping the highlights," and what it means is there are areas of your photo that are so bright, there will be no detail there whatsoever. Nuthin'. There will not be any pixels in those areas and if you printed the image, there would be no ink hitting the paper in those areas—it would just be paper. If that sounds bad (and it should), then you need to turn on your camera's highlight warning (yes, this is such a big problem that your camera can actually warn you if highlight clipping is occurring). Now, depending on your camera's make/model, this warning (sometimes referred to as the "blinkies" because when this feature is turned on, the clipped areas blink on/off at you when you view a photo on the back of your camera) could have a slightly different name. For example, on Fuji cameras it's called the Live View Highlight Alert, and on a Canon, it's simply the Highlight Alert. On most Nikons, in the Playback menu, under the Playback Display Options, you'll see a checkbox for Highlights (that's the one to turn on). Again, some cameras can show you the warning on your LCD after you've taken the shot (that's why you might turn on the warning in the Playback menu) and some show you the area where you're clipping in the viewfinder or LCD while you're composing the shot (there you'll see a zebra-like pattern, as seen here, rather than the "blinkies"). The important thing is to turn this warning on, and on the next two pages, we'll look at what to do if you see the blinkies, or zebra-like pattern, or if you're in Saskatchewan, a Bigfoot sighting.

Is the Highlight Warning You're Seeing Really Accurate? Well…No

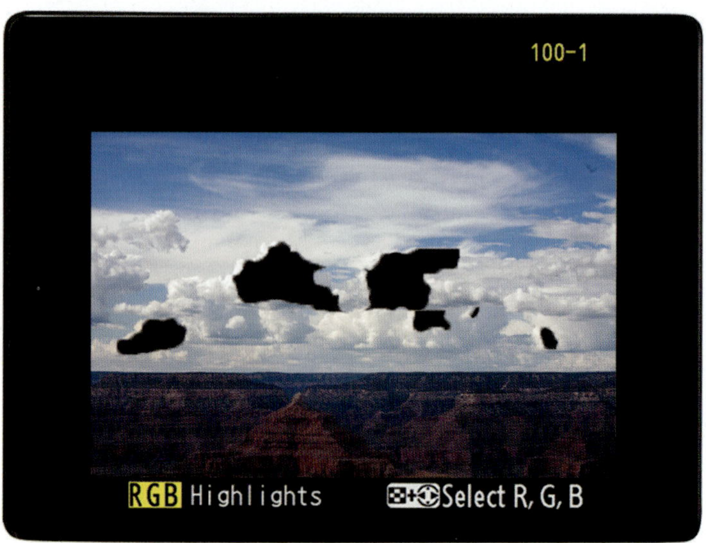

Okay, let's say you see a highlight warning/alert on the back of your camera (or a zebra-like pattern in your viewfinder before you start shooting). If it's not a ton of clipping (just an area here or there), chances are when you open the image in Lightroom or Photoshop the clipping will be gone (yes, both Lightroom and Photoshop's Camera RAW have highlight clipping warnings, too). So, why will the clipping be gone? It's because it was probably never really there in the first place. If you're shooting in RAW, the RAW format captures a wider tonal range than an image shot in JPEG would. Now, you might be thinking, "But, I'm shooting in RAW, and I'm still seeing blinkies on the back of my camera." That's because even though you're shooting in RAW, your camera shows you the lower-quality JPEG on the back of your camera, so what you're seeing is the JPEG image clipping, not the RAW image you shot. Now, what if there's a lot of clipping? Then, you're going to have to deal with it in-camera (and I cover that more on the next page): use your camera's exposure compensation to override what the camera thought was the proper exposure and darken it by 1/3 of a stop, take the same shot again, and see if you still have clipping.

How to Deal with Clipped Highlights

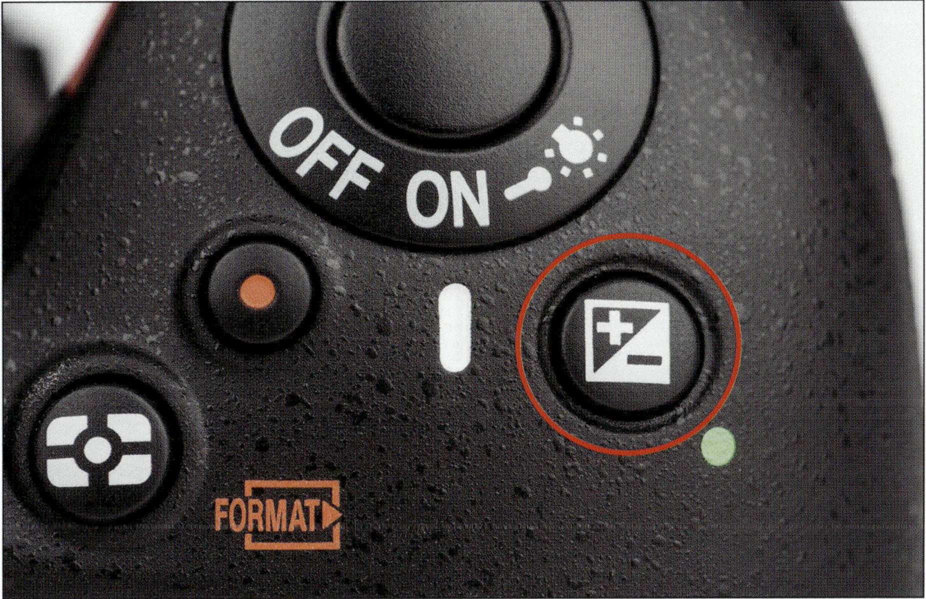

Spoiler Alert: you're going to darken your exposure a bit to recover those clipped highlights, and depending on your shooting mode (I recommend aperture priority for landscapes), you'll adjust it differently. Remember, in aperture priority mode, you set the f-stop and your camera chooses what it thinks is the right shutter speed for the scene. But, sometimes it's wrong, and you wind up with clipped highlights. If that happens, you're going to override what the camera thinks is the correct exposure by using an awesome, must-know feature for landscape photography called "exposure compensation." All that means is, "my camera's wrong (my highlights are clipping), so I'm going to compensate for that by making my shot a little darker (usually adjusted in 1/3-of-a-stop increments)." So, you'll darken the image 1/3 of a stop using the exposure compensation dial (depending on your camera make/model, it can be a dial, or you press a button and then move a dial), take a test shot, then look at the image and see if the clipping is still there. If there's a decent amount left, darken the exposure another 1/3 of a stop. If there's still a little clipping after all that, we just let it go because, as I mentioned on the previous page, you're looking at the JPEG photo, not the RAW photo (even if you're shooting in RAW), and chances are it won't have that little bit of clipping left. If you're shooting in manual mode, exposure compensation won't work on most (but not all) cameras, so you'll have to darken your exposure manually by changing your f-stop. If you're at f/11, raise it to the next available number (f/16 on most cameras), take a test shot, and see if you still have clipping. If you do, darken the scene a bit more until it goes away.

Which Metering Mode to Use

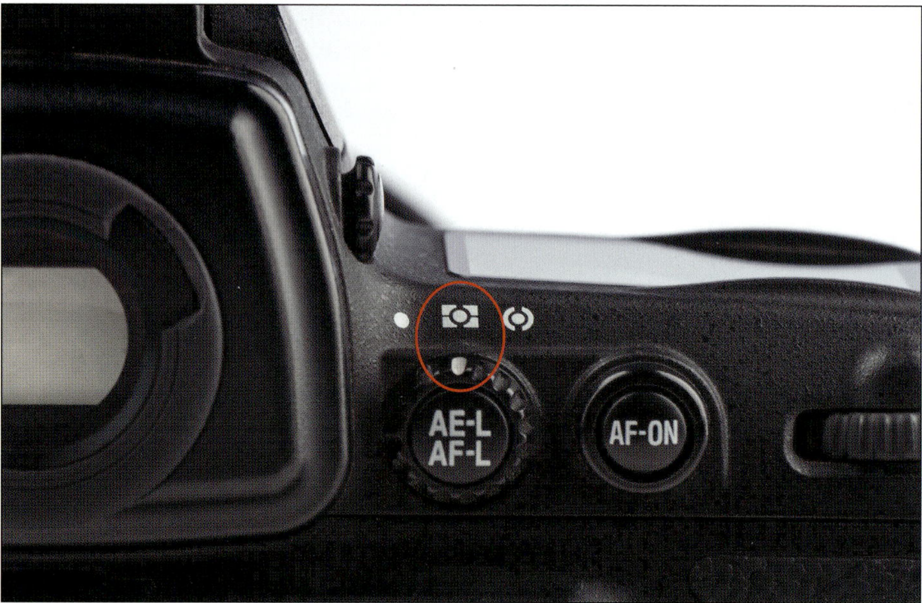

This is surprisingly easy, and although people really seem to overthink and sweat this part of the process, you don't have to. I use the metering mode that is actually the default on most cameras these days: evaluative metering (also known as matrix metering). The reason it's the default choice is because it's the most sophisticated metering system out there, and that's why it works so well for most lighting situations. When you're using evaluative metering, your camera analyzes the light from the entire scene you're aimed at, and then it combines the data from all those different areas to give you an overall great exposure. There was a time when this stuff was tricky, but thanks to evaluative metering, for the most part, it's a set-it-and-forget-it type of thing. I rarely—rarely—ever have to change my metering mode (and, really, only in one situation do I change it at all—see the next page). So, if you were sweating the whole exposure thing, don't (especially since you have exposure compensation—see the previous page). If you don't agree with how the camera exposed your image, you can override it yourself. Also, if you somehow missed it during your shoot, and you open an image later and realize that it's half a stop or more too bright or too dark, you can fix that in Lightroom or Camera Raw by moving a single slider 1/8 of an inch.

When to Switch to Spot Metering

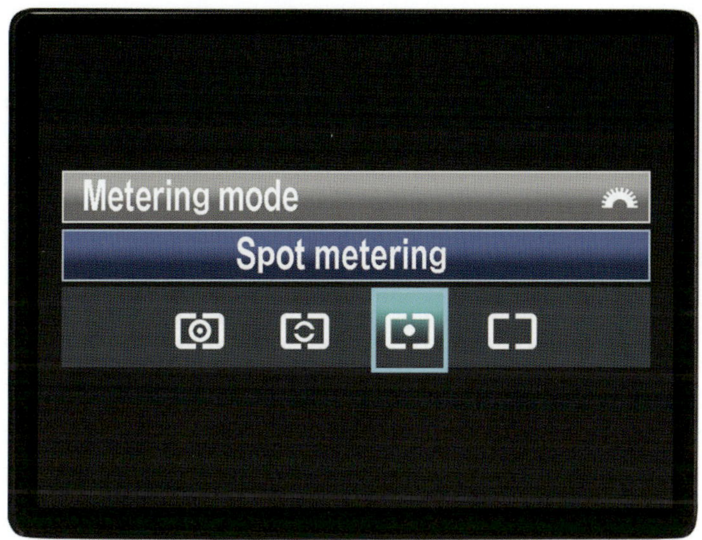

As I mentioned, the default metering on today's cameras (labeled Matrix or Evaluative on most cameras) is so good that I rarely have to switch metering modes. In fact, the only time I might is when I'm in a tricky lighting situation and my camera is either underexposing or overexposing the scene by quite a bit. The reason this happens is that your camera's default metering mode averages the light in the entire image to make what it thinks is an overall good exposure. But, when it's a tricky lighting situation, that average reading can sometimes be wrong, and you wind up with a really dark or really bright image. When you switch to spot metering, instead of averaging the light in the entire image, now it's just looking at the light in a small area of your image, right where you are aiming the center point of your focus area. By doing this (switching to spot metering—check your manual for how do that on your particular make and model of camera), you are telling the camera, "Only expose for this area—this is the important part." Again, you won't have to do this often, but if you wind up in one of those situations where you can't seem to get the overall exposure right, switch to spot metering, point at the important area, and see if that doesn't fix the problem.

Set Your White Balance to Cloudy

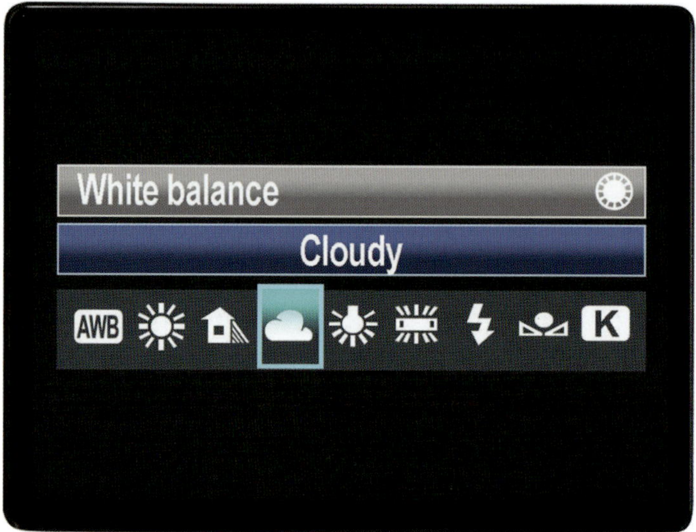

I picked up this trick out on a shoot with a top pro and I've been using it ever since: for landscape photography, set your White Balance to Cloudy, even if it's not cloudy. This makes your images look warmer overall, and generally, we find things that are a little warmer more pleasing, including flesh tones, but it works wonders for landscapes. Anyway, that's what I've been using for at least the past 10 years. Give it a shot—I think you'll like the results.

You Have to Check Sharpness During the Shoot

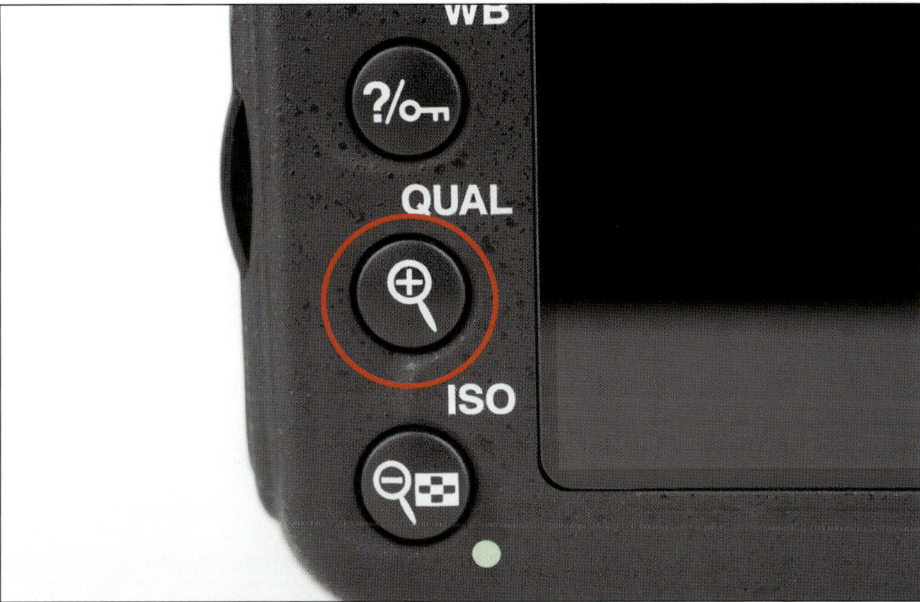

If I only had a dollar for every landscape shot I've taken on a tripod and found out later that I had done something (bumped into the tripod leg, didn't have my cable release with me and moved the camera just a tiny bit when I pressed the shutter button, etc.) that made the shot a little—or even a lot—out of focus. The problem is that everything looks in-focus on that tiny 3-inch screen on the back of your camera, but then later, when you open the shot at a larger size on your computer, that's when heartbreak sets in. That's why it's so important that you zoom in and check the sharpness of your shot now, while you're still out on location and you can take another shot. This is critical, and it just takes a couple of seconds, but it's so worth it. To make this process even quicker and easier, a lot of cameras these days allow you to set a nice, tight, zoom to one button on the back of your camera (like the Set button on a Canon Quick Control Dial, or the OK button on a Nikon). That way, you press it once, it zooms in tight, you check to see if it's sharp, then you zoom back out. One click in; one click out.

Live View Super-Sharp Focus Trick

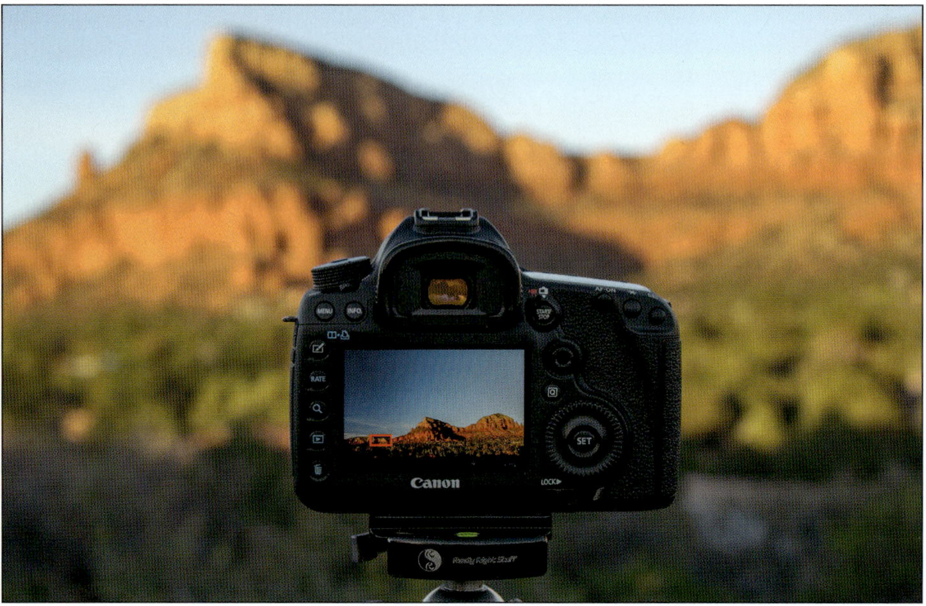

This is a trick that has been gaining popularity because it starts by using your camera's auto focus, but then you tweak that focus manually to ensure it's super-sharp. Here's how it's done: (1) Position your focus point, so it's about 1/3 of the way into your scene, then hold the shutter button down halfway to engage your auto focus on that spot. (2) Now, turn on Live View, so you're looking at the scene on the LCD monitor on the back of your camera. One cool advantage of Live View mode is that you can zoom in tight on the scene even before you take the shot (usually, you can only zoom in on an image after you've taken it), so press the zoom button (its icon looks like a magnifying glass on most cameras) and zoom right in on the spot where you focused in step one. Let's say, for example, you focused on a rock about 1/3 of the way into the scene, so zoom in right on that rock. Once you're zoomed in tight like that, you can really see how in-focus that area is. (3) On the barrel of your lens, turn off the Auto focus switch, so now you're in Manual focus mode. Now, you're going to look at that zoomed-in area as you turn the Manual focus ring on your lens, until that spot where you focused is super-sharp and crisp. You can now just take the shot, knowing you totally nailed that focus. If you absolutely need to know your focus is as sharp as it can be, this will help ensure that. All that being said, I must admit I don't use this trick very often—the auto focus on our cameras today is pretty darn good, so I save this technique for just those times when I've found a killer shot and I want to make absolutely 100% certain the focus is on the money. That's when I'll make the extra time and effort.

Which Focus Mode to Use

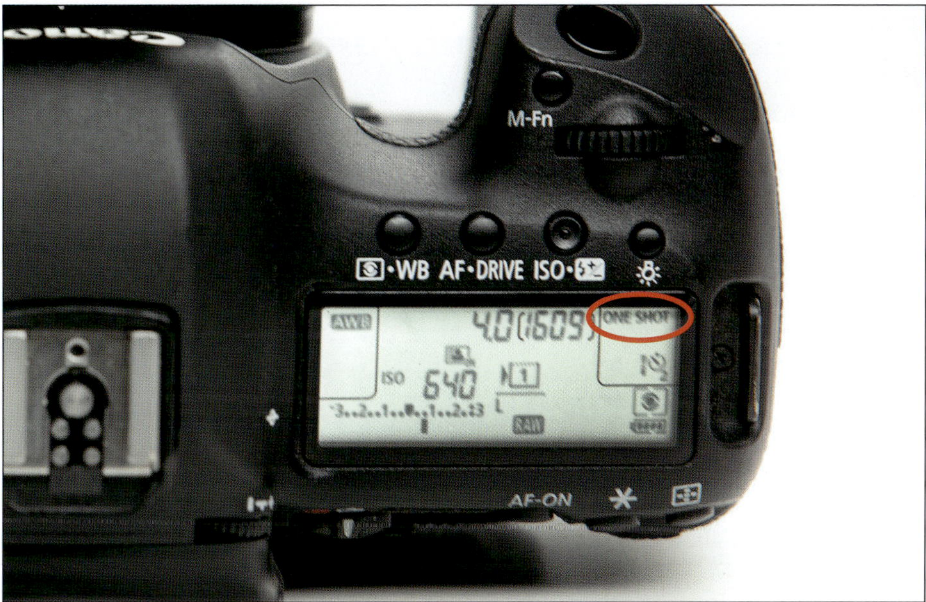

This is another setting where you simply set it and forget it, because it's not gonna change while we're shooting landscapes. Since your landscape is a still object, set your focus mode to single focus (rather than any type of continuous focus mode). You want to be able to choose the spot where your camera focuses—you don't want it to choose for you, since there's a reasonable chance it won't make an awesome choice. So, set your focus mode to single and you're good to go.

Mirror Lockup

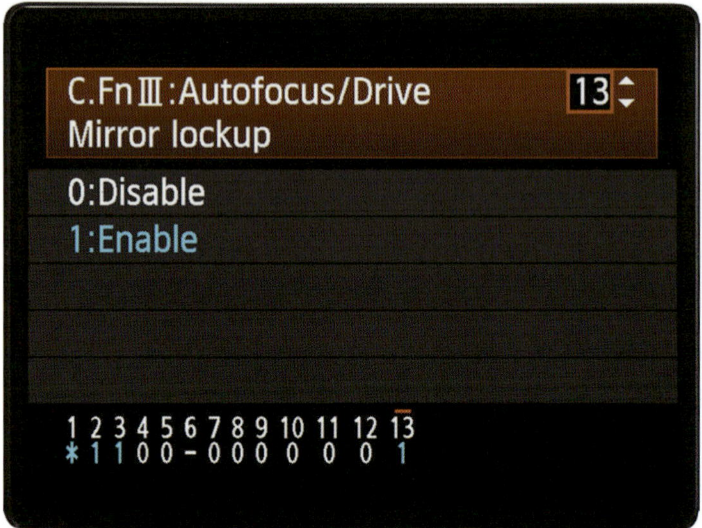

If you're trying to squeak out every possible amount of sharpness you can from your camera, you're shooting a DSLR (this trick isn't necessary for mirrorless cameras), and you're on a tripod (that's key), you can use a feature called "mirror lockup," which locks your mirror in the up position right before you take a shot, reducing the small amount of vibration that happens when the mirror flips up during the shooting process. It's easy use, but not every camera has this feature, so download the free PDF of your camera's instruction manual and do a search for "mirror lockup" (or "exposure delay mode" on some cameras). If your camera has it, it will tell you which menu it's found under, and you just have to turn it on. If your PDF search comes back with "not found," you can stop here, because your camera doesn't have it. Anyway, once it's turned on, you're good to go. Just remember to turn this feature off any time you're shooting hand-held.

Your Cable Release Alternative

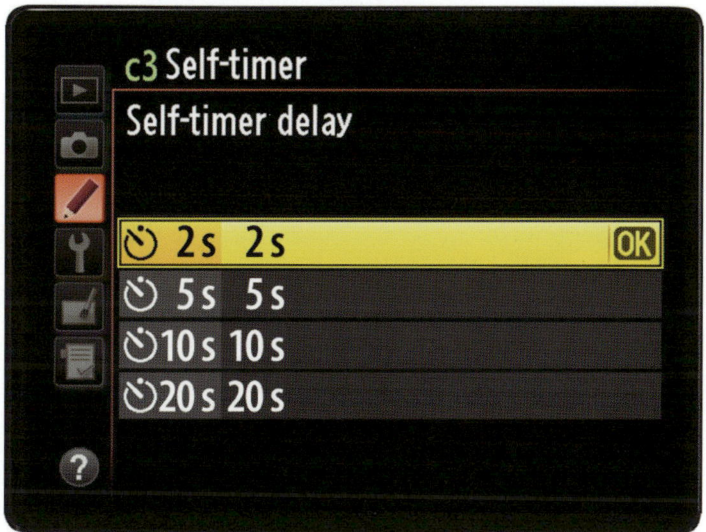

If you either don't own a cable release, you forgot your cable release, or you left it back in the car (which is a hike from where you are), here's your backup plan: use your camera's self-timer feature. That way, after you press the shutter button (which moves your camera a little bit), there are a few seconds for that movement to dissipate, so you can get a sharp shot. Now, most cameras have a few settings for how many seconds go by before your camera fires the shot for you: The default is usually 10 seconds, which is great for when you're using it for taking a group shot where you need to be in the picture. But, it feels more like six minutes when you're standing there waiting for it while you're shooting a landscape photo, which is why I change my setting to the two-second option. This two seconds still feels like two-and-a-half minutes, but that's better than the six-minute feeling by about three-and-a-half minutes.

Wide-Angle Lens (Why and Which One)

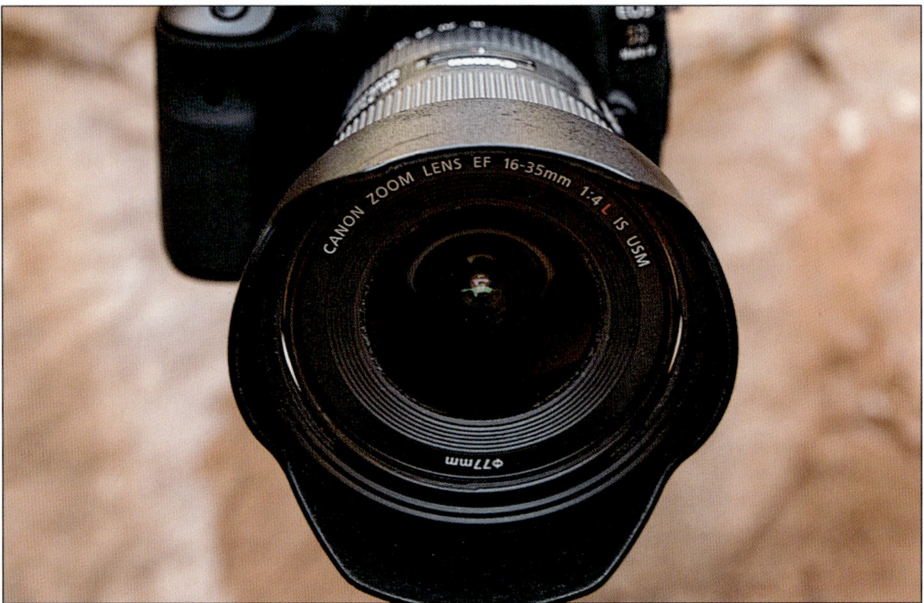

While there are instances where you'd want to use a longer lens, the mainstay of landscape photography is the wide-angle lens. The weird thing is, you don't want to go "too wide" because an ultra-wide-angle lens pushes things away from you, so mountains in the background look even farther away. Plus, those super-wide-angle lenses often have a bulbous, rounded lens that keeps you from using screw-on ND filters or polarizers without a large, more complicated bracket setup. This is one of those topics that people debate endlessly online, so I'll put it this way: if I had to choose an ideal wide-angle for landscapes, it would be around a 24mm wide-angle for full-frame cameras or an 18mm for crop-sensor cameras. Of course, you get a little more flexibility with a wide-angle zoom, so a 24–105mm works on full-frame cameras and so does a lighter 16–35mm (you don't need the heavier, more expensive f/2.8 for landscape work. I use the f/4—it's lighter and half the price. Unless you're shooting starscapes pretty often, you'll never use that f/2.8 of the more expensive version). For crop-sensor bodies, Tamron has a nice 10–24mm f/3.5–5.6 that is a bargain and has a lot of fans in the landscape community. In short, don't go too wide (on a full-frame camera, not wider than 16mm; on a crop-sensor camera, not wider than 18mm), and don't go too tight (don't go tighter than 35mm on a full-frame camera, or 24mm on a crop-sensor camera).

When to Use Ultra-Wide Lenses

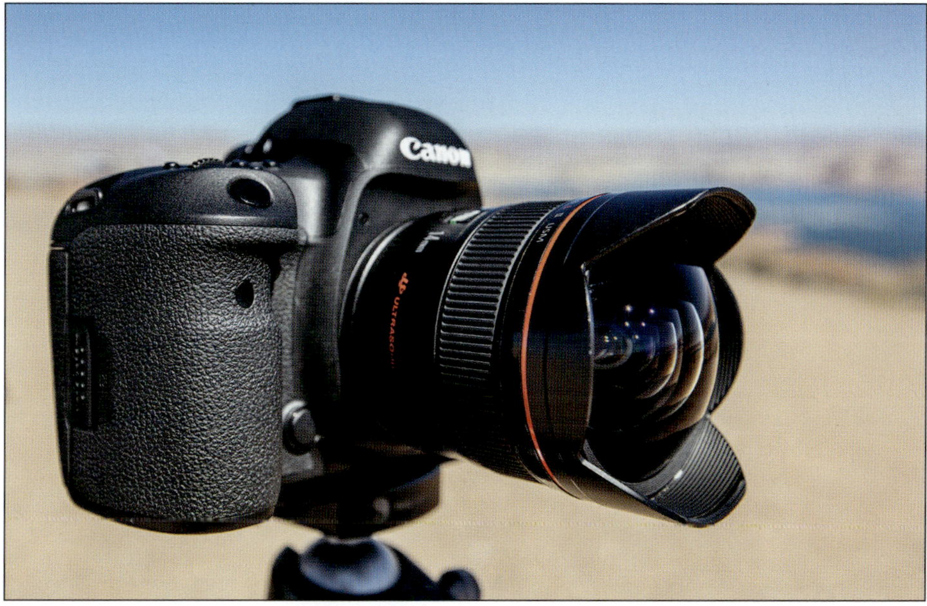

Although you now know my personal "sweet spot" for full-frame landscape lenses would be around 24mm (or 18mm on a crop-sensor camera), are there any times where you might want to go wider than usual? Well, if you have something really close as your foreground, like a large rock, or a piece of driftwood, then ultra-wides can look really great. Also, when you're shooting a waterfall, or shooting in a forest, or shooting in a canyon slot, or shooting the Milky Way (see Chapter 7), or…well…you can see there are a few times where an ultra-wide-angle might come in handy. It won't be your mainstay for landscapes because it pushes things away from the camera (so big mountains in the distance become much smaller), but if you're shooting with a full-frame camera, you can swing something like Tamron's 15–30mm, Nikon's 14–24mm, Sony's 12–24mm, or Canon's 11–24mm, and then you'll have a lot of options (but note that these lenses are all pretty large and heavy). Much smaller, lighter, and much cheaper are the crop-sensor lenses in the 10mm and 12mm range (Canon, Nikon, Sony, Tamron, and Sigma all make ultra-wide zooms in the 10–24mm or 10–22mm range for crop-sensor cameras), and yes, you'll need to go that wide on crop-sensor bodies to get what you'd call an ultra-wide field of view.

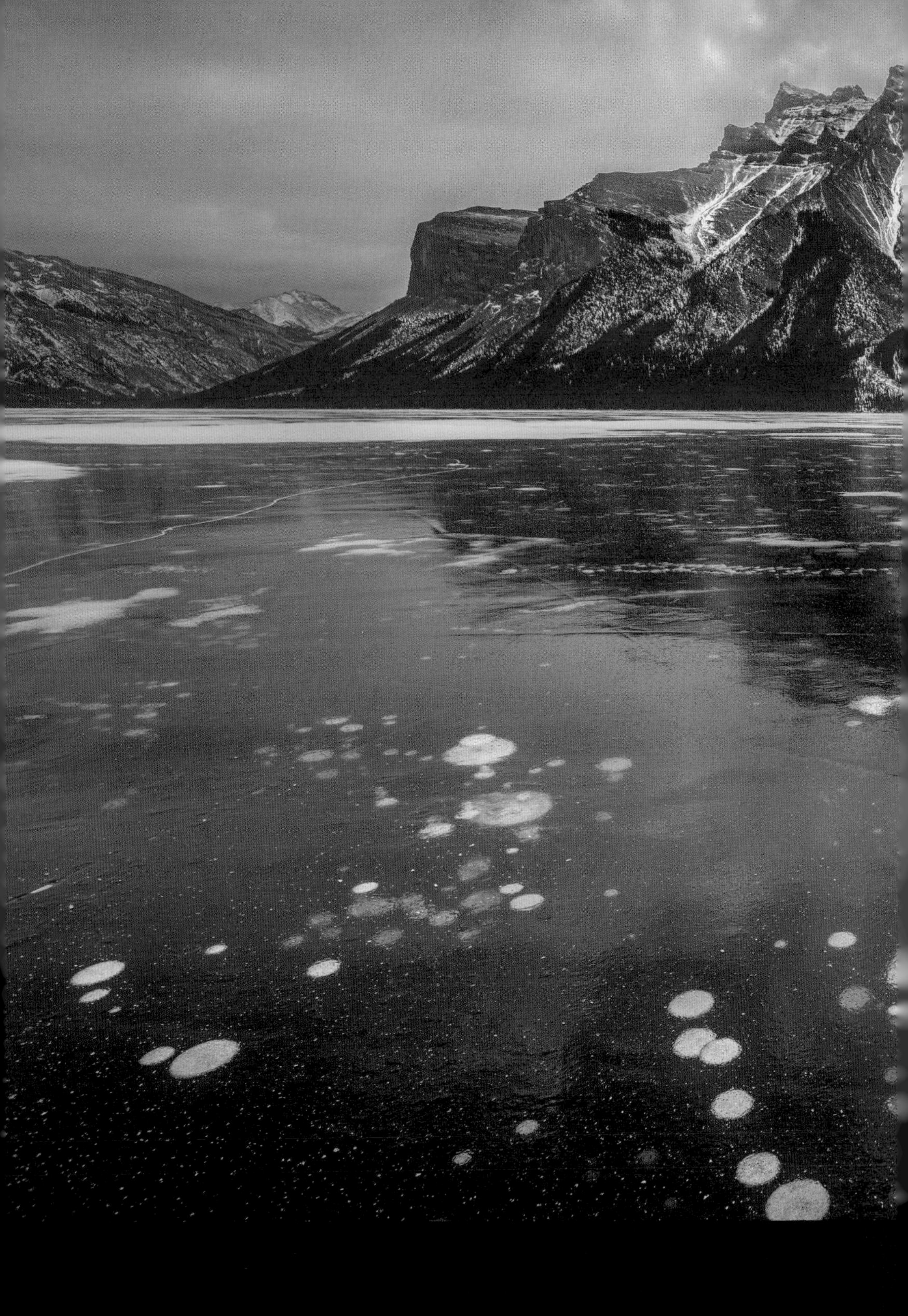

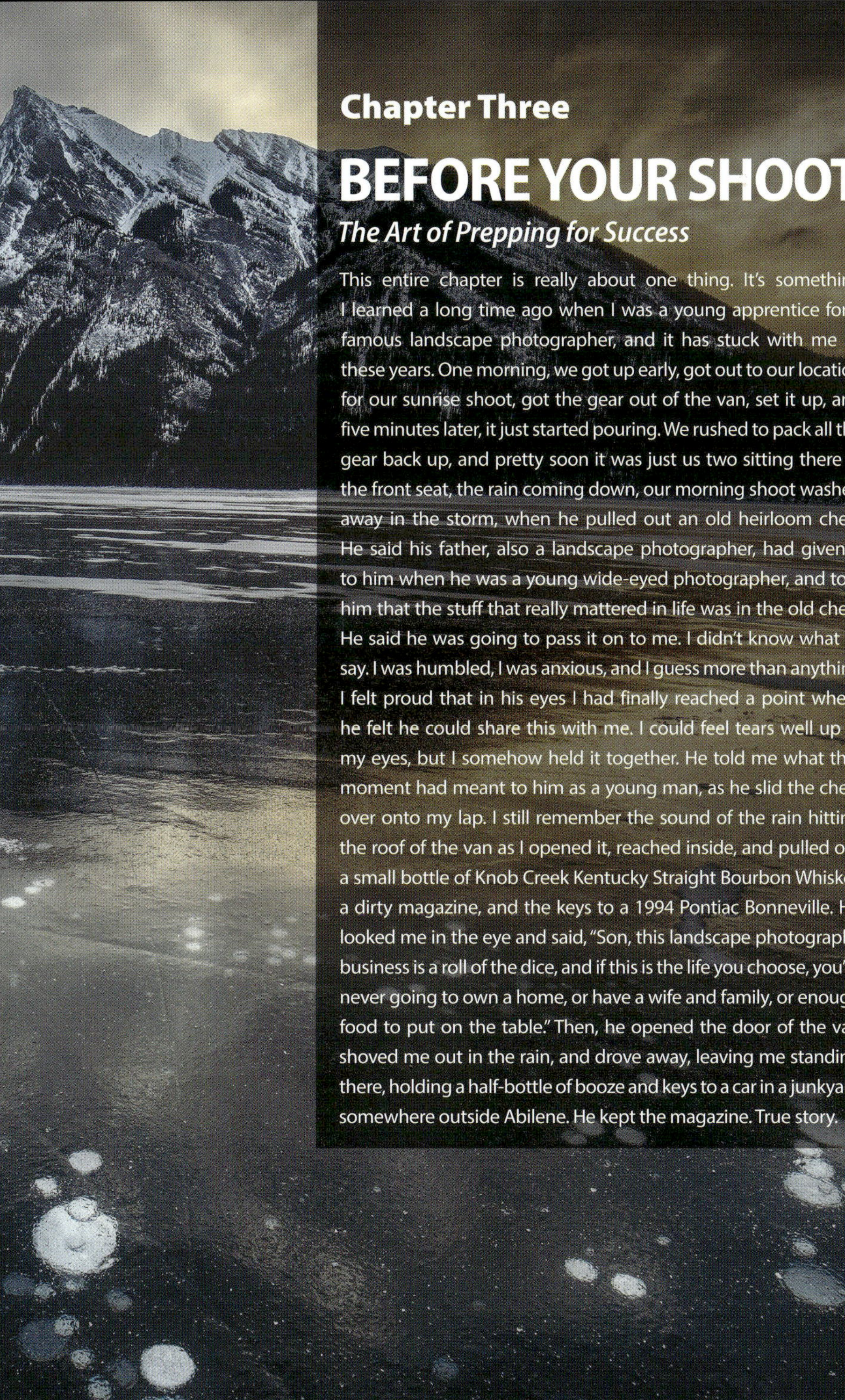

BEFORE YOUR SHOOT
The Art of Prepping for Success

This entire chapter is really about one thing. It's something I learned a long time ago when I was a young apprentice for a famous landscape photographer, and it has stuck with me all these years. One morning, we got up early, got out to our location for our sunrise shoot, got the gear out of the van, set it up, and five minutes later, it just started pouring. We rushed to pack all the gear back up, and pretty soon it was just us two sitting there in the front seat, the rain coming down, our morning shoot washed away in the storm, when he pulled out an old heirloom chest. He said his father, also a landscape photographer, had given it to him when he was a young wide-eyed photographer, and told him that the stuff that really mattered in life was in the old chest. He said he was going to pass it on to me. I didn't know what to say. I was humbled, I was anxious, and I guess more than anything, I felt proud that in his eyes I had finally reached a point where he felt he could share this with me. I could feel tears well up in my eyes, but I somehow held it together. He told me what that moment had meant to him as a young man, as he slid the chest over onto my lap. I still remember the sound of the rain hitting the roof of the van as I opened it, reached inside, and pulled out a small bottle of Knob Creek Kentucky Straight Bourbon Whiskey, a dirty magazine, and the keys to a 1994 Pontiac Bonneville. He looked me in the eye and said, "Son, this landscape photography business is a roll of the dice, and if this is the life you choose, you're never going to own a home, or have a wife and family, or enough food to put on the table." Then, he opened the door of the van, shoved me out in the rain, and drove away, leaving me standing there, holding a half-bottle of booze and keys to a car in a junkyard somewhere outside Abilene. He kept the magazine. True story.

Do Your Research

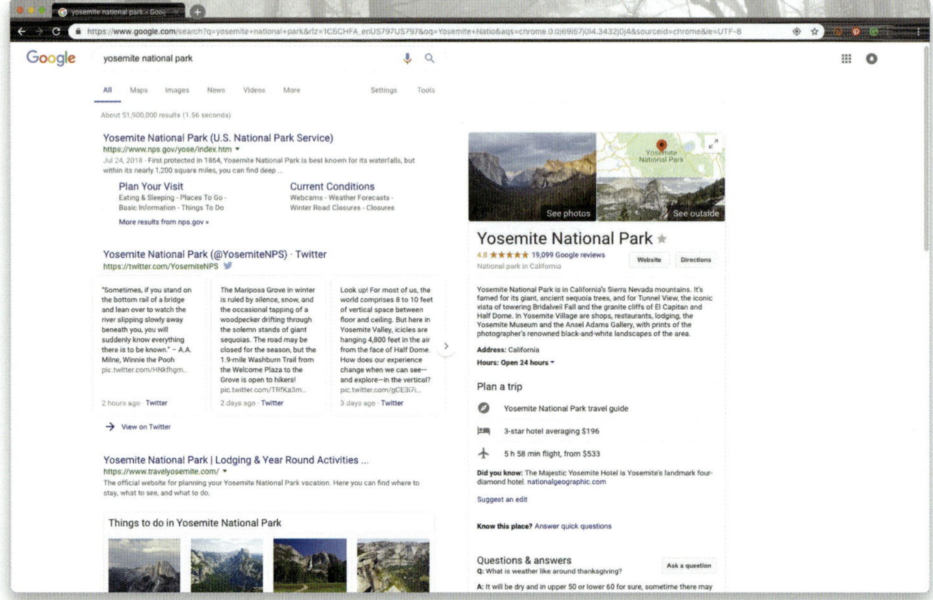

I can't tell you how much of a difference it makes to do some research in advance about shooting opportunities available in the area you'll be. I've skipped this step before, and once I got home and posted the first image online, people commented: "Did you shoot at [insert name of incredible shooting location I didn't know was right nearby]?" Sometimes that location winds up being way cooler than the obvious place you went to shoot. This is a heartbreaker and all it takes is a little work up front to avoid missing out on something awesome.

Start with Pinterest

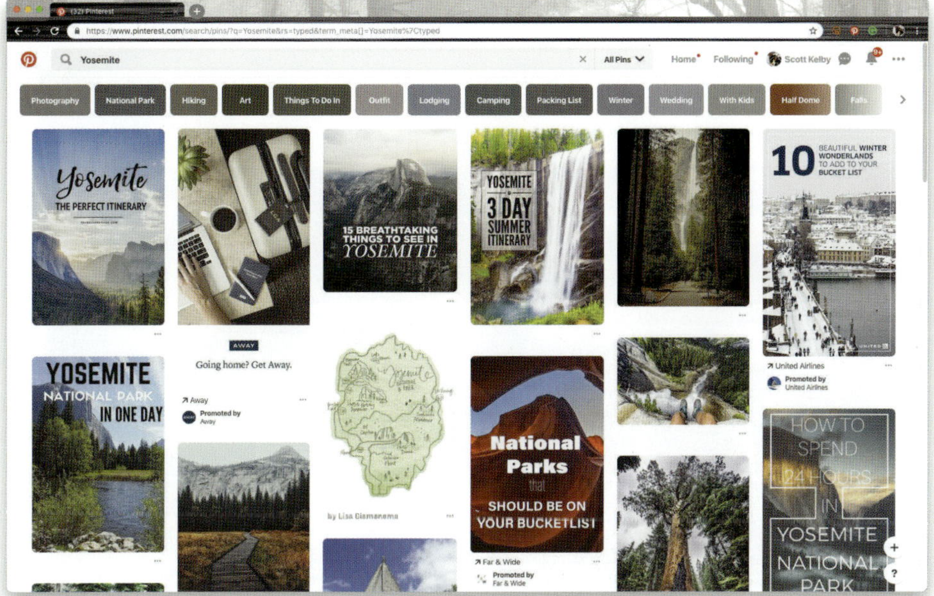

It's worth joining Pinterest, if you don't already have an account (it's free), because there you'll find people who love landscapes curating a bunch of their favorite shots and articles from the web, all together in one place. Start by typing in a search term for where you're thinking of going. For example, I just typed in "Yosemite,"and one of the very first results (the results all come back in the form of images) was an article called "15 BreathtakingThings to See inYosemite," where it tells you where to get its "cover shot" (it notes you can drive right up with easy access). As you scroll down this article's page, you'll find other locations in the area (ones you might miss if you just Google this location), with helpful notes, like "...easy 1-mile walk from the parking lot and gives you a 360-degree view ofYosemite" and "Take Mist Trail to gaze at this beautiful fall, but be sure you have hiking shoes on as the trail gets very slippery from all the mist" (by the way, here's the link to the article: https://localadventurer.com/best-things-to-do-in-yosemite-national-park/). Again, Pinterest gives you image-based results with links to articles, blogs, and images themselves that make this my first stop, well before the shoot, when researching an area I'm heading to.

Then, Check 500px.com

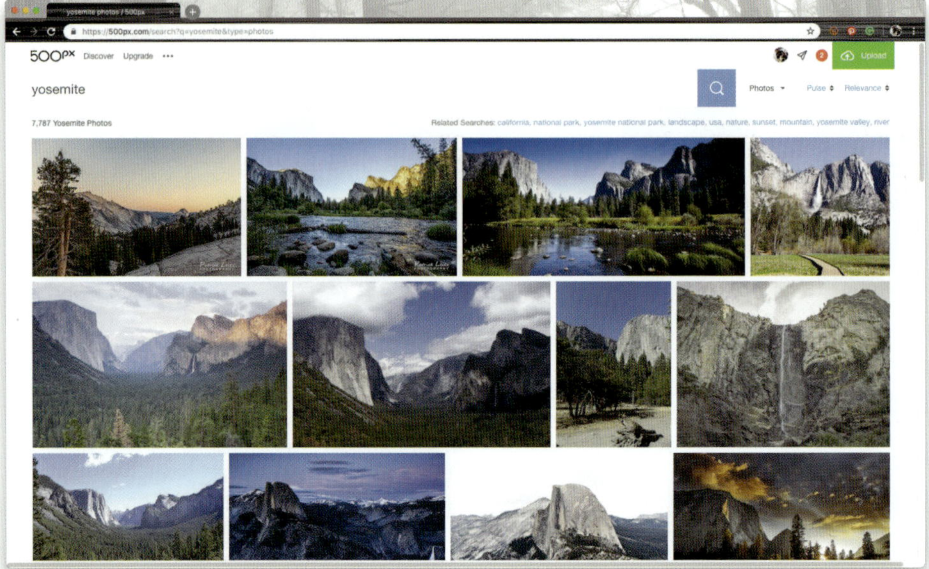

The website 500px.com is a huge, worldwide photography community of serious shooters, and when you type a location into their search field, you'll instantly find lots of amazing shots from that location. If you click on an image and look down at its provided details, you'll often get the exact location where it was shot (often with a map included), what equipment was used, and sometimes, some very specific information about how to reach that location (including the best times of year to shoot there, things to watch out for, etc.). I've made some great discoveries here I would have otherwise missed.

Google Images Search & Google Maps

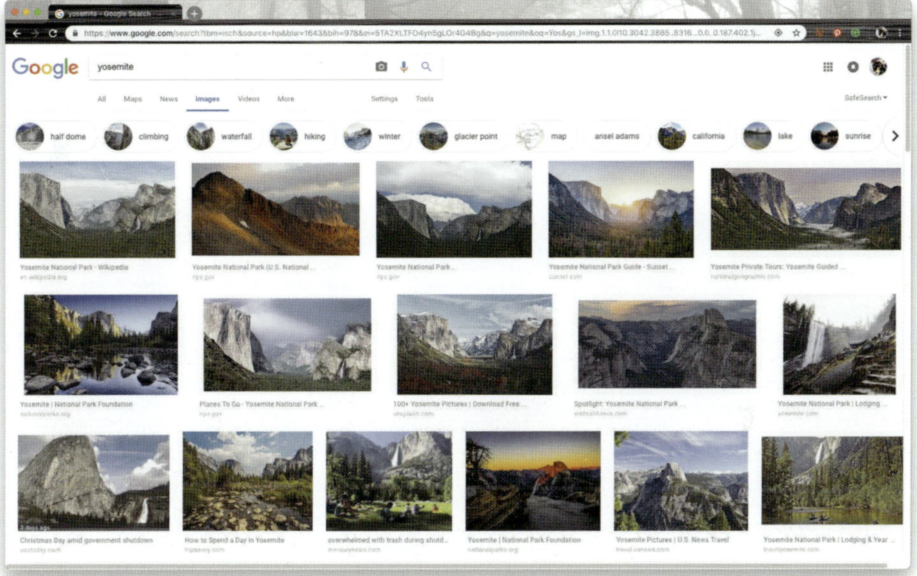

Both Pinterest and 500px bring you lots of great images in their search results. A Google Images search also brings you lots of images, and while they're not always great, that doesn't mean you might not get a lame photo of a great location you might have missed using the other two options. So, it's worth giving it a look as the third leg of your research chair. The fourth leg is Google Maps (or the Google Earth app). Once you've found a general location, this is a really great resource for things like where to find nearby parking, where various trails are, which areas are accessible, and lots of other helpful info. But, I don't turn to Google Maps until I've figured out the general location first, using either Pinterest or 500px.

Location Scouting

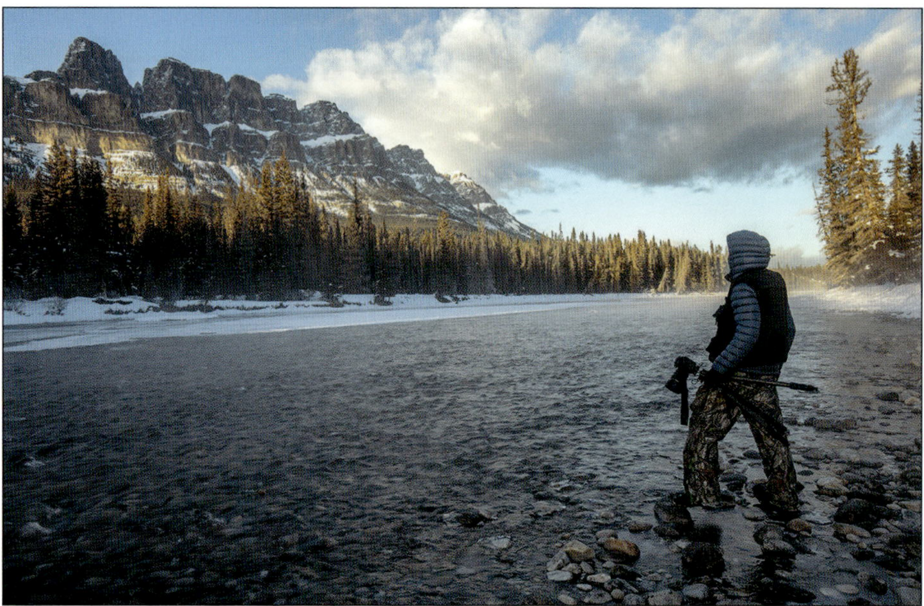

This is especially important if you're going to be shooting at dawn, because it's really hard to find the perfect spot in the dark. Sadly, I've been burned by this more than once. When I showed up where I thought I wanted to shoot, it wasn't as great a spot as I thought, and by then it was too late—I was stuck with that location and came away with shots I was really disappointed with. Had I scoped out the location the day before, I would have realized then that it wasn't that great and found a better spot. This is particularly important when you don't have a chance to return the next day and try again—if you only get one shot at it, it's worth scoping out the location the day before to see if it's really what you're looking for. You don't even have to pull out your gear—just take a quick snap with your cellphone and you'll know whether this is the spot to trek out to in the dark the next day. Now, you might be thinking you can skip this for sunset, but I've been burned skipping the location scouting for sunset shoots, too. The worst is getting there and finding out the location is closed off, or access has been limited, or there's currently something there (like there was for me one time when a huge utility truck was parked where there was no way to get the shot and keep it out of my frame). If I had driven by the day before, I would have realized that I needed to scope out a different sunset location. By the time you get there and see the obstruction, it might be too late to come up with a Plan B. Don't underestimate the usefulness of location scouting.

Great Landscapes Make Great Landscape Shots

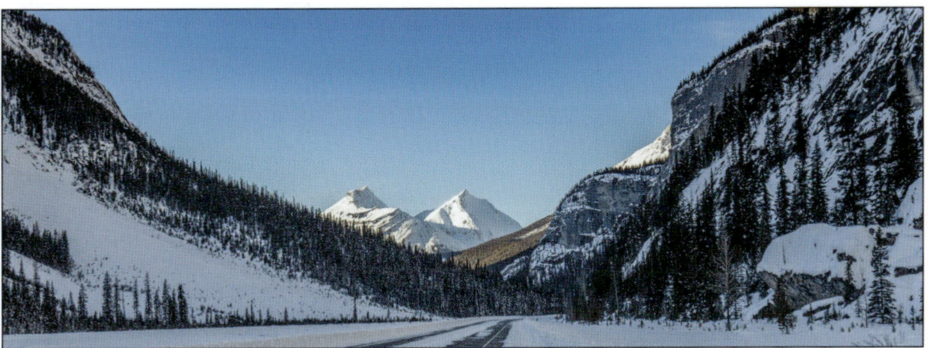

If you're a landscape wizard, you might be able to take lemons and make lemonade and make the most of an "iffy" landscape location. But, your chances for getting a great landscape shot go up exponentially when you're standing in front of a great landscape. If you're standing in a great spot in front of Yosemite's Half Dome at dawn, you're probably going to come away with a beautiful shot, especially if the weather cooperates and Mother Nature gives you an amazing sky full of clouds and colors. You've basically positioned yourself to come away with a spectacular landscape shot. Now, if you're not standing in one of the world's top 50 landscape photo locations, you're going to have your work cut out for you (there are a dozen lists like this online, but I like this international list from *U.S. News & World Report*: https://travel.usnews.com/gallery/the-50-most-beautiful-landscapes-in-the-world). Think of it this way: if you wanted to be a great automotive photographer, you'd ideally want to shoot Ferraris, Lamborghinis, Porsches, Jaguars, McLarens, etc., because these cars are so photogenic, with beautiful lines, brilliant finishes, and incredible wheels. Now, could you create a photo of a Toyota Prius? Perhaps, but you'd better be an incredible automotive photographer to make a photo of a Prius get a "wow" from someone. It doesn't take nearly as much to get a "wow" from a photo of a Ferrari. Yes, it takes more effort to find one to photograph, but your chances of creating a "wow" photo go way up. Yes, it takes more effort to get to an amazing landscape location, but your chances of creating a "wow" photo also go way up. What you're standing in front of when you press that shutter button makes all the difference in the world.

When to Shoot: Dawn

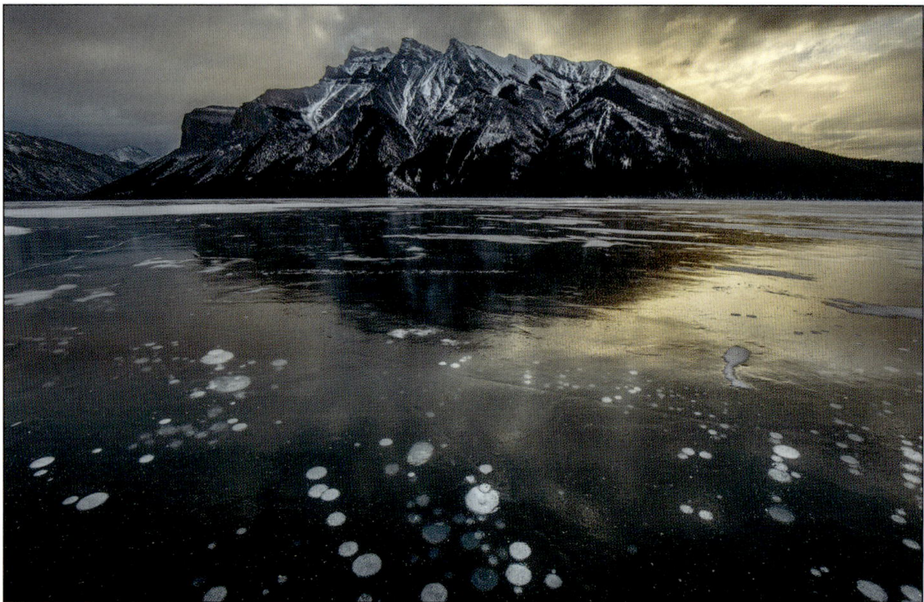

If you've fallen in love with an amazing landscape image, chances are it was taken near dawn or dusk—those are the two times of day when the light is beautiful, the shadows are soft, and landscapes far and away look their best. Doing a dawn shoot is harder because you have to get up so darn early, but it can pay off by presenting you with spectacularly colorful skies and smooth, glassy reflections. The key to dawn shoots might surprise you: most of your best shots will probably come before the sun actually rises. That is your prime shooting time—the 15 to 20 minutes before the sun actually breaks the horizon usually deliver the best light. You need to be set up, in place, and ready to start shooting at least 30 minutes before sunup, so set that alarm early. If you have some clouds in the sky to catch the color as the sun is getting ready to rise, it can truly be magical. Once the sun does come up, you'll usually have (depending on the location, and if you're in the mountains and such) around 10 to 15 more minutes to shoot before the sun gets up in the sky enough to where the beautiful sunrise light turns into bright, harsh light, and the shoot is over. The whole idea is to shoot when the light is beautiful, soft, and flattering to the landscape you're standing in front of. That window of "good light" totals around 30 to 35 minutes (20 minutes before sunrise and around 10 to 15 after it rises). These lengths of time are generally what to expect (or harsh realities, depending on how you look at it) and are based on where you're shooting (for example, in the summer in Norway, sunset light lasts for four hours) and what you're shooting (mountains can make the sunrise later than advertised).

When to Shoot: Dusk

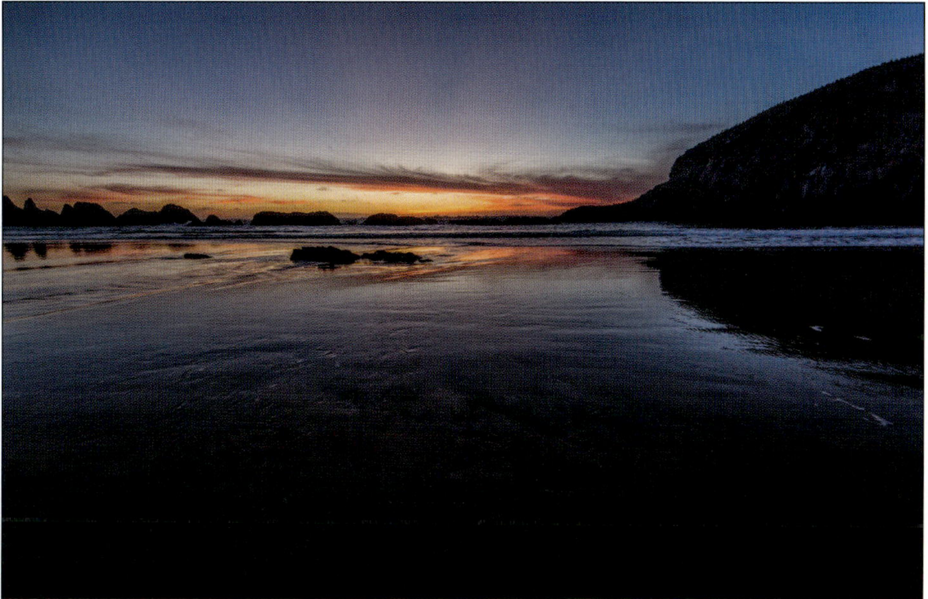

While this is something that is debated endlessly online (pretty much like every topic online now that I think about it), many landscape photographers prefer to shoot around sunset rather than at dawn. You still get that soft, beautiful, flattering landscape light, but (a) you don't have to get up crazy early; (b) you don't have to scout your location the day before—you can do it an hour before; (c) the "window of shooting" opportunity is longer—from around 45 minutes to an hour before sunset to around 20 minutes or more after, depending, of course, on what and where you're shooting. If you're shooting in the mountains, the sun will often tuck behind the mountains much earlier than the posted time for sunset that day. And, (d) shooting at sunset is easier—you're not traipsing around in the dark, location scouting is easier, a flashlight or head gear isn't needed, it's not as cold, you can sleep in (you get the idea). I generally try to shoot both if I can, and I'm usually shooting in two different locations because of the position of the sun—some locations are better suited to sunrise shoots and some look dramatically better at sunset. This is something that's usually pretty easy to learn (which to shoot when) when you're doing your research before the trip. You'll literally see people write "This is definitely a sunrise shoot…" and they'll explain why. This is another reason why it pays to do your research up front. That way, you don't show up to a popular location at sunrise and you're the only one there. For the first few minutes, you'll be like, "Man, this is amazing! I can't believe we're the only photographers here. We've got our pick of shooting spots. Whoo hoo!" and then as the sun goes up (or down), you'll see why everybody was someplace else at that time.

What to Shoot Other Times

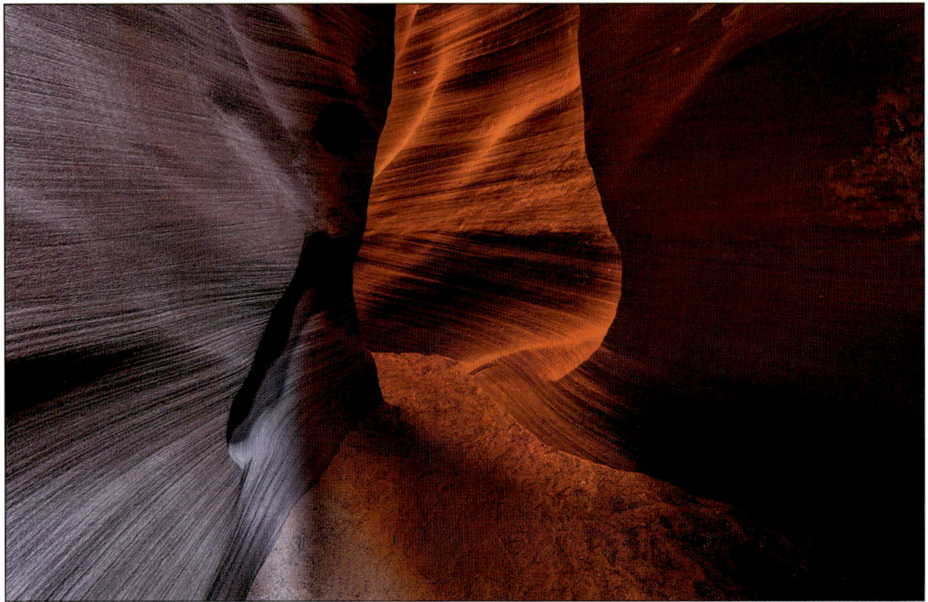

I will tell you this: I know a lot of landscape pros who will simply not shoot during daylight, period. They feel like the light is harsh, the shadows are hard, and this midday time is for location scouting or sitting back in the room sorting and post-processing. But, if you are dying to shoot in the day, and you want some good images, this is your opportunity to shoot things that don't rely on that beautiful dawn or dusk light. For example, this is a perfect time to shoot a waterfall or a stream in the forest. If you have enough cover from the trees, you can do long exposures to get soft, silky water (at my last waterfall shoot, it was bright and sunny all the way to the parking lot, but on our short hike in, there were so many trees that it was ideal for shooting in the soft light). If it's cloudy, or if you have dark, dramatic skies, you can make some nice high-contrast black-and-white images, especially right before or after a storm, when you'll often see some amazingly dramatic clouds. You can also shoot slot canyons in the day (if you're around any, of course), or in caves (I shot a waterfall in a cave in Iceland in the middle of a bright, sunny day—it was gloriously shady in there. Wet, but gloriously shady). Another thing that often photographs pretty well in direct, harsh sunlight is big bodies of water. Think about shots you've seen of tiny islands surrounded by crystal blue water (Bahamas, Bali, Hawaii, etc.) or how about a crisp beach shot with some palm trees? So, if you're near water, you might be near a pretty cool shot (and if you're in the Bahamas, Bali, or Hawaii, you're near a cool midday shot for sure. But if you can't find one, really, who cares? You're in the Bahamas, Bali, or Hawaii, so there's that).

Shooting at Blue Hour

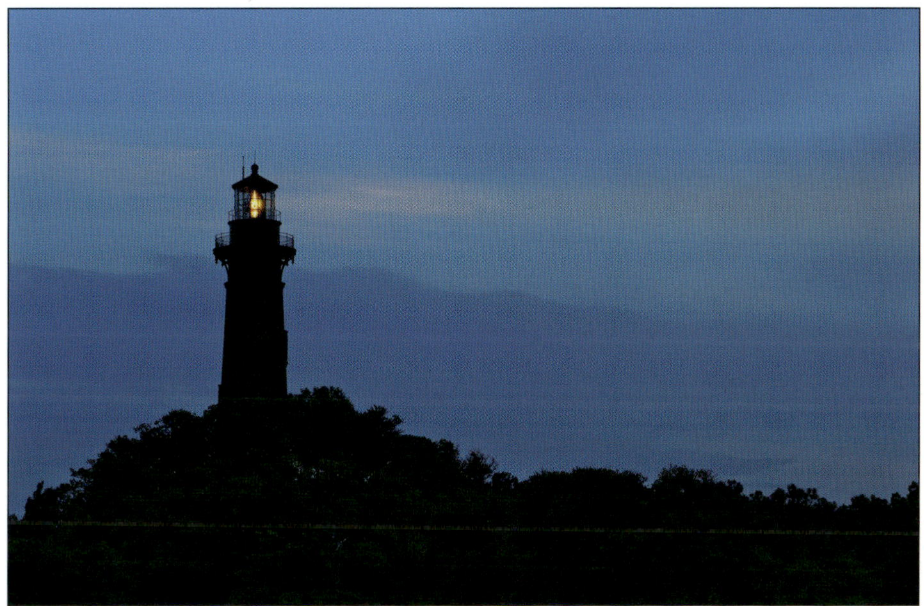

"Blue hour" had to be named by a marketing executive, because it's really more like "blue 30 minutes" (at best). This blue hour phenomenon happens around 15 to 20 minutes after the sun has already set and it lasts for around 30 minutes after that (the amount of time before it appears varies depending on where you're shooting, but if you wait patiently, it will appear, much like Santa). It gets the "blue" part of its name because, instead of the sky turning black (like the usual night sky), the sky literally turns a rich, beautiful shade of blue for this 30-minute "hour." This after-dark blue sky lets you keep shooting well after sunset, and can make for some spectacular images—especially helpful if you don't have a nice cloud-filled sky. The good news is you don't have to do anything special to shoot in blue hour light—you'll use the same settings (I use something like f/11 at 100 ISO in aperture priority mode, where your camera will set the shutter speed for you automatically), and the same setup (tripod, cable release, etc.), and you won't need any filters (no polarizer, no NDs, grads, etc.). So, it's a simple shoot, under a beautiful blue night sky (provided, of course, that the sky isn't so cloudy you can't see the blue hour sky, but I think you already knew that). By the way, there's often a shorter blue hour in the morning, right before sunrise, but it's a very short time, and it goes away when you're near sunrise, so most folks prefer the after-sunset blue hour.

What Time to Get There for Sunrise Shoots

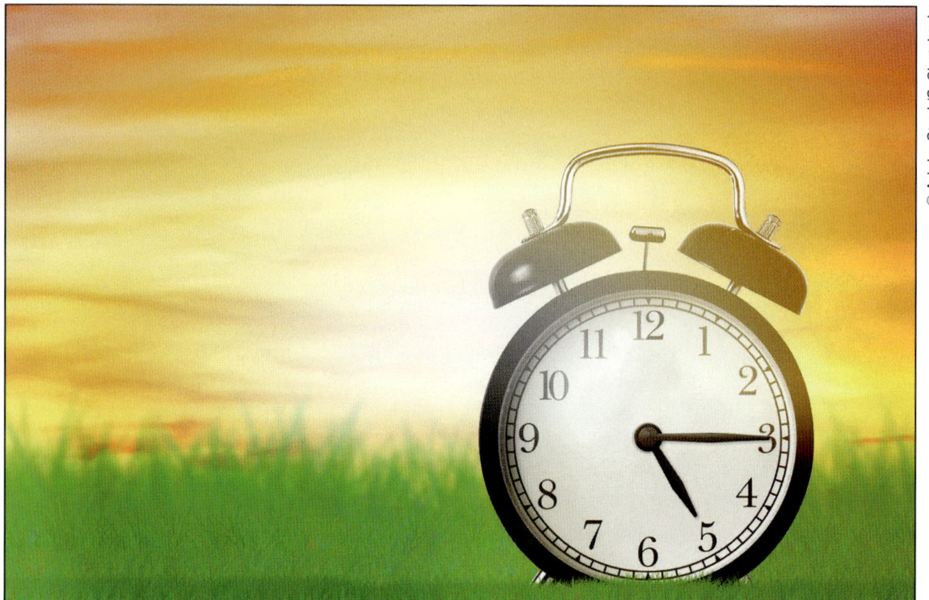

The biggest mistake you can make at a dawn shoot (besides forgetting critical gear) is to get there late. (Yes, this has happened to me. We underestimated how long it would take us to get to our sunrise location and we missed it altogether, which is a heartbreaker. There is nothing worse than driving down the highway, watching the sun rise over an overpass when you are supposed to be down on the beach, shooting some amazing rock formations.) You don't want to be rushed, or frustrated, or playing "beat the clock," so when it comes to sunrise shoots, the best advice I can give you is to get there 30 minutes earlier than you think you need to. That way, if something goes wrong, or you misjudge the distance, or traffic, or the length of the hike, you'll still have time to settle down, get in a creative mind-set, and enjoy the shoot. Also, before you set your clock for some crazy wake-up time, do a quick bit of research the night before. Check the weather for the time you'll be on location. I know, I know, weather apps are trying to predict the future, and they aren't always right. But, if you wind up taking a raincoat and it doesn't rain, that's not the worst thing in the world. But, if you don't check, and so you don't take a coat, and then find out it's colder and windier than you were expecting, it's not only a drag, it'll probably cut your dawn shoot short, or you'll ditch it altogether. Also, check your app for which way the sun will be rising, so you'll aim in the best direction. Once you get on-site, you might find that the way that looks best is facing into the rising sun, or not. Just depends on the location, but it's helpful to know which way it's coming up well before it comes up.

What to Do the Night Before Your Dawn Shoot

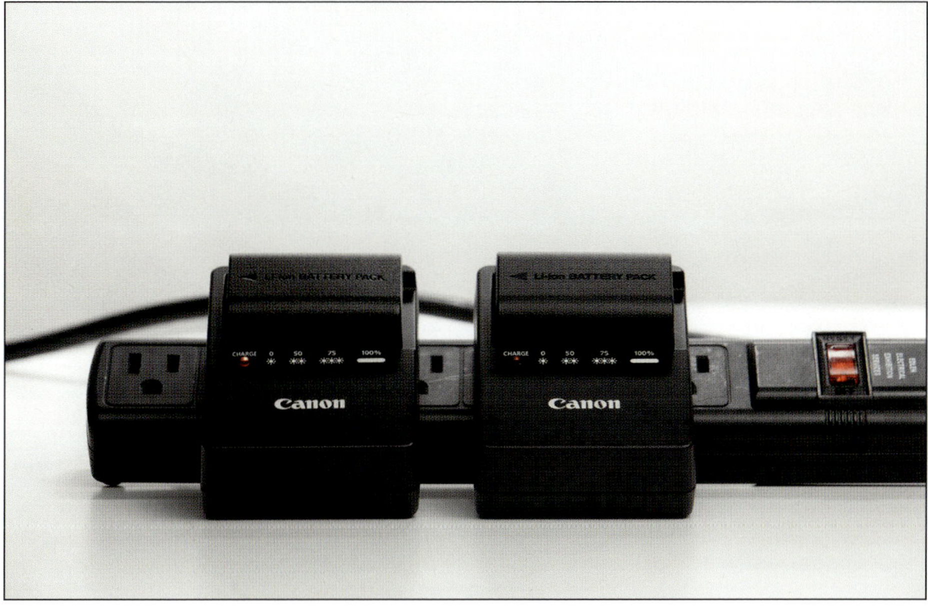

You're going to be grabbing your gear really early in the morning, while you're still a bit sleepy, so you'll be more likely to forget something or forget to do something, and that might mess up your dawn shoot. You don't want to get on-site, only to start hunting for your cable release in the dark or trying to borrow a camera battery from somebody, while everybody else is capturing that once-in-a-lifetime sunrise of your dreams. That's why, the night before, you need to get everything organized and ready, so when you step on the scene, you're ready to shoot. First, charge your batteries, and be sure to take extra batteries with you, especially if it's going to be cold at your sunrise shoot because you'll burn through batteries much, much faster when it's cold. Second, make sure you've got a memory card with enough free space in your camera, and a backup card standing by if that one gets full. Make sure your tripod is ready to go, and that you packed your cable release. Clean the glass on your lenses now, too. Double-check what time sunrise will be (I've gotten burned by this one). I also set my camera settings the night before (since I already pretty much know what they're going to be: 100 ISO, f/11, aperture priority mode, shooting in RAW, single-point focus, etc.). Forget any one of these things, and your shoot goes belly up. I've seen so many folks at workshops forget one or more of these things, and they were so upset and frustrated futzing around in the dark. Even if they eventually found (or borrowed) what they needed, it killed their creative mood. If you get this stuff set the night before, you can just grab your gear and go in the morning, knowing you're ready to set up and shoot.

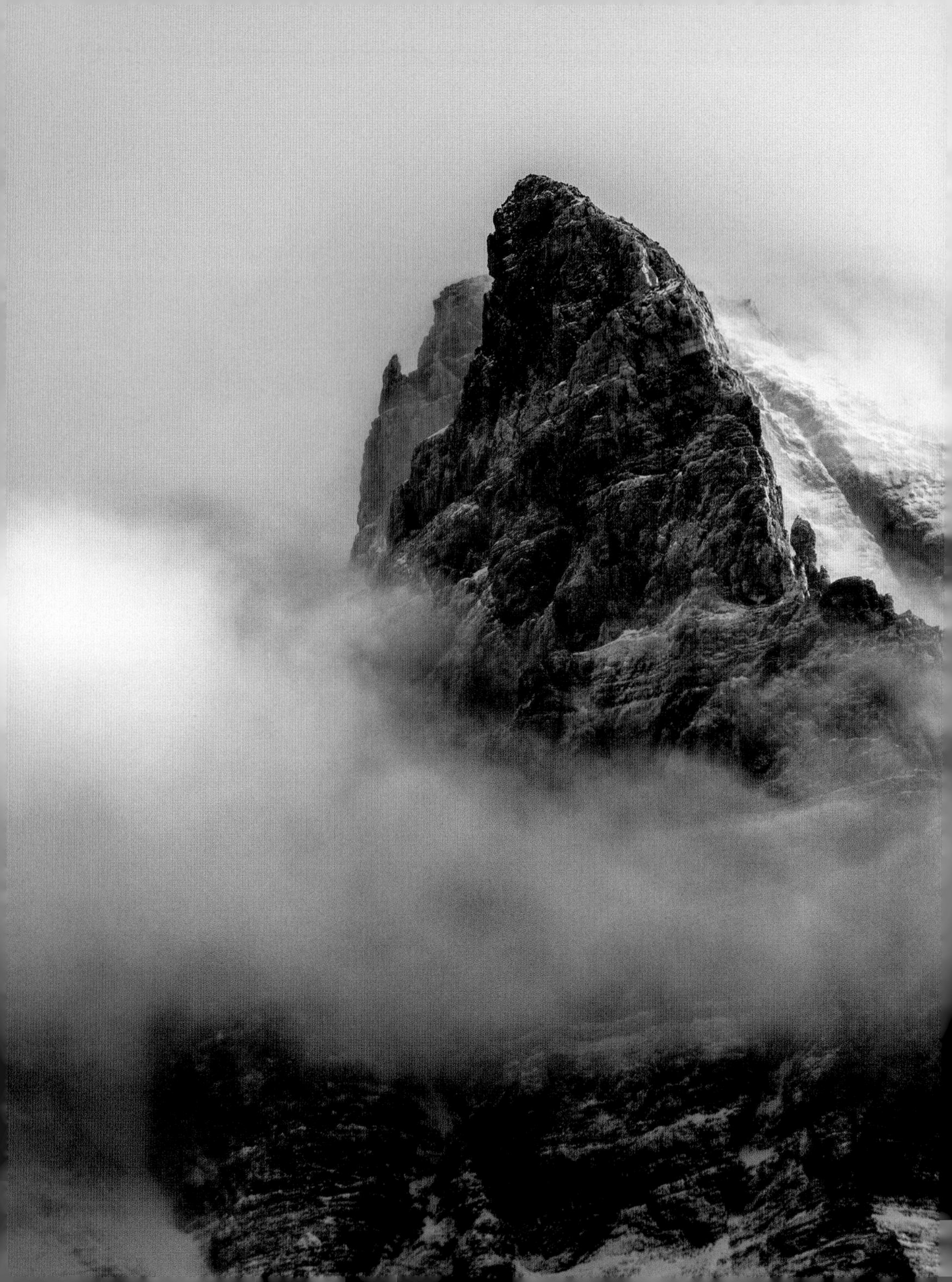

Chapter Four

COMPOSITION

Framing Is Everything!

So, these archaeologists go and exhume Beethoven's coffin. They open the coffin and find him in there erasing a piece of sheet music. Startled, they ask him, "Beethoven, what are you doing?" He says, "I'm decomposing." Get it? Decomposing? Ah, you guys don't get the jokes unless they're about photography. Okay, a photographer is walking by a lake and he sees a man drowning. He either has time to save the man or take a shot of the man drowning, which leaves him with a crucial question: which lens should he use? (I'm here all week. Try the veal.) Anyway, landscape photography is full of questions like this, and it's also chock-full of bad jokes (none of which have been displayed here. This is some of my top-shelf stuff). Anyway, part of being a photographer is practicing spontaneous laughter at jokes that other photographers make when it's 4:45 a.m., it's freezing outside, there are 14 mph winds, and all you can think about is tripping one of the other photographers, so they go rolling down the hill and you get their pancakes. Hey, pop quiz: How do you get a professional photographer off your front porch? Pay him for the pizza (rimshot!). Of course, I would never dream of harming a photographer (well, certainly not just for pancakes), especially because there's such a thing as hiring photo assistants. A lot of folks think of these assistants merely as Sherpas, who tote and set up your gear, but there's a hidden benefit. It's an unwritten rule among professional assistants that part of their role is to make sure other nearby photographers experience a serious lack of self-confidence, feelings of inadequacy, and just generally feel overall lower in the gene pool by making fun of them, their gear, and how they're dressed. When you find an assistant like that, man, they are worth their weight in warm Vermont maple syrup.

Choosing Your Shooting Position

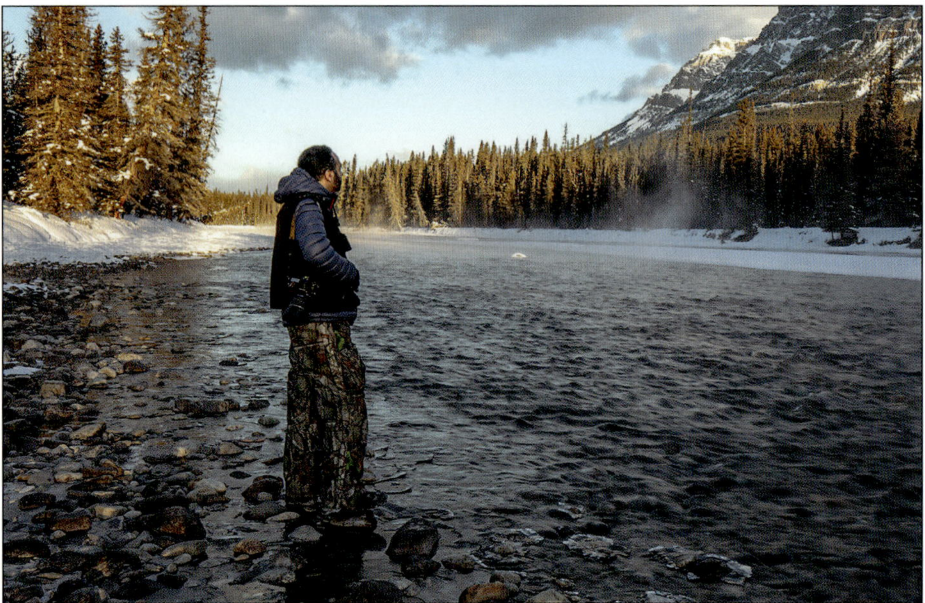

Once you get to the location where you'll be shooting, don't just take your tripod out and set it up where you think you'll be shooting from (rookie mistake). Instead, leave your tripod folded up, walk around with your camera in hand, and try out different angles to find which looks best. You're not going to take any shots during this scouting phase—you're just looking through the viewfinder to see which angle is most advantageous for that particular location. Once you've figured out where that is, then (and only then) do you set up your tripod. Walking around and scouting like this, with your camera in hand, is quick, easy, and effective. Walking around lugging your tripod with your camera on top is slow, it's easy to trip, and you'll end up settling on a spot that isn't necessarily the best shooting angle, but at least you're not carrying that heavy rig around anymore. Do yourself a favor and do the scouting first, then set up the tripod after. I promise you'll come away with better images.

Should You Shoot Tall or Wide?

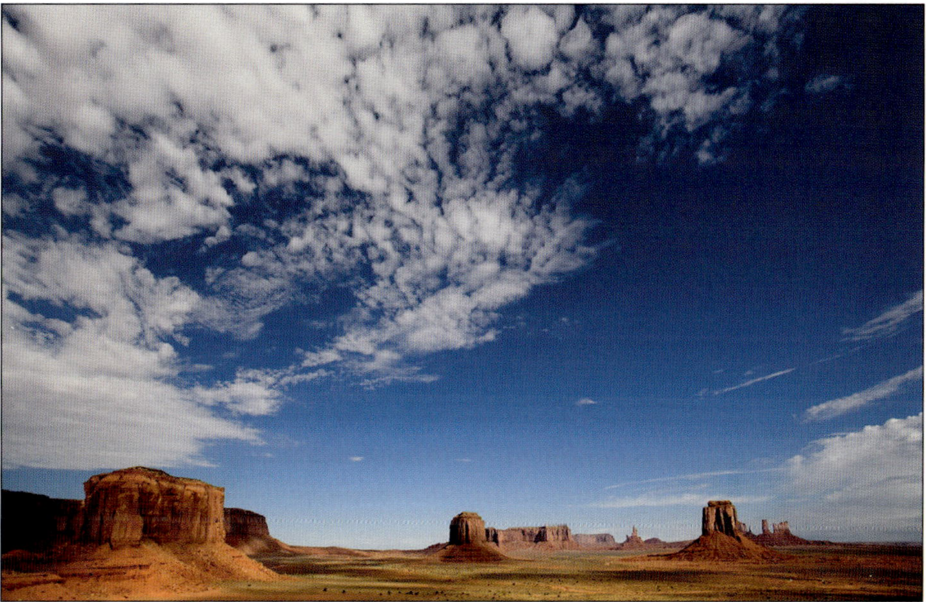

Of course, you can do both. There is an old saying: "When should you shoot a tall picture? Right after you shoot the wide one." But, I can tell you that unless I'm shooting something where it really requires me to shoot vertically (like a really tall, thin waterfall, for example), I'm shooting wide pretty much all the time. The landscape genre, in general, is wide (after all, shooting wide is referred to as shooting in "landscape" orientation, and shooting tall is referred to as shooting in portrait orientation). But, I feel that shooting landscapes in landscape orientation gives me flexibility, since I can crop a wide image to make it a tall image, if necessary, but it's rare that you can crop an image you shot vertically and make it into a successful wide image. So, while you can do both, if I were telling a friend how to shoot landscapes, I would say to shoot them wide for maximum flexibility (or unless, as I mentioned before, the subject requires you to shoot vertically).

Where to Focus

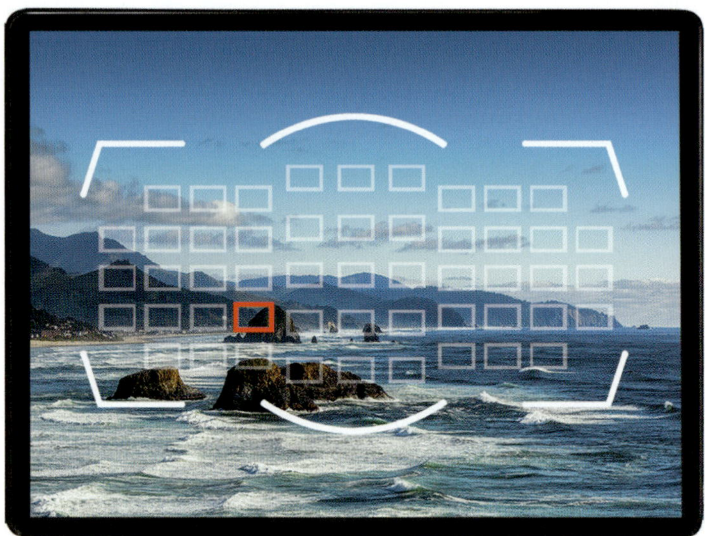

If you're using an f-stop to keep everything in focus from front to back (something like f/11 or f/16), you'll want to make sure you focus on the right spot to get the most of that depth, and that spot is about 1/3 of the way into the shot. Usually, we choose something on the ground in the foreground to focus on (and that will probably mean moving the focal point in the center of your viewfinder down to that spot on the ground), but of course, it depends on the photo. Regardless of what is in the frame, that's what we're looking to do—focus on something 1/3 of the way into our frame.

Or Use Infinite Focus, So Everything's in Focus

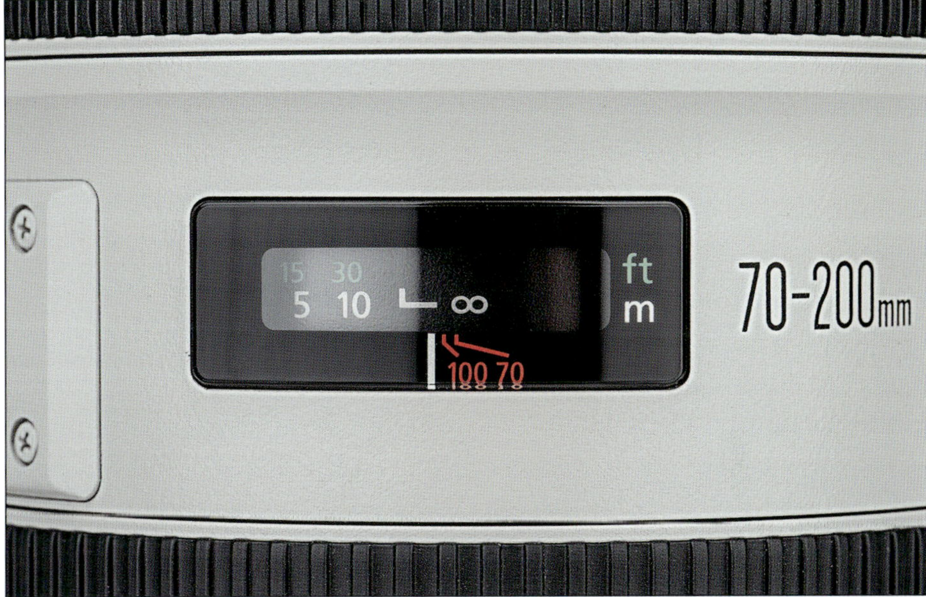

If you don't have something clear to focus on 1/3 of the way into your frame, another thing you can do is set your lens to focus on "infinity." This is made easier if you have a lens that has a focus distance indicator scale right on the outside of the lens itself. You simply use the switch on the side of your lens to switch from Auto focus to Manual focus, and then look inside that little focal distance scale, and you'll see an infinity symbol (∞). Rotate the Manual focus ring on your lens until you reach that infinity symbol, but then you turn it back slightly to the little vertical line that appears right before the symbol. That's the correct spot for focusing to infinity.

Where to Put the Horizon Line

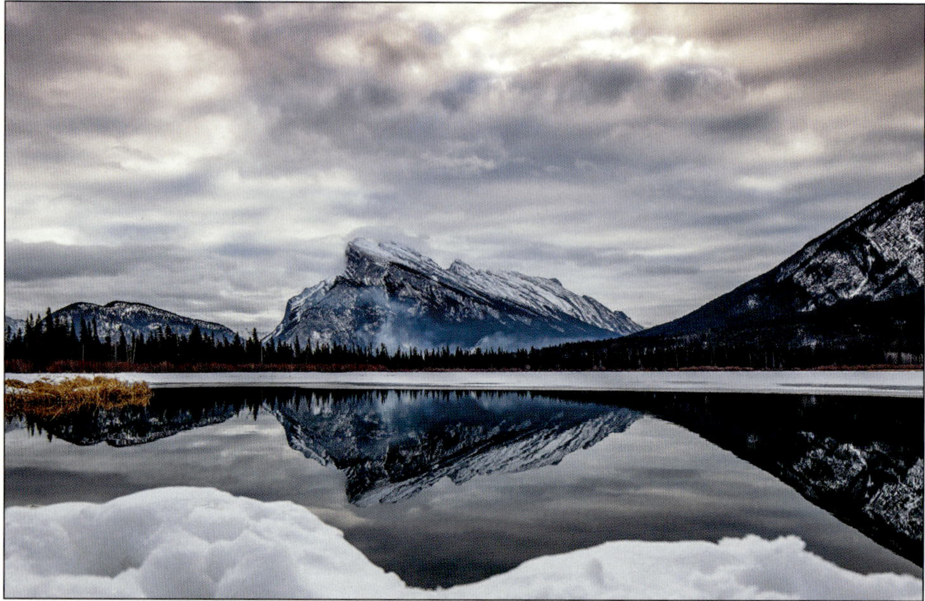

This is a key composition decision, but luckily we have a guideline that helps make this decision fairly easy—use a part of the Rule of Thirds composition concept, which works perfectly for landscape images. Start with this thought: generally, the worst possible place for you to place the horizon line in your image would be in the center. Now, that's not just for horizon lines—in general, dead center is dead boring—but it's particularly lame and average for horizon lines. So, where would be a more interesting place to position the horizon line in your image? Using the Rule of Thirds concept, it would be to position it either at the bottom third of your image or the top third. So, how do you know whether to position it in the bottom or top third? It's incredibly simple, because the rule is: show more of whatever looks most interesting. For example, let's say you have an interesting rock forma-tion in front of you as your foreground, but the sky above it is bland and cloudless. Well, you can pretty much figure what I'm going to tell you—show less sky, right? You do that by positioning the horizon line in the top third of the frame. That way, you'll see more interesting rock formation and less boring, cloudless sky. If the sky looks amazing, and you want it to be the hero of your shot, then you'd show more of the sky (and less of the foreground), putting the horizon line near the bottom third of your image, so you see more sky. By the way, these "thirds" don't have to be exact, so don't sweat getting a perfect third—it's a compositional concept, not a federal law, so you have some leeway (it might look better with the horizon line at 1/4 of the way from the bottom of the frame rather than at 1/3).

How to Lead the Viewer's Eye

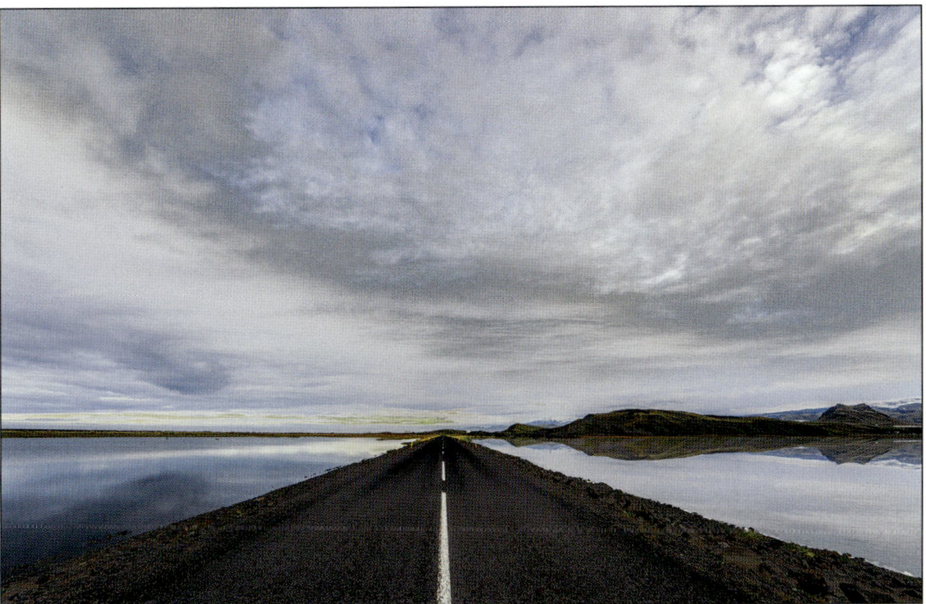

A really popular technique in landscape photography is to lead the viewer's eye to where you want them to look by using what are called "leading lines." Just the way a photo of a stream naturally leads the viewer's eye down the stream, that's what you want to do with either man-made elements in your image (like a country road winding through a forest, or a picket fence that leads you to a lighthouse, or a dock that leads you out into a lake) or natural elements (like the lines on the top of a sand dune, or a row of trees, or a shoreline that leads you down the beach toward a large rock out in the water). If you do it right, you should be able to draw a marker right down these lines, and they will lead the viewer to your subject, or some interesting part of your image. One thing to keep an eye out for is when you naturally have lots of leading lines in your image. Make sure you've positioned yourself to take the shot where the leading lines are leading the viewer to the same place. You don't want their eye to follow along one visual path, and then suddenly change direction leading them off someplace else. So, when you're composing, just be aware of how many leading lines are in the image, and make sure you are using them to lead the viewer where you want them, without them competing with each other.

Drawing the Viewer's Eye Using Negative Space

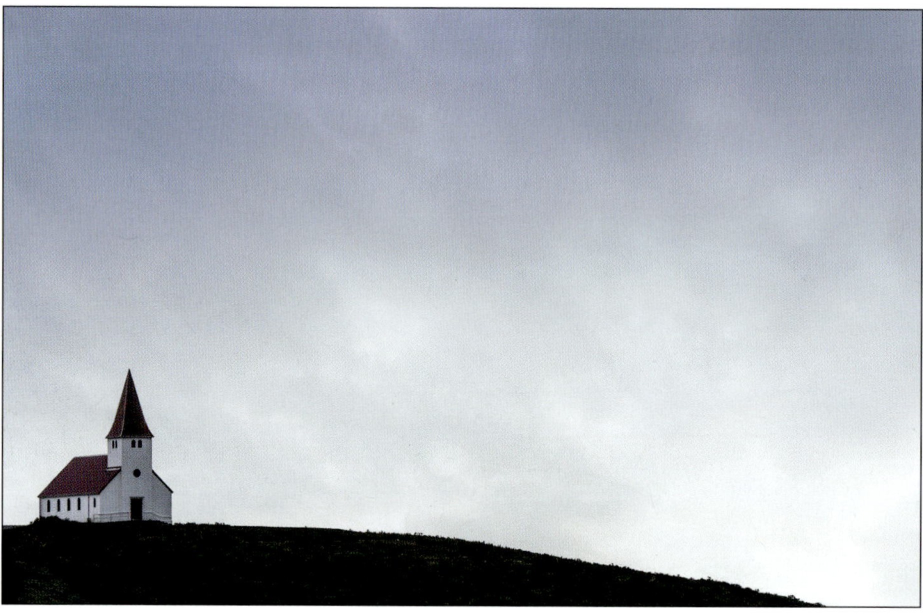

Another compositional technique we use to lead the viewer's eye to where you want them to look is to have a part of the image that really contains nothing, so the thing you want them to look at really jumps out at them. An example would be a hilltop with nothing else there but a lone tree, or a large blank sky with just the tip of a mountain peeking up into it. All that empty area is called "negative space" and since there's nothing in that empty space that surrounds your subject, it really pulls your viewer to it. In landscape photography, this can be a really useful and powerful composition technique. This negative space doesn't necessarily have to have nothing in it, it just has to have nothing of interest, so the subject of your image doesn't have anything to compete with—the rest of the image is "clean," so your object kind of stands alone. Give this one a try—it's often fairly easy to pull off, but it can make for a really intriguing shot.

Drawing Their Eye with Light

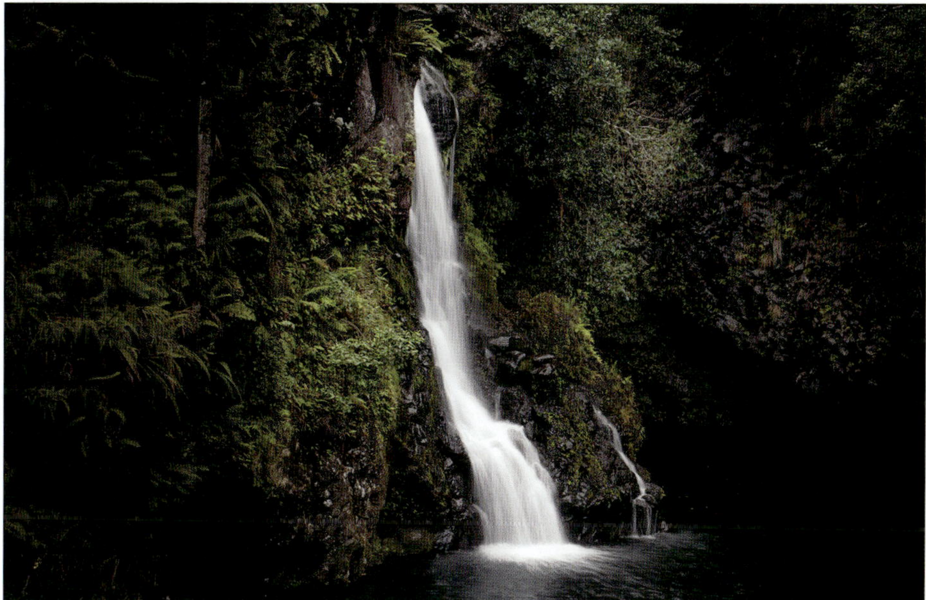

The first thing our eyes are drawn to is the brightest thing in an image. Right after that, they're drawn to the sharpest thing, and if the brightest thing is also the sharpest thing, well…that's pretty irresistible. So, how does this help make your composition stronger? You're going to compose the shot, so the focal point or subject is the brightest thing in the image, and you're going to compose it so any brighter parts are not in the frame. You might have to change your angle, or perspective, or it may be as simple as just aiming your camera to the left or right a little bit to keep that other bright area out of your frame. Another trick you can use to lead the viewer's eye is make your focal point brighter in post-production: in either Lightroom or Photoshop, using the Adjustment Brush with the Exposure increased by 1/2 stop to 1 stop, paint over the focal point in the image to make it jump out at the viewer.

Why You Need a Foreground Object

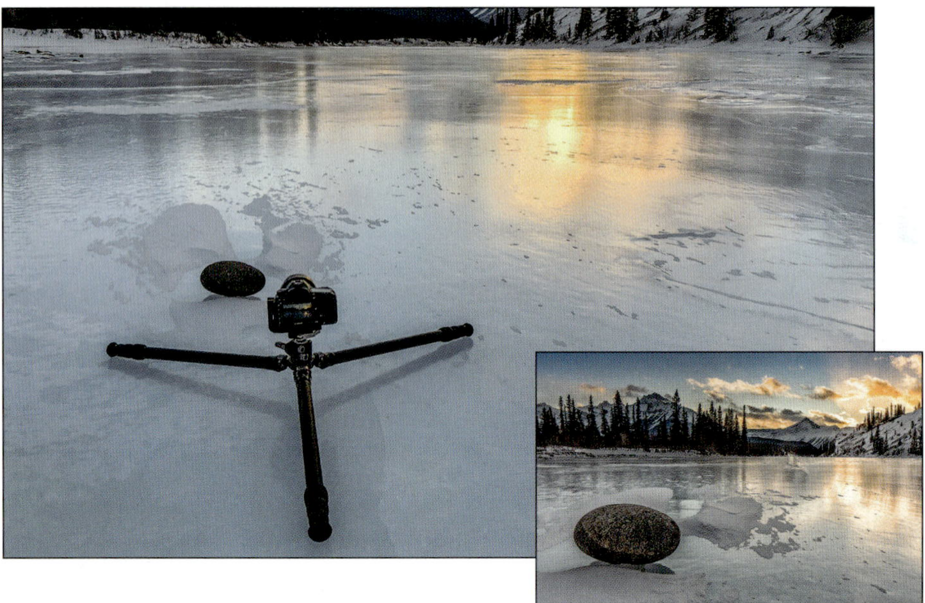

When you take a landscape image, you're telling a story. Hopefully, it's a big, epic, sweeping story that takes your viewer right into the image, and for that, it really helps to have all three of the key parts of the image in place: a foreground area, a middle ground, and a background. The foreground is what draws the viewer into the image, visually leads them, and makes them want to explore. It creates depth. A strong foreground is critical, so put something right at the base of your image (it could be rocks at the shoreline, or a log at the base of your image, or some wildflowers, or one of a hundred things that your viewer can connect with as you lead them to the middle ground). For example, if you were shooting a lake with a mountain behind it, you wouldn't want your composition to begin in the middle of the lake. That's like starting in the middle of the story. Instead, you might want to get down low at the shoreline, and maybe get some rocks right up close in the frame (or maybe you can see some interesting rocks through the still water near the shore), and then lead your viewer out to the lake (the middle ground), which will then lead them to the mountain and sky behind the lake (the background). You want all three pieces of the story: foreground, middle ground, background. Put something strong and, ideally, interesting right in the foreground, and it will make for a much stronger overall image, and help to lead the viewer and tell the full story.

You Need a Clear Subject

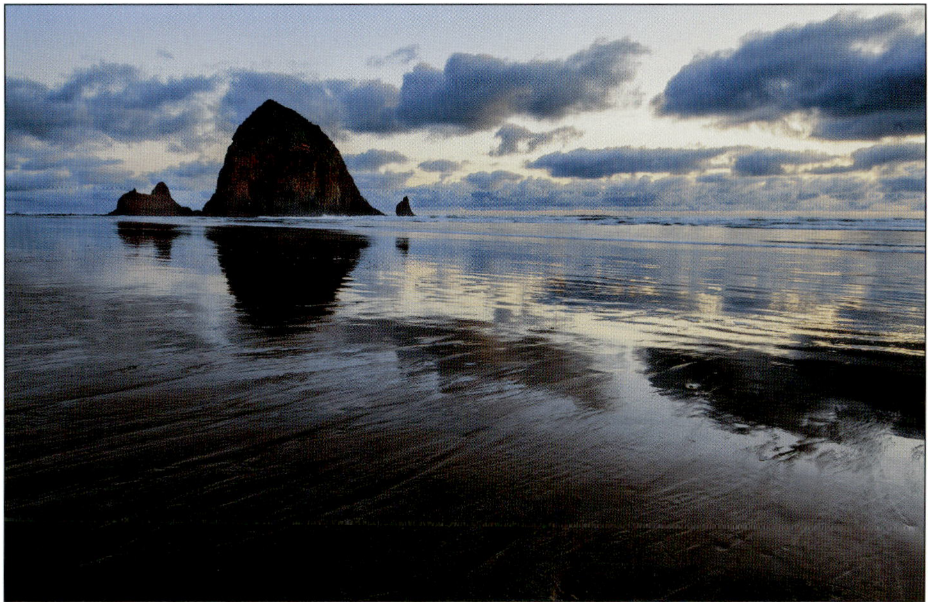

This is going to sound silly when I first say it, but so often I see landscape images that miss this simple mark, and that is: your image needs a subject. The person viewing your image has to connect with your subject immediately—they need to look at your image and go, "Oh, a stream" or "I love sunset photos" or "What a beautiful waterfall." If they look at your image and they're just quiet for a few moments, and then they say, "Well, this is nice. What is it?" you know, at that moment, your image has failed. The "this is nice" part is them being polite. Also, the subject can't be "it's the whole scene." That's not a subject. It has to be something within the scene (an arch, a mountain, a lake, a waterfall, a field of wildflowers, a lighthouse, a lone tree, a farmhouse, a country road—ya gotta give 'em something as a subject). Also, don't try to come up with a subject after you've taken the shot ("Oh, it's those trees on the left...I mean that mountain on the right," or maybe "It's those rocks on the ground"). If you want your image to be a success, have a clean, well-defined subject before you start shooting.

Simplify the Scene

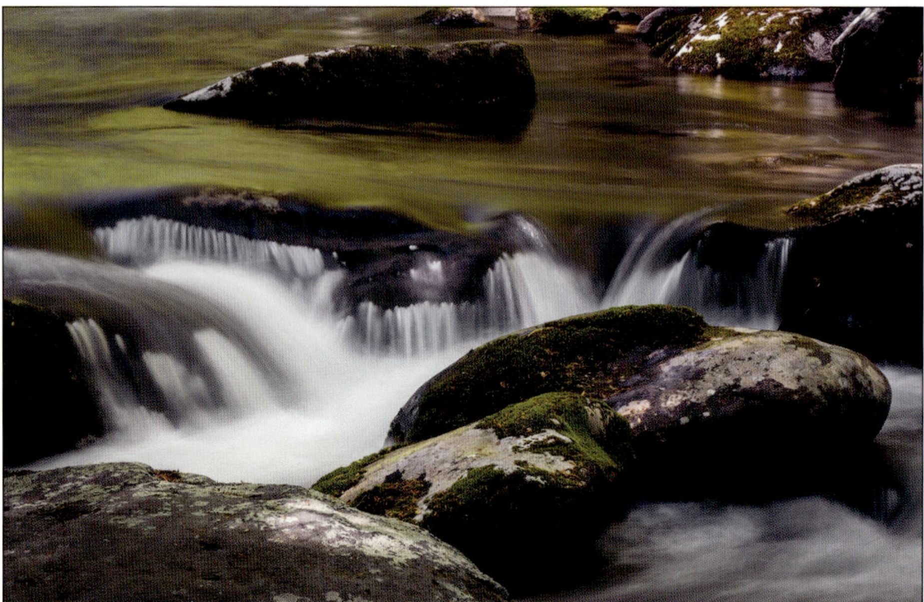

Landscape shots tend to get very messy. There's often a lot going on, which is why simplifying your scene can make your image so much stronger. Take a stream, for example. There are often lots of sticks and leaves and twigs and tree branches and all sorts of distracting elements that are in that stream, so the viewer isn't actually sure where they should be looking. If you simplify the scene and avoid as much clutter as you can, getting the image down to just a few elements, it makes for a really strong image. If you have the choice of a ridge top with either a clump of trees or one single tree, the shot with that one single tree will almost undoubtedly be the strongest. Simple shots have great power to connect with the viewer, and keeping your scenes simple and uncluttered will help you create images with great depth and visual interest. This is one of those "less is more" type of things.

Avoiding the Border Junk That Ruins Images

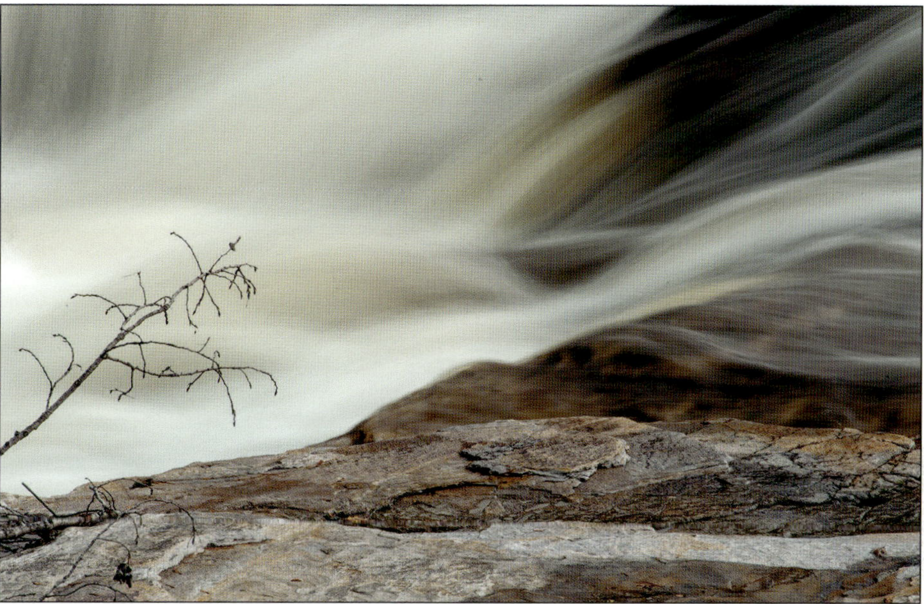

One of the biggest mistakes I see when I'm critiquing landscape images is one of the easiest to avoid, and that is keeping "junk" away from the outside edges of your image. We're talking branches or sticks that extend in from the sides (as seen above on the left), or a dead tree limb, or part of something, or any one of the little things that sneak in to ruin your photo. The reason this happens so often is that we're focused on the subject of the image. For example, let's say we're shooting a waterfall. We're focused on the waterfall itself, and getting the water smooth and silky, and while that's what we're looking at while we're taking the image, the viewer sees everything in the image—the dumb stick coming in from the edge or the tree branch on the other side. All these distracting things that we weren't even paying attention to jump out when other folks look at the image, and they are scene killers. I've heard it said that we are responsible for every inch of our image—not just the main subject of the image. Don't let that junk sneak in and spoil your otherwise beautiful image—get used to keeping an eye on the edges of your image, and if something does sneak by you, be prepared to remove it later in Photoshop (see page 172).

Why We Need Clouds in Our Shots

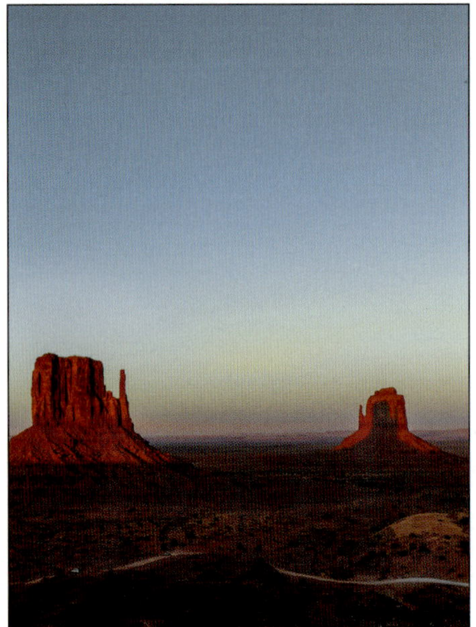 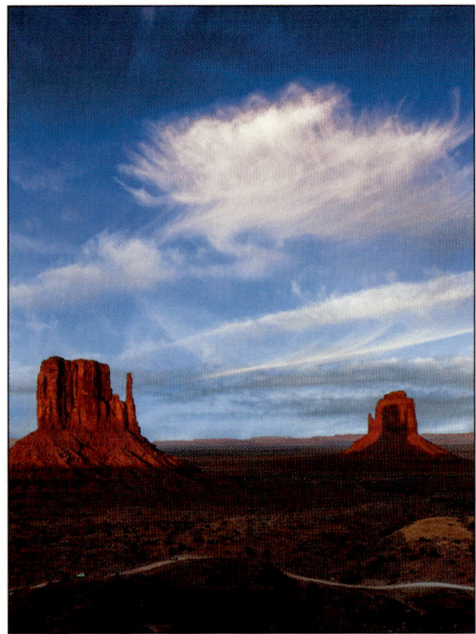

Leonardo da Vinci once wrote, "Once you have tasted the taste of sky, you will forever look up." Clouds are heavenly. We adore clouds. We're fascinated with them. We write songs and poems about them. We stand there and marvel at how they're lighter than air, we find faces and animals in their shapes, and entire photo books are published with nothing but clouds. Without clouds, we wouldn't look at the sky in awe or marvel over amazing cloud formations—the sky at sunrise or sunset would be…well…empty. Outside of shooting in great light, they're probably the most important thing to have in your image because the clouds are what hold the color of sunrise and sunset. The sky is just a canvas. The clouds are the art, and having them in your shot can literally make or break it. If you've got a killer sky with great clouds, honestly, the rest is easy. You can be photographing a big ol' ugly rock in a barren desert, and if an amazing sky shows up, you'll come away with an awesome image. That's how critical a great sky is for most landscape photography, and it's also probably the single biggest challenge for us because we have absolutely no control over when clouds appear whatsoever. It's what makes patience and perseverance the biggest assets for landscape photographers. If you've got a great subject, you might have to visit that same spot every dawn or every dusk, for days (day after day), until Mother Nature brings you a sky so marvelous that you can't believe you're standing there to see it. Does this mean that you can't make a great landscape shot without clouds? No, it does not. But, great clouds will almost always make it that much better.

Getting Still Water Reflections

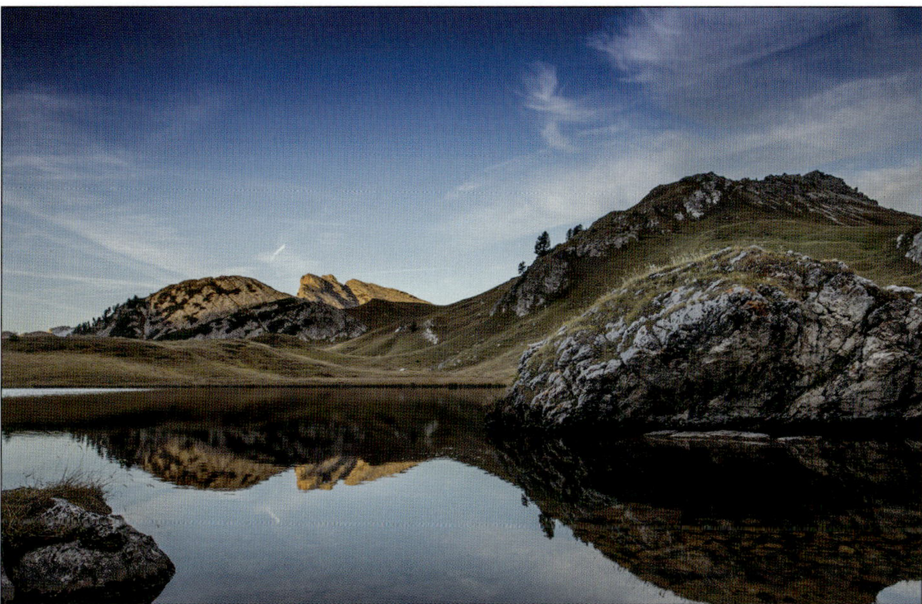

If you want a sure bet for a landscape image people will love, find some still water (in a lake, a pond, etc.), put a mountain in your background, and the magic will happen. People are drawn to images with reflections, and the more mirror-like and glassy the reflection, the better. The challenge is that water isn't often perfectly still to create those reflections, which is probably why we like them so much. Any minor bit of wind creates choppy water and you've lost that reflection. So, what's the secret to getting that still, glassy water? Get up super-early. First thing in the morning is your absolute best shot at getting still water, so you can nab that reflection. While there's great light twice a day (dawn and dusk), you've usually only got one shot to get that glassy water, and that's around dawn. So, set your alarm and hope for calm winds.

Taking Great Shots of Mountains

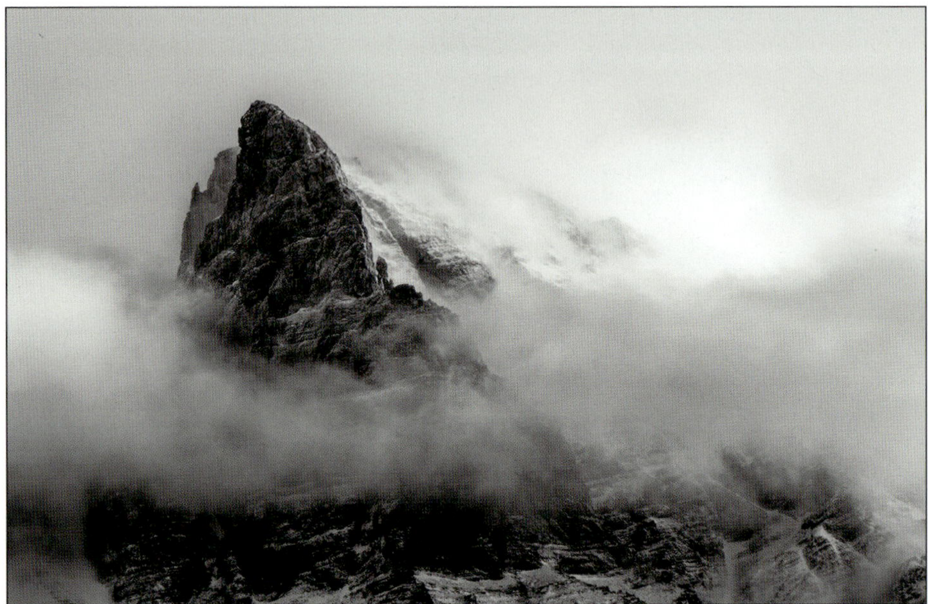

How are most mountain photos taken? From the ground. Probably from a standing position, and if you want your photos of mountains to look like everybody else's (boring), then do that. Shoot up at the mountains. But if you want to make more dramatic, compelling mountain images, don't stand there shooting up. Your images will have so much more impact if you can shoot the mountains from up in the mountains themselves. That way, you're either shooting across at them, or maybe even down at them. This is a view you don't see nearly as often, and that's what makes it much more interesting—and no, you don't have to climb a mountain to take these shots. Oftentimes, you can literally drive up them to lookout points and overlooks that give you a totally different perspective. I've taken ski lifts and cable cars to get up to some wonderful observation decks, and on a winter's day, the clear air is just amazing for landscape photography. This is the type of thing you want to research before you go out shooting, so you can see if there are high views where you can shoot without long hikes or scaling the side of a mountain (unless, of course, you love long hikes or scaling mountains. If that's the case, you're going to have some great shooting opportunities). Also, as an added tip: don't just "go wide." Pull out your longer lens for some great shots of mountain tops—it can create some really dramatic looks.

Mountains as Backgrounds

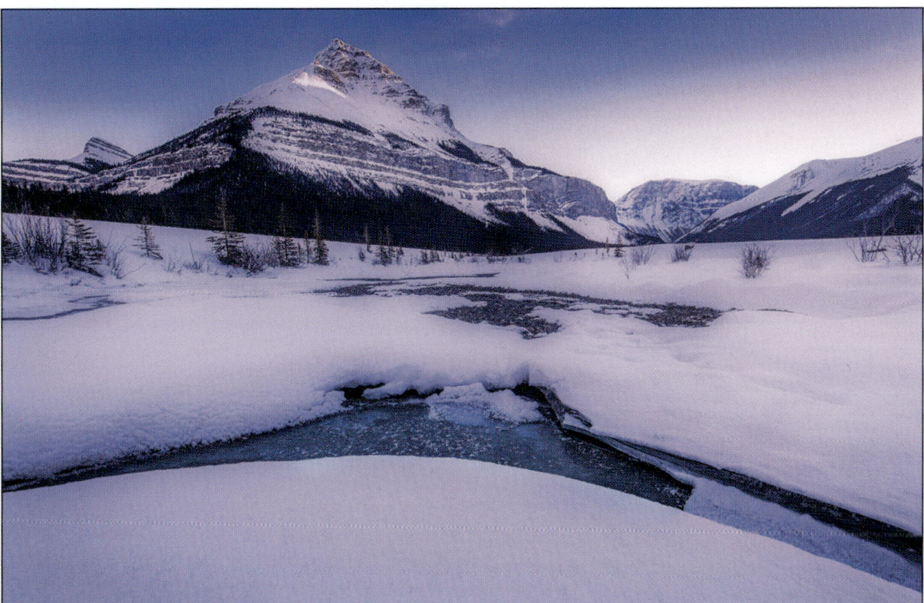

If you don't want to make the mountains your foreground, try making them your background. They make awesome background elements with other things in the foreground. For example, that old barn that everybody shoots up in Wyoming with a line of mountains in the background. The reason everybody shoots it is, it's almost too perfect. You have an interesting, timeless old barn (which has an interesting shape itself), and then you have this beautiful mountain range behind it that takes the image to a whole different level. Photo of an old barn in good light? Eight out of 10. Some beautiful clouds show up? Nine out of 10. Put some beautiful mountains as a background behind it? Ten out of 10.

Photographing Mountains from Down Low

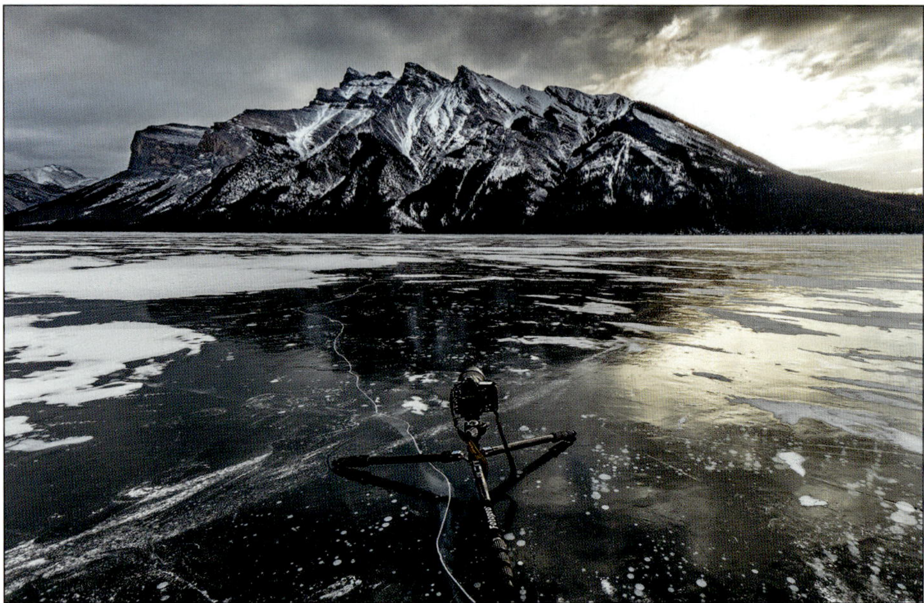

If you don't want to go up high to photograph mountains, then do the extreme opposite: get really low to the ground. Either splay your tripod's legs all the way, so you're just 6" or 8" from the ground, or get something like a Platypod, so your foreground is big right in front of you, and the mountain is your background. But, because you're down so low, the mountain will loom large in the photo. You'll want to use a wide-angle lens to take it all in, but don't go too wide or the mountain will look like it's far away. This is another great method for photographing mountains, because you're not shooting from a standing position—you'll still have that big, sweeping, epic feel because you're down low with a strong foreground element, but for anybody looking at your image, they'll still know it's about the mountain.

Shooting with the Sun in the Frame

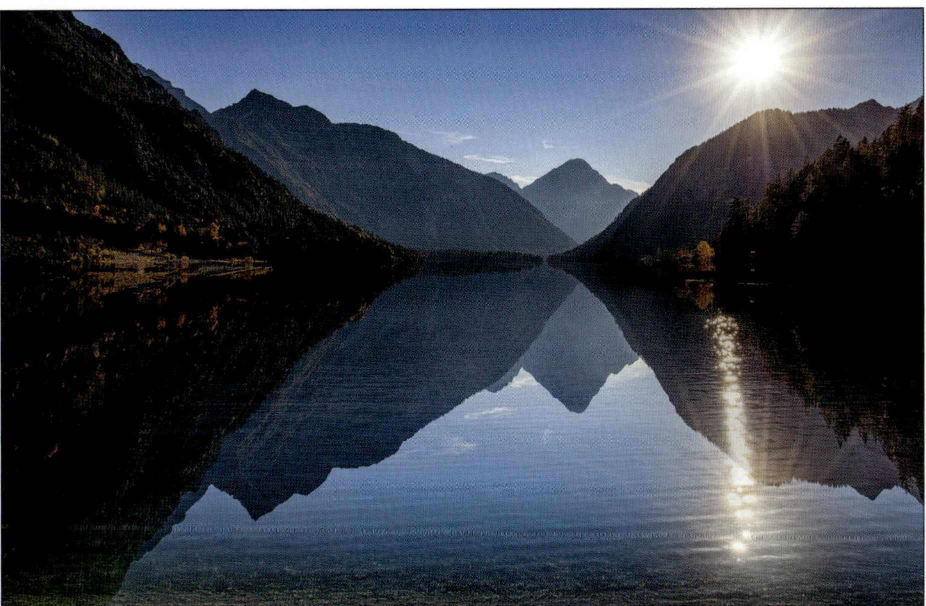

The "don't shoot with the sun in your frame" warning is really an outdated concept from the early days of digital photography. There was a fear back then that the brightness of the sun might somehow damage the sensor, and heck, back then it might have been true. But, today, we shoot into the sun all the time without fear of damaging our gear. The sun is such an important part of our landscape life, it would be a shame not to include it in daytime shots—especially since including it can add more depth and interest to your scene, and if you position it right in your frame, you can have it help lead the viewer's eye. This is especially helpful since we know that our eyes are drawn to the brightest part of an image (see page 67), and if you have the sun in your image…well…I'm not sure there's anything brighter, so use this to your advantage. Compositionally, I prefer to have the sun in either one of the corners, or I like it touching some object in the image, so it's not fully exposed, and then I can use the trick on page 190 for creating starbursts. But, of course, the placement of the sun, as always, pretty much depends on the scene. I try not to let the sun appear as just a giant blob of light in the frame (which it easily can), so I normally use exposure compensation or a high-numbered f-stop to give some sort of shape to it. I've also found it's better to deal with this in-camera than to try to do it in post-processing because when you pull back the highlights or exposure, it doesn't make the sun less bright. Instead, it turns the ball of the sun gray, which looks pretty bad. So, getting it right in-camera works best.

Shoot Right Before or Right After Bad Weather

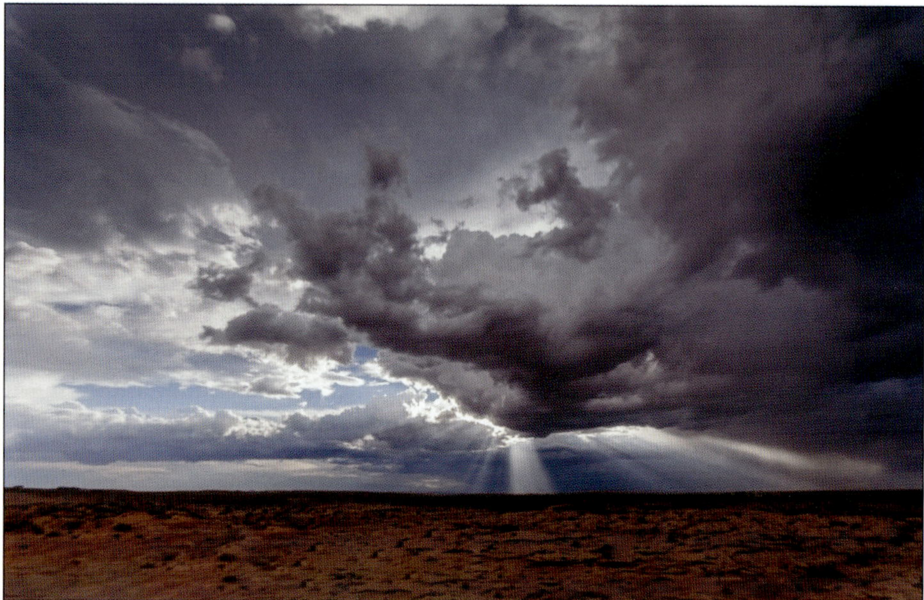

Some of the most dramatic clouds appear right before or right after a storm, and while everybody else is sitting this one out, this is your chance to make some incredibly dramatic landscape images. A sky full of dark, ominous clouds makes for a really interesting sky, so don't miss out on this opportunity. Just remember to keep yourself and your equipment as dry and safe as possible (stay away from lightning—it's just a photo; it's not worth risking your life over).

Study Other Landscape Photographers' Work

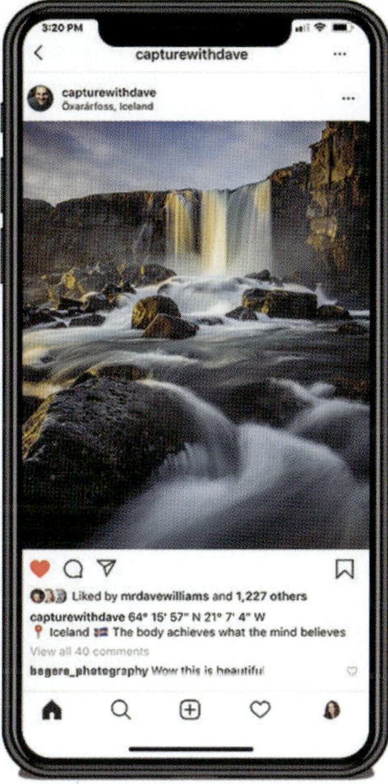
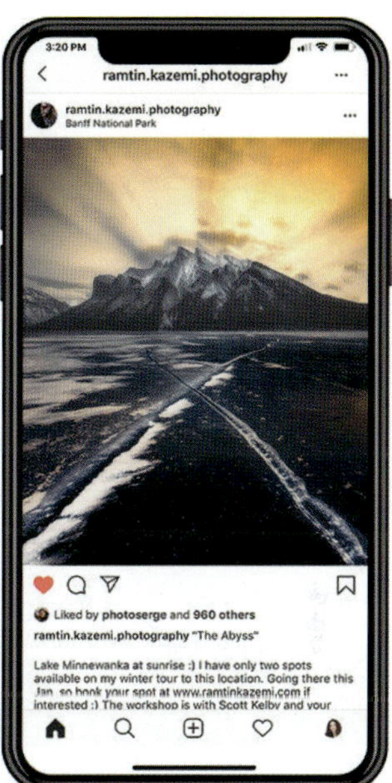

I truly believe that studying the work of other landscape photographers you admire is one of the best things you can do for your landscape photography. Don't just look at their photos—dissect them, break them down. For example, look at the light. See if you can figure out if they shot at sunrise or sunset. Maybe they shot in late morning or early morning light, but after sunrise. Look at what they use for their foreground. Rocks? A lake? A tree? Look at how they use leading lines. Look at their post-processing. Figure out what type of lens they used (how wide or how tight). Look at their locations. There is so much information in their images—you just have to look for it and be aware of it. It's one of the best learning tools we have, and thanks to Instagram, we can easily follow a lot of different photographers. You'll quickly find out which ones are taking the kind of landscape images you want to take, and learning that (which particular style of landscape photography you like) is a big help. Once you figure out which style of landscape images you want to make, you can focus on shooting that one style, and you'll see a big leap forward in your own photography because now you're focused on the exact type of images you want to take. As far as following landscape photographers on Instagram, if you're looking for a place to start, here are a few of my favorites:

@maxrivephotography @LarsVanDeGoor @sofyan_adi2805 @chrisburkard @liang.dennis @danielkordan @alexstrohl @jamieout @kilianschoenberger @antonyspencer @noriegaphotography @marcadamus @capturewithdave @ramtin.kazemi.photography @bernabephoto

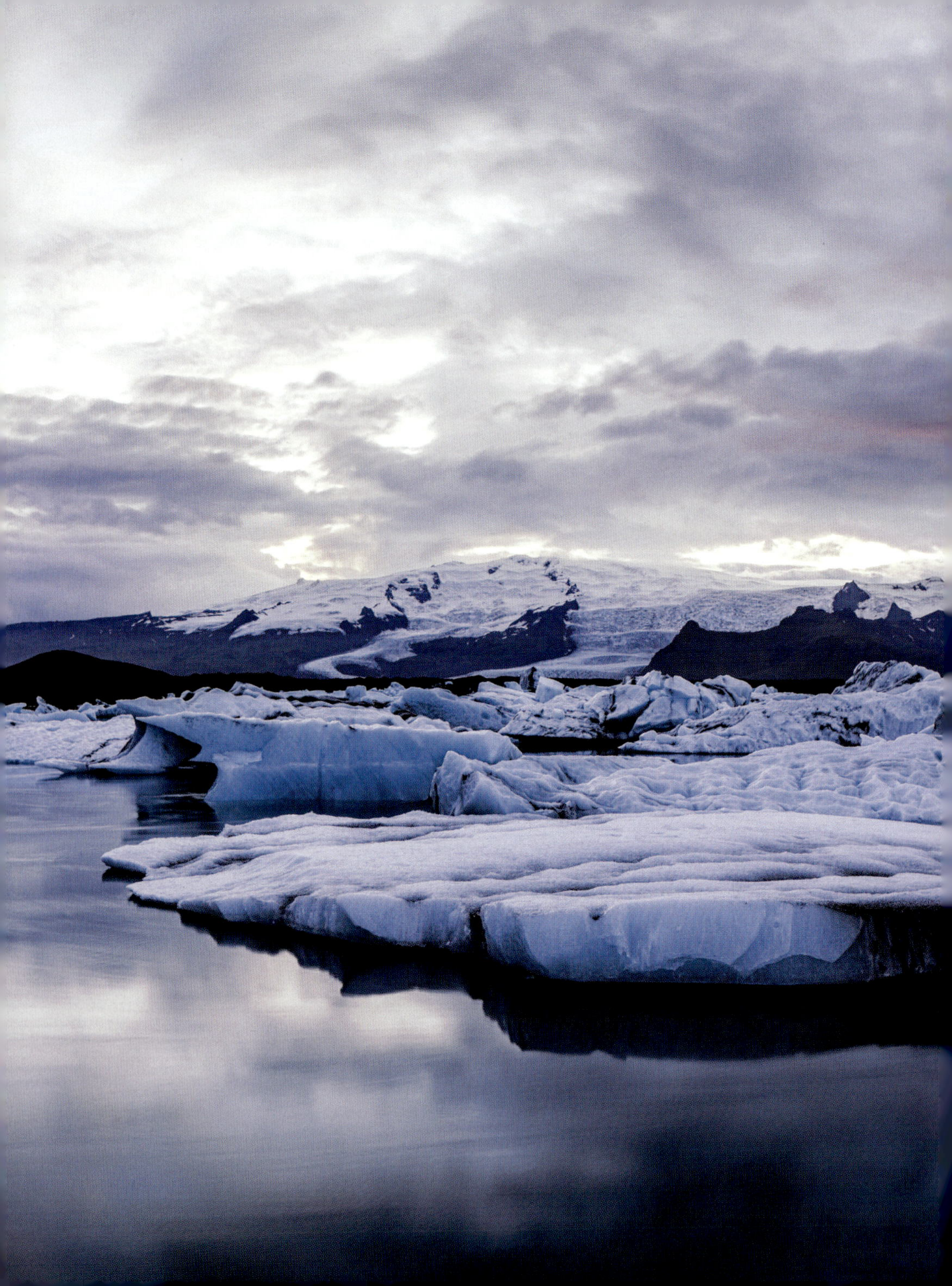

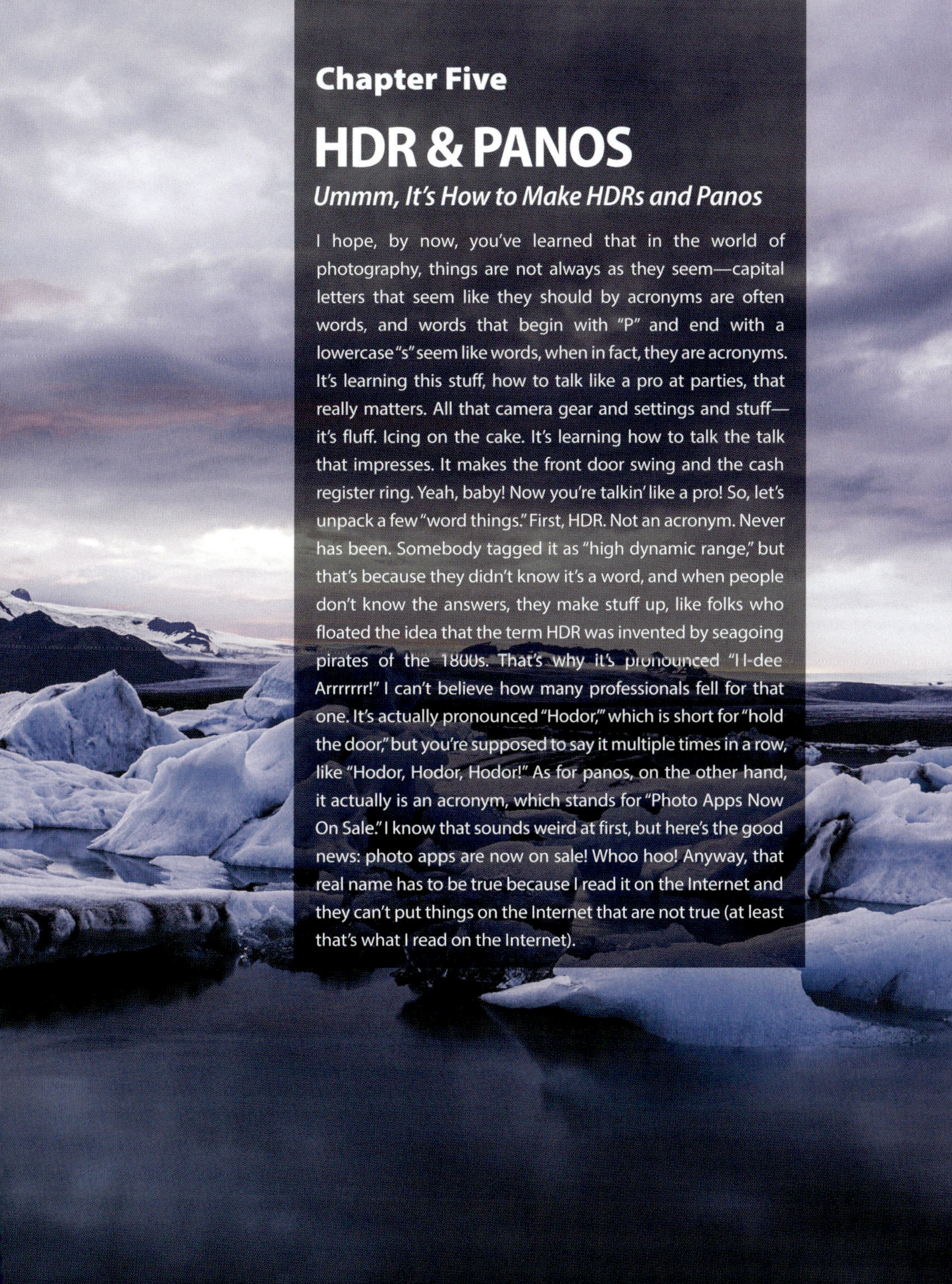

Chapter Five

HDR & PANOS

Ummm, It's How to Make HDRs and Panos

I hope, by now, you've learned that in the world of photography, things are not always as they seem—capital letters that seem like they should by acronyms are often words, and words that begin with "P" and end with a lowercase "s" seem like words, when in fact, they are acronyms. It's learning this stuff, how to talk like a pro at parties, that really matters. All that camera gear and settings and stuff—it's fluff. Icing on the cake. It's learning how to talk the talk that impresses. It makes the front door swing and the cash register ring. Yeah, baby! Now you're talkin' like a pro! So, let's unpack a few "word things." First, HDR. Not an acronym. Never has been. Somebody tagged it as "high dynamic range," but that's because they didn't know it's a word, and when people don't know the answers, they make stuff up, like folks who floated the idea that the term HDR was invented by seagoing pirates of the 1800s. That's why it's pronounced "H-dee Arrrrrrr!" I can't believe how many professionals fell for that one. It's actually pronounced "Hodor,'" which is short for "hold the door," but you're supposed to say it multiple times in a row, like "Hodor, Hodor, Hodor!" As for panos, on the other hand, it actually is an acronym, which stands for "Photo Apps Now On Sale." I know that sounds weird at first, but here's the good news: photo apps are now on sale! Whoo hoo! Anyway, that real name has to be true because I read it on the Internet and they can't put things on the Internet that are not true (at least that's what I read on the Internet).

The Advantage of Panos Versus Wide-Angle

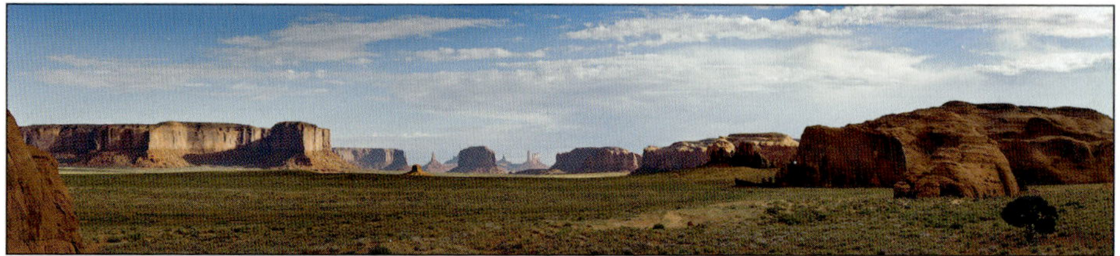

I've had people ask me why we even do panos, and wouldn't it be easier to just shoot a wide-angle lens and crop it like a pano? Well, there are three big advantages to shooting a pano over a wide-angle, but to me, the first is the most important: (1) panos make big things look big and help maintain their scale, while wide-angle lenses push the scene farther way, making big mountains look smaller, huge arches look regular, and tall waterfalls look small. Panos keep that sense of scale and big-ness. Plus, there's (2): panos have really high resolution, and you can print them at huge sizes because you're combining a bunch of high-resolution photos into one image. Lastly, (3) shooting a pano can capture more of a scene than a wide-angle lens. You can make your panos as long, tall, or wide as you want. You can do multi-row panos (see page 94), and even panos where you combine multiple wide-angle lens shots, so you have more options on how to capture the scene you're standing in front of. There's also a bonus reason: (4) people love panos. The viewing public loves to see a printed pano in person, because that's something you just don't see every day (for a tip on printing, see page 98).

Camera Settings for Shooting Panos

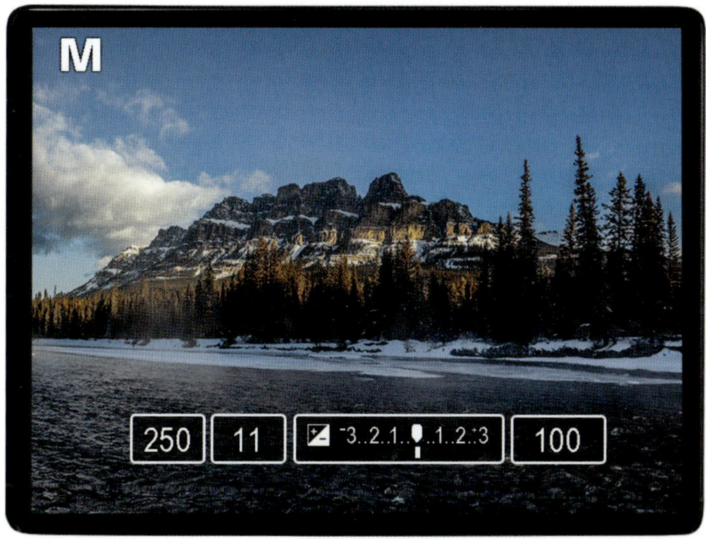

We use specific settings for shooting panos because each frame of the pano has to have the exact same exposure and focus. If you shoot 11 frames, they all have to look the same. If you let the camera determine the exposure and auto focus point of each different frame while you're shooting your pano, you'll wind up with a pano where some areas are darker, some parts are focused at one depth, and others look soft at the same depth, and basically you wind up with a mess. So, let's set our camera for panoramic success. First, if you're on a tripod, set your ISO to your cleanest setting (probably 100 ISO). If you're hand-holding, you might have to go higher (see page 26). Then, switch your camera to aperture priority mode and choose f/11 for your f-stop, so everything will be in focus. Now, aim your camera at a key part of the scene, hold the shutter button down halfway, and look through the viewfinder to see what shutter speed it chose to properly expose the scene. Remember that number (let's say it showed 1/250 of a second). Switch your camera to manual mode, leave your f-stop at f/11, and set your shutter speed to that number you remembered (1/250 of a second). Okay, your exposure is set. What about your white balance? Don't use Auto white balance because it could change from frame to frame. Choose an actual white balance preset (I generally choose Cloudy white balance. See page 36). Hold the shutter button halfway down, so your Auto focus locks on the scene, then switch your lens focus to Manual, so your focus doesn't change. Take a test shot or two to see how it looks (and, yes, zoom in to check sharpness, just in case), and now you're all set to shoot without having any surprises later on.

Picking a Lens for Panos That Limits Edge Distortion

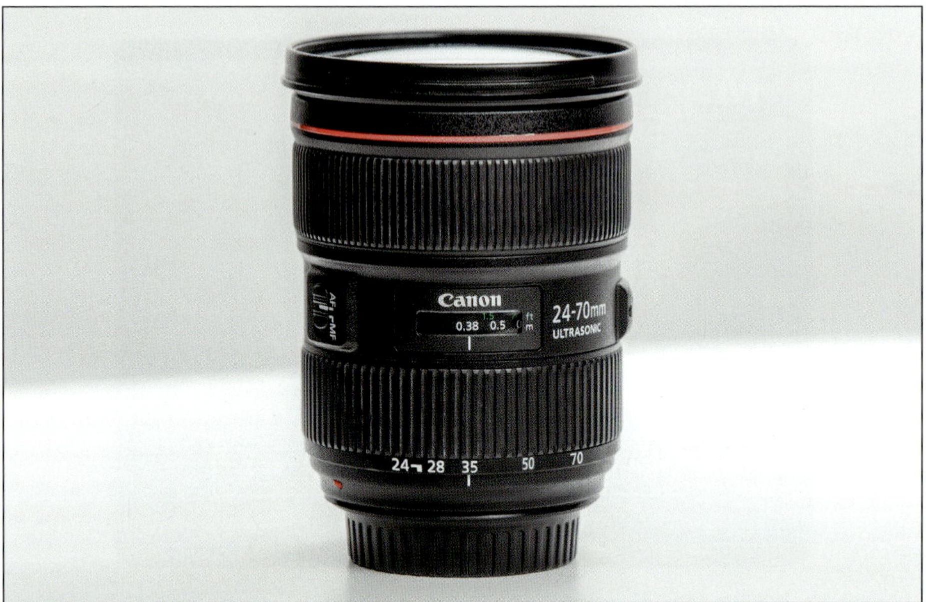

While you can use a wide-angle lens to shoot panoramas, to limit any edge distortion, you should ideally try to use a lens that is a minimum of 35mm (on a full-frame camera), but shoot for 50mm or more. This distortion, which you might not notice all that much on a single image, gets magnified in a panorama. So, instead of trying to "fix it in Photoshop," pick a lens that works best for panos, like something 50mm or longer (I often use the 70mm on my 24–70mm lens that I have with me for landscape shoots).

Make Certain Your Camera Is Level

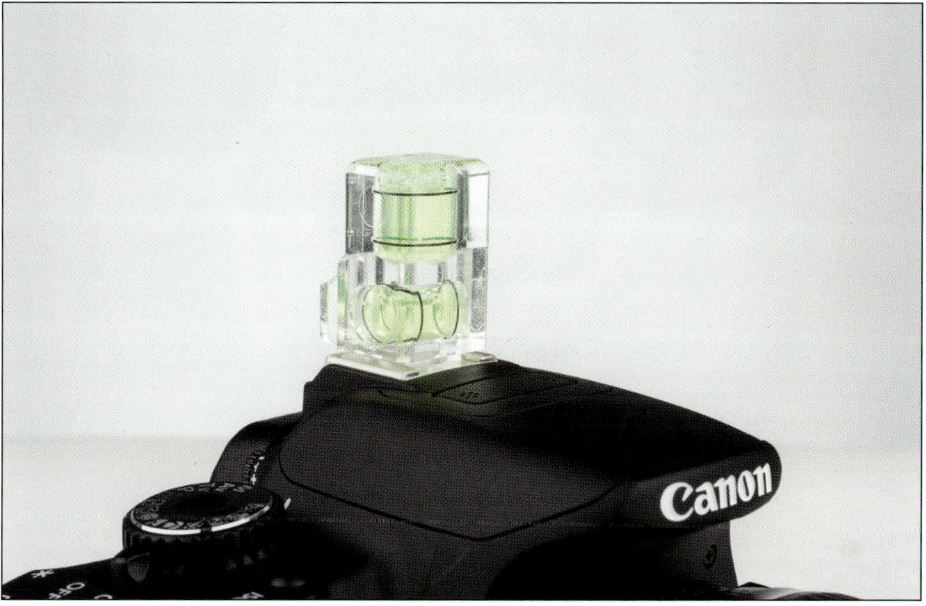

One of the things we always try to do when shooting panos is to keep as much of what was shot of the scene without having to crop a bunch away. One big thing that will help is to make sure that when you're shooting on a tripod, your camera is perfectly level. If it's even a little crooked, as you take each pano segment, your pano will start to tilt more and more, causing you to have to crop off quite a lot because you'll have big gaps around your tilted, skewed pano image. This is why keeping your camera straight and level is really important. A lot of newer cameras have built-in leveling features (see page 11), so if yours does, make sure you level your camera right on the money before you start shooting. If yours doesn't have a built-in feature, you can buy a bubble level that slips right into the hot shoe mount on the top of your camera and you can level it that way (the Vello 3-axis hot shoe bubble level is around $22). A lot of ballheads these days have bubble levels built-in, too, so check for that. Also, another thing that will help keep things level while you're shooting is a ballhead that has a panning adjustment at the bottom of the unit that lets you smoothly swivel your camera around the vertical axis of your rig to take your pano images. It's usually a small extra knob at the bottom that you loosen to let it swivel (look near the bottom of your ballhead for a set of vertical lines—if you see that, yours has this swivel/pan feature).

Keeping Your Camera Centered

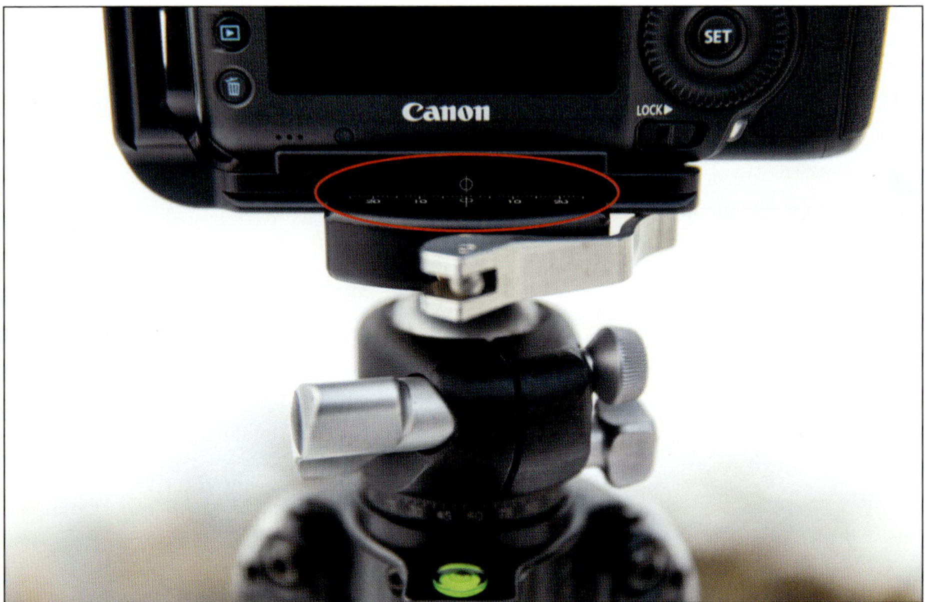

To get the best results from your panos (and to limit the amount you have to crop away once the pano is stitched together), one thing that will help is to make sure your camera is perfectly centered on your tripod. Depending on your tripod's make and model, this might be a no-brainer, but if you're using one of the popular L-brackets or quick release plates, it's easy for them to get just a little out of line, and then you pay for that later when you're having to crop away more than necessary. That's why most L-brackets and quick release plates have a scale on them with the center marked—both on the bracket and the top of the ballhead (as seen here)— so you can easily line those two points up and know that your camera is right at that center point. It's a little thing, but they're pretty much all little things—they just start to add up quickly.

Three Advantages to Shooting Them Tall

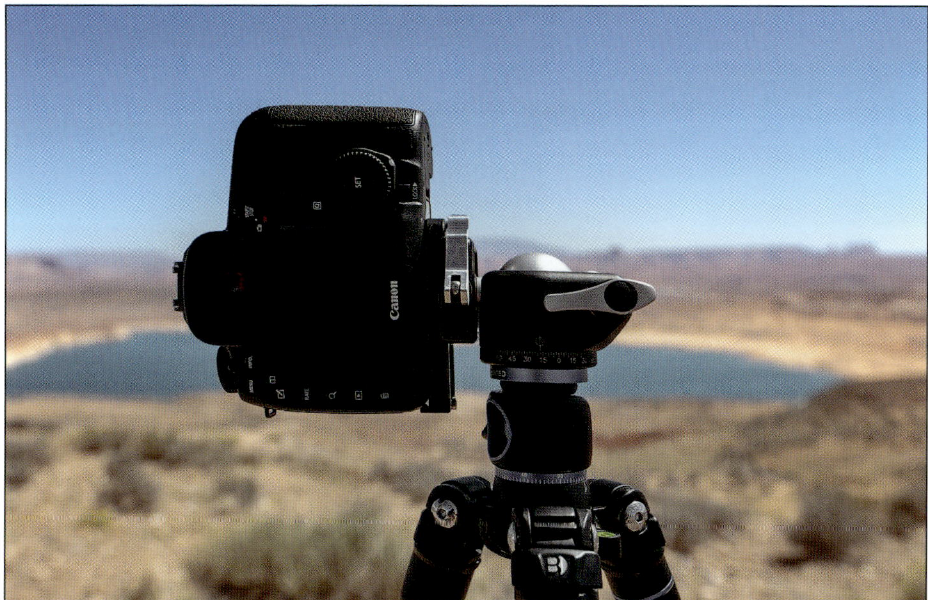

There are three advantages to shooting your panos in tall orientation (portrait ori-entation) rather than shooting them wide: (1) You get less edge distortion when you shoot tall. (2) If you have to crop your pano (and, by the way, you almost always have to crop your pano after it's stitched together), shooting tall usually gives you more breathing room at the top (more sky) and bottom (more foreground), so you're not cropping away something important in the image (like a mountain top or the foreground of a lake). Can you get away with shooting your panos in wide (landscape) orientation? Absolutely. Do I sometimes shoot in wide orientation when I take my panos (and I shoot a lot of panos)? I do. Has anything bad hap-pened to me when I've done that? I've lost a couple of mountain tops I wish I hadn't. And, (3) you wind up with a higher resolution final image when you shoot tall. For example, let's say it took five frames shooting wide to cover the scene in front of you, and you're shooting a 24-megapixel camera. Stitched together (before cropping) that would yield around a 120-megapixel image (but take off 20% or 30% for the overlap). If it took eight frames shooting tall to capture that same scene, your result would be around a 192-megapixel image, and you'd have enough resolution where you could print that bad boy on the side of a bus, and it would look awesome (well, depending on the bus, of course). So, those are three fairly compelling reasons to shoot tall. The only downsides are: (1) it takes more segments shooting tall to cover the same ground as shooting wide, and (2) your final file sizes will be larger. Not too bad a trade-off.

Put Your Ballhead's Notch on the Left for Tall Panos

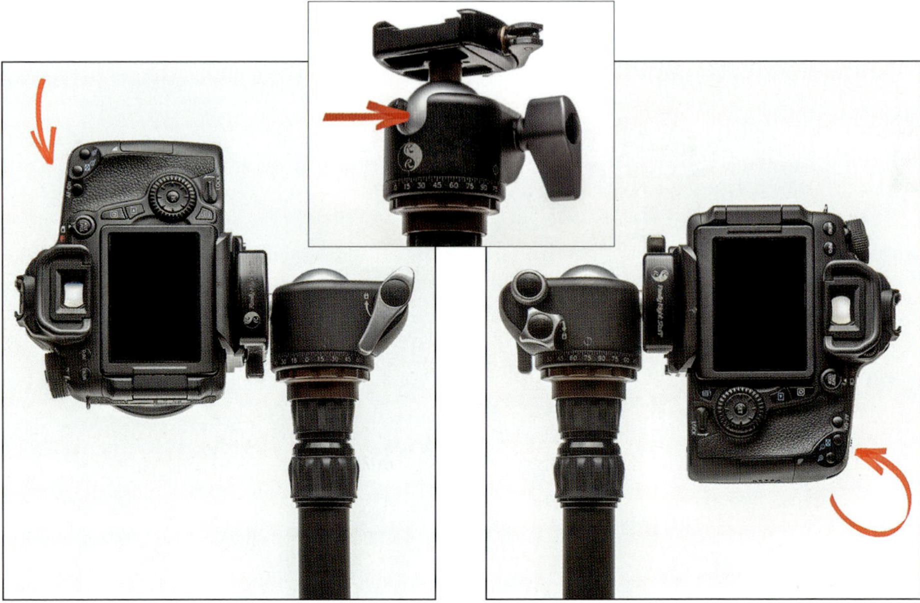

Most ballheads come with a notch cut out of the side of their base, so you can fully tilt your camera on its side for things like vertical panos (well, not just for those, but it sure comes in handy). This is just a quick tip that will help you make shooting vertically more comfortable, and that is to rotate the base of your ballhead so the notch is always on the left side from your shooting position. That way, when you use the notch to shoot vertically, your shutter button is near the top of your camera and easy to reach. If the notch is on the right side, your shutter button winds up near the bottom of the camera and getting to it is more of a pain when it's on that side.

The Key to Panoramas That Stitch Together Perfectly

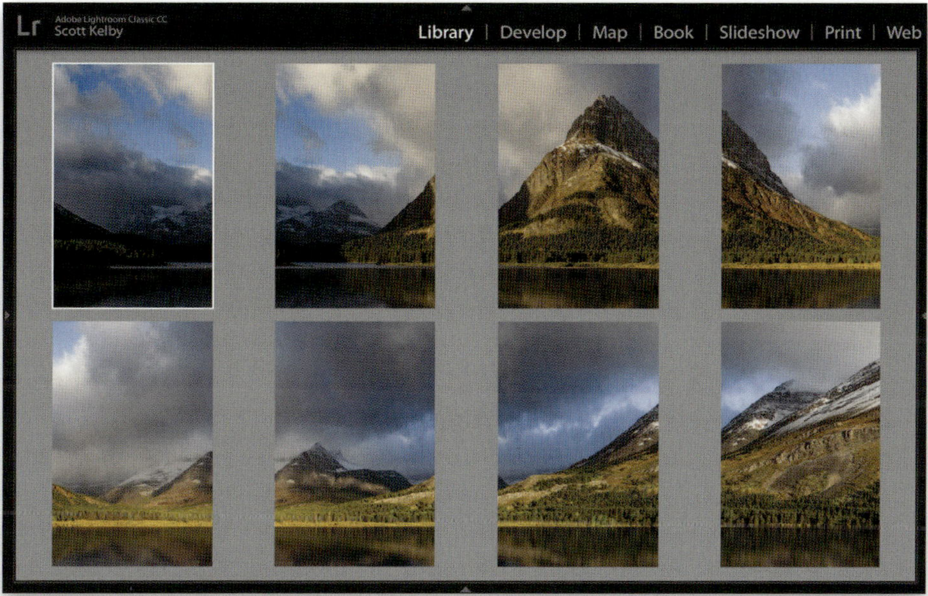

Lightroom (and Photoshop's Camera Raw) does an amazing job of taking multiple frames and combining them into one seamless panoramic image, as long as you follow this one simple rule when shooting your pano shots: you need to overlap each image by around 30%. Notice I said "around"—you don't have to calculate this precisely, just keep in mind that around 1/3 needs to overlap. Easy enough. The reason you need to do this is that both programs use the same technology, which needs to see some overlap, so it knows those two frames go together. It sees part of the same image at the edge of both frames and that's its cue that they go together. If you do more than 30%, no problem—it'll still work fine. If you do less than 30%, then it might not join all the segments together (you'll get a warning that says, "[some number] of the images were unable to be merged"). So, just keep the 30% minimum overlap thing in mind and you'll be good to go.

The Two-Finger Trick Pano Helper

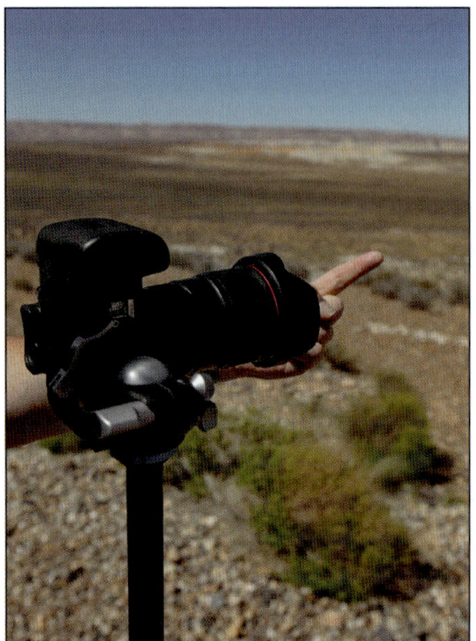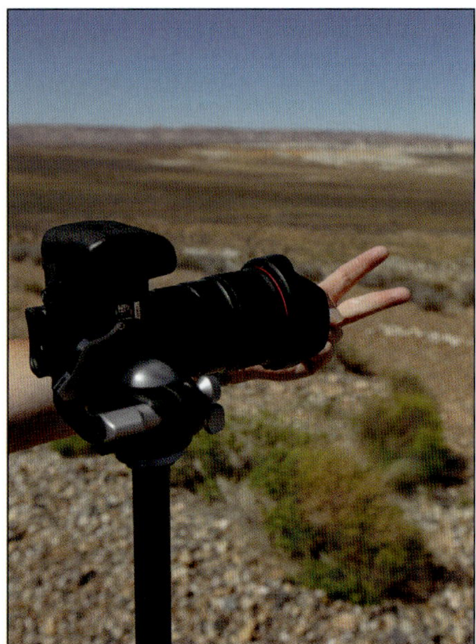

This is a trick I've been using for years, and it's way more handy than it's going to sound (I get emails from people I've taught this trick to thanking me for it, so you have to at least give it a try). Before you shoot your pano, hold one finger up in front of your lens and take a shot, so your finger is clearly visible in the shot. Then shoot your pano segments, and when you're done, take one more shot, but hold up two fingers in front of your lens, so they're clearly visible in the shot. Where this pays off is later, when you're looking at your image thumbnails in Lightroom or Adobe Bridge. When you see a shot with one finger held up, you'll instantly think, "Oh, that's right, I shot a pano there," and you'll know exactly where the segments for that pano end because you'll see that shot of two fingers. When you're scrolling through hundreds of thumbnails from a shoot, you'll be so glad you did this.

Pano Trick for Keeping More with Less Cropping

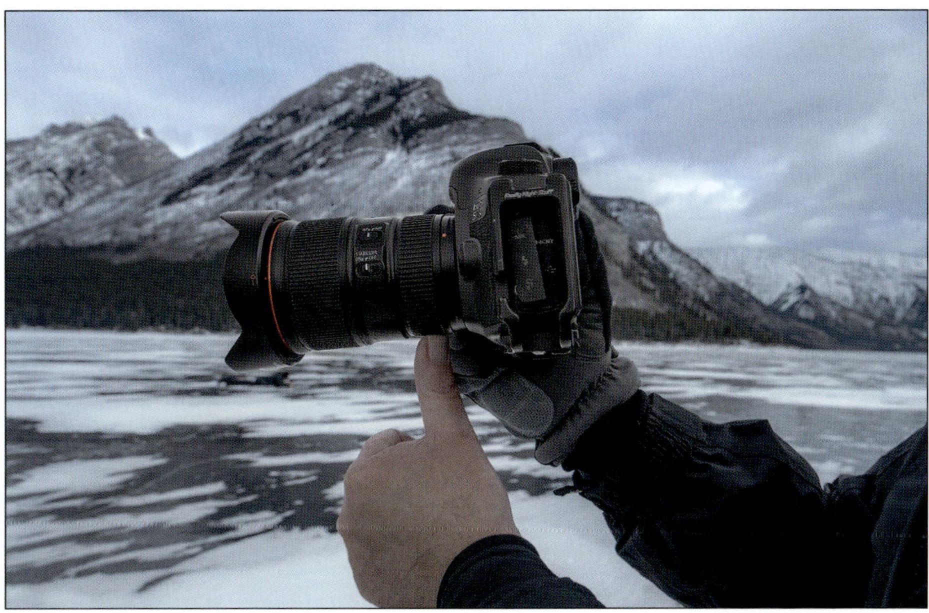

I learned this trick from my dear friend, French photographer Serge Ramelli, and what it lets you do is keep more of your pano by not having to crop as much. Now, you can buy specialized panoramic heads that are designed to help with this, but for some reason they are among the most-expensive camera accessories out there. For a good one (not a killer one, just a good one), you're talking $600+ and for a really good one, well over $1,000 (don't shoot the messenger), which is why Serge's trick is so awesome because it works so well, and it's free. (*Note:* To do this, you have to hand-hold your pano—it doesn't really work if you're on a tripod.) Here's what you do: You hold up your thumb like you're giving a "thumbs-up" and you place it directly below the center of the lens, touching the bottom of it (like your thumb is acting like a tripod), and then you take your pano segments by simply rotating the top of your camera with your other hand. Take a shot, rotate it a bit, take another shot, rotate it, and so on. The result is a pano where you have to crop away very little. It works like a charm (thanks, Serge!).

Be Quick About It

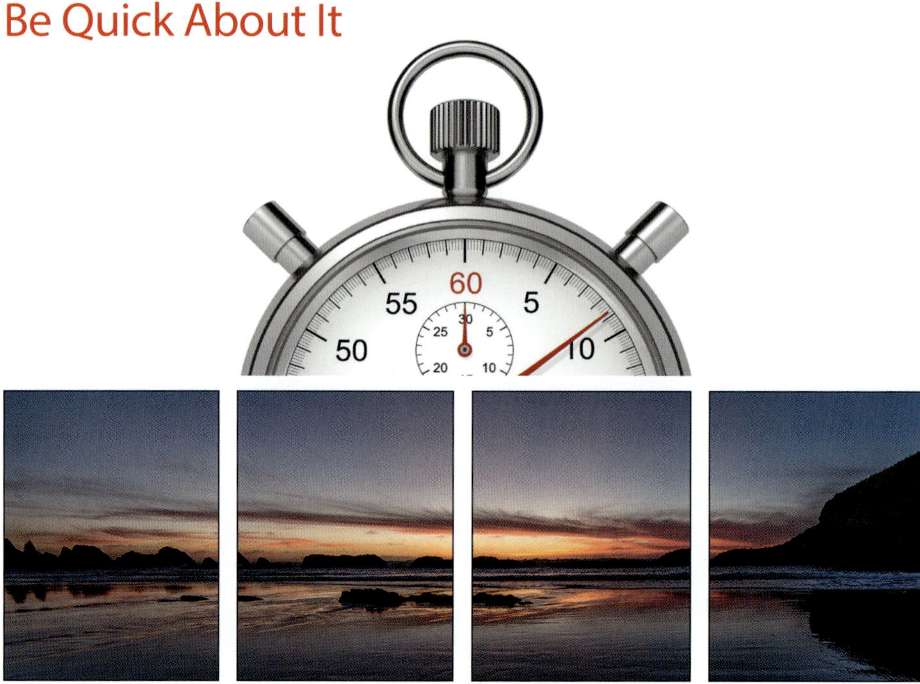

When you start to take your panorama, be quick about it. If there are things moving in your image (like clouds, or water, or trees swaying in the breeze), you need to take your pano segments fairly quickly, so you don't wind up with a blurry mess in those areas. Again, this is only if things are moving in your image. If you're shooting, say, a six-segment pano, it should take 10 seconds or less to shoot all six segments, not 30 seconds. If something does move a bit, you can often "fix it in Photoshop," but sometimes not. So, just shoot it fairly quickly, and you won't have to worry about it.

Shooting Vertical Panos

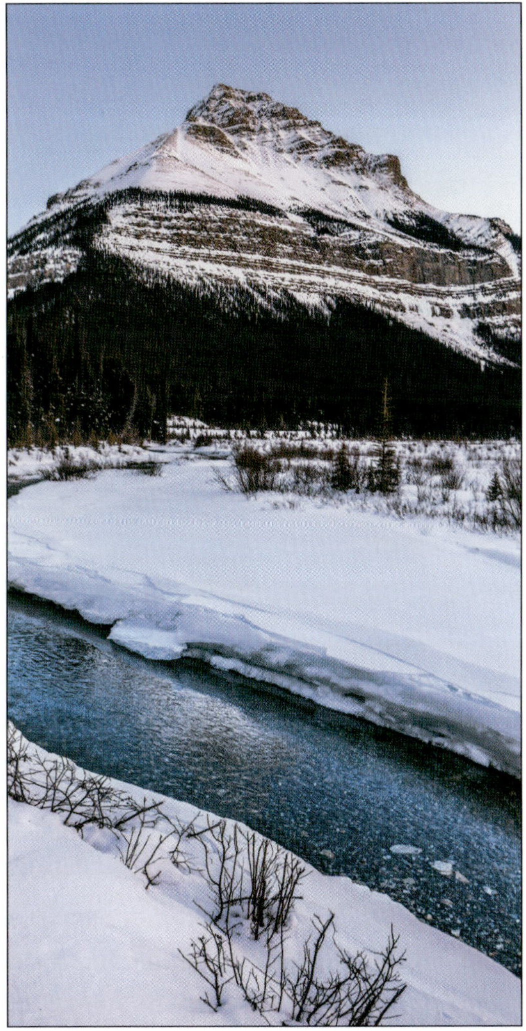

Vertical panoramas (where instead of creating a wide, horizontal panorama, you create a tall, vertical one) have become so popular that they have their own name: vertorama. You shoot and stitch a vertical panorama, errr…vertorama, the same way you would a panorama (with at least a 30% overlap between frames). But, instead of shooting from left to right, you start at the bottom of the scene and shoot moving upward, one frame at a time (don't forget the overlap), until you reach the top. Once you're done, you'll stitch it together in Lightroom or Camera Raw just like you would with a regular horizontal panorama (see page 95).

Shooting Multi-Row Panos

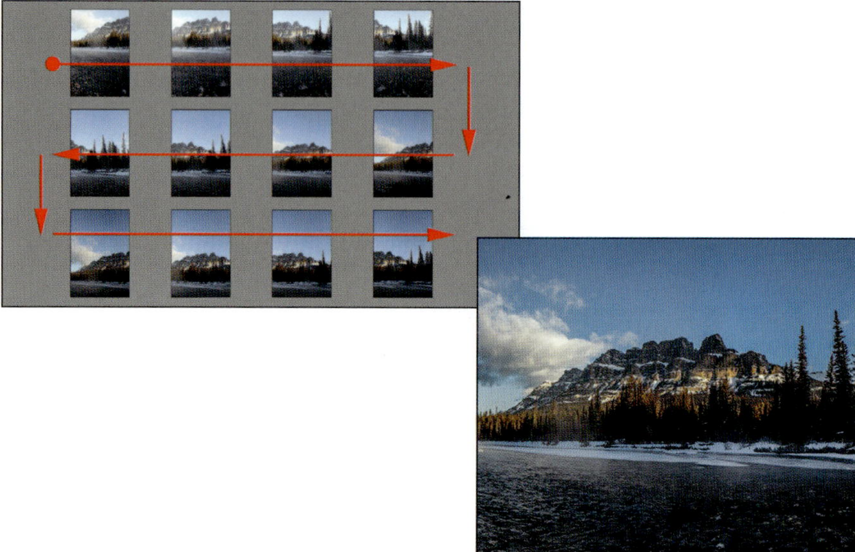

Imagine stacking two or three panos, one on top of another, to create a giant, seamless über-pano (I think I just coined a new name). You don't have to imagine it because multi-row panos are easy, and they let you cover so much of the scene you're capturing. You can have the top pano be the foreground, the middle pano be the subject, and the bottom pano be the sky. All it takes is a little bit of planning. First, let's start with the foreground: angling the camera downward, going from left to right, take your pano frames and stop when you get to the last frame. Now, tip the camera up to get the center of the scene (make sure you're overlapping the top and bottom at least 30%), but this time, you're going to shoot from right to left (the opposite direction), taking your frames, but once again stopping when you get to the end. Lastly, tilt your camera up again for the final pass—we're back to just going from left to right for this one. So, you're kind of making an "S" pattern with this technique (as seen above on the left). Now, when you open all of these images in Lightroom or Camera Raw and process them as a regular pano, it will put all three rows into one giant über-pano.

How to Stitch Your Shots Into a Pano

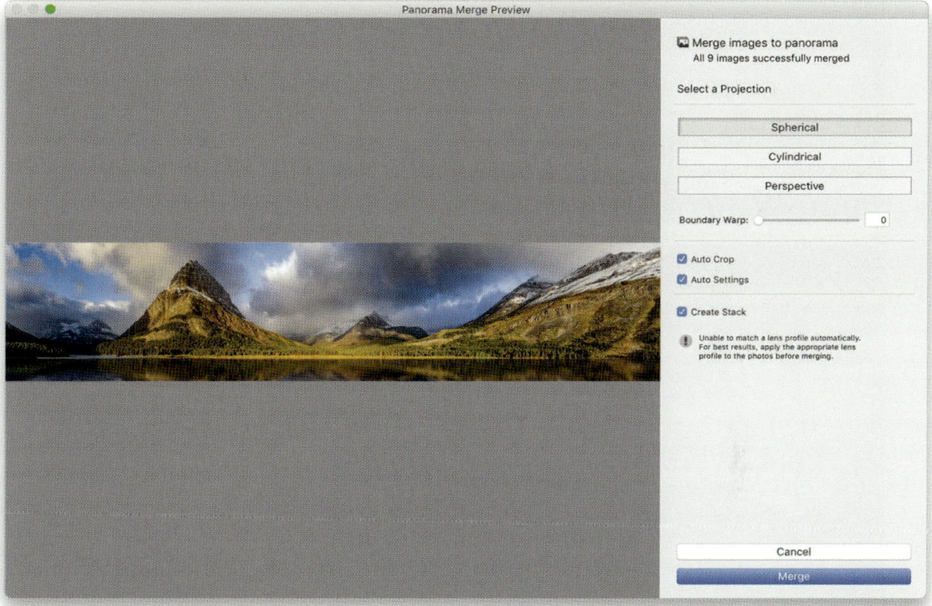

You can combine your individual frames into a single panoramic image (we call this "stitching") in either Lightroom or Adobe Camera Raw, and it's pretty much the same except for how you start the process, so I'll cover both. In Lightroom: Press-and-hold the Shift key, click on the first thumbnail in the pano (not the one with your finger in it—the frame after that), then click on the last frame in the series (the one before your two-finger shot) to select them. Now, go under the Photo menu, under Photo Merge, and choose **Panorama**. If you're using Camera Raw, press-and-hold the Command (PC: Ctrl) key, click on your pano images in the filmstrip along the left side of the window, and then press **Command-M (PC: Ctrl-M)**. No matter which program you're in, this opens the Panorama Merge Preview dialog, which shows you a preview of how your final stitched image will look. You have a choice of three different types of pano processing, and usually, it will choose Spherical, as that one is often the best for most panos. The middle choice, Cylindrical, is really more for architectural panos, so I don't generally use that one, but there's no harm in clicking it to see if you like the results better. You can also try clicking on Perspective, which tries to keep your lines straighter. (*Note:* It won't always be able to render this choice, so if it doesn't work for you, don't sweat it—our first choice will almost always be Spherical anyway.) If you turn on the Auto Settings (or Apply Auto Tone and Color Adjustments) checkbox, it applies the Basic panel's Auto adjustment when the pano is complete (I usually leave it on as a starting place, but lower the Shadows and raise the Contrast back up immediately).

Which Is Best: Auto Crop or Boundary Warp?

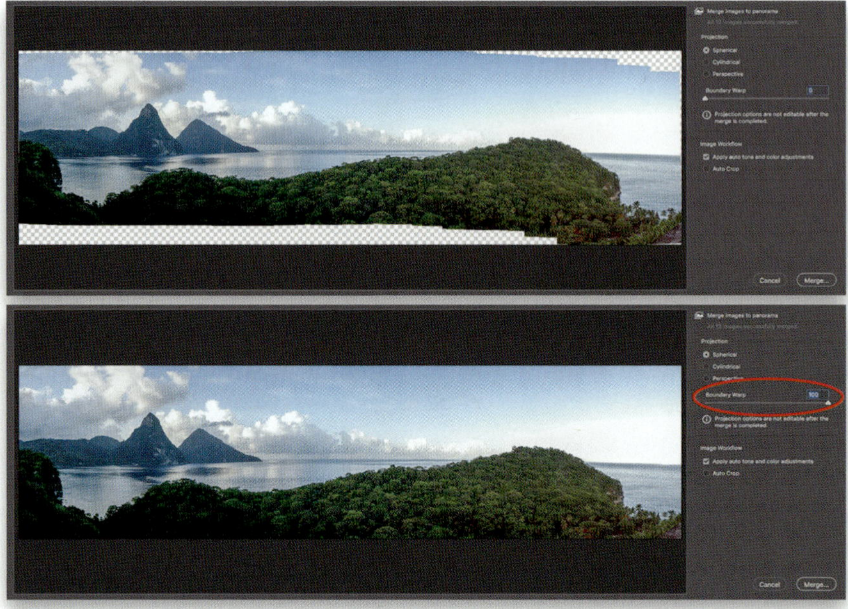

When Lightroom/Camera Raw stitches a pano together, it will have to massage (for lack of a better term, or my just wanting to use a term that sounds somehow naughty) the images quite a bit to combine them into a single, seamless image. This usually leaves white gaps along the outside edges of your images that range from little gaps to really big ones, depending on the image. This is normal pano stuff, and that's why you get two options for dealing with these gaps. One is called "Auto Crop," and if you turn this one on, it just crops your image down on all sides, so you don't see any white gaps. Unfortunately, this can sometimes crop off important stuff in your image (like the top of an arch, or the tip of a mountain, etc.), plus it usually makes your pano very skinny because of the tight crop. That's why I prefer to use the miracle that is Boundary Warp instead. When they talk about "Photoshop magic" this is the type of stuff they're talking about. Simply drag this slider to the right (I normally drag it all the way to the right, as seen here at the bottom) and watch how the pano repositions itself to somehow fill in all those gaps without you having to crop the image down at all. It truly is amazing, and it's my preferred way of dealing with those gaps. Of course, this is just a preview window, so you can try both to see which one you like and go with the one that looks best for that particular image. But, my money is on you trying Boundary Warp, picking your jaw up off the floor, and then going with it.

Stacking Your Panos to Keep Things Tidy

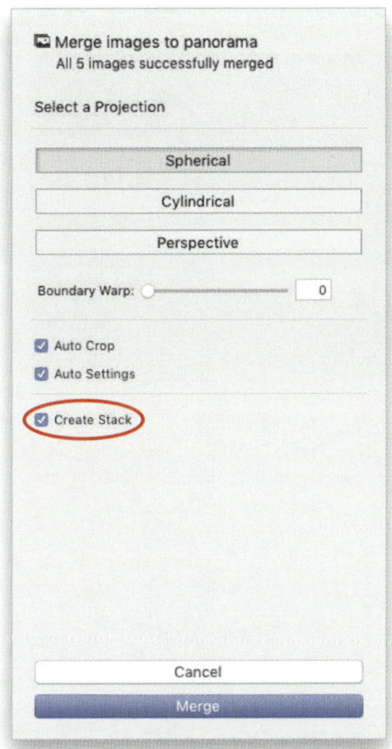

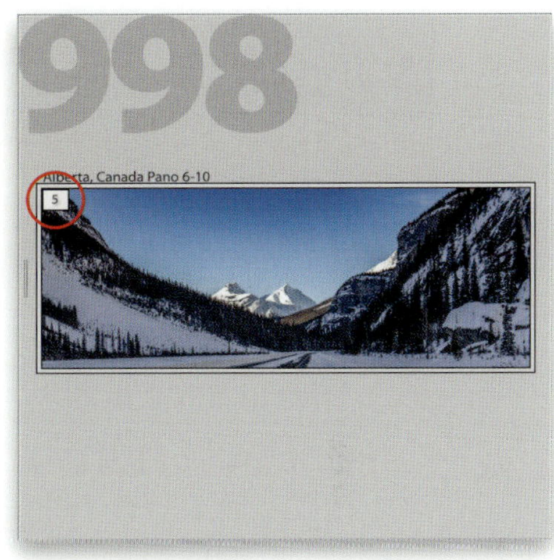

In Lightroom's Panorama Merge Preview dialog, you'll see a checkbox for Create Stack, and I highly recommend you turn that checkbox on because it will help you stay visually organized. What this does is it tidies things up by stacking all those frames you used to create your pano behind the final pano thumbnail. So, for example, let's say you used four photos to create your pano. Instead of seeing all four thumbnails and your pano, you just see your pano with the number "5" appearing in the top-left corner of its thumbnail. That lets you know that there are four more images stacked beneath that one thumbnail. This is so handy because once you've stitched that pano together, what do you need those four thumbnails for? Nuthin', right? Well, we're not going to delete them (after all, they are our originals), but we don't need to see them either—they're just cluttering up our view. So, by tucking them out of sight like this, it tidies up your thumbnail grid. If you want to see those four frames again, just click right on the number 5 and it expands the stack to display all five like usual. To collapse them back into a stack, click where that number was (it will now say "1 of 5"). There's a keyboard shortcut if you'd prefer that: just click on the thumbnail and press the letter **S** on your keyboard to toggle back and forth between seeing your pano frames or just the final pano image with the others stacked behind it. Great for helping you stay organized.

Printing Panoramas

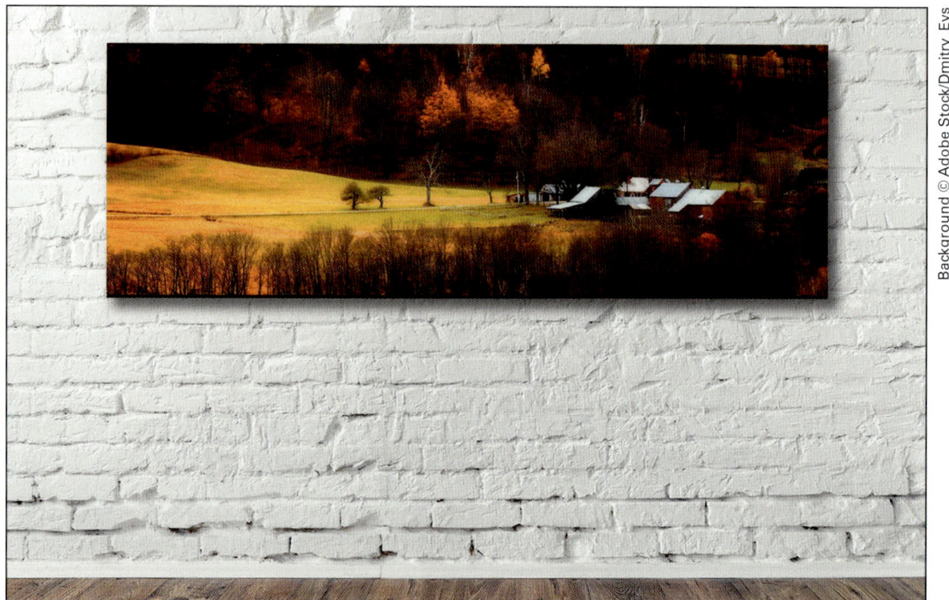

There are some online printing labs that will print panoramic sizes, but my go-to for printing panos is to have them printed on canvas. One advantage of canvas is that it's the most forgiving printing surface known to man. If you don't quite have enough resolution to print something really big, print it on canvas and they'll never know. Plus, I love giving a pano as a gift—the people receiving it literally lose their minds. I have two sources (here in the US) that I use for printing panos. If you want the most awesome canvas you've ever seen, like gallery-quality stuff, try ArtisticPhotoCanvas .com (I'm not affiliated with them in any way, besides just being one of their customers). Their customer service is top notch, and all you have to do is upload the file to their site, and they'll prep it for you. The canvas is wrapped around a wooden mounting frame, and you can have them wrap the image around the edges, or choose to have it mounted in a white or black frame. They are the best I've ever used. Great folks, too. The other one I use when I want the best possible price for a canvas pano, and the quality isn't critical. The site is CanvasDiscount.com and their deals are pretty insane (I'm not affiliated with them either, just a customer). If you sign up for their newsletter, you'll get deals that will blow your mind (not just on pano sizes). The last deal I got from them was for a 30x40" wrapped canvas on a wood frame for $30 (I am not making this up—I just looked it up in my email). It's crazy! The quality is good. It's not amazing. It's "good." But to send as a gift to a non-photographer (we're so picky), it's ideal. Anyway, just wanted to share how I print my panos.

How to Shoot HDR Images

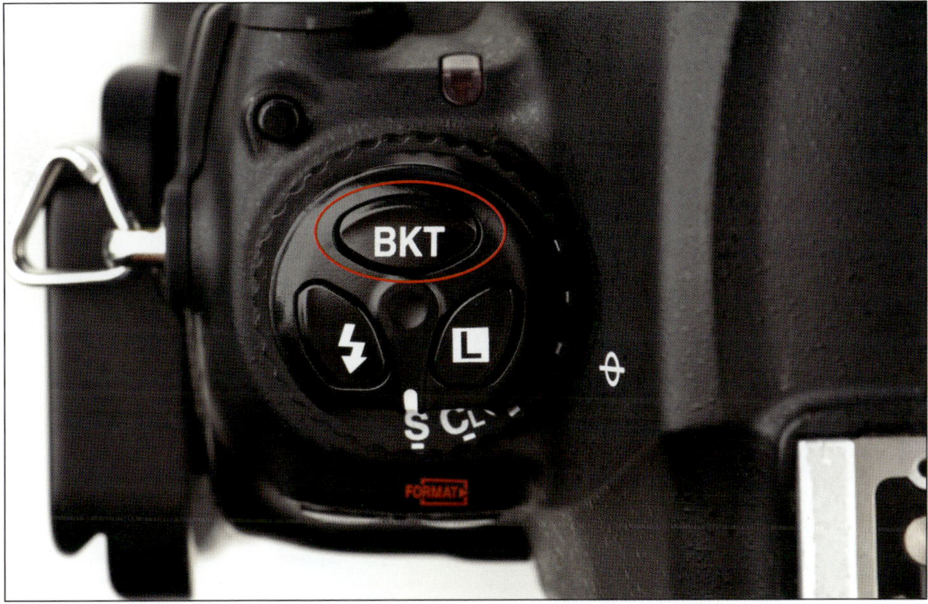

You'll be merging multiple shots of the same image into a single image, so while you could shoot HDR bracketed images hand-held, for the best results, shoot on a tripod. Set your camera to its lowest, cleanest ISO, switch to aperture priority mode, and choose an f-stop that keeps everything in focus, like f/11. The key to this technique is setting your camera to shoot bracketed exposures. When you turn on this feature, called "Auto Exposure Bracketing" or "AEB," you take one photo, and then your camera automatically takes at least two more of the same photo, but darker and lighter. On my camera, I set it to take a 2-stop bracket, so it takes the normal exposure, and then it takes another shot that is 2 stops darker, and another that is 2 stops brighter. These are the three images needed to make an HDR. Now, my particular make and model of camera allows me to do a 2-stop bracket, but some cameras will only do a 1-stop bracket. No problem. Instead of shooting just three photos (that are 2 stops apart), you'll need to shoot five 1-stop shots, so when you're done, you'll have a 2 stops darker shot, a 2 stops brighter shot, and the regular exposure. The two others left over (the one that's 1 stop darker, and one that's 1 stop brighter), you can ignore. If you want to just press the shutter button once and have it take all the photos for you, there are two things you'll need to do: (1) Turn on continuous shooting mode. That way you keep holding down the shutter until it takes all the bracketed shots. However, I prefer to also add one more thing: (2) turn on your camera's self-timer, too. That way, with continuous shooting mode turned on, it will take the first picture, and then take the rest of the bracketed frames for you (without you having to hold anything down).

How to Merge Those Into a Single HDR Image

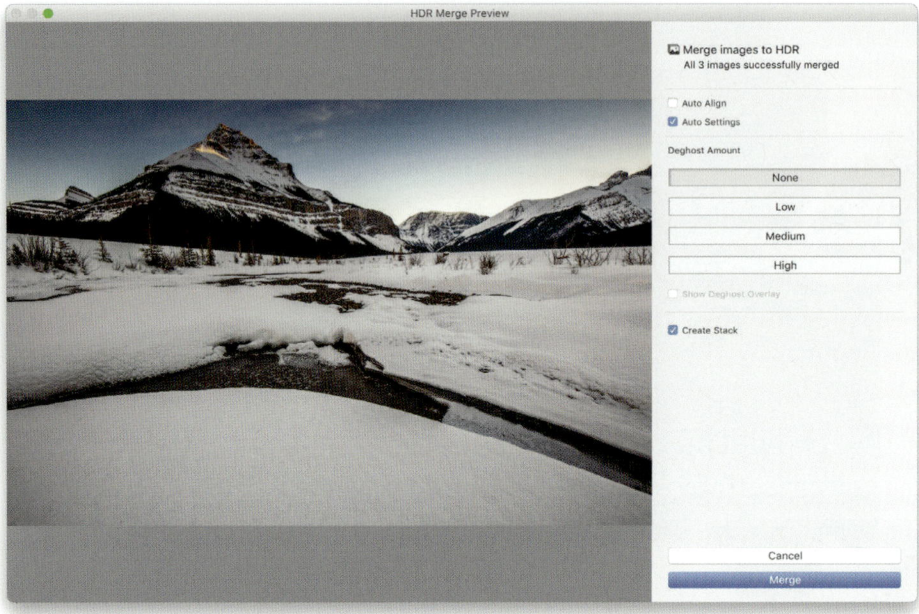

If you're using Photoshop or Lightroom to make your HDR image, you actually only need the 2 stops darker and 2 stops brighter photos to make the image—just those two images—you don't even need to use the normal exposure. (*Note:* Most other HDR applications will need that normal exposure image though.) Anyway, in Lightroom select your two bracketed images, then go under the Photo menu, under Photo Merge, and choose **HDR** to bring up the HDR Merge Preview dialog. If you're using Photoshop's Camera Raw, instead, select the two images in the filmstrip on the left and then press **Option-M (PC: Alt-M)** to bring up the HDR Merge Preview dialog. If you hand-held your HDR (it works much better if you shoot on a tripod, so I hope you didn't), turn on the Auto Align (Align Images) checkbox, or just click the Merge button and it'll take the best parts of both of those two images and combine them into a single image with a greatly expanded tonal range (and—bonus—you can open the shadow areas way up without introducing a bunch of noise. A hidden advantage of Lightroom's and Camera Raw's built-in HDR feature). One more thing (and this is really cool): the resulting HDR image that Lightroom or Camera Raw creates is a DNG image (well, provided that you started with RAW images), so it retains the properties of a RAW photo. Mind. Blown.

Creating HDR Panos

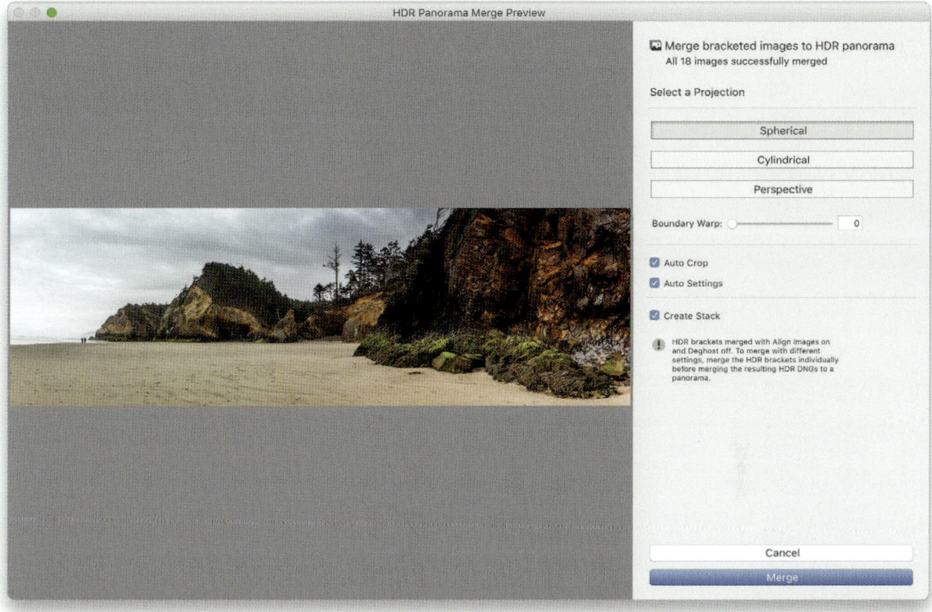

Now yer takin' things up a notch. Not just an HDR image. Not just a pano. It's both, in one image, and it's surprisingly easy to do (especially since Lightroom and Photoshop have built-in features for processing and stitching HDR panos). Here's what you're going to do: You're going to shoot a pano like you normally would (going from left to right across a scene), but instead of just taking one shot for each frame of your pano, you're going to turn your camera's exposure bracketing on, and let it take three bracketed shots. Now, you'll swivel your camera to the next frame over, let it shoot another three bracketed shots, and so on, until you reach the end of your scene. Then, import all of those bracketed pano images into Lightroom or open them in Photoshop's Camera Raw. In Lightroom, select them all, then go under the Photo menu, under Photo Merge, and choose **HDR Panorama**. In Camera Raw, select all the images in the filmstrip on the left, then click the four lines icon at the top right of the filmstrip and choose **Merge to HDR Panorama**. It opens what looks like the same Panorama Merge Preview dialog as always, but if you look in the top-right corner, you'll see, sure enough, it's for HDR panoramas. No special tricks here—just pretend it's a regular pano—but when you click Merge, behind the scenes it merges the HDRs first, and then stitches the pano for it. It definitely takes longer than just stitching a pano, so this is a great opportunity to brew a fresh cup of coffee (or drive to a Dunkin' Donuts in the next town over).

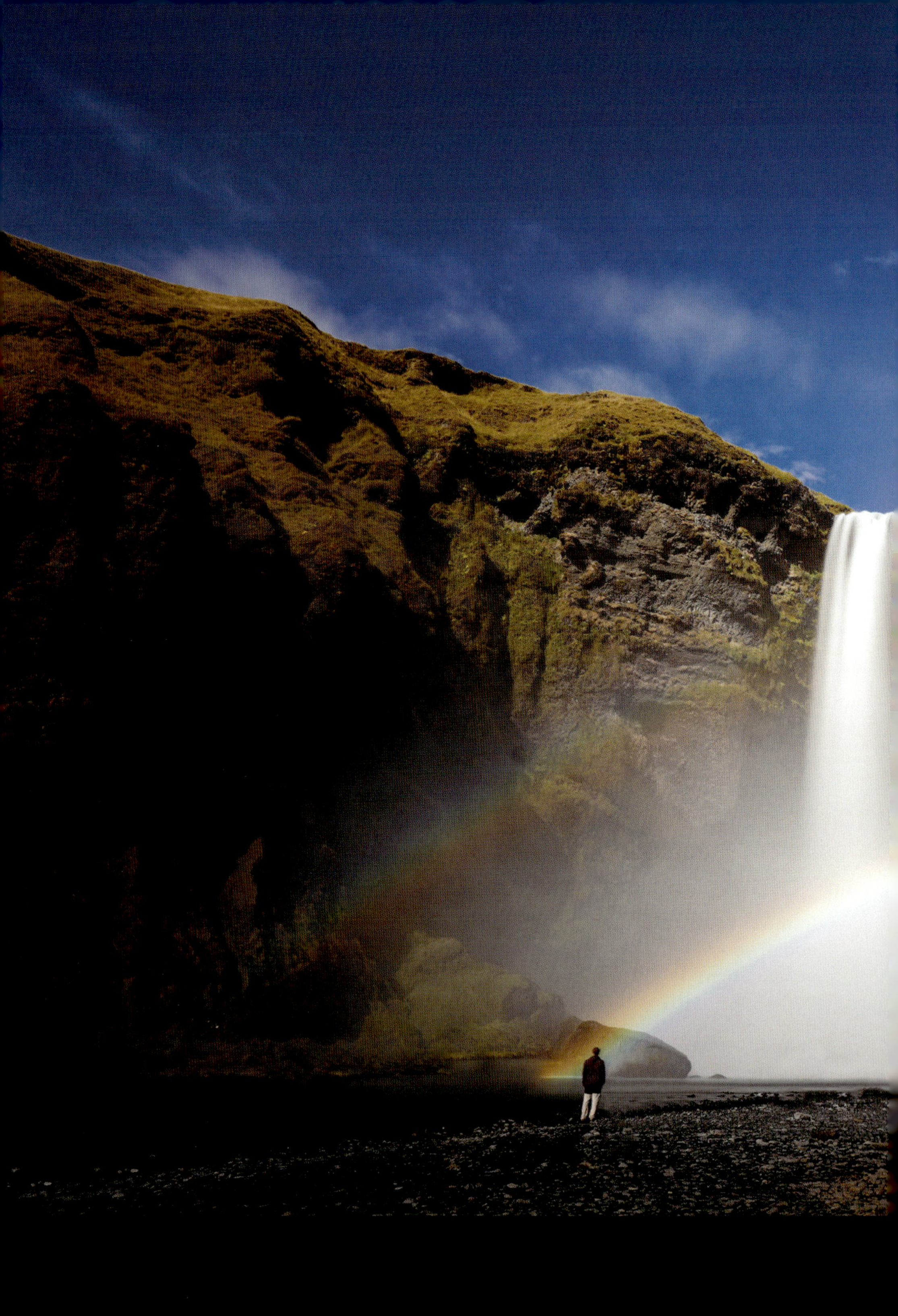

Chapter Six

LONG EXPOSURES
The Art of Showing Movement

I gotta tell ya—I am a huge fan of long exposures, and for me, the longer the better, which brings up an idea I've had for an invention. I've never told anyone about this, but I'm going to share it here with you (and if you run with it and do a Kickstarter campaign to get it made, I will be among the first to buy it). I had the idea for this invention during a 14-minute-long exposure of a canal (I used a 10x ND stacked with a 6x ND on top). Anyway, I'm standing there doing nuthin', and then it hit me—"I'm standing here doin' nuthin'. I could be sitting and relaxing, if only someone had created The Long Exposure Chair." Something small and lightweight that you could deploy quickly right after you press the shutter button, with a drink holder and a side pocket for snacks, and no, it can't be just a glorified camping chair—we're photographers and camping stuff is affordable. When It comes to photography, you have to jack up the price (triple it if it's for use in video). Anyway, just imagine how many more long exposure images you'd take if, immediately after pressing the shutter button, you could melt into a gloriously comfortable, tricked-out, pro-photo-shooting chair/chaise lounge/napping apparatus. Imagine the other photographers' envy as you reach into the side pocket and exclaim: "Oh, what's this? Cheetos!" Or, take it up a notch: "Oh, what's this? Warm biscuits with sausage gravy?" Or, perhaps even: "Oh, what's this? Lobster Thermidor with an oven-browned Gruyère cheese crust." You know and I know that they would spontaneously black out and be on the floor in the fetal position if they saw that. If you really want to take things over the top, sew in a sleeve on the left side to hold a roll of Ritz Crackers, and on the other side, a can of Easy Cheese spray cheese in a can, and get ready for it to rain benjamins! You heard it here first, folks.

It Starts with a Tripod and Cable Release

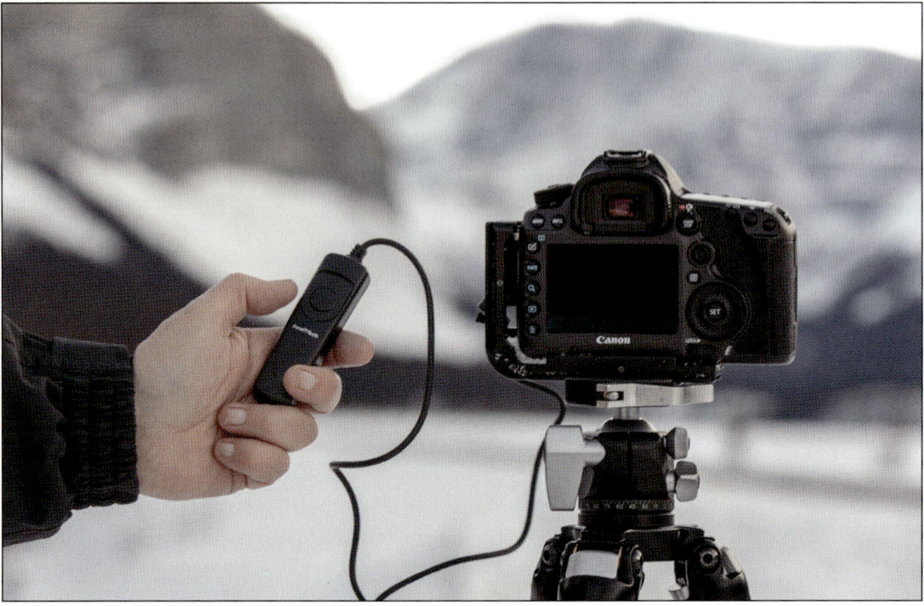

The whole long exposure thing is based on your camera's shutter being open for a long time (from a few seconds to a few minutes), and while that shutter is open, you can't have your camera move even the tiniest amount. Any movement, however incredibly small, and your shot will be blurry and go in the trash. So, you definitely need to put your camera on something stable. You're also going to want to make sure you don't move the camera while pressing the shutter button, so you're going to want a cable release, wireless shutter release, or at the very least, you'll want to use your camera's self-timer (see page 41), so you don't move the camera at all.

Start with Auto Focus, Then Switch to Manual

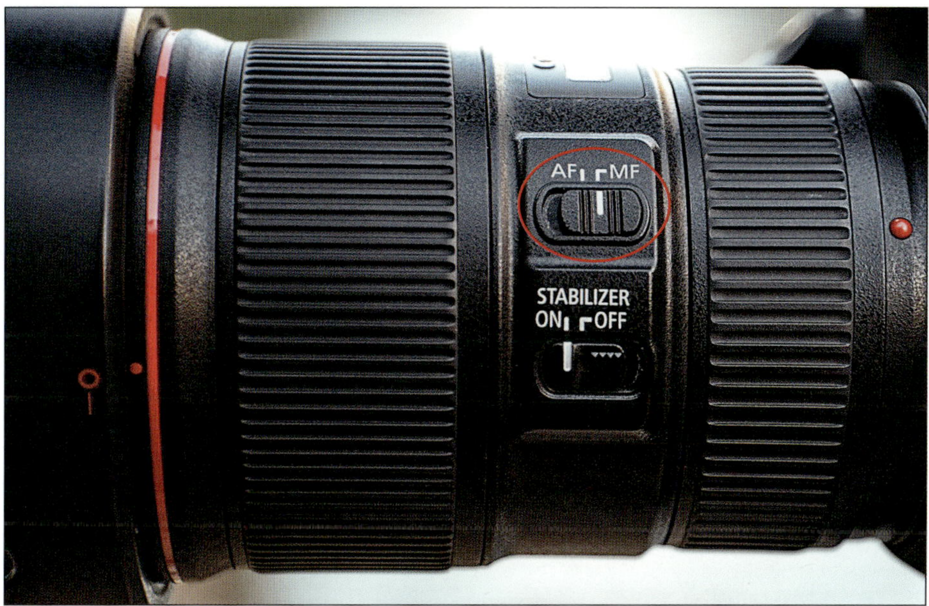

You're going to be putting a really dark filter over the end of your lens—so dark, that your camera's auto focus won't be able to see to set your focus. So, you're going to use Auto focus on your lens to set your focus before you put the filter on. Then, once your focus is set, you're going to turn the switch on your lens (the one on the side) to Manual mode. That's all there is to it. Well, to this part anyway.

Turn Off IS/VR

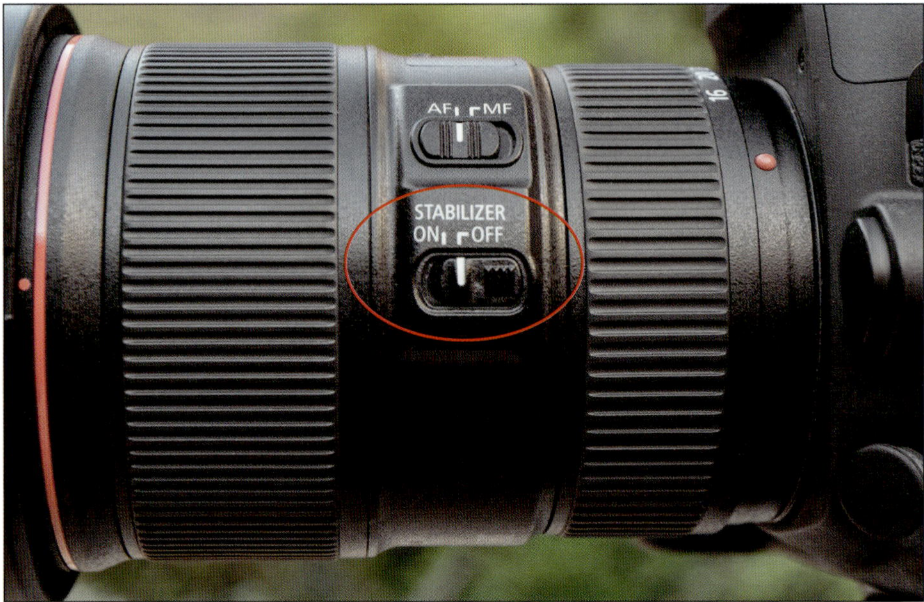

If your lens has built-in vibration reduction or image stabilization, turn it off when you're shooting a long exposure. The reason being, you're on a tripod, so your lens doesn't need stabilizing (it should be perfectly still on that tripod). With VR or IS turned on, the motor inside the lens will be searching for vibration for it to counteract, and when you're on a tripod, that searching causes a slight bit of movement. It's mostly unnoticeable when you're hand-holding your camera, but when it's on a tripod, it can make your image less sharp (yikes!). So, simply turn this switch off right on the lens itself.

Where to Set Your ISO

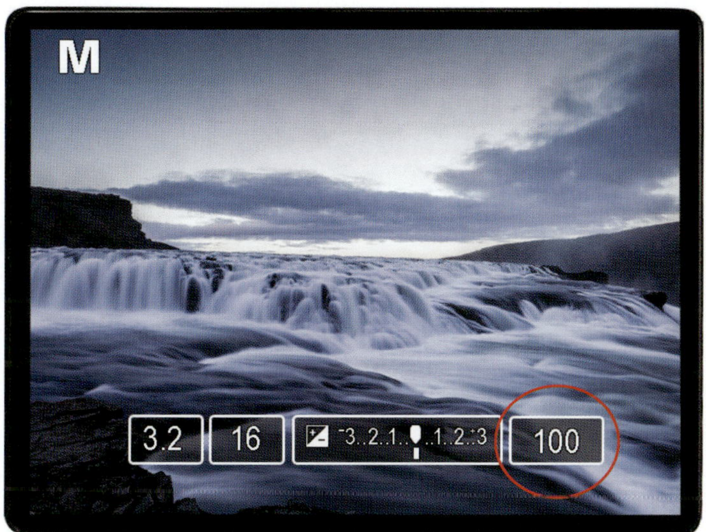

The longer the exposure, the more chance you have for noise, so you want to start with the cleanest ISO possible. You're shooting on a tripod, and your camera won't be moving at all. So, unless you're shooting the Milky Way at night (see Chapter 7), set your camera to your cleanest, lowest native ISO for the sharpest, most colorful and contrasty images (raising your ISO affects everything from color to contrast to noise). For most cameras, your cleanest native ISO is around 100 ISO, although for some, it will be 50 ISO and others 200 ISO. To find out what yours is, just Google your camera's make and model and "Native ISO," and you'll know in about 2 seconds. If you're still not sure, go with 100 ISO.

How Long to Keep Your Shutter Open

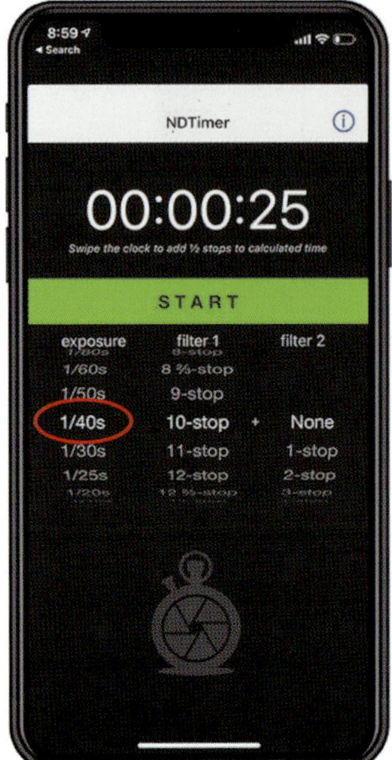
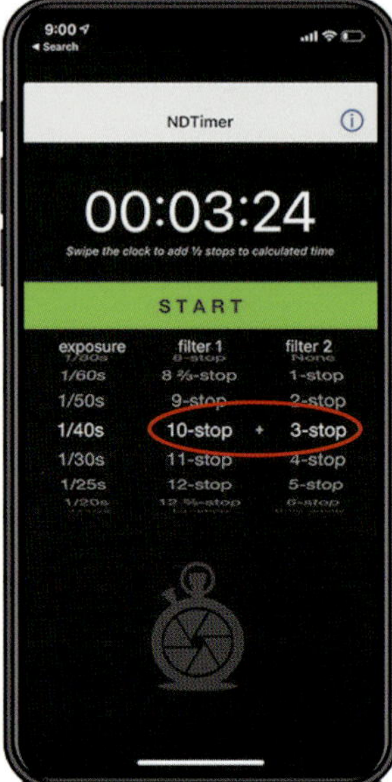
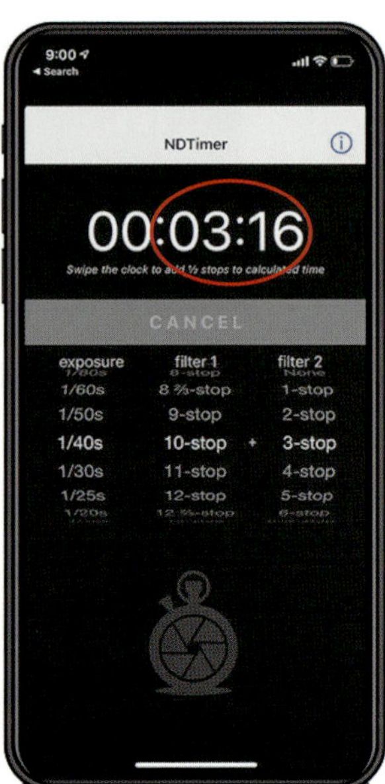

Believe it or not, you'll start to get a feeling for how long to keep your shutter open for particular situations fairly quickly, but until then, it's nice not to be totally guessing (it just wastes a lot of time). That's why you'll want to download one of the incredibly handy apps out there that will do all the math for you. Not only will they tell you exactly how long to keep your shutter open for the current scene you're photographing, they will even do the timing for you, and alert you when it's time to close your shutter. My favorite timer for iOS (iPhone) is called NDTimer. I've been using it for years, and here's how it works: Before you put your ND filter on your lens, put your camera in aperture priority mode, set your f-stop to f/11, and then hold the shutter button on your camera halfway down. Now, look through the viewfinder to see what shutter speed your camera chose for the proper exposure. Let's say it was 1/40 of a second. Go to the ND timer app, and in the first column, where it says "Exposure," enter 1/40 of a second (you just scroll down to 1/40s, as seen above left). Then, in the second column, you tell it how dark an ND filter you'll be using (3-stop, 6-stop, 10-stop, etc.). You'd only use the third column if you're stacking ND filters (let's say, for example, you're using a 10-stop, and then putting a 3-stop on over that. So, you'd enter "10-stop," and then "3-stop," as seen above middle). At the top of the app, it instantly displays exactly how long to leave your shutter open for a proper exposure (as seen above right). When you're ready to take your long exposure shot, tap the onscreen Start button, and the timer starts counting down. When it gets to zero, it dings. The equivalent for Android phones would be the ND Filter Timer app.

How to Shoot Longer Than 30 Seconds

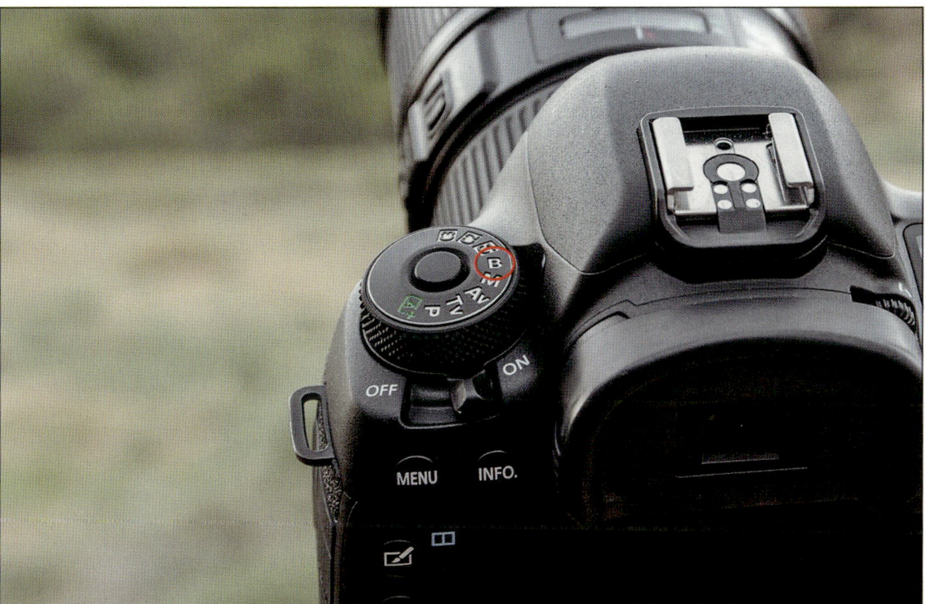

Most cameras will let you set your shutter speed to a maximum of only around 30 seconds—the dial literally stops at the 30-second mark and won't let you set it any longer than that. So, how do you get exposures longer than 30 seconds? You switch to Bulb mode. This mode was created expressly for doing long exposures. When you're in Bulb mode, you can keep your shutter open as long as you hold the shutter button down. Five minutes. Ten minutes. Whatever. Bulb mode is a major mode on most cameras, so if you have a physical mode dial on top of your camera, look for the letter "B." Otherwise, it will be on a mode button, or depending on your camera's make and model, it could be in a menu. Now, what happens if your particular camera's make and model lets you choose any shutter speed without having to go to Bulb mode? Just be happy that's one more thing you don't have to mess with when it comes to long exposures.

Cover Your Viewfinder to Avoid Light Leak

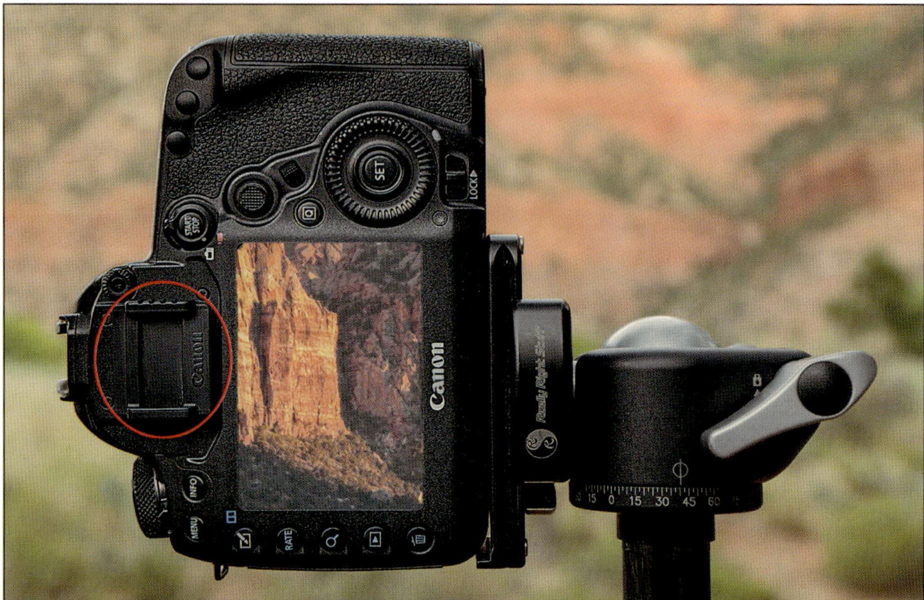

If you leave your shutter open for a long time, there's a decent chance that light will leak into your image through your viewfinder (unless you're shooting a mirrorless camera, in which case, you can skip this page altogether—this is a DSLR thing). Depending on which make and model of camera you're using, you might have a little lever you can use that puts a cover over your viewfinder (it's there for this exact purpose). If yours doesn't have this feature, then you can simply cover it with…well…whatever. I've seen people slide a small piece of card stock over the opening, or a piece of black gaffer's tape (see page 18), or (get this) some cameras have a little piece of plastic attached right to the camera strap (the one that came with the camera) that is designed to detach and fit right over the viewfinder to keep light out. It doesn't matter which method you use, as long as you use one. By the way, I don't recommend using the "I'll just cover the viewfinder opening with my thumb" technique because you'll run the risk of accidentally bumping the camera at some point and ruining your shot.

Why You'd Want to Lock Your Shutter Release

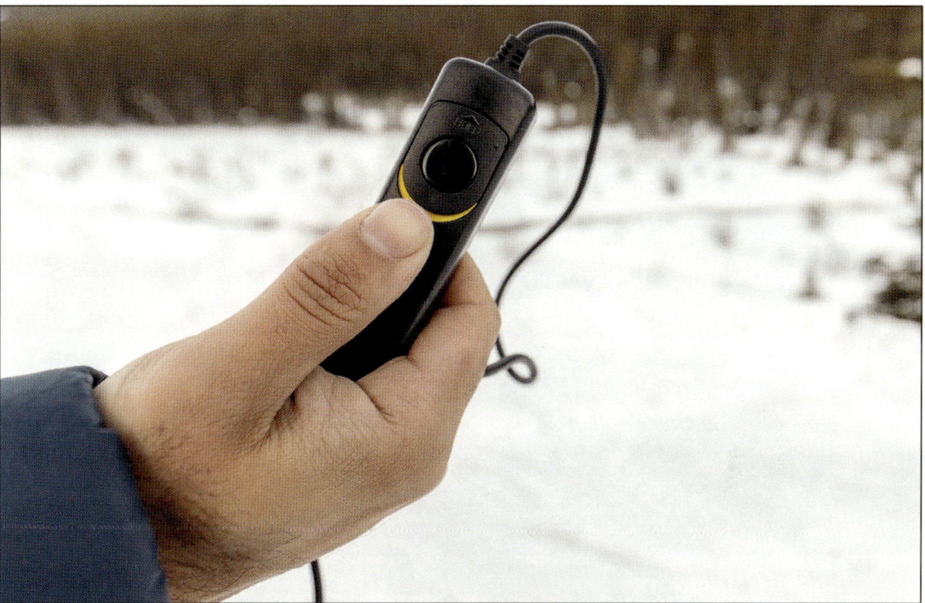

If you're doing a really long exposure (let's say 10 or 11 minutes), standing there and holding your shutter button down for 10 minutes is a drag. That's why most shutter releases have a lock button on them, so you can press the shutter button, and then lock it in place without having to actually hold it down the whole time. With some models, you press the button, and then slide it upward to lock it in the open position (as seen above, where the yellow color under the slider lets you know your shutter is locked in the open position). I've been in long exposure shooting situations where I'm doing such a long exposure, that I press the shutter release, turn on the lock button, and then go sit in my car until the exposure is done (hey, it was pretty chilly out there). Anyway, the important thing to know is there is a lock on your shutter release cable, and it's really handy if your long exposure is more than just a few seconds.

You'll Need an ND (Neutral Density) Filter

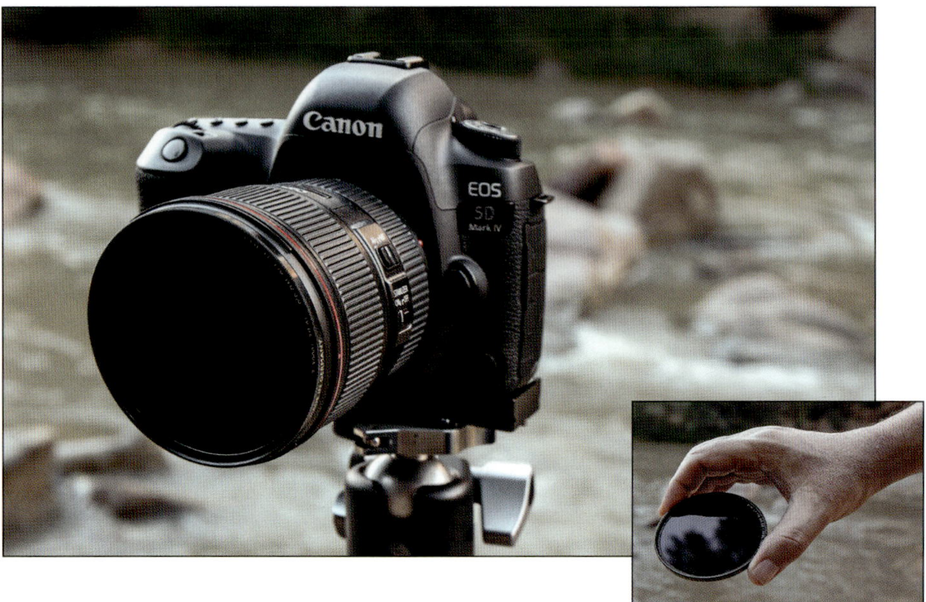

The key to taking long exposures during daylight hours (when your camera wants to use a very short shutter speed) is to make your camera keep your shutter open longer than it thinks it should to make a proper exposure. We do this by putting a really dark filter—a neutral density filter (ND filter, for short; we looked at these in Chapter 1)—over our lens. They come in different darkness amounts, from a 1-stop filter (that just makes your exposure 1 stop darker, so as you might imagine, 1-stop filters aren't very popular) up to 12- to 15-stop filters (I've never used one darker than 15. Heck, I don't even know anyone with one darker than 15 stops. That's really, really dark). I'm a 10-stop ND filter guy myself—that's my go-to amount of darkness. It allows me to shoot long exposures in almost any light. You can get this as a screw-on filter, which is great if you're on the go a lot (I use a Haida), but if you buy a screw-on filter like this, you can only use it on lenses that are that exact size (the actual size of the glass—mine only fits my 77mm lens). That's why I also have a different style Haida ND filter—it's a square sheet of glass that slides into a holder system that goes in front of your lens (seen on the next page). The advantage of this system is I can buy inexpensive adapters, which let me use that filter on smaller or larger lenses. It's not as convenient as using the simple screw-on filter, but it's still easy to use (it just takes more steps and it's larger to carry around). By the way, what I like about the Haida ND filter is that the color is right on the money. Many ND filters introduce some sort of color cast (for example, my B+W brand ND filters make my long exposures have a brown tint, which actually can kinda look good, but it's not accurate color).

Stack ND Filters for Even Longer Exposures

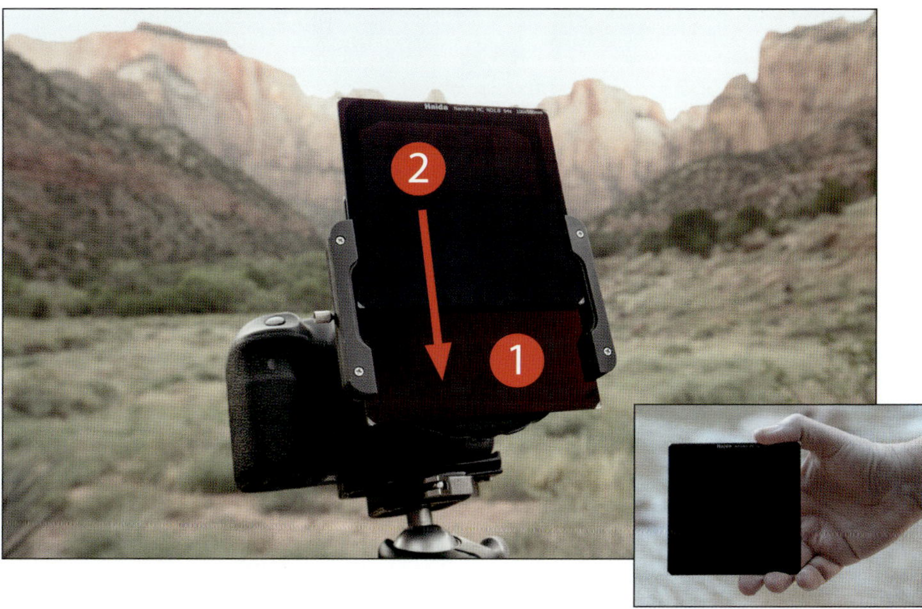

I mentioned I had a 10-stop ND filter, and that does an awesome job in most cases, but what if you need to keep your shutter open for longer than your 10-stop ND will keep it open? Then you stack—you put another ND filter in front of the ND filter you already have on your lens (you literally stack one in front of the other, hence the name). This is why, in addition to my 10-stop ND filter, I also have a 3-stop ND filter I only use for stacking when I need to keep my shutter open even longer (especially handy on a really bright day). Here's an example of how well stacking works: If your shutter speed is 1/60 of a second before you put your 10-stop filter on, when you put your 10-stop filter on (#1 above), you'd only have to leave your shutter open for 17 seconds to get a proper exposure. Now, stack a 3-stop ND filter on top of that (#2 above), and the time you'd need to leave your shutter open for a proper exposure jumps up to 2 minutes and 16 seconds. That's a pretty big jump (and you can see why having that extra 3-stop ND filter can make a big difference).

Try Using Live View to Focus

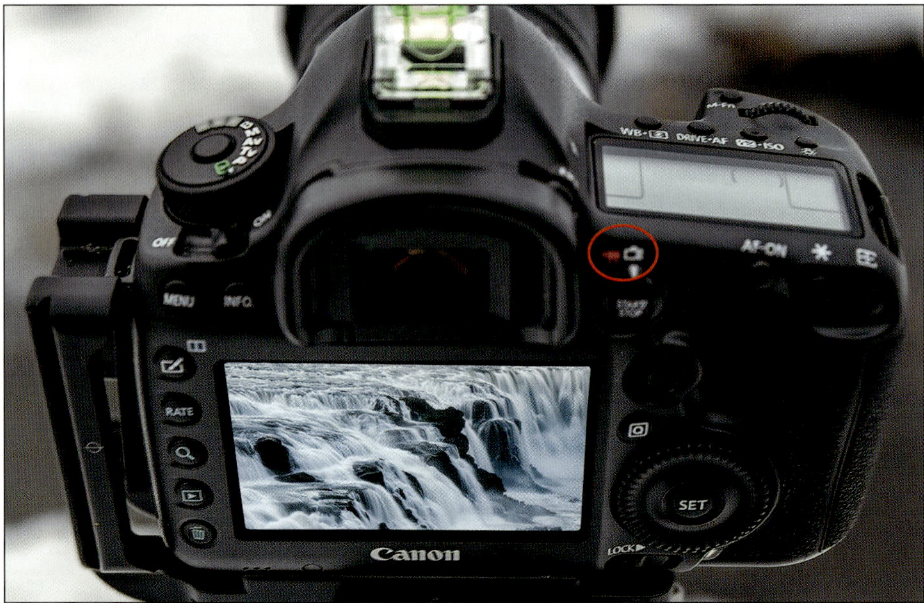

When you put an ND filter over your lens, you can look through your viewfinder and the scene will probably just look solid black. That's why we have to focus before we put the filter on—that ND makes the scene nearly black and your camera can't "see" to auto focus. However, depending on your camera's make and model, you might be able to use Live View to get a preview of how your long exposure image is going to look. For example, on most Canon cameras, even with your ND filter on the lens, switching to Live View mode (where you see the image on the LCD monitor on the back of your camera, rather than through the viewfinder) lets you see a preview of the final exposure. Same thing if you're shooting a mirrorless camera, but you can also see it in the electronic viewfinder as well, which is nice. This is helpful once you get comfortable with shooting long exposures, so you don't have to use a timer app any longer—you can turn on Live View (or look through your EVF on a mirrorless camera), look at the live preview, and by seeing how dark or light the exposure is, you can make a pretty decent guess at how long your shutter should stay open. Again, this is for after you've been doing this long exposure thing for a little while, but at least you know it's there when you're ready.

Take a Second Shot in Aperture Priority Mode for Sharp Detail

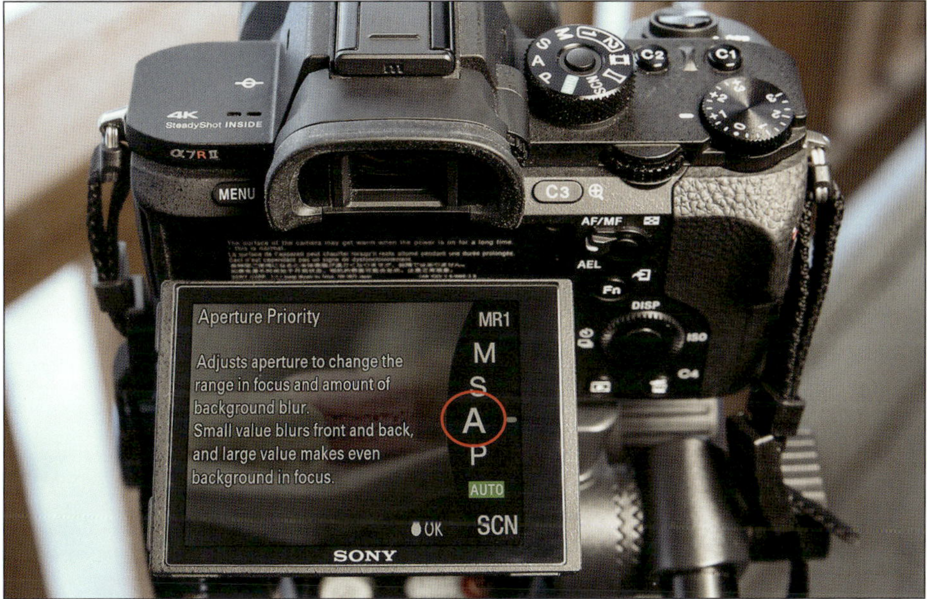

This is a trick I learned from my dear friend, and long exposure expert, Mimo Meidany: after you've taken your long exposure image, take the ND filter off your camera, switch to aperture priority mode, and take a regular photo (not a long exposure). This second image is there in case you need to add sharp detail back into your photo later in Photoshop (Lightroom can't do this trick). Sometimes, with a long exposure, the water will look super-smooth, or the sky will look wonderfully streaky, but other parts of the image might be a tiny bit blurry. Any little bit of movement that happens while your shutter is open, even a tiny vibration from a passing car, or people walking on a bridge you're shooting on, can make the detail areas just a little blurry. That's why having a second shot with all that stuff perfectly tack sharp can come in handy. If the water and streaky sky are a little blurry, you generally won't notice because they're supposed to be soft, but detail areas have to be sharp, and that's why this second shot can be a lifesaver. This little trick has saved me more than once. In the Post-Processing chapter (Chapter 8), I'll show you how to combine these two images (the long exposure shot and the same shot taken in aperture priority mode) to create a super-sharp, super-detailed long-exposure image (it's incredibly easy—anyone can do it). But, if you didn't take the second shot, you won't be able to do the trick. So, when you get a shot you like with the right framing and composition, stop right then and get that second shot while still on the tripod in the exact same position. You might be really glad you did.

Long Exposure Noise Reduction

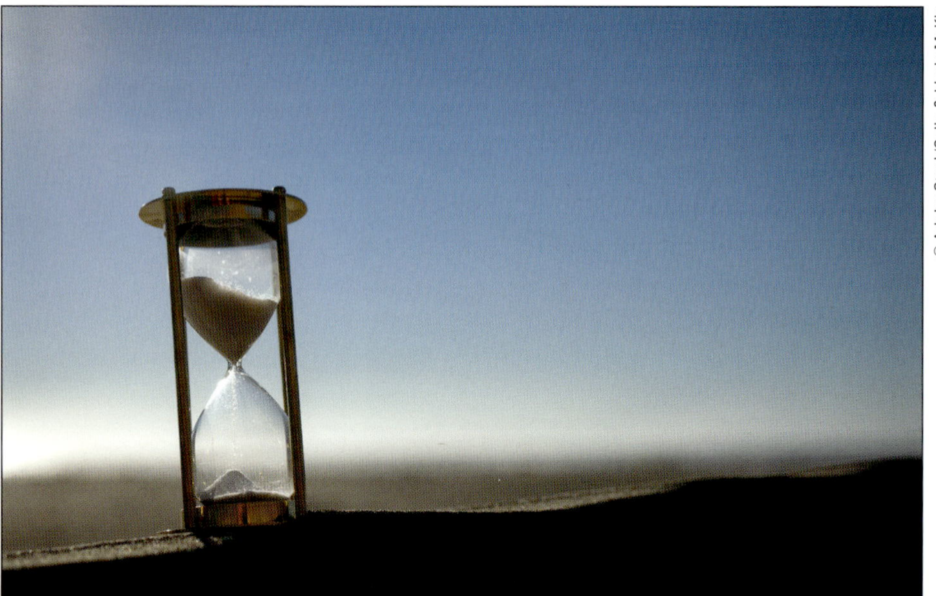

Many cameras have a feature called Long Exposure Noise Reduction and as tempting as that name may sound, I don't recommend using it. The first downside is that the noise reduction is applied in your camera immediately after you take the shot, and it doubles the amount of time needed before you can take another shot (or in many cases, before you can even see your shot on the back of the camera). For example, if you took a 6 1/2-minute exposure with Long Exposure Noise Reduction turned on, you'll have to wait an additional 6 1/2 minutes for the noise reduction to be applied, so now you're waiting 13 minutes to see if your shot came out okay. Worse yet, the noise it reduces is a slightly different kind of noise than you're used to, so you might have to do some regular noise reduction afterward in post-processing anyway. So, in short, I don't turn this feature on in my camera. If I have to do some noise reduction, I do it in Lightroom or Photoshop's Camera Raw. I apply the noise reduction to the original RAW image, and then only in the spots where it really needs it (see page 173), which is something your camera can't do—it's going to apply that noise reduction to the entire image.

Making Waterfalls and Streams Look Silky

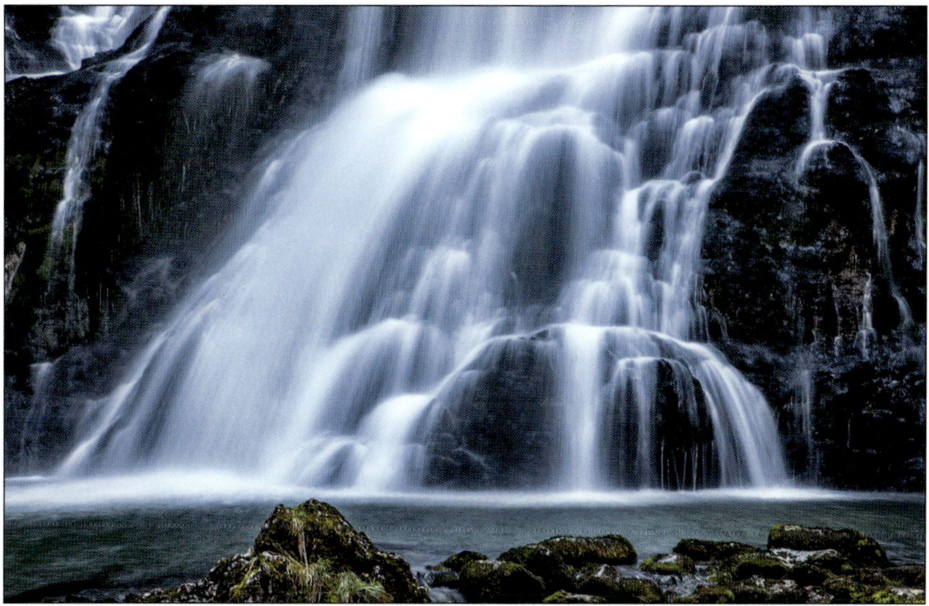

When it comes to shooting waterfalls, we're looking for that smooth, silky water (freezing the water looks…well…let's just say it's not what a pro would do), and there are some different ways to go about it. The good news is the water usually moves so rapidly you don't need a very long exposure to get that silky water look—usually only two or three seconds, but sometimes even less. In fact, sometimes, you can get a long exposure like this without even using an ND filter, especially if the waterfall is in a forest, or if it's a very overcast day—just set your f-stop to f/22 and if it's not too bright outside, you'll have instant silky water. Sometimes even a polarizing filter (see page 13) will darken the exposure enough to get you some decently silky water by keeping your shutter open a little longer than normal. Of course, you can always pop an ND filter on, but you probably won't need something like a 10-stop ND—this is one of those rare situations when a 3-stop will probably do the trick. Just wanted to give you a couple of options when it comes to shooting waterfalls and streams.

You Want the Clouds Moving

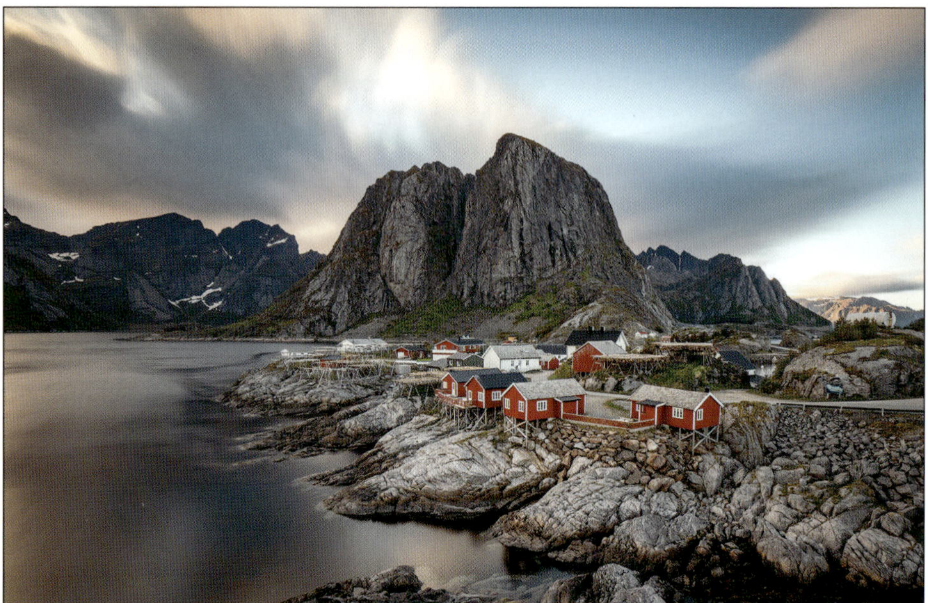

There are two main things that long exposure brings to the table when it comes to daytime landscape photography, and they are: (1) smooth, silky water, and (2) awesomely streaked skies. However, to get that awesomely streaked sky, the clouds have to be moving, and the faster the better. If the clouds aren't moving—they're just kind of sitting there still in the sky (as is sometimes the case)—there's no sense in even doing a long exposure because all you'll get are some slightly out-of-focus clouds. Of course, if you don't have clouds at all, just keep your gear in your car and keep driving.

How to Do Light Painting

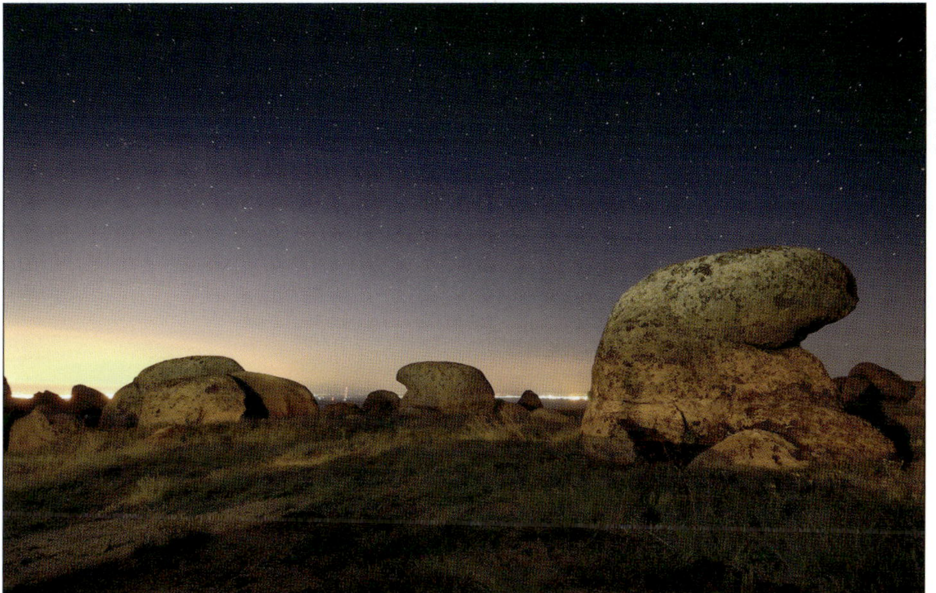

This is a particularly interesting (and fun) genre of long exposure photography, usually done at night, and you use it to illuminate a foreground object (for example, some rocks in your foreground) while your shutter is open. You literally take a small flashlight and "paint" over an area with a few strokes, and when your exposure is complete, that area where you painted is "lit" and clearly visible. You can go from subtly lighting an area to making it look like you set up studio strobes, and it's all based on how long you paint with that light on. First, you'll need a flashlight of some sort (see page 142 in the night and Milky Way photography chapter for some recommendations). Once you have your light, and your shutter is open for your long exposure, you'll start painting over the object you want lit in your nighttime image. It takes a bit of trial and error to find out exactly how long you'll need to paint, so expect to shoot a few practice frames every time you do a light painting, as you figure out how long to paint (the longer you paint, the brighter the lit area will be. So, in most cases, you'll only be painting for a very short time, but again, it's based on how large the object is that you're light painting). Also, once you start painting, don't stop or pause, or you'll get bright hot spots on those areas—keep it moving and fluid the whole time.

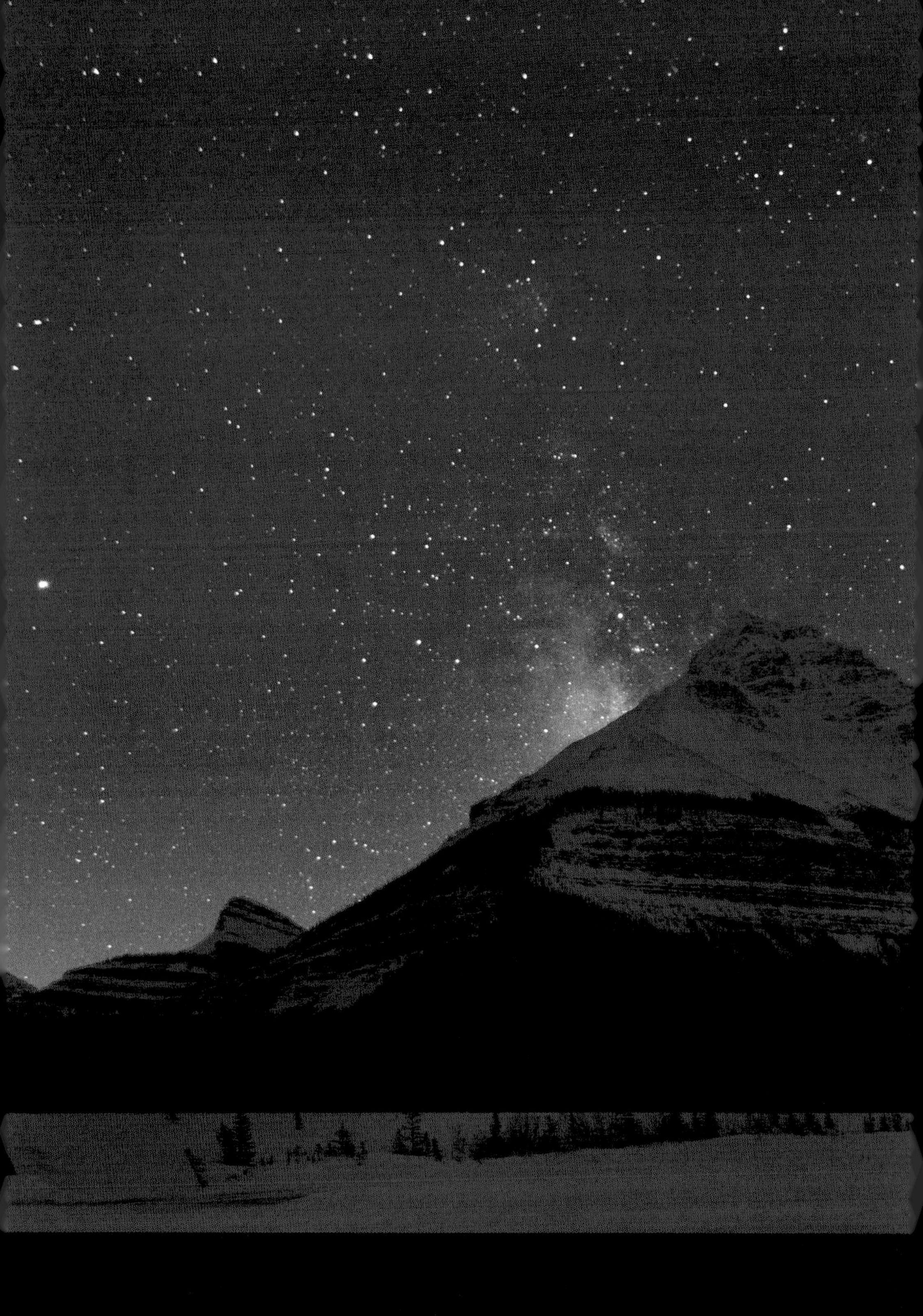

STARRY SKIES & THE MILKY WAY

Shooting the Heavens

The ancient Romans had a saying: *"Omnes una manet nox,"* which means, "Same night awaits everyone." They also had this saying: *"Permitte divis cetera,"* which roughly translated means, "What ever happened to Peter Cetera, the old bass player for Chicago, who sang that duet with Cher?" Apparently, the Romans were big fans of night skies and the original line-up for Chicago, but shooting the night sky is something that has always drawn landscape photographers. The problem is that it's a little tricky due to these main issues: (1) The earth is moving. (2) The stars are moving. (3) Things inside your camera are moving. (4) Things inside you are moving. (5) Aliens are real. It's mostly numbers 2 and 5, but regardless, when things are moving, there is an excellent opportunity for things to get blurry. If you do wind up with a blurry photo, there are only so many things you can do with it. For example, you could: (1) Sharpen it in Photoshop using the Unsharp Mask filter. (2) Sharpen it using Lightroom's Detail panel. (3) Try Photoshop's Shake Reduction filter. (4) Try Photoshop's High Pass filter. Or, (5) offer the image as a sacrifice to the alien overlords. There's also some gear that's absolutely essential for capturing crisp photos of the stars and Milky Way, like: (1) A very sturdy tripod. (2) A headlamp to operate your camera in complete darkness. (3) A cable release to trigger your camera without introducing any movement. (4) A wide-angle lens to capture both the landscape and the sky. And, (5) a beryllium sphere used to power the alien craft with enough force to break free from Earth's atmospheric ring, so it may return to Klaatu Nebula. The most important ones there are probably numbers 1 and 4. Number 3 is pretty big, too.

Your Goal: a Landscape Shot with a Starry Sky

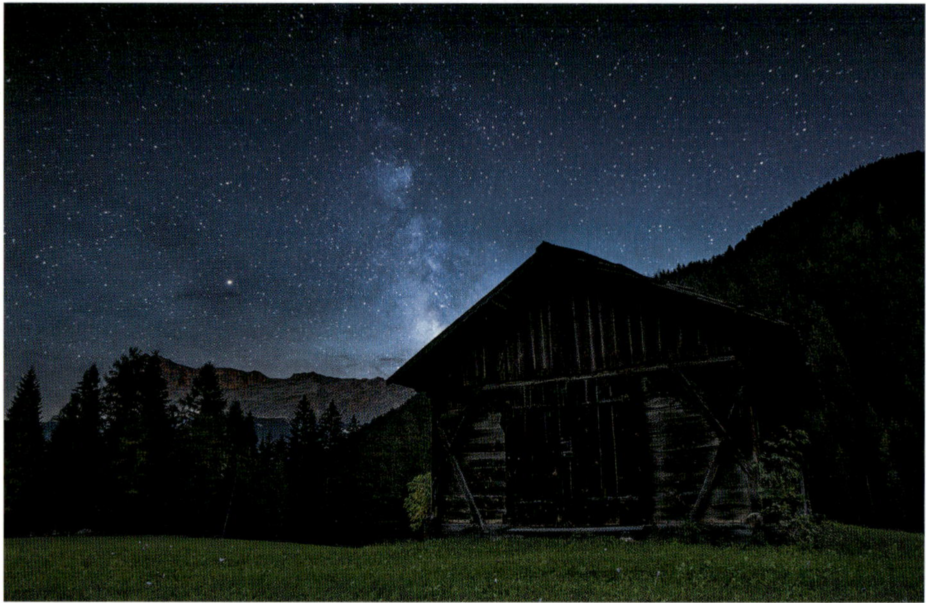

Just like in regular landscape photos, a starry sky or Milky Way shot will generally be stronger if you have an interesting foreground element, and what you'll often see is either a recognizable silhouette (mountains, a rock formation, a building, barn, arch, lake, ocean—something clearly recognizable even when silhouetted), or that same type of object artificially lit (more about that on page 142). Having a landscape foreground of some kind at the base of your shot gives interest and context to the image, rather than just pointing straight up at the dark sky. Search Google for "Milky Way photography" (then click the Images link), and you'll see that nearly all the results have something in the foreground that brings it all together.

Avoid Light Pollution

Before you even pull out your camera and tripod, you're going to need to find a shooting location that will put you in position to capture a star-filled sky and/or the Milky Way (the "home run" of night sky shots). This is significantly harder than it sounds because to get the type of shots you probably want, you're going to have to be far away from cities, highways, and basically any signs of civilization. These "signs of life" (houses, farms, billboards, highways, etc.) generate an amazing amount of "light pollution," which masks the stars, makes them appear very faint (if they're visible at all), and pretty much ruins your chances of making a great shot. Even if the city or houses are way off in the distance, you're still hosed—you literally have to get miles away from civilization to get that deep black, unpolluted sky that makes great images. There is actually an official scale that rates the quality of the night sky and your chances of getting a great shot. It's called the Bortle scale and it numerically ranks the brightness of the night sky at your current location, using a scale from 1 to 9. A rating of 9 means the sky is so bright that you can't really see any stars at all, and if you can see any, they're so weak you can pretty much forget about it (say that in a New Jersey accent to really make it hit home), and a rating of 1 means "this is the night sky you've always dreamed of." What are you looking for? A 3 or lower (the lower the number, the better the sky). So, start with finding a location far enough away from other humans that you have a shot at making a great image. I can't overstate the importance of a good sky.

Check the Weather, 'Cause You're Gonna Need a Cloudless, Clear Sky, Too!

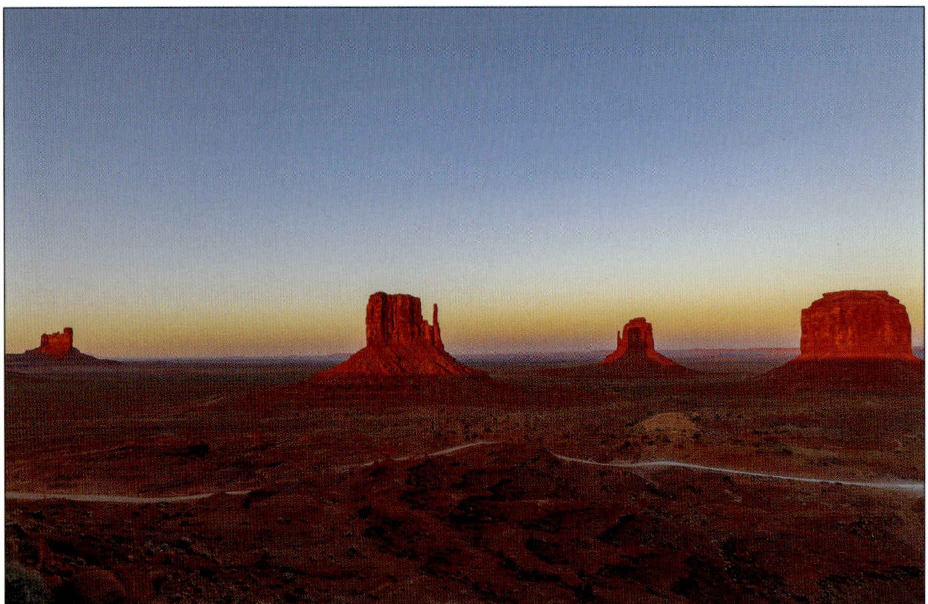

Not only do you need a location without any light pollution, you're going to need a clear, cloudless sky—if you have a bunch of clouds (or fog or haze) blocking even part of the sky, you're not going to be happy with the results. So, you're going to need to know the weather in advance for the location you scouted. You're looking for an empty sky, like the one you see above, which is the opposite of what we want for nearly every other type of landscape photograph, where we desperately need clouds or fog for atmospheric effects. I know, there's a lot of up-front research and planning, help from Mother Nature, and a bit of luck that goes into creating a successful night sky shoot, but that's partially why people love seeing these shots so much. It takes a bit of doing (even before you touch your camera gear) to create a great night sky shot, but when it all comes together, it's a pretty magical thing.

The Moon Is Your Enemy

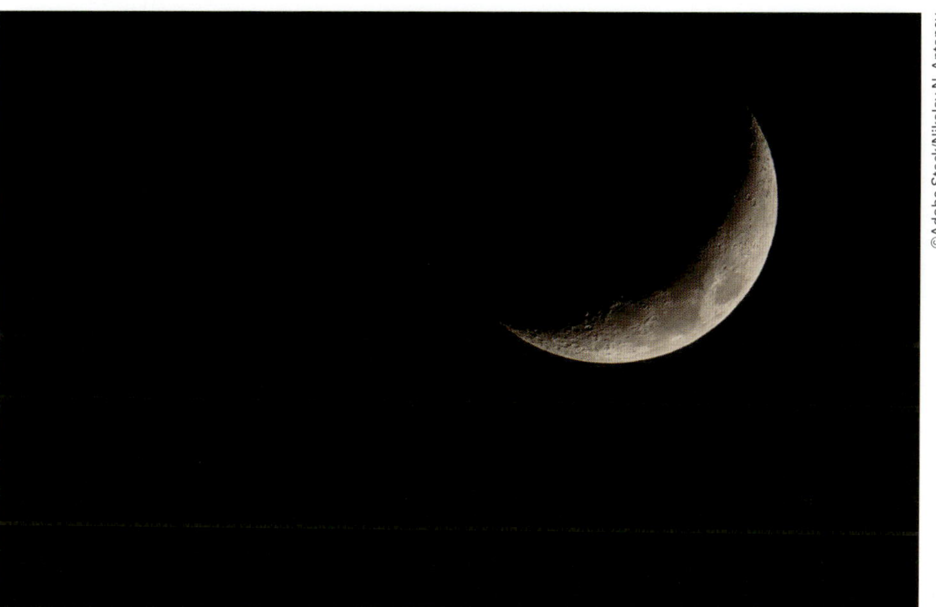

The moon creates a ton of light pollution and can kill your Milky Way and starlit sky shots by overpowering them with its light. The fuller the moon, the worse it makes shooting conditions in the sky, so what you're really looking to do is avoid shooting on nights when the moon is visible, or at the very least, try when just a sliver of it is visible. Ideally, you want to shoot when it's a new moon, because during this part of the cycle, the moon is completely invisible. You might be thinking, "So, let me get this straight, I need to get far away from civilization to avoid light pollution, and it has to be a clear, cloudless night with no haze, and I need to do all of this on a new moon night where the moon isn't illuminated at all, and that only happens about once every 29 1/2 days, is that correct?" Ummm, yeah, that's pretty much it. Well, there are times when you have something like a half- or quarter-moon in the sky on a particular night, but it's actually below the horizon line at some point during that night, and that window of opportunity is when you can shoot. The PhotoPills app I talk about on page 127 will tell you what time at night the moon will dip below that horizon line, and for how long, and that's when you can avoid light pollution from the moon, even though there's actually a moon out that night. Hey, I never said this was easy. Actually, I did, but I meant after you're already on location, with no light pollution or clouds, and it's a new moon night. You can find out when the next new moon is scheduled at timeanddate.com/astronomy/moon /new-moon.html.

The Milky Way Is Only Visible for a Few Months Each Year

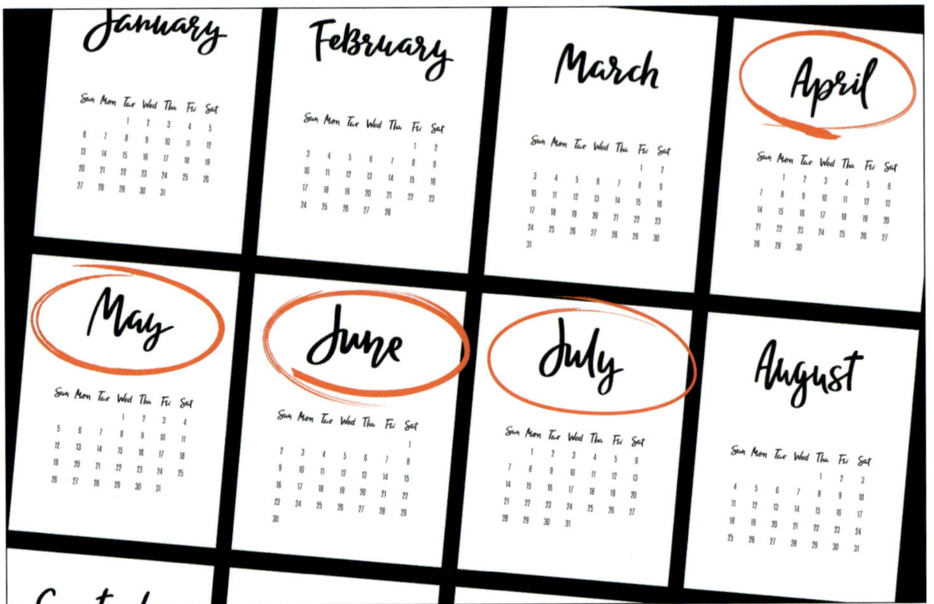

If you're in an area without light pollution on a clear night, you'll be able to capture a starry sky, no problem, but the Milky Way is only visible at certain times of the year from certain areas on earth. For example, the Milky Way is only visible to the Northern Hemisphere from around March to September, with the prime viewing time from around April to the end of July (that's when the galactic center of the Milky Way is at its most gloriously photogenic). The Milky Way appears like a horizontal band across the southern sky. In the Southern Hemisphere, it will appear as more of an arc with the center being nearly right overhead. Also, in the Southern Hemisphere, chances are you'll get more detailed shots because the temperatures are cooler, so the air is clearer. If you're not sure which hemisphere you're located in, perhaps shooting the Milky Way shouldn't be your biggest concern.

Where Exactly Will the Milky Way Be?
There's an App for That

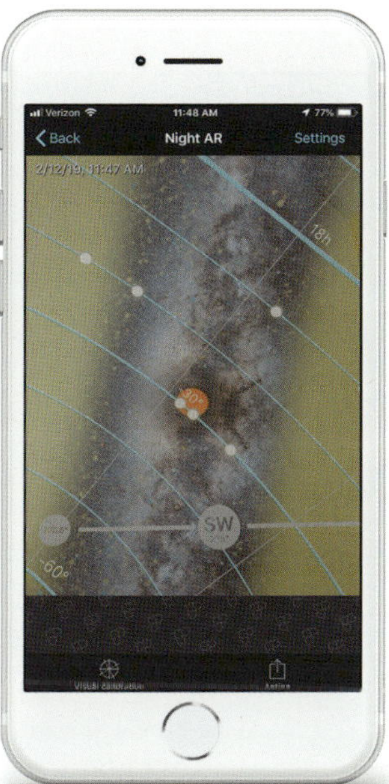
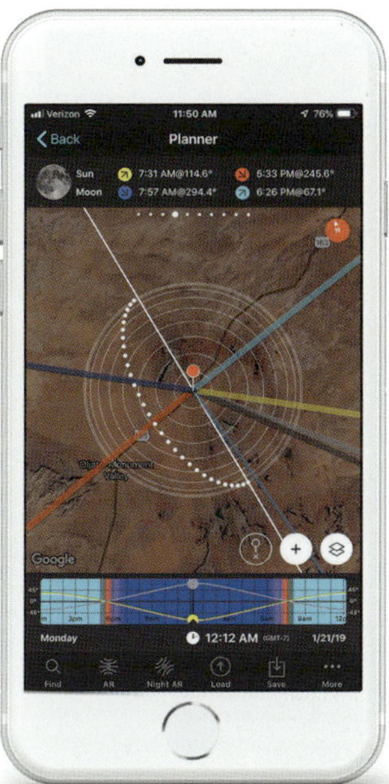

My buddy Erik Kuna turned me on to the PhotoPills app and it's absolutely brilliant (and pretty indispensable for finding where the Milky Way will appear in the sky). But, it doesn't just add an arrow that says, "It'll be over here." You can point your phone's camera at the scene where you want to shoot and it uses augmented reality to superimpose an image of the Milky Way onto your camera screen right where it will appear in the sky at that location. It's really something to see, and incredibly helpful in planning where to set up when you're scouting your location while it's still daylight. The app is available for Apple iPhones (iOS) and Android phones. It's $9.99, but worth its weight in gold for the night sky photographer.

Red Light Headlamp for Night Shooting

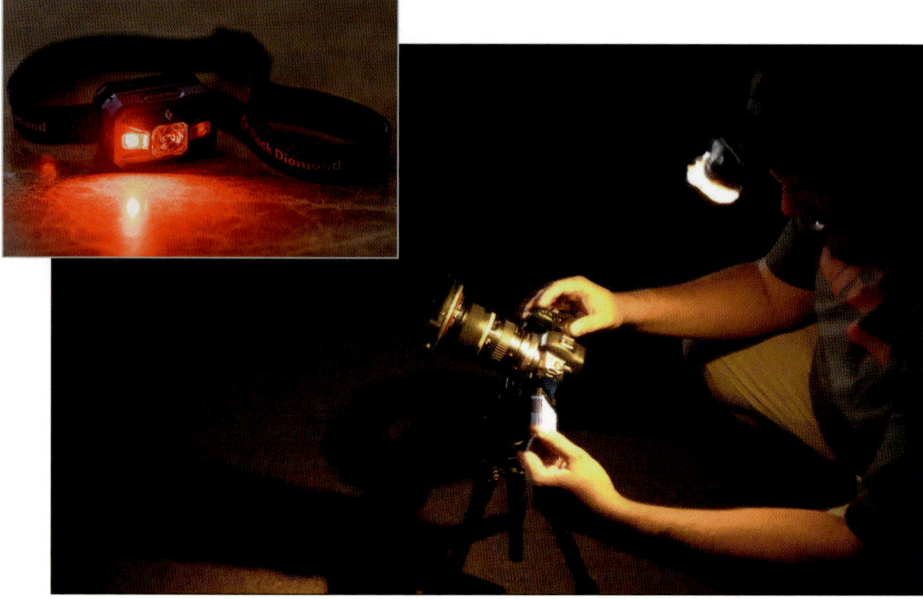

You've gone through the trouble of getting far away from light pollution, but you can ruin it all by pulling out a big ol' flashlight. Not only will it create light pollution, it's going to take up one of your hands, and you're going to need both of them to get all this set up. So, what I recommend is picking up a headlamp that has an option to use a red LED. Besides keeping your hands free and limiting the light around your camera, it serves another purpose: it lights your way as you're walking through the brush, or the desert, or over rocks, or somewhere away from the highway where you'll be shooting your Milky Way shot. Plus, once you've reached your shooting spot, you can switch the beam to red to help preserve your night vision while you're working with your camera. Lots of folks swear by the popular Petzl Tikka headlamp. It has brightness controls, width of beam controls, it's weather resistant, you can change the beam to red, it can tilt, and it uses regular ol' AAA batteries you can get anywhere. It's around $38 on Amazon. Another nice one (shown here in the inset) is the Black Diamond Storm Headlamp, which is also around $38.

Hold Your Camera Steady

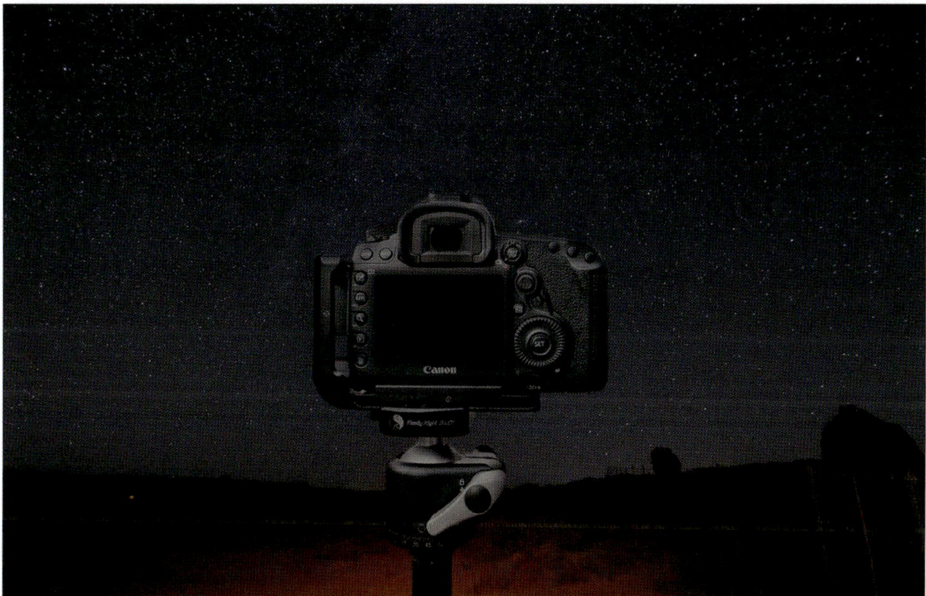

Your shutter is going to be open for a number of seconds and, by now, this probably goes without saying, but you're going to need a tripod and a cable release (or wireless shutter release) to hold your camera perfectly steady while that shutter is open. The reason I'm having to repeat this is because you might be interested in shooting the sky, and maybe you turned right to this chapter and missed it earlier, so…ya know (this is the stuff you have to think about when you're writing a book, and believe me, authors hate to repeat stuff, but sometimes ya gotta).

You'll Need to Shoot in Manual Mode

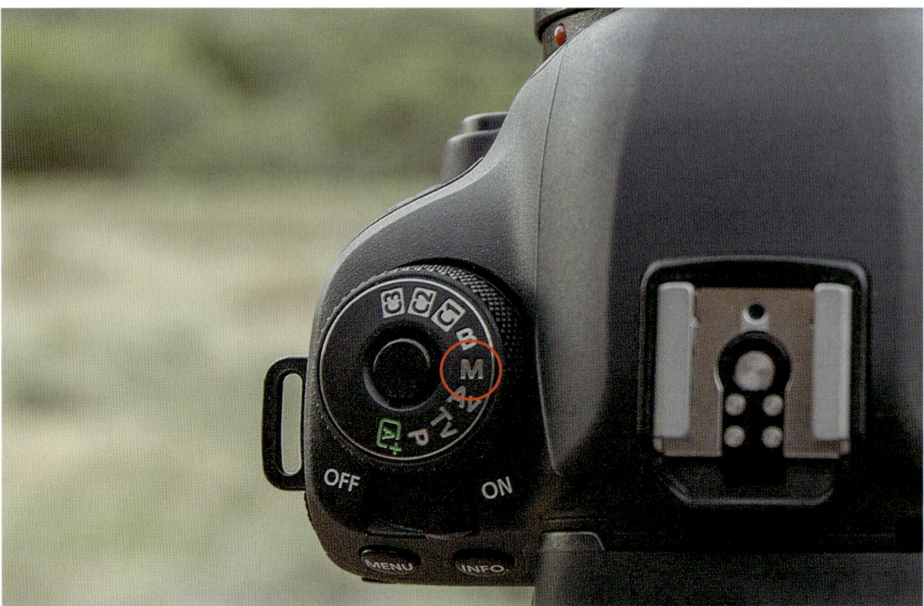

If you've never taken a single shot in manual mode, don't worry, this is so easy you'll absolutely be able to do it the first time, no sweat. We need to shoot in manual mode on our camera because we're going to need to lock in our f-stop and shutter speed (rather than letting the camera make any of its own decisions). So, switch your mode to M, and then you'll only need to do two things: (1) choose your f-stop, and (2) dial in your shutter speed. The good news is, once you do that, you may not have to mess with them again (and if you do, it will be a very simple, minor change).

Here's the F-Stop to Use

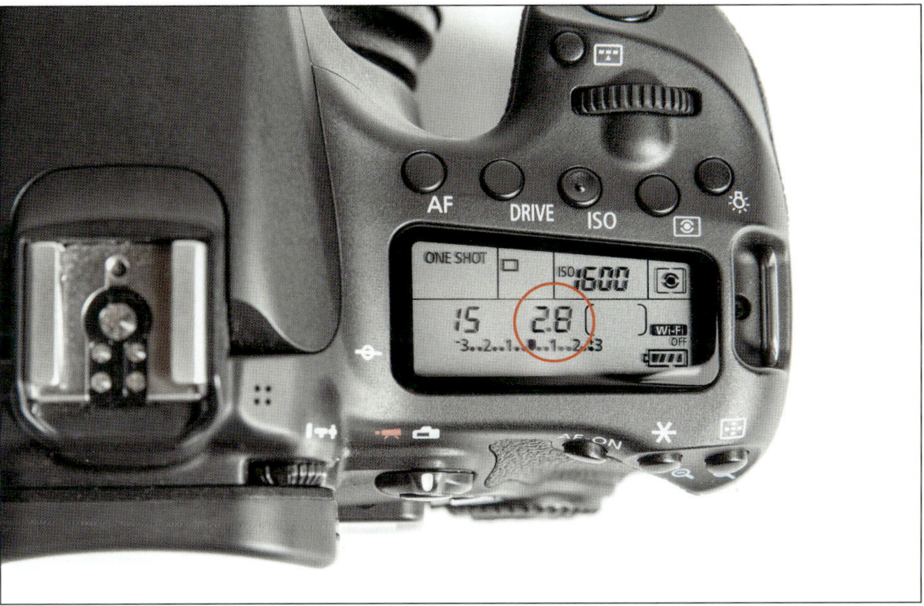

This is an easy one: use the lowest numbered f-stop your lens will allow. So, if your lens will let you go as low as f/2.8, or even f/1.8, then there ya go. Now, the lowest f-stop your lens will go might only be f/3.5 or f/5.6, but whatever that number is, that's the one to use. The stars themselves don't produce a whole lotta light, so you'll need all the help you can get (plus, using a fast f-stop like this will help keep you from having to bump your ISO up too much to where you start to introduce a bunch of noise). So, the lower the number, the better, when it comes to f-stops.

Here's How Long to Set Your Shutter Speed

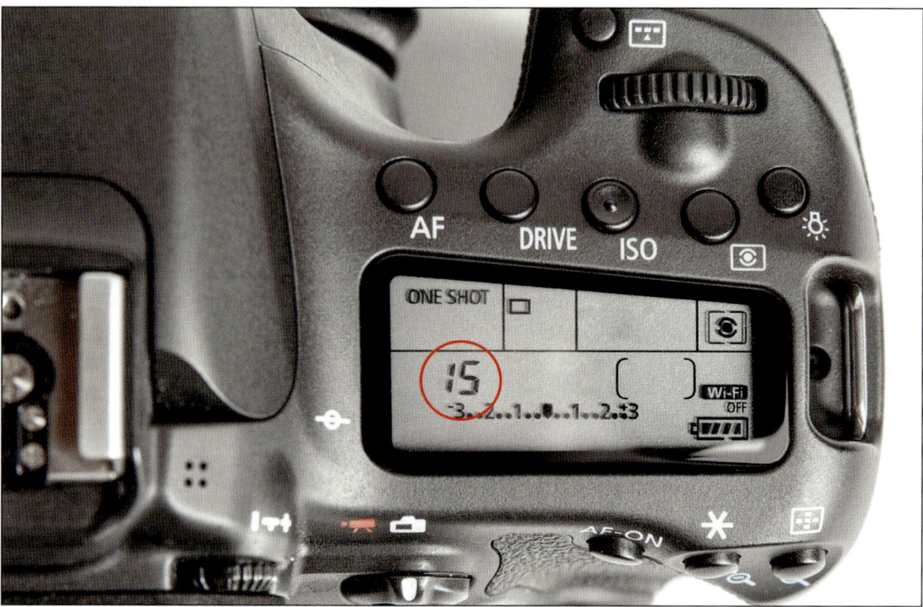

How long do you need to keep your shutter open for great starry sky and Milky Way shots? Usually around 12 to 15 seconds. If you leave it open any longer, you'll get blur from the natural movement of the earth and stars—go with a shorter shutter speed than 12 seconds and you'll have to crank the ISO on your camera so high you'll get lots of noise and you probably won't be happy with the results. So, start at 15 seconds, and then zoom in and check to see if the stars are nice and tack sharp. If not, then try a second or two shorter shutter speed and take a test shot. It might take you a few test shots to nail it, trying a 12-second or 13-second shutter speed, but you'll have it nailed down really quickly, and then you won't have to mess with it again. Now (nerd alert), if you're the type of person that says, "Scott, I can't experiment. I must know the exact proper setting for my lens, my f-stop, and my particular size sensor or I won't be able to sleep at night," don't worry—there's an app for that (see page 127). The PhotoPills app has a feature in it where you tell it how many megapixels your camera is, and how wide your lens is, and it will tell you exactly how long to leave your shutter open.

When to Bump Up Your ISO

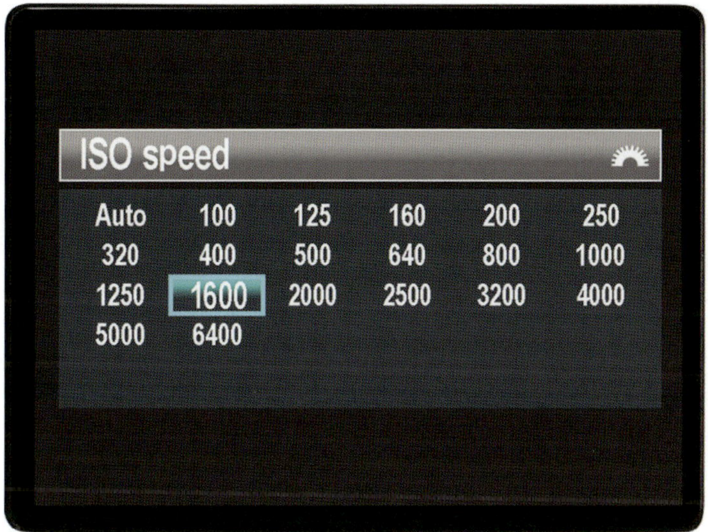

Okay, so we know we're going to be at around 15 seconds for our shutter speed, and generally when we're on a tripod, we try to keep our ISO at its lowest number (usually 100), but this is one of those cases where, to bring out the dimension and detail of the Milky Way and stars, you're going to need to crank the ISO. Start at 1600 ISO and see if the Milky Way and stars look bright enough to you. You might need to crank it up to 3200, which I know sounds high, but luckily, most of your sky will be very dark, so the small amount of noise that does appear will be just that—a small amount of noise. Take a test shot at 15 seconds shutter speed, ISO 1600, and see what you think. You can always raise (double) it and see how that looks for you. A 6400 ISO is as high as most folks will want to go, unless your camera is notoriously clean at high ISOs like this. Also, remember, we'll be doing some serious post-processing later on in Photoshop or Lightroom, so if your sky image just looks a little dark overall, don't sweat it—we can brighten things quite a bit in post while limiting the amount of noise.

You Need to Shoot in RAW

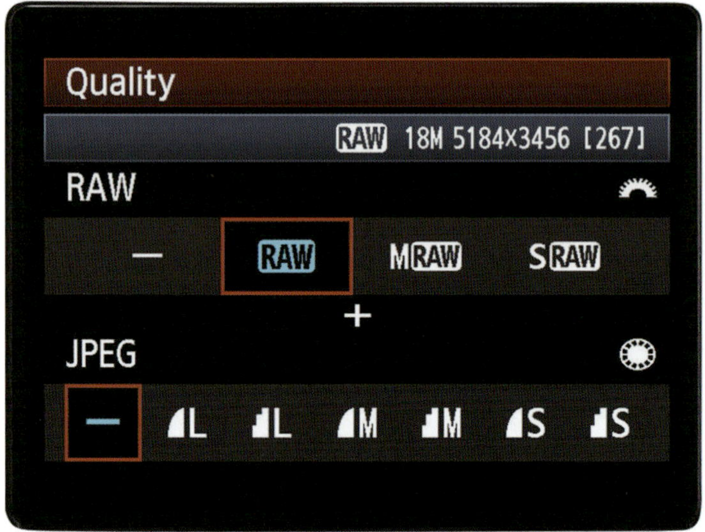

The images you see on the web don't come out of the camera the way you see them online. They've all been post-processed (some very heavily), and to make sure you have the best quality files to work with (especially important if you're going to be tweaking your images in post-processing a lot), you definitely want to be shooting in RAW mode on your camera. Not only do RAW images capture a wider tonal range, they are much more forgiving and do less damage to your image when you need to make a lot of adjustments (and you are going to make a lot of adjustments).

Use a Very-Wide-Angle Lens

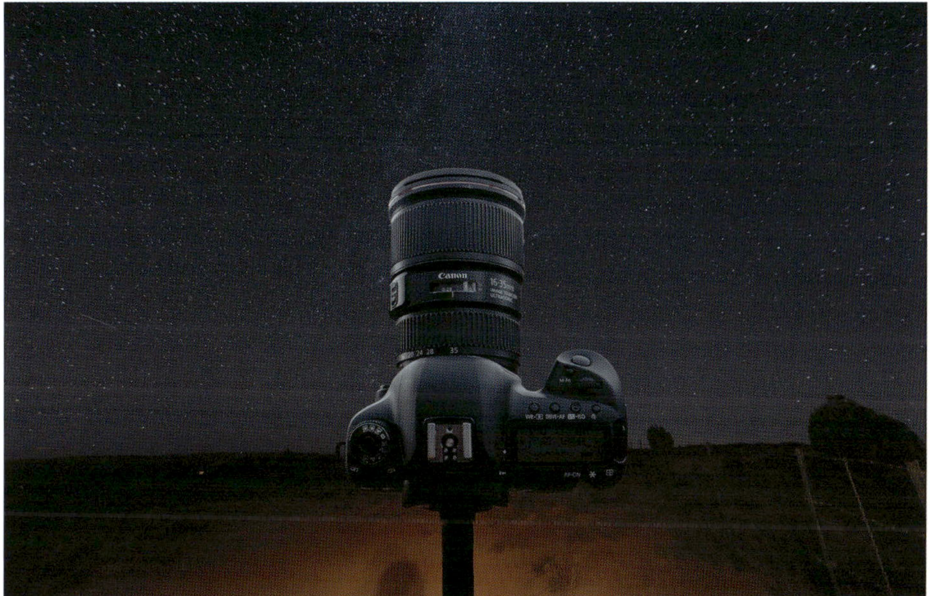

You're trying to capture the sky. It's really big. Especially, if you're trying to capture the Milky Way, too, which covers a lot of territory. So, you're going to want a really-wide-angle lens to capture it all (remember, you can always crop in later in post). On a full-frame camera, while you can get away with a 24mm, you're right on the edge of catching a large enough portion of the Milky Way. A 16mm wide-angle would definitely do the trick. If you've got a 15mm or 14mm ultra-wide-angle, all the better (and if you have a wide-angle zoom, like Nikon's 14–24mm, Canon's 11–24mm, or Tamron's 15–30mm, then you've got some flexibility when it comes to composition, too). On a crop-sensor camera, an 18mm wide-angle would be okay, but a 12mm or 10mm wide-angle would be even better. You want to go really wide, especially if you want to include some foreground in the shot. So, when you're packing your gear for your nighttime sky shoot, make sure you pack your widest wide-angle lens.

Turn Off IS/VR

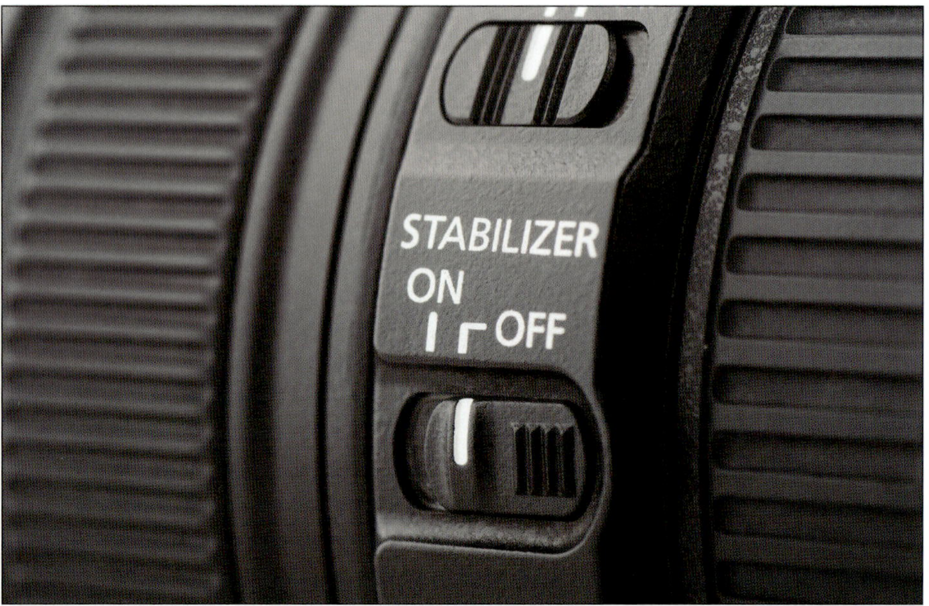

Your shutter will be open for up to 15 seconds, so you'll be on a tripod, and the last thing you want is the tiny motor inside your lens searching endlessly for vibration. That can actually cause vibration when you're on a tripod, and with any tiny bit of movement, you'll take a hit on sharpness. And, yes, there are a few newer lenses on the market that have a built-in feature that senses when your camera is on a tripod and they disable the vibration reduction/image stabilization feature, but they are few and far between. If you're not certain that your lenses have this auto off feature, just move the switch for VR/IS on your lens to the off position. Sharper shots await.

How to Set Your Focus on Stars, Method 1

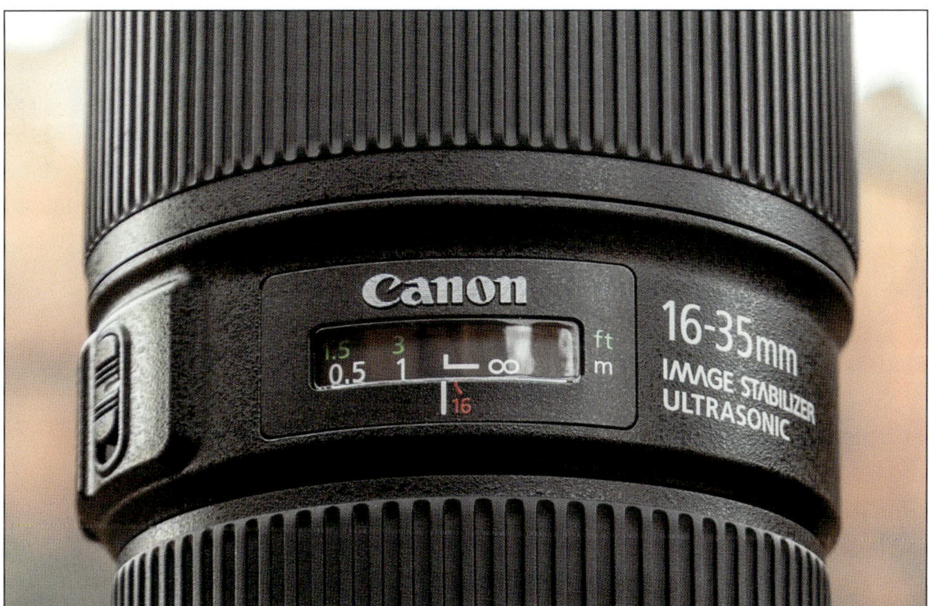

We don't actually set our focus on the stars—they're too small, too far away, and too dark to actually focus on. So, we use a technique called "focusing to infinity" (we looked at this back in the Composition chapter, as well). Depending on which type of lens you're using, this might be an incredibly simple technique because some lenses have a little window with a focus distance indicator scale on it, which is used with Manual focus (so, first, switch your lens to Manual focus). In that scale, you'll see an infinity symbol (∞). I know what you're probably thinking: "So, I just turn the focus ring on my lens to that infinity symbol, right?" Well, close. You do turn it to the infinity symbol, but then you turn it back slightly to the little vertical line right before the infinity symbol. That's the correct spot for focusing to infinity.

How to Set Your Focus on Stars, Method 2

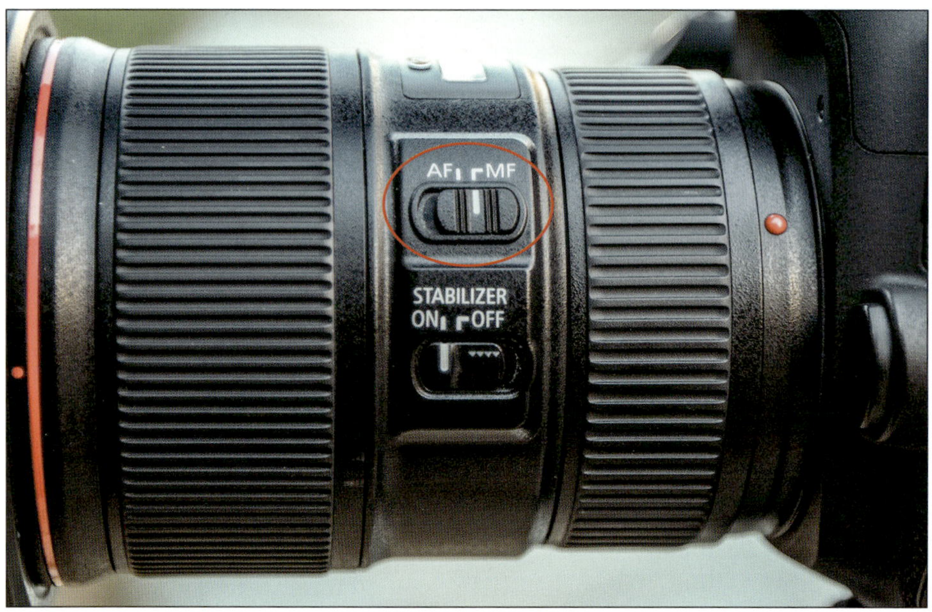

If you don't have a lens with a distance scale window on it, then you'll use a different method (and it actually works really well). First, set your f-stop to its lowest number (f/2.8 or f/1.8), then crank up your ISO to some crazy high number (just for this focusing part) to make the area as bright as possible, and then turn on Live View mode (so you're looking at the image on the LCD on the back of your camera). You're going to leave your Auto focus turned on, and aim your lens at the farthest object you can see—it can be a far off mountain, a tree, whatever the farthest thing away from you is that your camera will lock focus on. Hold your shutter button halfway down to lock focus on this faraway object, then immediately switch the Auto focus button on your lens to Manual focus. Use the magnifying glass button on the back of your camera to zoom in tight right on the area where you focused. If that area isn't tack sharp, turn the Manual focus ring on your lens to get that area really sharp and in focus. Now your stars will be sharp. Don't forget to reset to your ISO. If you're concerned that, where you're shooting at night, there won't be anything bright enough to focus on (which is good, really, because there won't be any light pollution), then you can do this same trick during the day. But once you get your focus really dialed in (you've switched to Manual focus, zoomed in tight on the area where your camera autofocused, and tweaked the focus ring so that faraway spot is as in focus as you can get it), take a silver sharpie marker and mark that spot right on your lens itself (just a tiny dot will do). So, when it's night and there's nothing bright enough to focus on, it won't matter—just turn on Manual focus, rotate the ring to that dot, and you're good to go.

Use Live View to Focus

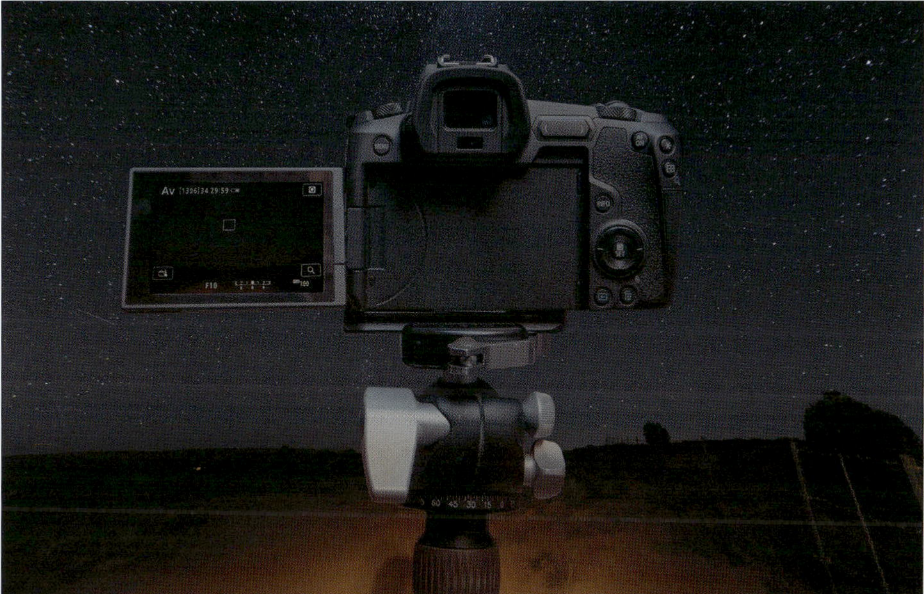

A lot of folks find the whole focusing process much easier with the Live View feature on their camera turned on (the one where you're looking at the scene via the LCD on the back of your camera, rather than looking through your viewfinder). Now, if you want bonus points, if your camera has a full articulating swivel screen, it makes this whole night-shooting process so much easier. Think about it—your camera is tilted way up toward the sky, and to look either through your viewfinder or at your Live View on the LCD, you'll need to squat down low behind your camera. However, if you have that pop-out LCD, you don't have to—you can stand there and see everything on that swivel screen, which makes the process of shooting the sky on a tripod that much easier and more convenient.

Use Focus Peaking for Super-Sharp Stars

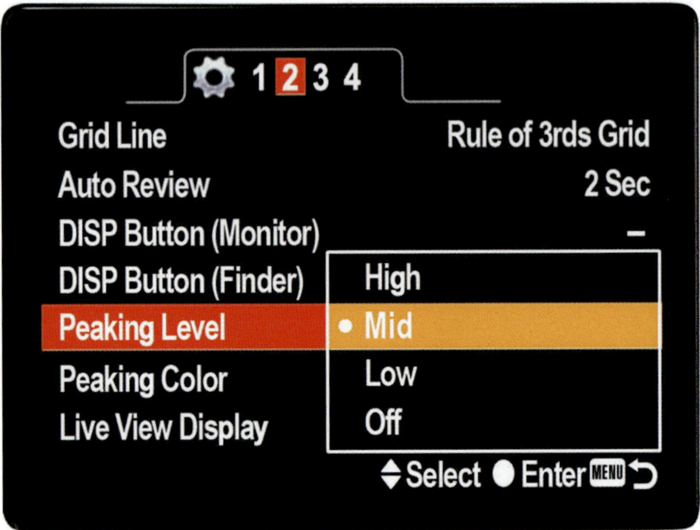

You're going to want your stars to be really sharp and crisp, and while setting your lens to focus to infinity does a decent job (see page 137), if your camera has a focus peaking feature (it's appearing in more cameras these days, especially in mirrorless cameras), you can get a more precise "next level" of sharpness. Focus peaking works when you're using Manual focus (which is what you'll be doing when shooting the night sky), and it aids in getting a sharp focus by highlighting areas with high contrast edges—the sharpest objects in your photo appear brightly lit on your screen, so you see exactly what's in focus. This works particularly well for getting your stars in focus because everything should be black, and then when you start tweaking your focus, if you see a bunch of stars appear onscreen, you know those are in sharp focus. Here's how I use focus peaking: First, turn on Live View, so you can use focus peaking with the large LCD on the back of your camera. Then, with the lens set to Manual focus, I completely de-focus (turning the barrel focus ring to the left), and then start turning the focus ring until I start to see the stars "come out" on my otherwise dark screen. When you see those areas appear while focus peaking is turned on, you know your stars are sharp and in focus. That's all there is to it.

Lighting Your Foreground Landscape, Method 1

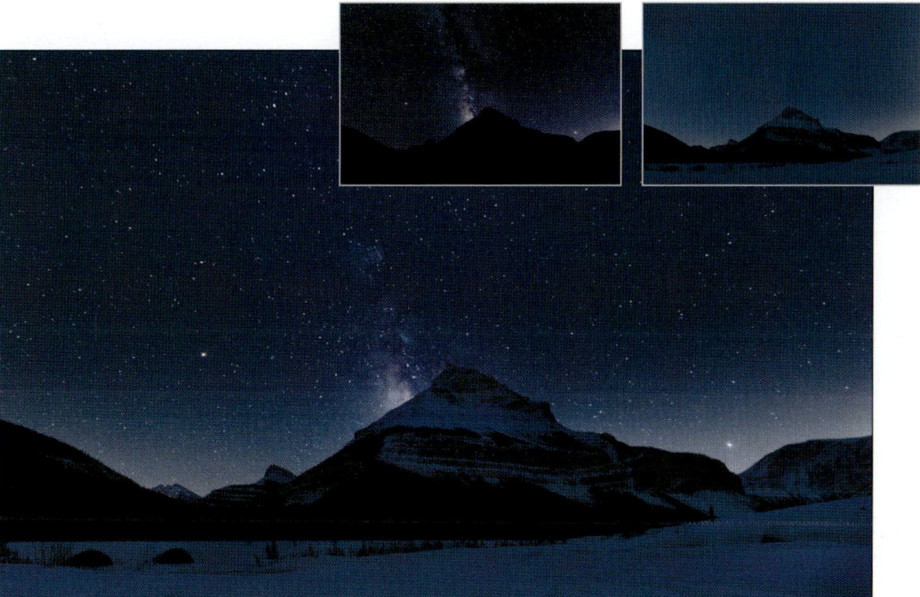

This one might either be the hardest or easiest method depending on your personal level of patience. This first method has you getting to your location before dusk, setting up all your gear, getting your image composed, and once sunset arrives, but there's a still a little light from the recently setting sun on your landscape, you take a few shots. That way, you've captured the foreground while it's dimly lit (you don't want to have a brightly lit landscape foreground, and then stick a dark Milky Way above it—that will look like…well…it won't look awesome and that's being kind. Instead, you want that late light on the landscape, after the sun has already gone down). Keep shooting that same shot until it's fully dark. Don't move your camera! It's set up, on the tripod, and you've got everything composed for the night sky. Now, you'll wind up with two photos: one where you've got the dimly lit foreground landscape, and one with the pitch black sky. You're going to put those two images together in Photoshop (it's simple to do—and yes, I made a video for you. It's at **kelbyone.com /books/landscape**).

Lighting Your Foreground Landscape, Method 2

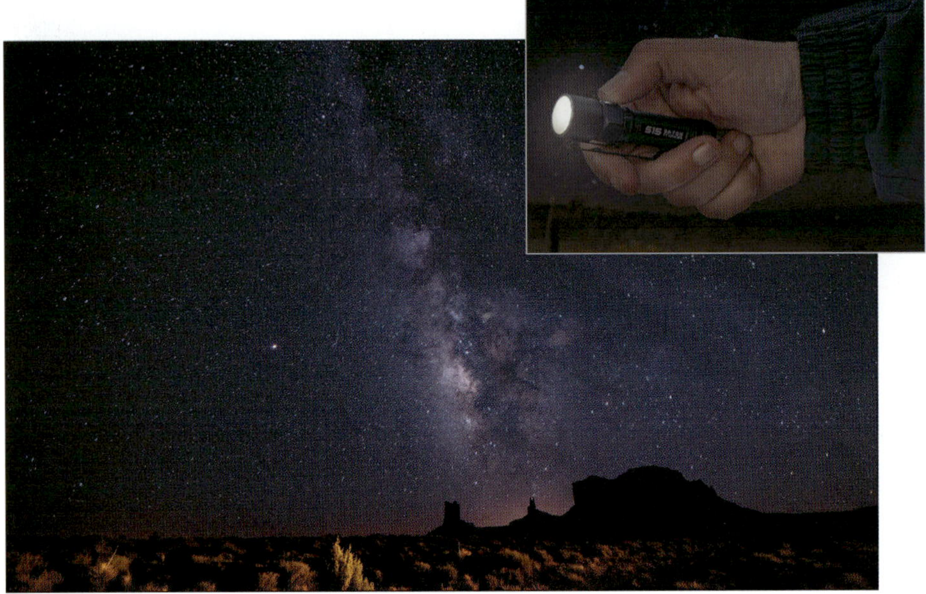

Another popular method of displaying your foreground is to "light paint" it (we looked at this earlier in the Long Exposures chapter, as well). This is easier than it sounds, but it might take you a few tries until you come up with a scene that is lit the way you want it. The basic idea here is to use a small, handheld LED flashlight, and while your shutter is open on your camera that is shooting the stars, you're going to "paint" with that light over a close rock formation, or foreground area, or tree, etc. You don't have to paint very long, usually just a few seconds, but enough to light those foreground areas. Again, you'll have to try it a few times to figure out how many seconds to paint, but it'll just be a few in most cases. It sounds kinda crazy, but it works like a charm. Now, if you want to light up something big that's far away (like an arch or a large rock formation, or Mount Rushmore, or an alien spacecraft), my friend and colleague Dave Black (known by many as the father of modern light painting) uses a super-bright handheld rechargeable halogen spotlight that will light paint really big objects up to 900 feet away (it ought to, it's literally 5-million candlepower!). It's not cheap either, at $198, but like Dave says, "Go big or go home!" (You can find it at www.larsonelectronics.com.) If you don't want to spend that much, and you want a smaller light that's still crazy bright, check out this bad boy: the A15 from CoastPortland.com. It'll throw its beam up to 429 feet, it's pen-sized (only 4" long and 5 oz.), and it's just $65, which is still a lot for a small flashlight, but think of it as your "light painting engine," and then it doesn't hurt nearly as much.

Post-Processing Milky Way Shots

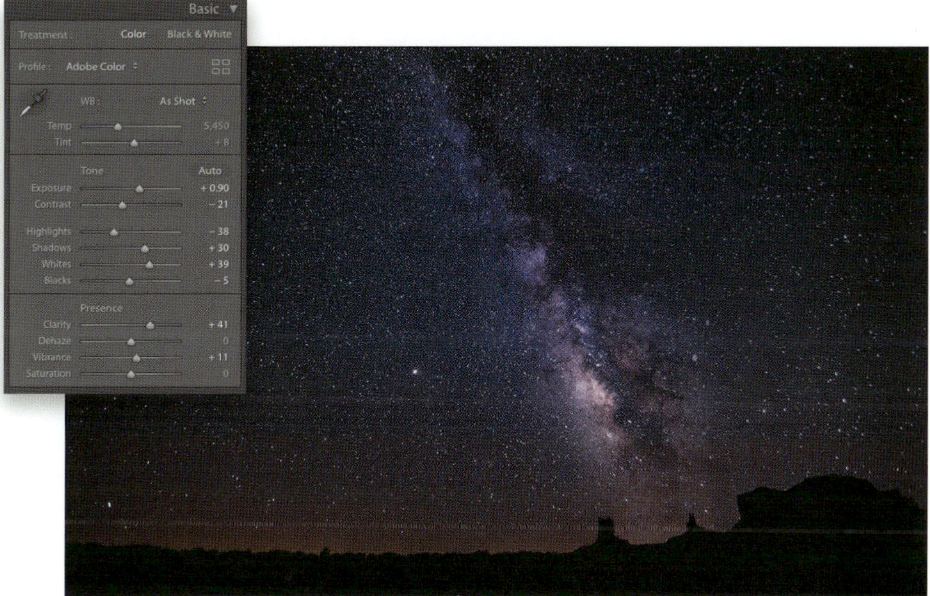

I made a short video that takes you through the techniques I use for post-processing a starry sky/Milky Way shot (I use Adobe's Lightroom and/or Photoshop). It isn't hard (it's just moving a few sliders), but don't be surprised if you have to make a number of adjustments to get things looking the way you want it to (they don't come out looking that way "out of camera"). Your main tools in either Lightroom or Photoshop's Camera Raw are: (1) The Exposure slider. You'll either wind up darkening the sky or brightening it—it depends on the image and how it looks after you make other tweaks. (2) The Dehaze slider. This works wonders on night skies (it's a specialized form of contrast) and it's probably the best thing that's happened to Milky Way post-processing because it literally cuts through the haze and boosts the color a bit, too. (3) The Clarity slider. Another powerful tool for starry skies. Dragging it to the right adds midtone contrast and can really help bring out your stars. (4) Sharpening. You're going to sharpen every sky image using Lightroom's Detail panel sharpening or Photoshop's Unsharp Mask filter. (5) White balance. You're going to adjust this using the Temp and Tint sliders to remove weird color casts you sometimes get (where your sky looks reddish) by making the white balance more neutral or, like I do, you can add in a little color tint (like blue or magenta) for artistic purposes. (6) Contrast (drag it to the right), and the Whites and Blacks sliders. Dragging the Whites to the right helps boost the brightness of the stars; dragging the Blacks to the left gives you a richer, darker sky around your stars. You'll be using these three a lot. Make sure you watch the video I made for you at **kelbyone.com/books/landscape**.

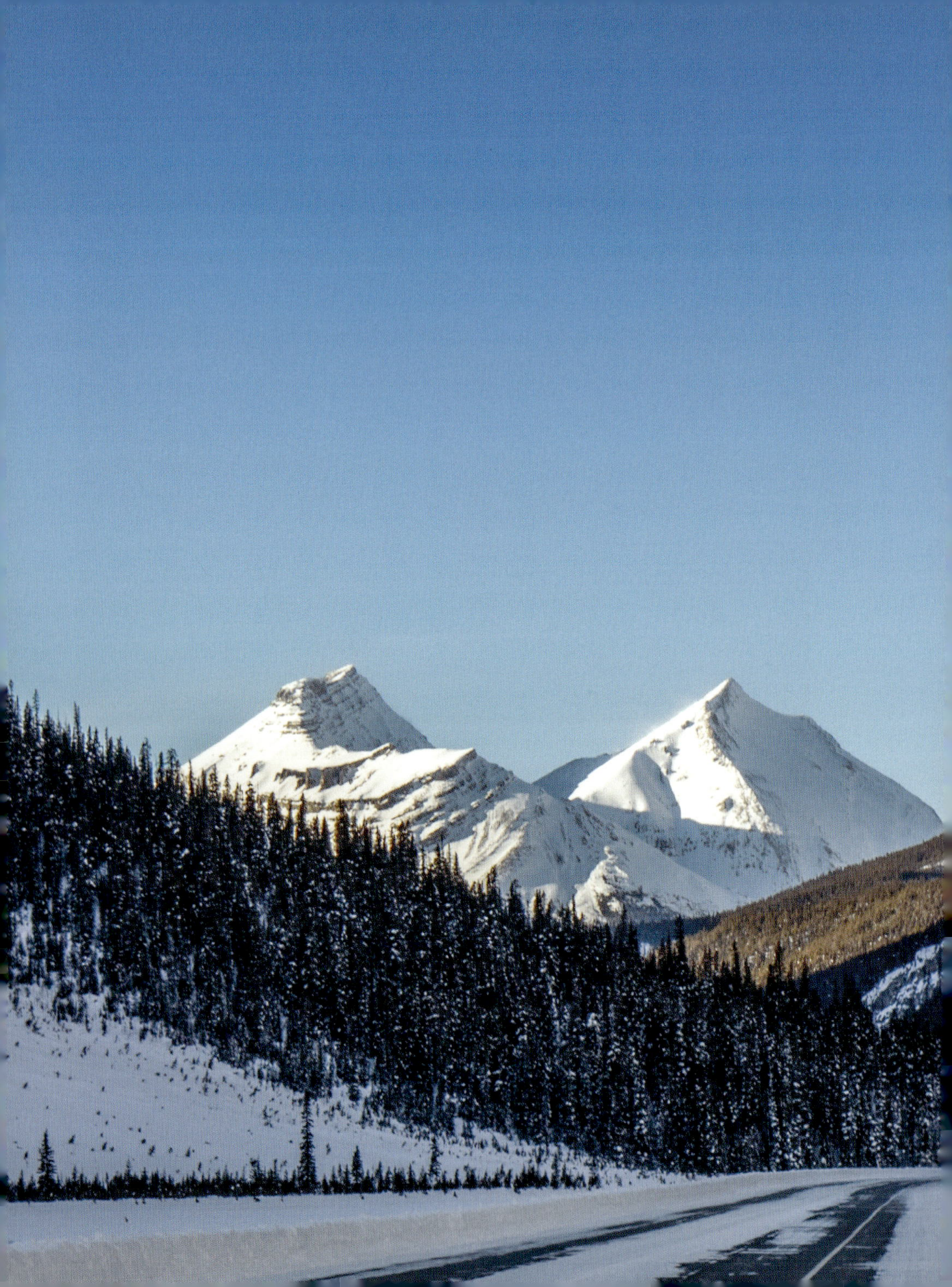

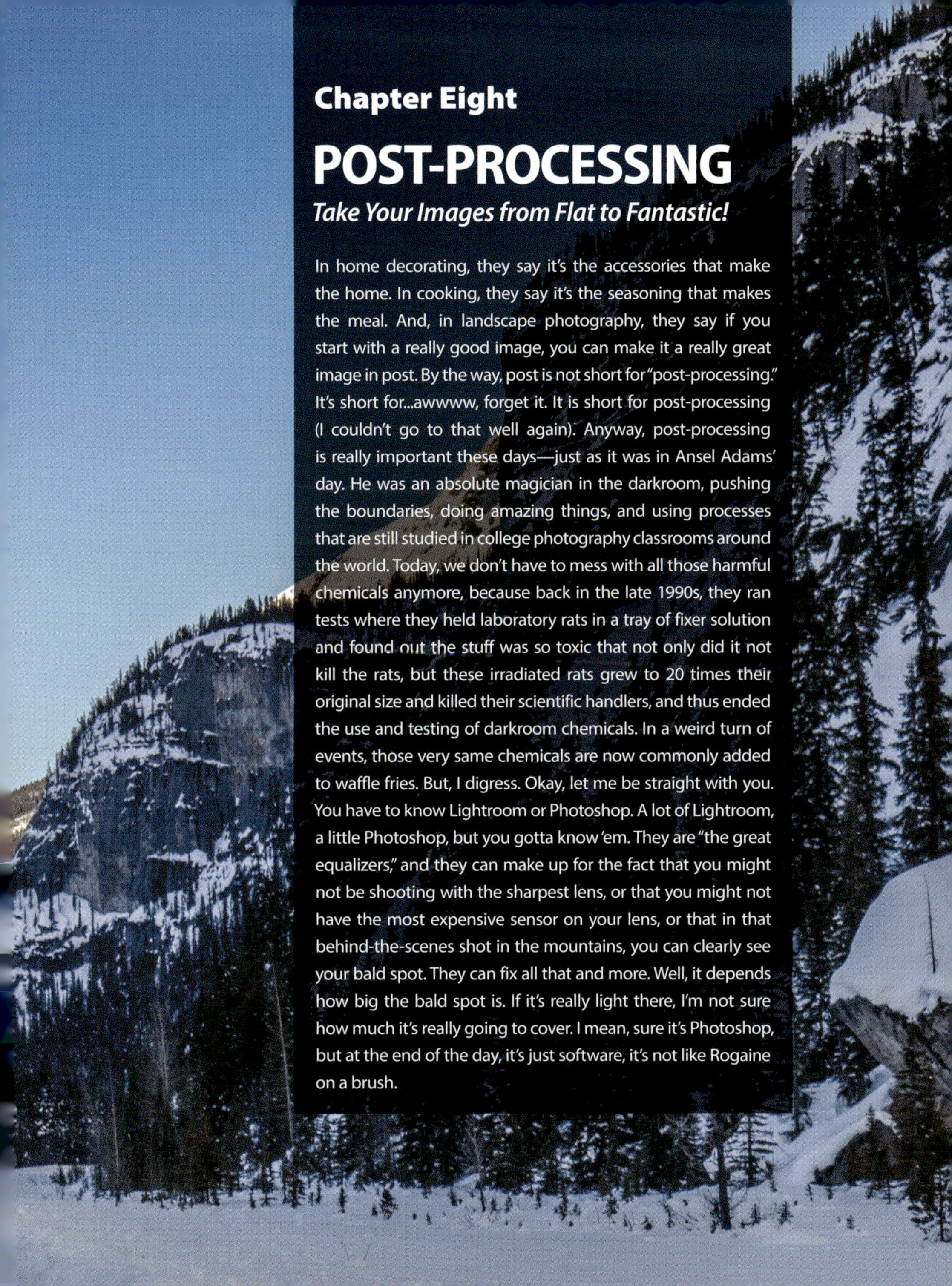

Chapter Eight

POST-PROCESSING

Take Your Images from Flat to Fantastic!

In home decorating, they say it's the accessories that make the home. In cooking, they say it's the seasoning that makes the meal. And, in landscape photography, they say if you start with a really good image, you can make it a really great image in post. By the way, post is not short for "post-processing." It's short for...awwww, forget it. It is short for post-processing (I couldn't go to that well again). Anyway, post-processing is really important these days—just as it was in Ansel Adams' day. He was an absolute magician in the darkroom, pushing the boundaries, doing amazing things, and using processes that are still studied in college photography classrooms around the world. Today, we don't have to mess with all those harmful chemicals anymore, because back in the late 1990s, they ran tests where they held laboratory rats in a tray of fixer solution and found out the stuff was so toxic that not only did it not kill the rats, but these irradiated rats grew to 20 times their original size and killed their scientific handlers, and thus ended the use and testing of darkroom chemicals. In a weird turn of events, those very same chemicals are now commonly added to waffle fries. But, I digress. Okay, let me be straight with you. You have to know Lightroom or Photoshop. A lot of Lightroom, a little Photoshop, but you gotta know 'em. They are "the great equalizers," and they can make up for the fact that you might not be shooting with the sharpest lens, or that you might not have the most expensive sensor on your lens, or that in that behind-the-scenes shot in the mountains, you can clearly see your bald spot. They can fix all that and more. Well, it depends how big the bald spot is. If it's really light there, I'm not sure how much it's really going to cover. I mean, sure it's Photoshop, but at the end of the day, it's just software, it's not like Rogaine on a brush.

Opening JPEG or TIFFs in Camera Raw

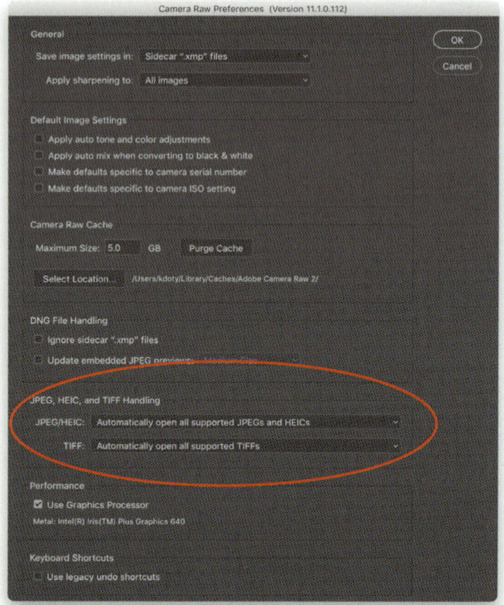

If you're not using Lightroom, if you're a "straight-up Photoshop user," and you shoot in RAW format, those RAW images open automatically for you in the Camera Raw editing window (Adobe's Camera Raw is part of Photoshop and is the tool that today's photographers use for most of their basic image editing). However, if you shoot in JPEG or TIFF, you still want to be able to open and edit those images in Camera Raw, so here are a couple ways to do that (you won't need to do this if you're a Lightroom user passing your images from Lightroom to Photoshop and back): (1) In Photoshop, go under the File menu and choose Open (PC: Open As) to bring up the standard Open dialog. Find the JPEG or TIFF image(s) you want to open in Camera Raw, select it, then choose **Camera Raw** from the Format pop-up menu near the bottom of the dialog (on a PC, choose it from the pop-up menu near the bottom right), and that selected image(s) will open in Camera Raw. (*Note:* On a Mac, if you don't see the Format pop-up menu, click the Options button in the bottom-left corner to reveal it.) Another way to do this is (2) to have Photoshop open JPEG or TIFF images in Camera Raw automatically. It's just a simple change to the Camera Raw preferences. Go under the Photoshop (PC: Edit) menu, under Preferences, and choose **Camera Raw** to bring up its preferences. In the JPEG, HEIC, and TIFF Handling section (PC: JPEG and TIFF Handling, on the File Handling tab), choose Automatically Open All Supported JPEGs and HEICs from the first pop-up menu, and then Automatically Open All Supported TIFFs from the second. Now, all your JPEGs and TIFFs will open directly in Camera Raw.

Choosing a Better Starting Place

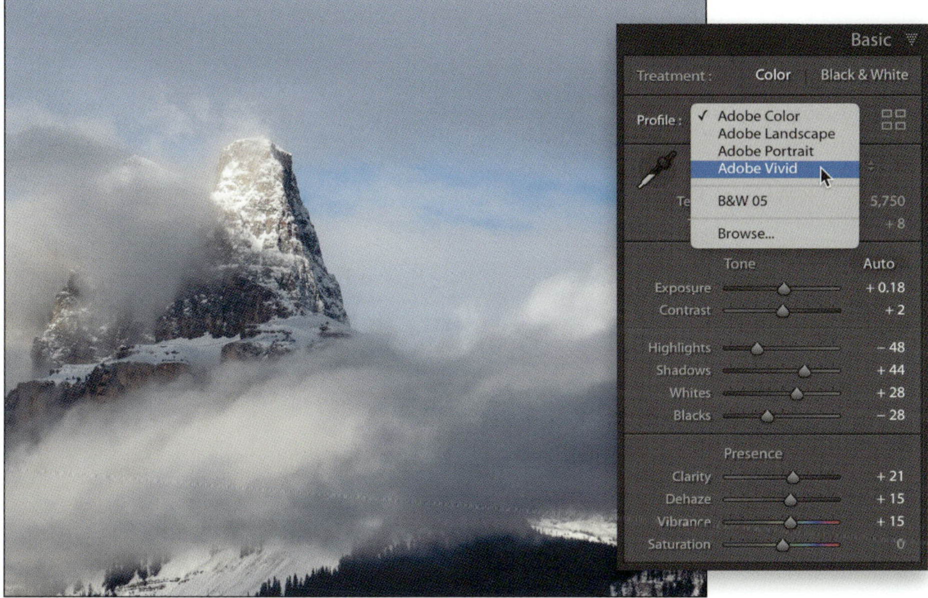

This first step in post-processing here is just for folks who shoot in RAW format on their camera, so if you shoot in JPEG or TIFF, you can totally skip this page. Okay, RAW shooters, we're going to jump back in photographic history for just a minute to help you understand what we're about to do. Back in the film days, we pretty much all used standard Kodak film. Well, to get better-looking landscape photos with rich, saturated colors, the pros had a trick. They would switch to a different type of film—Fuji Velvia—which boosted the overall vibrancy and contrast, and just flat-out made their landscapes look better. Well, we can kinda do the same thing in Lightroom and Photoshop. When you open your RAW image, Adobe has to interpret that RAW file and, by default, it uses a color profile called Adobe Color, which does a pretty decent job of giving you a nice-looking RAW file as your starting place for editing. However, it's kind of the "Kodak" of starting places when it comes to landscape images. It looks good, but there's a trick to getting a better starting place, and that is to choose either the Adobe Landscape or Adobe Vivid RAW profile, which both give you a more vivid, more contrasty image to edit. You can try out these profiles near the top of the Basic panel, where you'll see a pop-up menu for choosing them (as shown above). So, which of the two profiles should you use? I would try them both and see which one looks best for the particular image you're working on. Whichever looks best, go with that one, and now you've got a better starting place for editing your images. It's like you just popped in a fresh roll of Velvia 50.

Set Your White Balance First

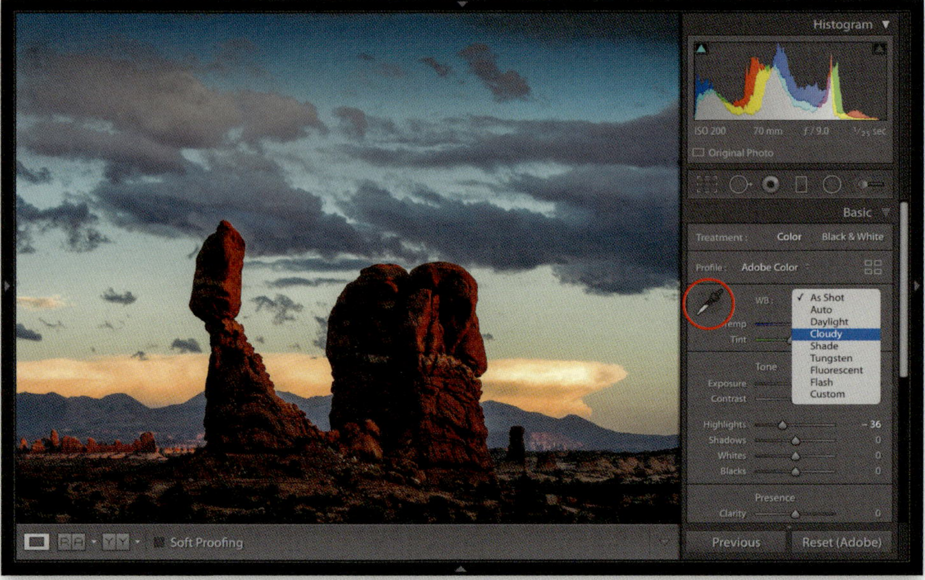

I think it's important to set your white balance first because if you change it later in your editing process, it can change your overall exposure (open an image and drag the white balance sliders back and forth while looking at the histogram—you'll see major changes to the exposure as you drag them). So, let's get it where you want it right from the start. If you shot in RAW, you'll be able to choose the same white balance presets you could have chosen in your camera from the WB presets pop-up menu (shown above). So, try out a few to see which one looks the best to you (luckily, there is no international committee on proper white balance—you're the photographer, this is your art, you get to choose which one looks best to you). Another method for setting your white balance (and the one I use most) is to use the White Balance Selector tool (shown circled above in red; it's found in the top-left corner of Lightroom's Basic panel, or in the left side of the toolbar at the top of Photoshop's Camera Raw). How it works is simple: you just click the eyedropper on something in the image that's supposed to be a light gray. If there's nothing in your image that looks light gray, then try to find a neutral color (something tan, beige, cream colored, etc.) to click on instead. If you click it somewhere and don't like how it looks, just click somewhere else until it looks good to you (it usually takes me a few clicks until I come up with a white balance I like). It's a really simple way to set your white balance and I highly recommend it.

Choosing a More Creative White Balance

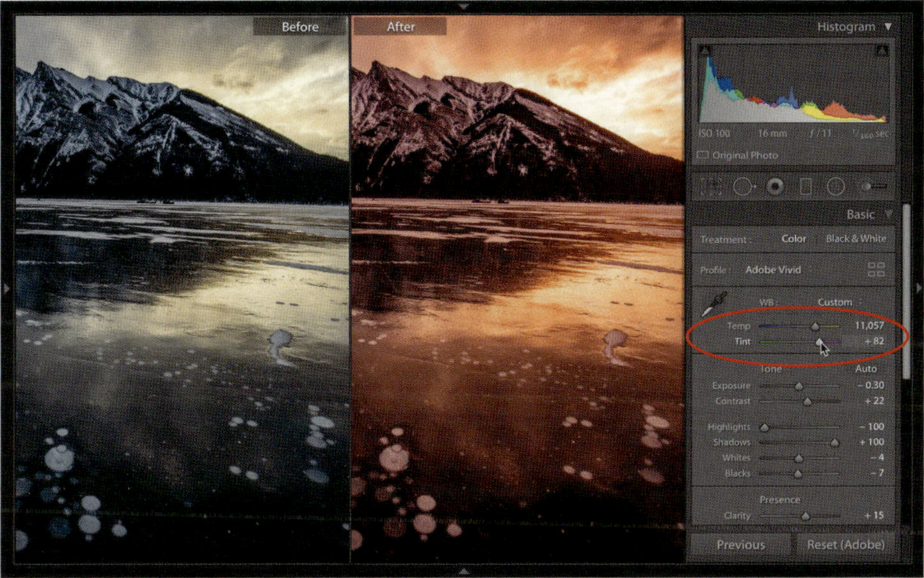

If, instead of picking an accurate white balance, you want to pick a more creative one (making the white balance look better than it did when you actually took the photo), then I would switch to the two white balance sliders, Temp (Temperature) and Tint, found near the top of the Basic panel. The nice thing about these sliders is that the color bars that appear right under the sliders themselves let you know which way to drag to get which color. For example, if you want more blue in your white balance, simply drag the Temp slider over toward blue. If you want less blue (you want a warmer color), drag to the right toward yellow. Super-easy to use (thanks to those color bars).

Now Set Your White and Black Points

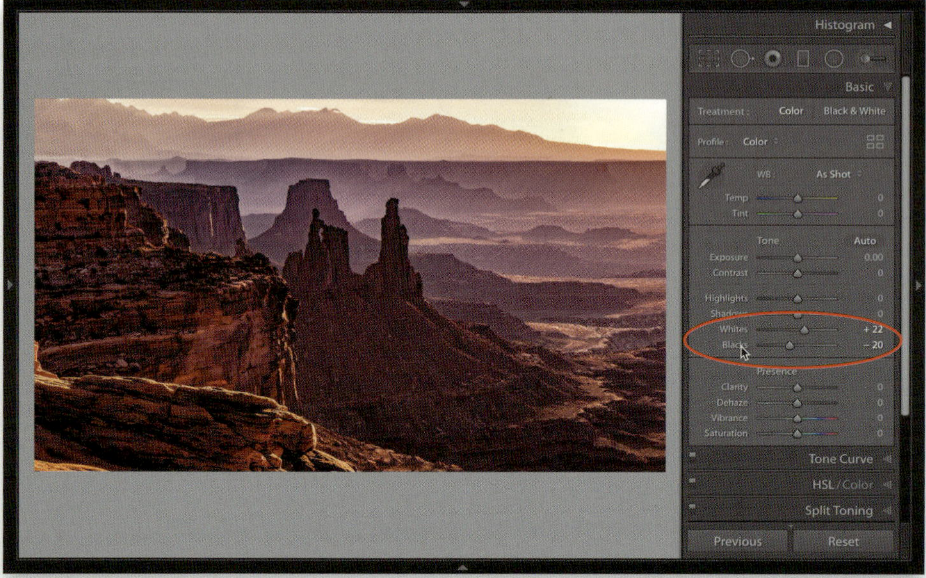

Now that the white balance is set, the next step is to expand the image's overall tonal range (getting the most out of it without clipping the whites or blacks) by setting the white and black points. What that means is I get the whites in the image as bright as I can get them without blowing them out. Then, I get the blacks as dark as I can get them without turning them solid black. There is a manual way to do this, but thankfully, Lightroom (or Photoshop's Camera Raw) will do this for you automatically, as long as you know the "secret handshake": In Lightroom, press-and-hold the Shift key, then simply double-click directly on the word "Whites," and then on "Blacks" in the Basic panel. In Camera Raw, you Shift-double-click on the slider knob itself. Either way, they both do the same thing—you'll see the Whites and Blacks sliders move to automatically set your white and black points for you. If you don't see a slider move very much, that's okay, it just means the tonal range for that image is already pretty well expanded (the Blacks slider is more likely to move very little or not at all). Just in case you're curious, the manual way of setting your white and black points is to press-and-hold the Option (PC: Alt) key, and then start dragging one of the two sliders. As you do, the screen turns black (for whites), and any areas that start to appear in white are clipping (blowing out the pixels). If you just see red, green, or blue areas appearing, it's not as bad—you're just clipping detail in those channels, not overall. For the Blacks slider, the screen turns solid white as you drag, and any areas that appear in black are clipping the blacks (turning them solid black, so there's no detail in those areas).

Setting the Exposure Slider

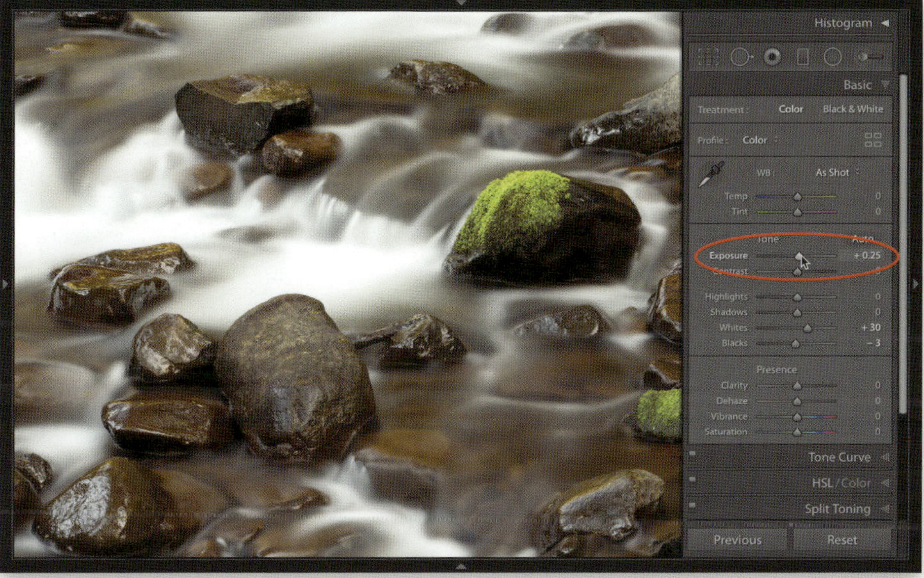

Now that your white and black points are set, evaluate the image. If you think the overall image is a little too bright or a little too dark after setting the white and black points, then you'll use the Exposure slider to fix that (it's found in the Basic panel; you drag it to the right to brighten the image, and to the left to darken it). Because you set the white and black points first, you normally won't have to move the Exposure slider very much, especially since this slider is so powerful—it controls the overall midtones for your image, so dragging it one way or the other has a big effect.

Fixing Damaged Highlights (Clipping)

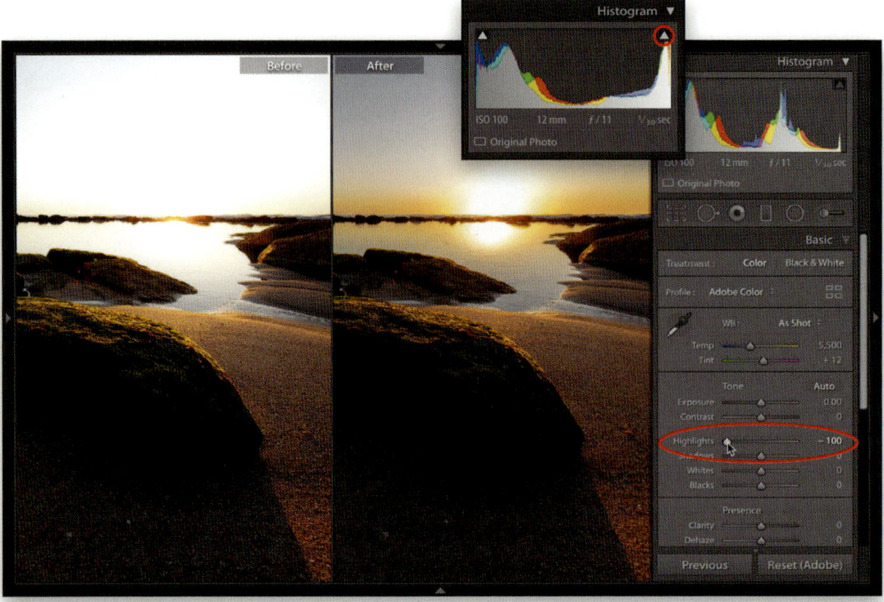

About the worst thing that can happen to an image is to blow out (called "clipping") the highlights. It's such a big deal that most cameras include a built-in Highlight Warning (see page 31) to let you know if you're clipping them when you take the shot (and, yes, you should turn this on because with landscape shots, we're most likely to clip the highlights in clouds, or a waterfall, or snow-capped mountains). If your highlights are clipped, there is no detail at all in those areas. There are literally no pixels, and if you printed the image, those clipped areas wouldn't have any ink on them. That's how serious clipping is. Obviously, we'd like to catch this clipping in-camera and fix it by lowering our exposure a bit (I shoot landscapes in aperture priority mode, so I use my Exposure Compensation dial to darken my exposure if I see a clipping warning), but if we don't catch it in-camera, luckily, in many cases, we can recover those clipped highlights in Lightroom or Camera Raw using the Basic panel's Highlights slider. First, to see if we have highlight clipping, look up at the histogram at the top right of the window—in particular, look at the triangle up in the top-right corner (circled in the inset above). If that triangle is filled with white, some parts of your image are clipping. To see which parts, click on that triangle and those clipped areas will have a red tint over them. Now, drag the Highlights slider to the left until the red areas are gone and your clipping is taken care of. Yes, it's that easy. By the way, if you see a red, green, or blue triangle in your histogram, that means just that color is clipping, which isn't nearly as bad as clipping in all channels where the triangle is solid white. I don't usually worry about clipping in just one channel.

Opening Up Dark Shadow Areas

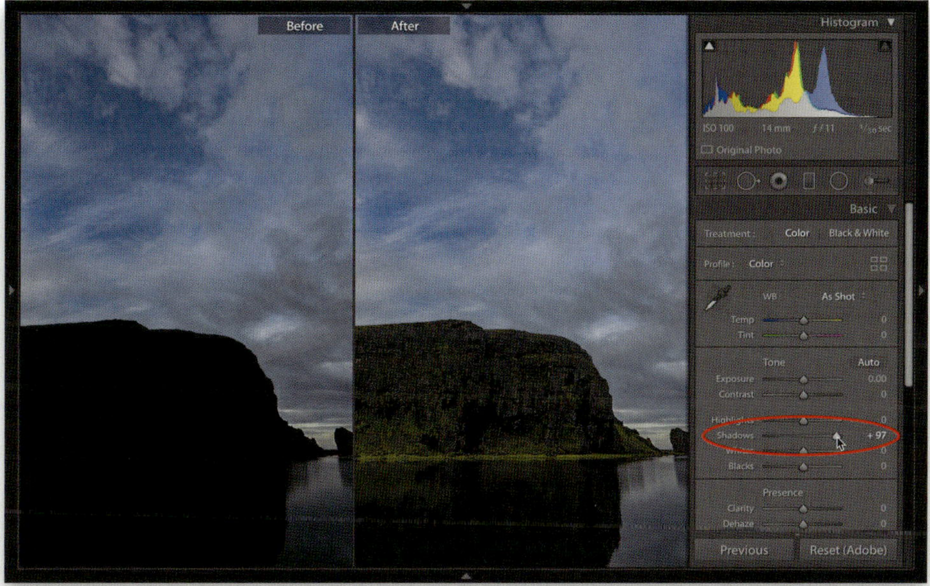

If there's one thing people love seeing in landscape images, it's detail. However, if some of the shadow areas in your image get too dark, they'll turn solid black and you'll lose detail. Luckily, there's a slider for that in the Basic panel. It's called "Shadows" and dragging it to the right will open up those shadow areas big time. I would caution you about dragging too far to the right, though. It might be just what the image needs, but depending on the image, dragging too far to the right can kind of give your image an "HDRed" look (and I don't mean the good HDR), so just keep an eye on that. Again, it just depends on the image, but this is an easy slider to overdo because its effect is pretty powerful. Also, sometimes, if you have to drag it way over to the right, the image starts to look kind of flat, like you've lost contrast, and if that happens, drag the Contrast slider a little to the right to bring some of that lost contrast back—just drag it a little or it will clog up your shadow areas again. This Shadows slider works particularly well if you have a backlit image—drag it to the right and it kind of works like magic to bring those dark areas back. Your eye sees those areas just fine while you're standing there taking the shot, but that's because your eyes have a much wider tonal range than your camera's sensor. This is also why we take so many shots where our subject is nearly a silhouette. When you're standing there, you can see all the detail, no problem. When you put a DSLR up to your eye, it looks the same, but then you take the shot, and your subject looks like a silhouette. Again, it's the sensor's fault, not yours, but now at least you know how to deal with it in post.

Enhancing Detail and Texture

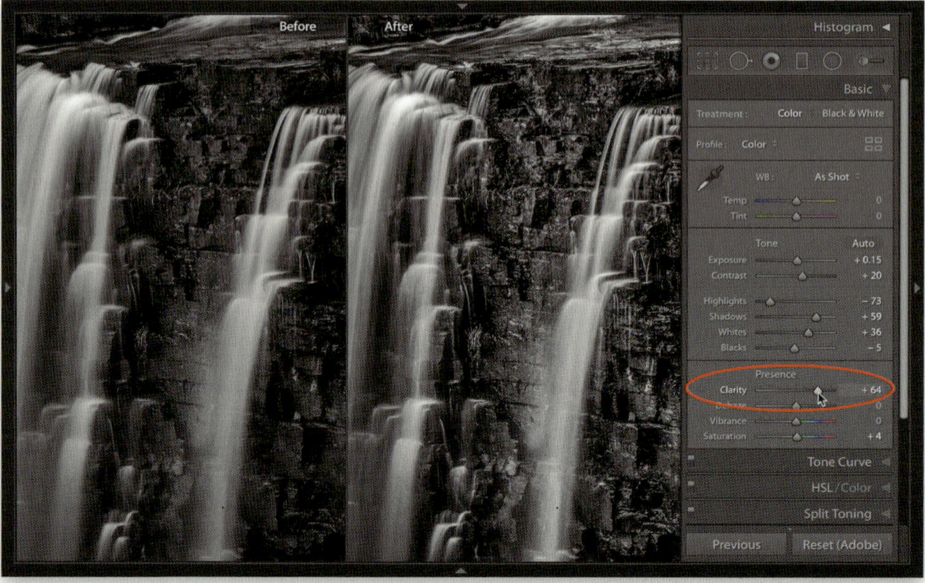

One of the most powerful tools we have for enhancing detail and texture is Lightroom's (and Camera Raw's) Clarity slider (found near the bottom of the Basic panel). Technically, it boosts midtone contrast (well, it does if you drag it to the right), but I just think of it as the detail enhancer. It really brings out texture and dimension and it totally rocks for landscape images, bringing out details in rock formations, making water shiny, and making foliage look more well-defined—it's like our secret weapon. Now, how do you know when you've applied too much Clarity? If you start seeing glows around the edges of things in your image, or if you start seeing what looks like a drop shadow behind your clouds, you've gone too far. I use a pretty liberal amount of Clarity in most cases, so I'm not scared to use it a bunch, but again (and I know I've said this a million times or so in this book), it just depends on the image. The more edges there are in the image, the more Clarity it can take. If the subject of the image is of a softer nature, like a flower, you might not crank it as high. Also, since Clarity does boost the midtone contrast, if you apply a lot of it, it can make your midtones look a bit darker. If that happens, increase the Exposure slider by around +0.20 to +0.30 to compensate and open those midtones back up a bit.

Making Your Colors Look More Vibrant

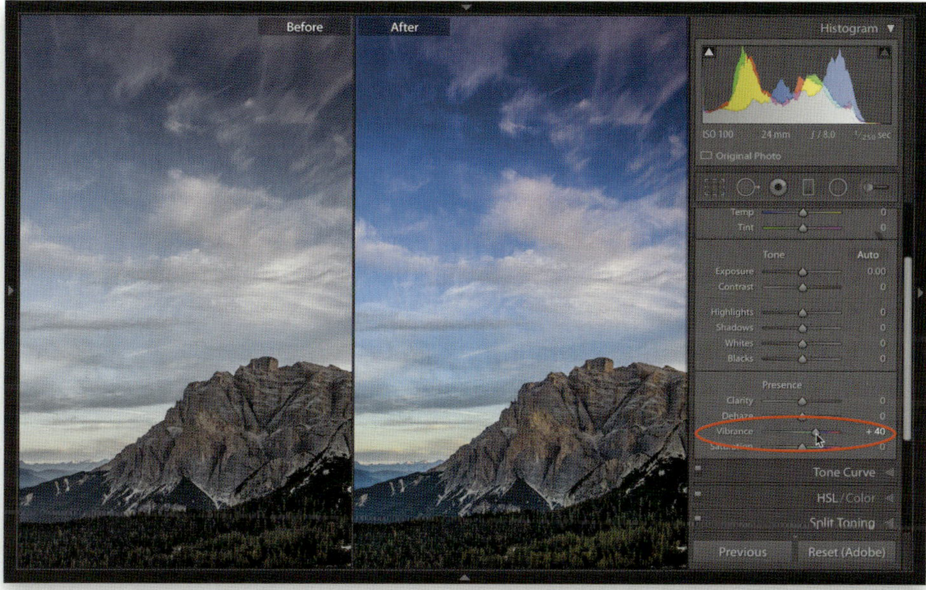

If you want to make the colors in your image even more vibrant, drag the Vibrance slider (it's near the bottom of the Basic panel) to the right a bit (or a bunch—it's your call). Vibrance is kind of like a smart saturation slider in that it doesn't just boost all the colors in your image across the board like the Saturation slider does (which is why we don't ever use the Saturation slider to add more color; we only use it to take away color—to desaturate an image). Instead, it evaluates the image and if it sees areas of dull color, it boosts the color in those areas a lot, and if it sees areas where the colors are already pretty vibrant, it boosts those just a little. It has a special mathematical algorithm that automatically avoids boosting flesh tones, so if there's a person (or people) in your photo, it won't make them look all sunburned or weird. That's one pretty smart slider. So, if your color needs a little boost, drag this slider to the right.

Adding a Graduated ND Filter in Post

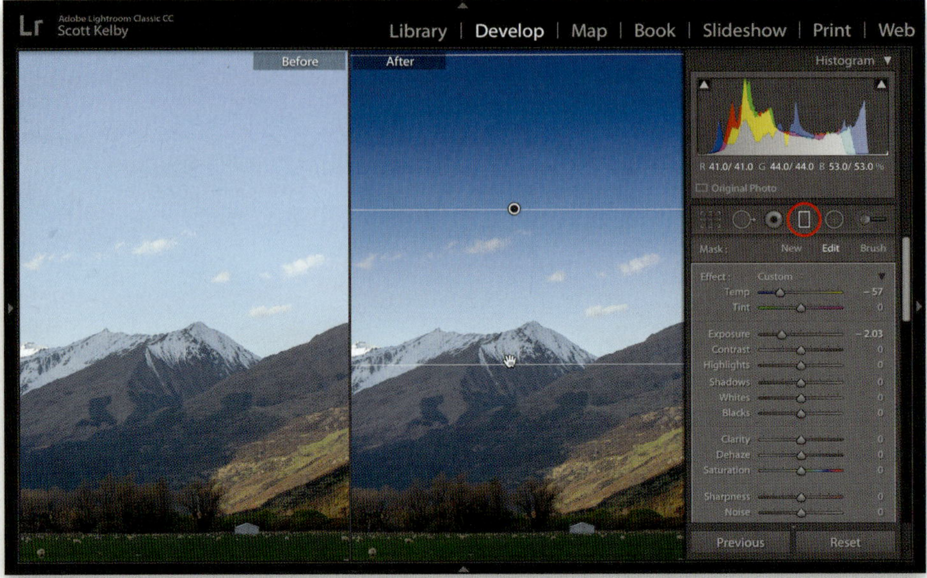

Remember the neutral density gradient filter we talked about back on page 14 that darkens the sky, and then graduates down to transparent at the horizon line, so both your foreground and your sky look properly exposed? Well, if you don't own an ND grad filter (or you accidentally left it back in the trunk of your car before you hiked out to the shooting location, like I have more times than I care to admit), you can use the Graduated Filter in Lightroom or Camera Raw to do the same thing (with some extra advantages). The Graduated Filter is found in Lightroom's toolbar, right below the Histogram panel (its icon looks like a gradient), and in Camera Raw, it's found near the right side of the toolbar at the top of the window. When you choose it, its sliders appear on the right side of the window, and you'll notice it has the same sliders, in the same order, as the Basic panel. You'll want to reset all the sliders to zero first, so to do that in Lightroom, double-click on the word "Effect" in the top left of the panel. In Camera Raw, click on the minus sign to the left of Exposure and all the sliders reset to zero, except for Exposure, which is set to –0.50. Okay, now drag the Exposure slider to –1.00 (a full stop), and then press-and-hold the Shift key, click in the top center of your image, and drag downward until your cursor reaches the horizon line. This darkens the top of your sky, but then it slowly graduates down, darkening less and less until it reaches the point where you stopped and there's no effect all—the same way an actual ND grad filter works. If you want the sky darker, drag the Exposure slider to the left. *Cool tip:* If you want the sky bluer, drag the Temp (Temperature) slider to the left a bit.

Cropping and Straightening

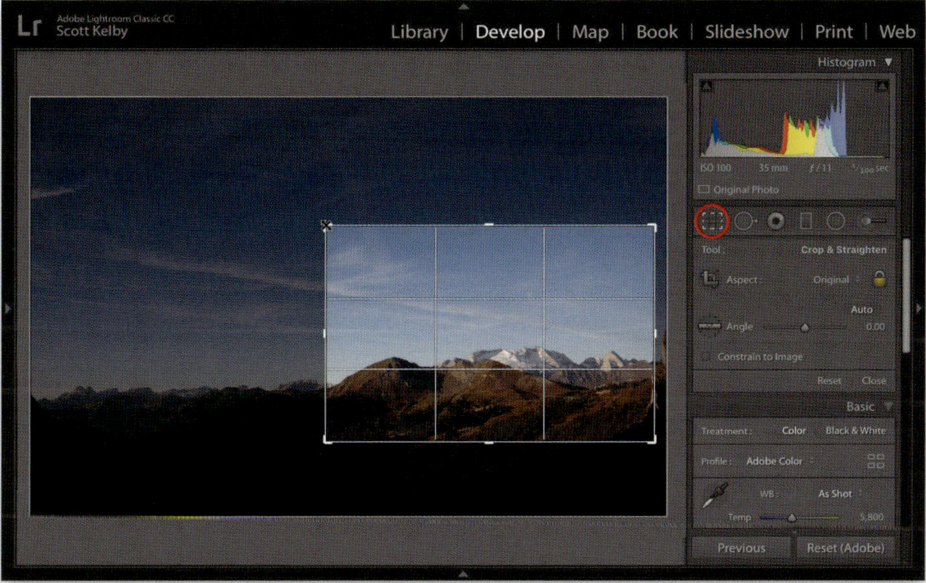

This is the single most-used tool in all of Photoshop and Lightroom, and it's super-easy to use. I prefer to use the Crop tool in Lightroom or Camera Raw because if you change your mind later, no sweat, you can always undo it, whereas Photoshop's is more permanent. Oddly enough, the tool works a little differently between Lightroom and Camera Raw (and it's actually called the Crop Overlay tool in Lightroom). We'll start with Lightroom, where all you do is click on the Crop Overlay tool (in the toolbar right below the histogram in the right side Panels area) and it puts a cropping border around your image. By default, it will crop to keep things proportional, but if you want a freeform crop, without it staying proportional, click on the gold lock icon in the top right of the tool's panel. Now, you can just click-and-drag one of the side or corner handles inward to start cropping. If you need to rotate your crop (to straighten the image), move your cursor just outside the cropping border (but still near it) and it will change into a two-headed arrow, and then click-and-drag up/down to rotate. There's also a straighten tool in the Crop Overlay panel in Lightroom: click on the Angle icon, then click-and-drag it across something that's supposed to be straight (either horizontally or vertically), and it will rotate the crop, straightening the image. The Crop tool in Camera Raw works pretty much the same way, except that when you choose it, it doesn't automatically add a cropping border around your image: you have to click-and-drag the cropping border out over your image. Also, in Lightroom, when you click inside the cropping border to reposition it, you actually move the image behind it; in Photoshop, you move the cropping border.

Converting to Black and White

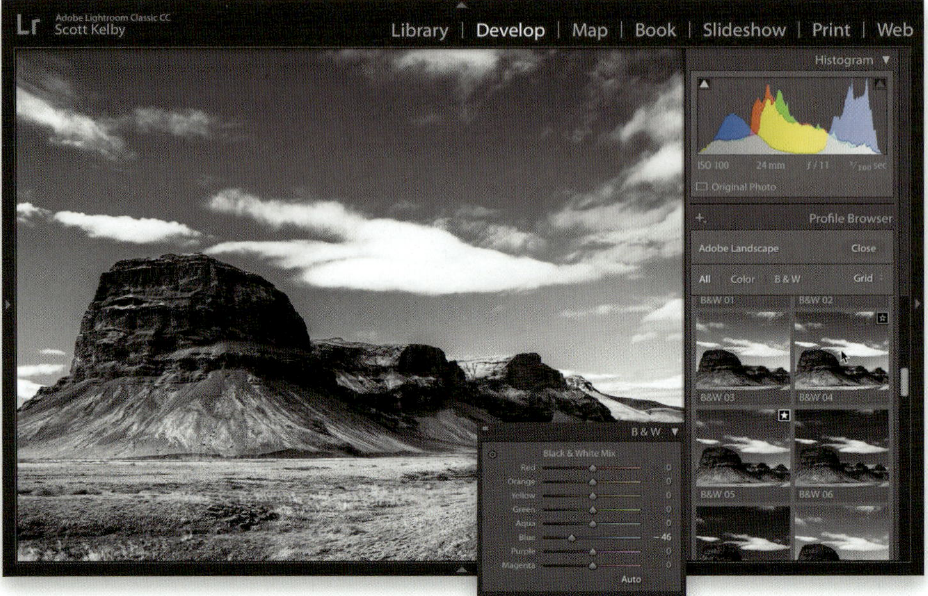

Don't use Lightroom's or Camera Raw's Black & White treatment option. There's a better way to make your black-and-white conversion, and you can tweak it later using the B&W (Black & White Mix) panel. The better way is to apply a B&W profile. There are 12 different ones (they all look quite a bit different), and you can quickly preview them to see which one looks best for your image. These creative profiles are found at the top right of the Basic panel. Click on the icon with the four squares to bring up the Profile Browser (seen here), then scroll down and open the B&W profiles. Now, just move your cursor over each profile to get an onscreen preview of how your image would look with that particular profile. Give 'em all a quick look (this should take about 10 seconds), then click on whichever one looks best, and now you've got a great starting point for editing your black-and-white image. Click on the Close button (at the top right) to close the Profile Browser, then scroll down to the B&W panel (in Camera Raw, click on the Black & White Mix icon, the fourth one from the left, below the histogram). Each of these color sliders controls a different area of your image. For example, if you wanted the sky darker, you'd drag the Blue(s) slider to the left. Want it brighter? Drag it to the right. Some adjustments are obvious like that, but honestly, the best thing you can do here is quickly drag each slider back and fourth a couple of times to see what each one affects in the image, and decide as you drag them if they help make the image look better. When you're done here, finish off the tweaking in the Basic panel (contrast is king with black-and-white images, so don't be shy), and then, of course, sharpen the heck out of it (we'll look at sharpening on page 163).

Two Methods for Adding Contrast

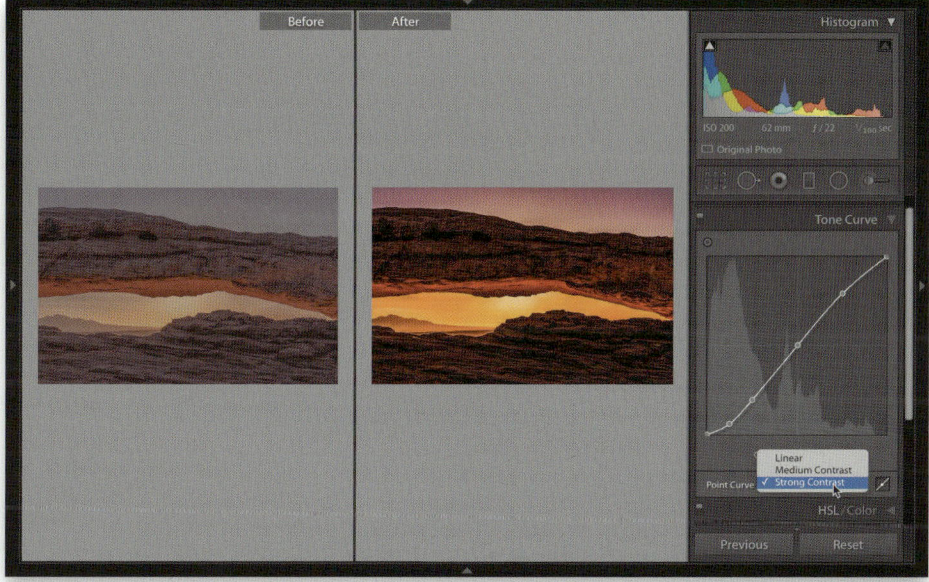

The most obvious is the Contrast slider (in the Basic panel), and I lean on this slider *a lot*—drag it to the right to add contrast; drag it to the left to remove it (great for that Instagram look). I love really contrasty images, so I often crank the Contrast amount quite a bit (especially on B&W images), which makes your whites whiter and blacks blacker. Those things together have the byproduct of making your colors more vibrant, so it's all good. Now, don't add contrast until you've set your white and black points because increasing the amounts of Whites and Blacks adds contrast already, so do that before you grab the Contrast slider. That's the easiest method of adding contrast—just drag the Contrast slider to the right. If you're more discerning about your contrast, you can also add it (in place of, or in addition to, the Contrast slider) using the Tone Curve panel. Below the curve, you'll see the Point Curve pop-up menu set to Linear, which means it's not doing anything. To add contrast, click on that pop-up menu and you'll see Medium Contrast and Strong Contrast presets. When you choose one of these, it plots a curve shape (in the shape of an "S") within the grid. If you chose Medium Contrast, the angle of the "S" is very subtle. If you chose Strong Contrast, it's more pronounced, and if you click-and-drag the points on the curve to make it steeper, that adds even more contrast. You can add more whites by dragging the top-right point upward. The midtones are made brighter or darker using the center point (upward to brighten them; downward to darken), and you can drag either of the two points on the bottom left upward to lighten the shadows or downward to darken them (adding more contrast).

Removing Haze from Your Scenes

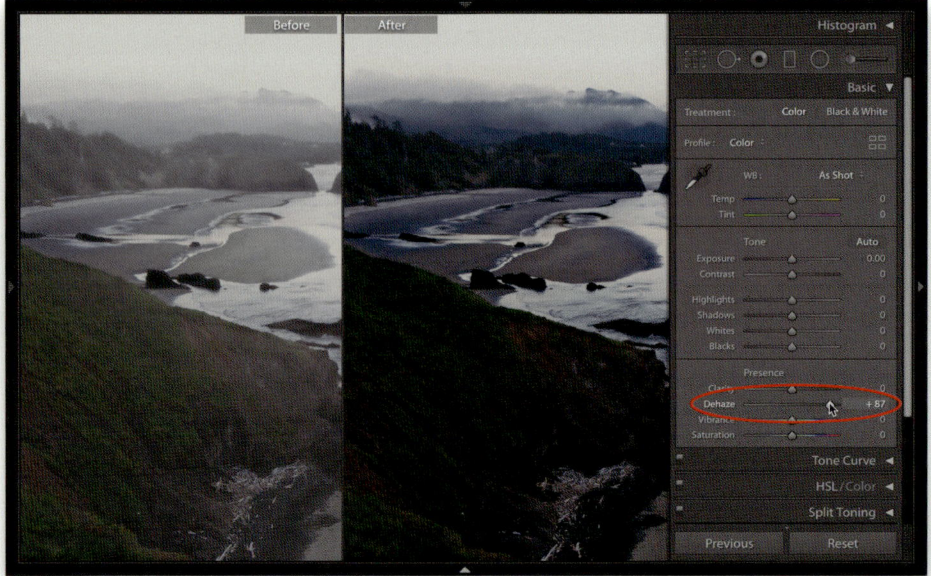

If it's a hazy day, or there's haze off in the distance, there's a really easy fix for it. It's a slider simply called "Dehaze," and the farther you drag it to the right, the more haze it removes. Take a look at the example here, shot at Cannon Beach in Oregon. It was a pretty hazy day, but dragging the Dehaze slider to the right makes easy work of it. There are two side effects of using a lot of Dehaze on an image: (1) it tends to add a blueish tint to the areas it affects, and (2) it tends to exaggerate any dark vignetting you have in the corners of your image. So, if you have vignetting, I would remove that first (usually turning on the Enable Profile Corrections check-box, in the Lens Corrections panel, will do the trick. See the next page) before applying a bunch of Dehaze. To reduce the amount of blue that adding a lot of Dehaze sometimes creates, you can go to the HSL (Adjustments) panel, click on the Saturation tab, and drag the Blue(s) slider to the left a bit to remove some of that blue it added.

Correcting Lens Problems

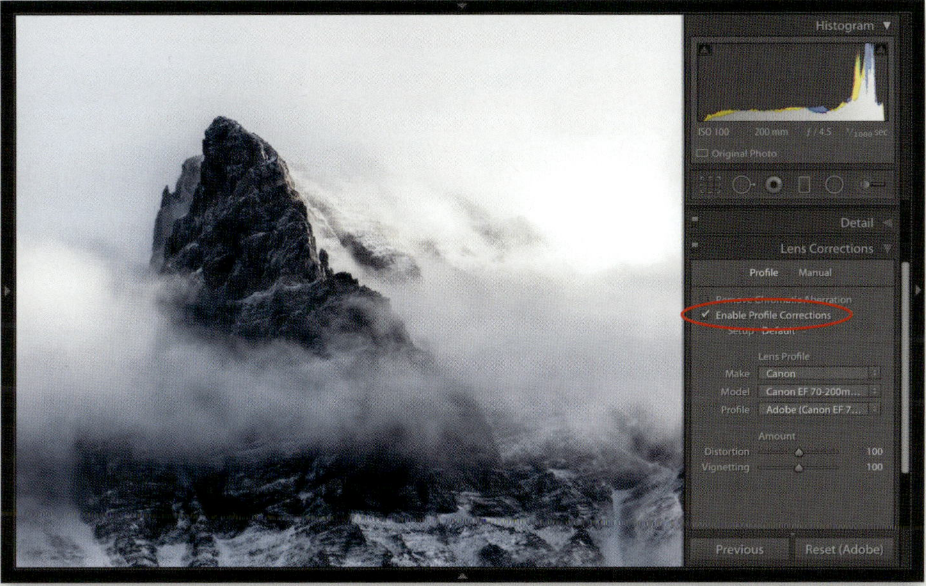

Since you'll be shooting with a wide-angle lens a lot, you're going to want to know how to fix some of the most-likely lens distortion problems you're going to run into. Luckily, this is pretty easy these days. Start by going to the Lens Corrections panel, clicking on the Profile tab, and turning on the Enable Profile Corrections checkbox. Lightroom and Photoshop's Camera Raw have huge built-in databases of lens correction profiles, and can read your camera data to know which lens you used to take the shot. So, when you turn on that checkbox, it finds the right profile (well, it usually does) and applies a fix to your image. It helps a lot, but it often doesn't do the whole job. Before we look at the next part, if Lightroom (or Camera Raw) doesn't recognize your lens, you can help it by just choosing the make of lens you used (Canon, Nikon, Tamron, Sigma, etc.) from the Make pop-up menu, and it will then usually find the profile for you. If you don't see your exact lens listed there (hey, it could happen), try to choose one that's close in focal length to the one you used. If there are still some distortion issues, you can usually fix them manually. In that same Lens Corrections panel, click on the Manual tab and you'll see a Distortion Amount slider (for that bloated look you get from barrel distortion). If you just drag this slider back and forth a couple of times, it'll be obvious what it does, and you'll be able to use it to fix any leftover distortion.

Dealing with Purple or Green Color Fringing (Chromatic Aberrations)

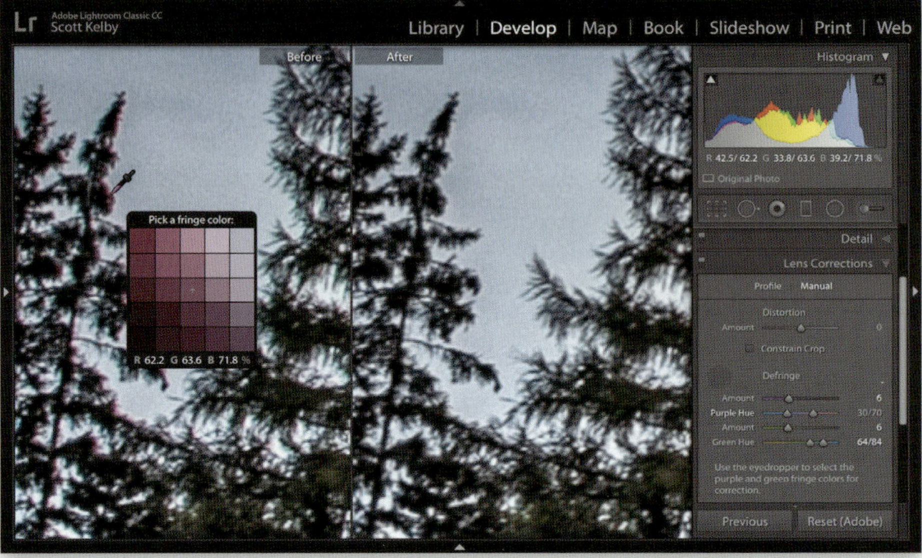

If you notice purple, magenta, or green fringe around the edges of things in your images (like the edges of a mountain, for example, or along a tree line, as shown above in the Before image on the left), you're experiencing a lens problem called a "chromatic aberration." In many cases, Lightroom or Photoshop's Camera Raw can remove this color edge fringing automatically—just go to the Lens Corrections panel, click on the Profile tab, and turn on the Remove Chromatic Abberration checkbox (in Camera Raw, click on the sixth icon from the left, below the histogram, to get to the Lens Corrections panel). If that doesn't fully remove the color fringing, zoom in tight on the area with it, then click on the Manual tab where you'll see a Defringe section with Amount sliders, which you can drag to remove the color fringing. Drag one to the right just enough to where the fringe goes away. If dragging an Amount slider doesn't fix the problem, then you might need to target exactly the right Hues. In the Defringe section, click on the Fringe Color Selector tool (this isn't available in Camera Raw), then click it once directly on the color fringe to target that exact color (you'll see a color loupe that shows the pixels zoomed in, as seen above, so you'll have no trouble finding them. There's no way the blue sky should have those purple pixels, right)? Those Hue sliders below each Amount slider are there to help you target the exact hue of purple or green that's causing the problem, and when you click with the Fringe Color Selector tool, it moves those sliders to the proper settings. You can also slide the Hue sliders around manually, and/or expand the range of hues each slider affects by dragging their two knobs out away from each other.

Sharpening Your Landscape Images

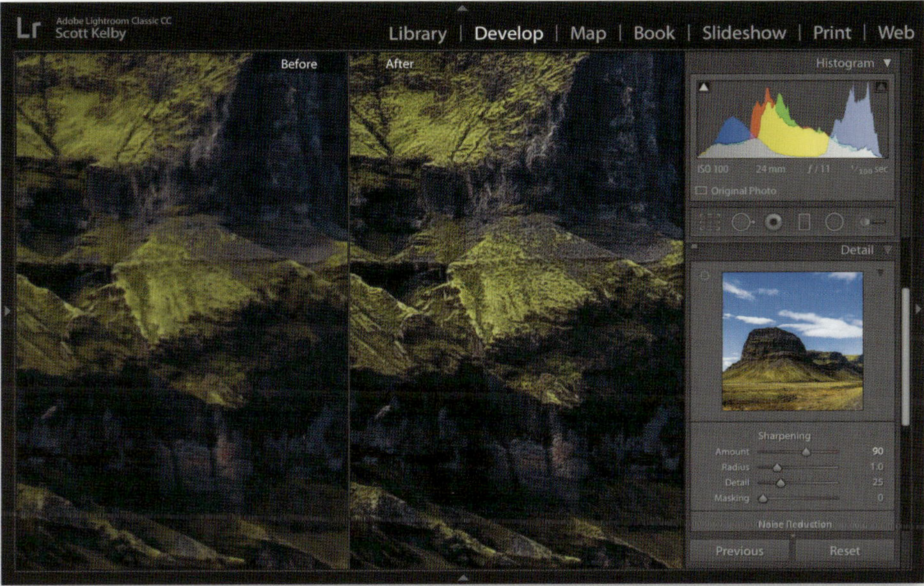

I sharpen every landscape photo—every one, without fail—and since there's a lot of detail and edges and texture, landscape photos can usually handle having a lot of sharpening added. There are built-in presets in both Lightroom and Photoshop's Camera Raw for sharpening, and you can find them in Lightroom in the Develop module's Presets panel (in the left side Panels area). Once you're in this panel, scroll down, click on Sharpening, and you'll see presets for Light, Medium, and Heavy. I generally use Heavy for most landscape images, but if you feel it's a bit too much for your image, try Medium (don't use Light—it's too light). If you think Heavy isn't enough, go ahead and apply it (by clicking on it), then go to the Detail panel (in the right side Panels area) and drag the Sharpening Amount slider to the right to increase it. If that doesn't make a big enough difference, increase the Radius to 1.1 (or if you're using a 50-megapixel or so camera, bump it up to 1.2). You can find these Sharpening presets in Camera Raw by clicking on the Presets icon (the second one from the right) beneath the histogram, and then clicking on Sharpening in the Presets panel. If you need to add some creative sharpening (sharpening added in just a few particular areas now that the whole image has a base layer of sharpening), get the Adjustment Brush **(K)**, set all the sliders to zero, then drag the Sharpness slider to the right a bit and paint over the areas you want spot sharpened.

Creating Reflections

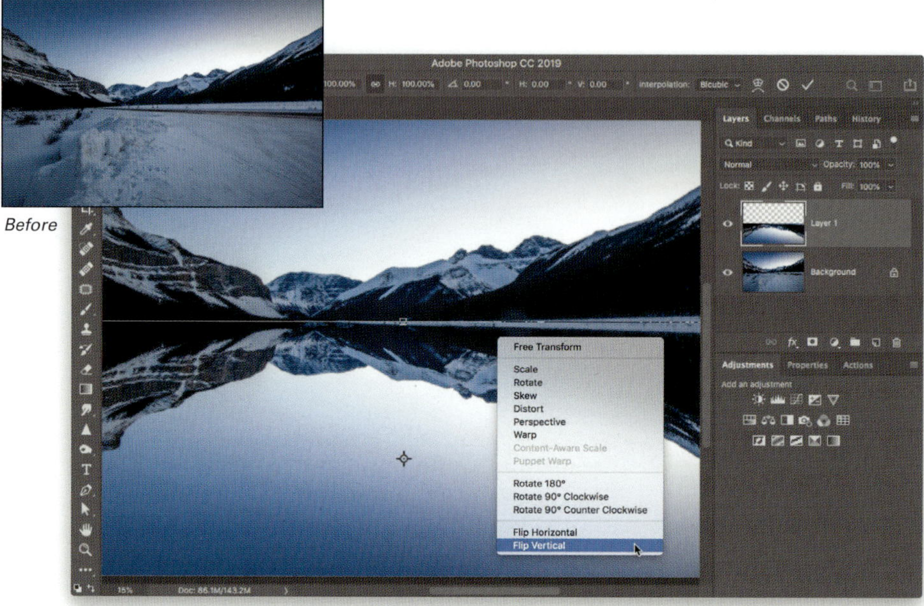

Before

Okay, this is totally cheating (but everybody does it. Well, not everybody, but enough photographers out there that you should know how to do it, too…ya know…just in case). You do this in Photoshop (Lightroom can't do this one). Step one is to use the Rectangular Marquee tool **(M)** to select from the top of the water's edge (or the horizon line if there is no water) up to the top of the image, so you're selecting everything from the water on up. Now, press **Command-J (PC: Ctrl-J)** to put that selected area up on its own layer. Press **Command-T** to enter Free Transform, Right-click inside the bounding box, choose **Flip Vertical** (as shown here), and then hit **Return (PC: Enter)** to lock in the transformation. Switch to the Move tool **(V)**, then press-and-hold the Shift key (to keep it perfectly aligned) and drag it straight down until the two waterlines meet. That creates the reflection. The one final thing you might want to do (well, I do it anyway…ya know…if I were ever to actually do this cheating thing) is to darken the reflection a little bit, so it doesn't stand out. You can do this using Camera Raw as a filter by going under the Filter menu and choosing (you guessed it) **Camera Raw Filter**. When it opens, just drag the Exposure slider a little to the left to darken the reflection, click OK, and you're done.

Dealing with Glows

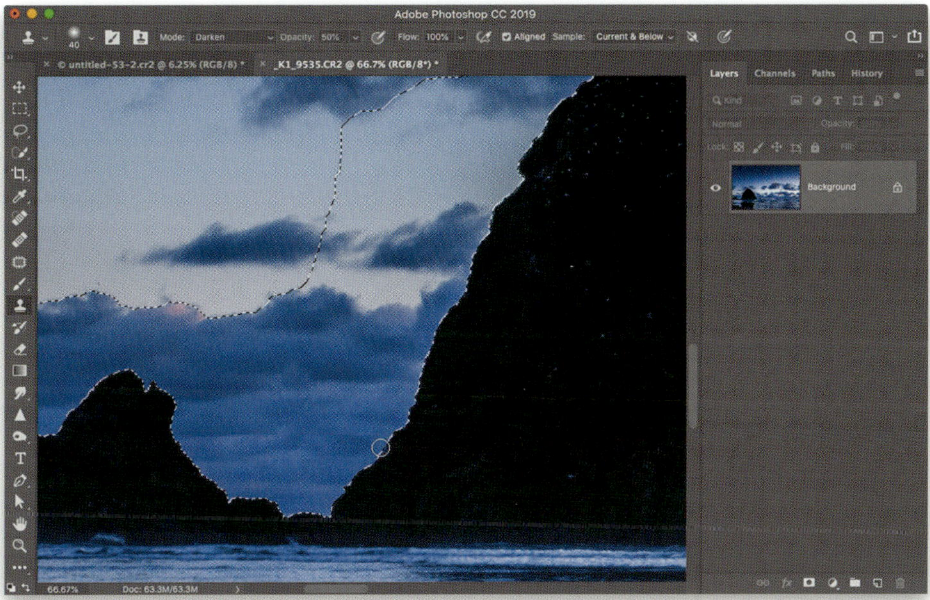

Sometimes, if you do a lot of post-processing, including adding lots of contrast or clarity, you might get a white glow that appears along the edges of things in your landscape—like along the edges of mountains or rocks—and it doesn't look awesome. That's why I always fix these glows, because they're distracting and they signal to other Photoshop users everywhere, "I've overcooked this image." Luckily, hiding those glows (while somewhat tedious) is actually pretty easy, but you have to do this one in Photoshop. Get the Quick Selection tool **(W)** and paint the area around the glow (so, in this instance, you'd paint over the sky in that area, all the way up to the edge of the rock, to select it. That's what the Quick Selection tool does—it lets you paint selections, and it uses smart technology to keep you from accidentally selecting things like the rock). Now, get the Clone Stamp tool **(S)** from the Toolbar (its icon looks like a rubber stamp), then go up in the Options Bar and lower its Opacity to 50% and change its blend mode to **Darken** (that way, it only affects pixels that are lighter when you paint in the next part). Press-and-hold the Option (PC: Alt) key, and click once right near the white glow to sample a clean area. Now, move your cursor over the glow and start painting, and as you paint, it copies (clones) that nearby area of sky without the glow, right over the edge glow. When you're done, press **Command-D (PC: Ctrl-D)** to Deselect. Like I said, you might have to do this a lot for a large landscape, and it takes a little time to do it piece by piece, but when you're done, and you see your image without the glow, I bet you'll think it was worth it.

Post-Processing Focus-Stacked Images

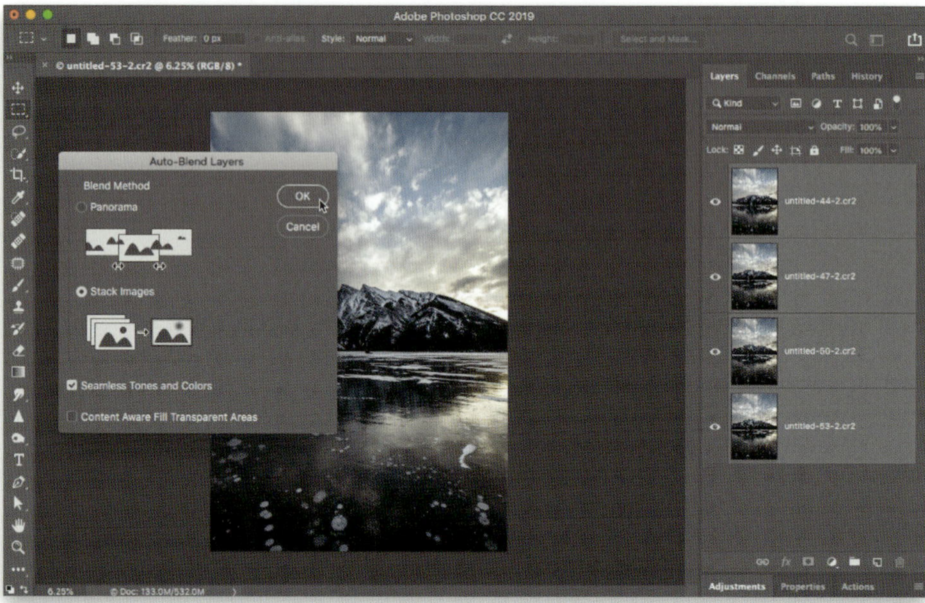

If you shot your image using the stacked photo technique (see page 191), here's what to do in post-processing: First, open the images in Photoshop (this is a Photoshop thing; Lightroom can't do this). Then, go under the File menu, under Scripts, and choose **Load Files into Stack**. When the Load Layers dialog appears, click the Add Open Files button, then click OK, and it will combine those stacked images into a single document, with each image on its own layer. Since you shot these on a tripod, they will be perfectly aligned with one another, so now we just have to mask in the sharp areas from each layer to create an image that has tremendous depth of field and sharpness throughout. Let's say, for example, that you opened four images, so you now have four layers in the Layers panel (as seen above). Click on the top layer, then press-and-hold the Shift key and click on the bottom layer to select all four layers. Then, go under the Edit menu and choose **Auto-Blend Layers**. When its dialog appears, click the Stack Images radio button, turn on the Seamless Tones and Colors checkbox, and click OK. Now, something amazing is about to happen— Photoshop analyzes your images, finds the sharp areas of each photo, and adds layer masks. So, the only thing that now shows are the sharp parts of each image, with everything else hidden behind a black layer mask, leaving you with an image that has tremendous depth. It does most of the hard work for you. All you have left to do is go to the Layers panel's flyout menu (at the top right of the panel) and choose Flatten Layers. Boom. Done.

Blue Sky Trick

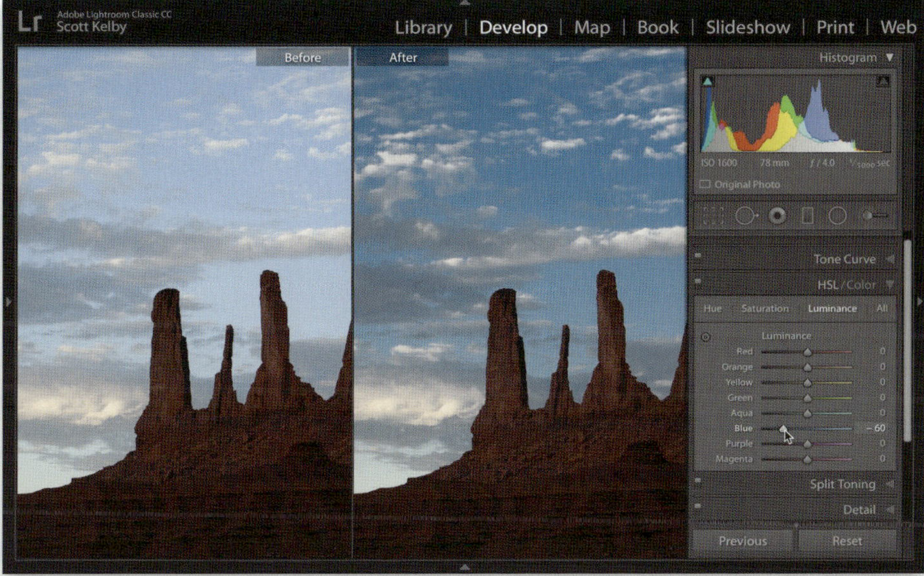

If you have a weak sky, meaning it's blue but it's that kind of a washed-out, lame blue, instead of that nice rich blue sky you wish you had, try this: Go to the HSL (Adjustments) panel, either in Lightroom (in the right side Panels area) or Photoshop's Camera Raw (click on the fourth icon from the left beneath the histogram). At the top of this panel, click on the Luminance tab, and then drag the Blue(s) slider to the left and watch the magic happen. Okay, "magic" might be overselling this one a bit, but your sky will get anywhere from more blue to awesomely blue, which is a good thing.

Using the Auto Button as a Starting Place

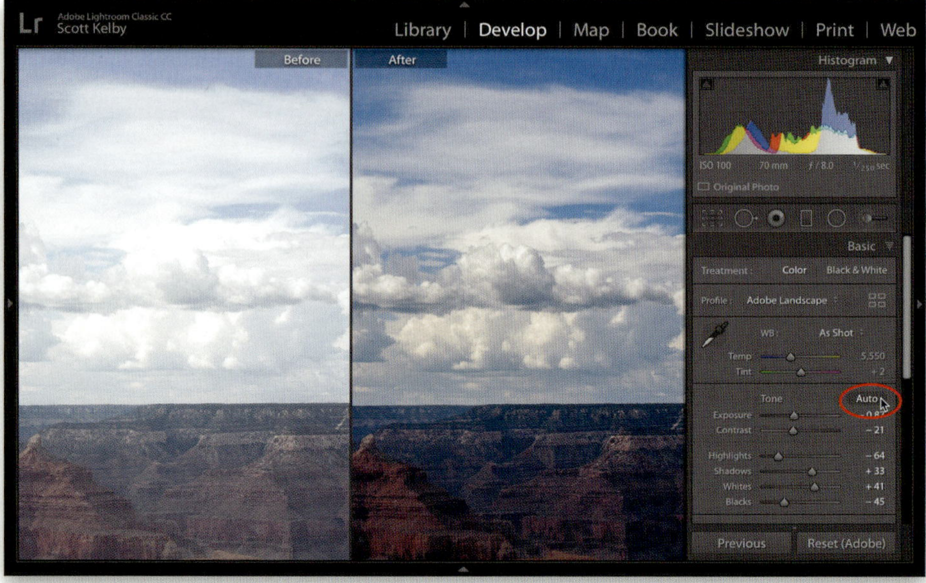

Both Lightroom and Photoshop's Camera Raw have an Auto button in the Basic panel, and although it used to be pretty darn awful, they've majorly updated how it works, so now it's just awful (and not "pretty darn"). Okay, it's not awful, it's actually (finally) pretty decent to use as a starting place. It doesn't give you a finished image, but if you're not sure where to start, this is as good a place as any. My problem with how it works is this: it opens up the shadow areas too much and it lowers the contrast. Say that last line aloud: "it lowers the contrast." Whoever thought of that idea at Adobe was not a landscape photographer. So, for better results, do this: right after you click the Auto button, raise the Contrast slider back up to at least zero (if not higher), then lower the Shadows amount (dragging it to the left) by at least 1/3 to 1/2 of what it boosted, and then it will look pretty decent. I think you can do better on your own, using the tools I've taught you in this chapter, but again, if you're not sure where to start, click the Auto button, then follow it up with these two moves, and you'll at least be in the ballpark. Also, make sure you choose your RAW profile first (moving it off Adobe Color to either Adobe Landscape or Adobe Vivid; see page 147 for more on profiles) before clicking the Auto button.

Adding That "Dreamy Look"

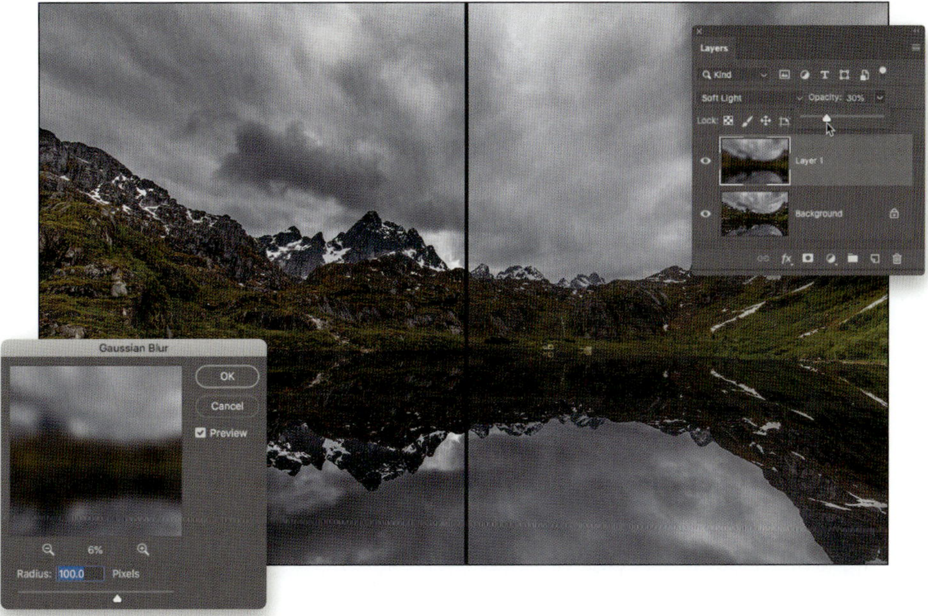

This is a popular look photographers are adding to their landscape images in Photoshop—it's a blurring that's applied mostly in the highlights, and a little in the shadow areas. You may have heard this dreamy look referred to as "The Orton Effect," as it was created by Michael Orton back in the 1980s. But, this look is having a renaissance—we're seeing it all over Instagram from some of the top-ranked photographers. So, I wanted to share it in case you want to add it to your image. There are a number of different ways to get this look, and one I've been teaching for use on HDR images (because it takes the edge off some of the overly sharpened native look of some HDRs) is to duplicate the Background layer **(Command-J [PC: Ctrl-J])**, and then apply a large Gaussian Blur (under the Filter menu, under Blur, choose **Gaussian Blur**). I'm talking 80, 100, or even 120 pixels of blur for those really high-res images from 50+ megapixel cameras—really blur all the detail. Then, change the layer blend mode of this blurred layer to **Soft Light** (from the pop-up menu at the top left of the Layers panel), and lower its Opacity to 30% to complete the effect (Soft Light applies a contrast effect, making the highlights and shadows more intense). Or, you can also try leaving this layer in Normal blend mode, lowering its Opacity to 20%–30% (depending on how much dreaminess you want), and then opening Levels **(Command-L [PC: Ctrl-L])**. Drag the white (highlights) Input Levels slider to the left quite a bit to boost the highlights, and then drag the black (shadows) Input Levels slider to the right a bit to boost the shadows. Try both methods and see which one "speaks" to you and your style.

Cloud Replacement, Technique #1

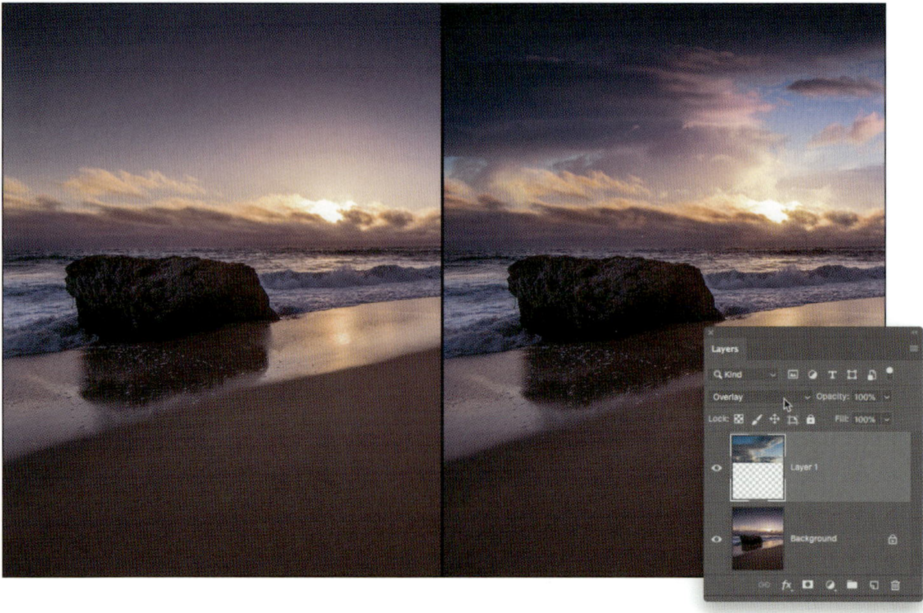

Because we can't control whether clouds show up at our shooting location or not, the art of cloud replacement (taking a beautiful or interesting sky from a different image and adding it to your original, empty, cloudless sky image in Photoshop) has become incredibly popular—many top pros now do this without batting an eye. So, since this has become so commonplace, I wanted to give you a couple of techniques for how to do it. Before you start, there are a few things to keep in mind, so the sky you're bringing in looks natural: (1) Make sure the sun is hitting the clouds from the same side as in the bald sky image. If it's not, once you've made a selection of the cloud image, bring up Free Transform (found under the Edit menu), then Right-click inside the bounding box and choose **Flip Horizontal** to flip the clouds, so the sun (and any shadows) are on the proper side. (2) The clouds you're bringing in should match the overall tone of your image. Don't bring a sunset sky into a daylight shot, and vice versa. (3) Ideally, the clouds you're bringing in should be shot with a similar lens, so their size and shape look right. Images shot with a 200mm lens will probably look out of place when added to a wide-angle shot. With all that in mind, here's a Photoshop technique you should try first: Copy-and-paste the cloud image over the bald sky, then click on the layer blend mode pop-up menu (in the top left of the Layers panel) and scroll through each blend mode to see an onscreen preview of how those clouds will look blended with that image. I usually find that Multiply, Soft Light, or Overlay look the best, but of course, it depends on the image. Also, consider lowering the opacity of this layer a bit, too, to help it blend in.

Cloud Replacement, Technique #2

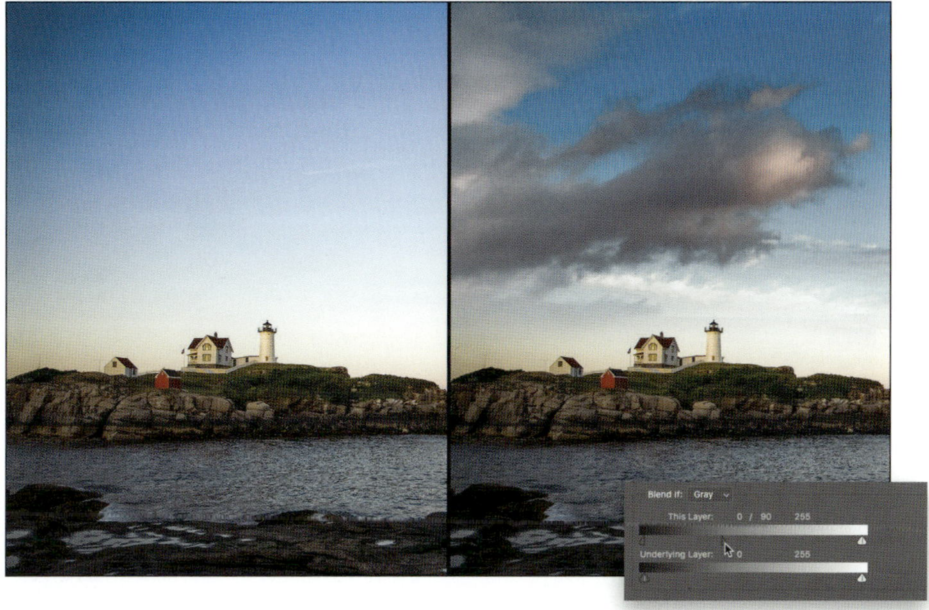

Here's another technique to try. Well, it's kinda 1 1/2 techniques. Maybe two. I dunno, but here goes: (1) Copy-and-paste the good clouds over the bald sky in your original image. Then, go to the Layers panel and double-click on the cloud layer to bring up the Blending Options in the Layer Style dialog. Near the bottom, you'll see the Blend If sliders, and we're going to use those two sliders to find a nice blend. But, before you just start dragging sliders around, press-and-hold the Option (PC: Alt) key and, as you drag a slider, it splits the slider knob in half, giving you a much smoother transition. Don't drag these sliders without pressing-and-holding the Option key! Since every image is different, I can't tell you which of these sliders will be the right one to make a perfect blend, so you'll just have to drag them back and forth a couple of times and see what works. It's a trial-and-error kind of thing, but usually, this can get you pretty close if the previous technique doesn't. The other technique (the 1/2) is to copy-and-paste the clouds into the bald sky document, then press-and-hold the Option key and click on the Add Layer Mask icon at the bottom of the Layers panel (the third icon from the left; it looks like a rectangle with a circle in the center). This hides your clouds layer behind a black mask, so you can't see the clouds now at all, just the original image on the layer below it. Get the Brush tool **(B)**, choose a soft-edged brush from the Brush Picker up in the Options Bar, make sure your Foreground color is set to white, and then paint in the clouds just where you want them. You still might need to change the layer blend mode of this clouds layers to blend it better, or lower the opacity a bit, but this one's worth trying, too.

Removing Distracting Stuff

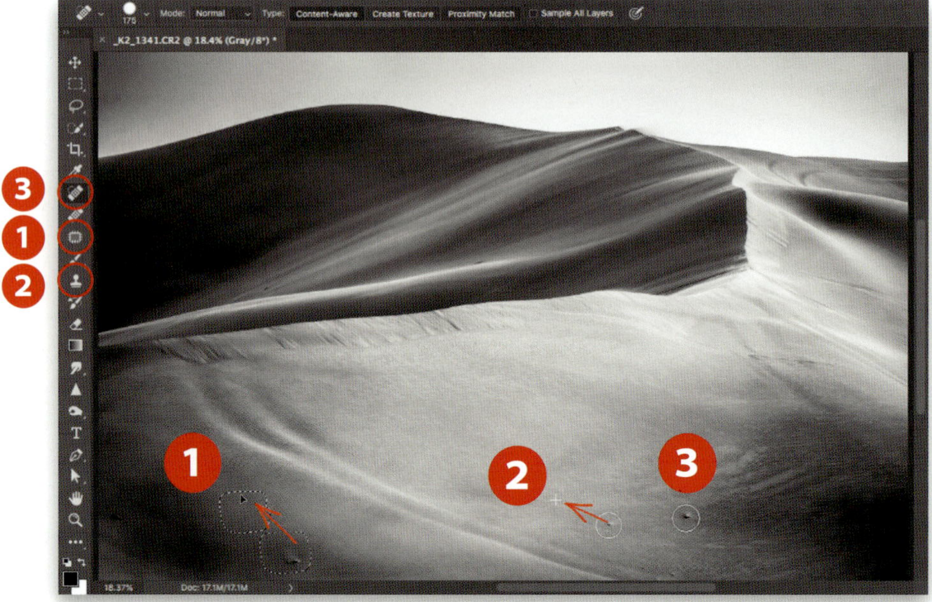

If you're just removing a small spot or speck, then you can use Lightroom's Spot Removal tool—just click it over a spot and it's gone. Usually. It's not the most accurate and sometimes it does a pretty lame job, which is why I always recommend using Photoshop instead, because its tools for removing distracting stuff are awesome. The three main tools we use are: (1) The Patch tool. I use this for removing larger-sized things. Click-and-drag a loose selection around the thing you want to remove, then click inside your selection and drag it to a nearby, clean area. When you release your mouse button, it snaps back to the original position and your distracting stuff is gone. I love this tool! (2) The Clone Stamp tool. It lets you clone part of your image right over the thing you want to remove. Just find a clean, nearby area, then press-and-hold the Option (PC: Alt) key and click once to sample that area (you'll see a crosshair where you Option-clicked, as seen above). Then, move your brush over the thing you want to remove, click once, and that should do the trick. This is great for removing larger stuff, too. Just remember, it's making a copy, a clone of where you Option-clicked, and covering what you want to remove with that, so be careful not to create a visible pattern of cloning. (3) The Spot Healing Brush tool. This is an incredible tool (and *way* better than Lightroom's Spot Removal tool). Simply make your brush a little larger than the thing you want to remove (as seen above) and just click. That's it. Just click once, and it's gone. You don't have to choose a sampling area or anything like that, which is why it's so popular. Ideal for removing small things, or power lines, or branches sticking into your image.

Noise Reduction Just Where You Need It

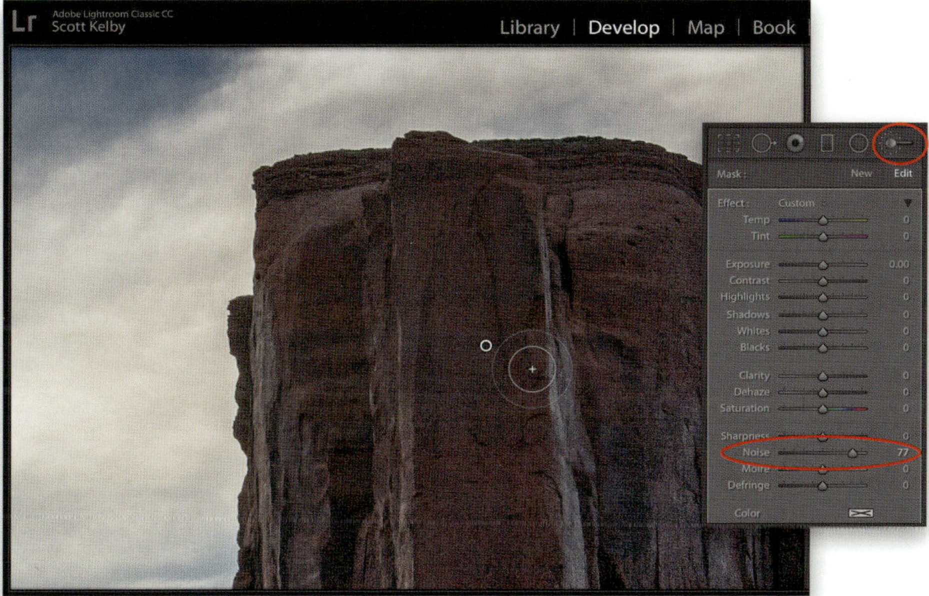

There's a pretty serious problem with applying noise reduction to your image, because the way noise reduction works is it applies a level of blurring to hide the noise. It does work for the most part, but you wind up with a soft image, which goes against everything we try to do in landscape photography, which is to create tack-sharp images. So, you have this lame trade-off where you either have a less-noisy image that's blurry, or a noisy image that's sharp. Neither choice is awesome. That's why I think this trick is so handy because, in most cases, the noise in our images lives in the shadow areas, and the more you open up those shadow areas (or just make the whole image brighter), the more you see noise in them. So, instead of applying noise reduction to the entire image and making the whole image soft, we're going to use the Adjustment Brush **(K)** in Lightroom (or in Photoshop's Camera Raw) to paint noise reduction just in the areas where we actually need it. Like in the big ol' rock above. The sky is fine—you really don't see any noise in it at all—so there's no need to apply noise reduction to that area. Get the Adjustment Brush, drag the Noise slider (circled above in red) way over to the right, and just paint over those noisy areas, like the rock, and leave the rest of the image nice and sharp. This way, you're only applying noise reduction where you actually need it, and you wind up saving much of the sharpness of the image, while still reducing the noise.

Combining Long Exposure Images

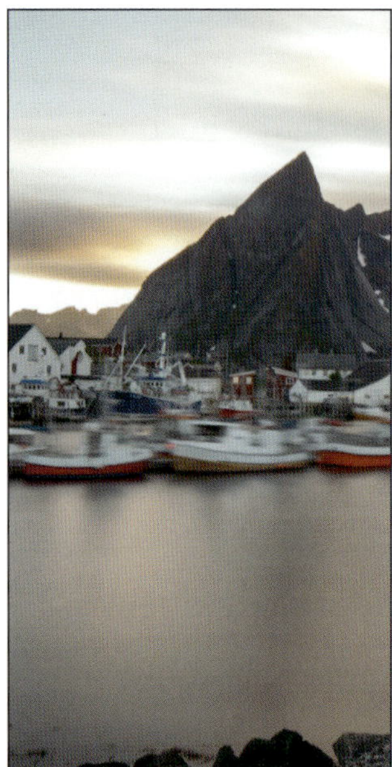 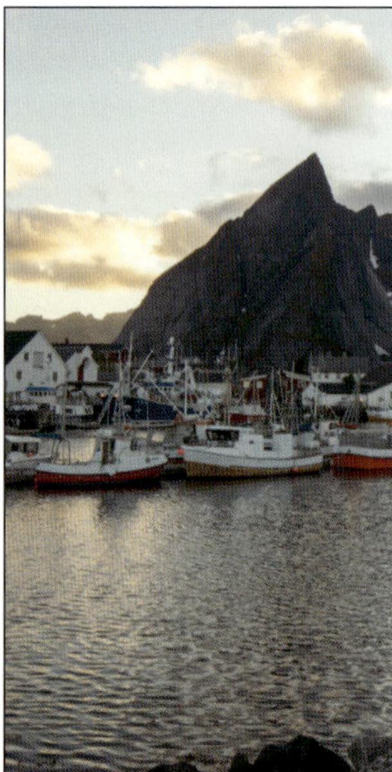 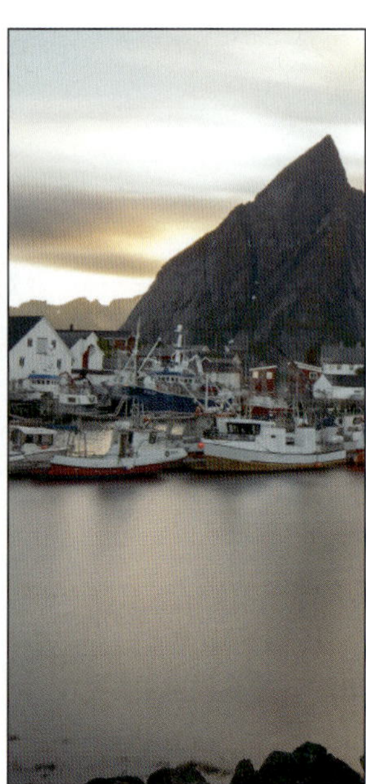

I mentioned back in the Long Exposures chapter that it's a really good idea, when you're done taking your long exposure shot, to take a regular shot, in aperture priority mode, so you have a shot with sharp detail. It's super-helpful if anything in your image is moving, like these boats in the harbor above. The shot on the left is the long exposure shot for the moving water and, of course, the boats are all blurry because they were moving while I had my shutter open for the long exposure. The middle shot is the regular shot I took in aperture priority mode at a normal shutter speed, and you can see it froze the movement of the boats. The shot on the right is a combination of the two—the best of both worlds because I have the soft, silky water, but the boats are in focus. This is done in Photoshop and it's way easier than you'd think. Open both images in Photoshop and copy-and-paste the aperture priority sharp shot on top of your long exposure shot (it will appear on its own layer). Then, press-and-hold the Option (PC: Alt) key and click on the Add Layer Mask icon at the bottom of the Layers panel to hide the sharp, crisp layer behind a black layer mask. Now, get the Brush tool **(B)**, make sure your Foreground color is set to White, and then paint over the moving boats, revealing the sharp non-moving boats from the top layer. And, yes, I made a short video for you showing you exactly how to do this. You'll find it, along with other videos, on the book's companion webpage, mentioned in the book's introduction.

Get Detail in the Moon by Combining Images

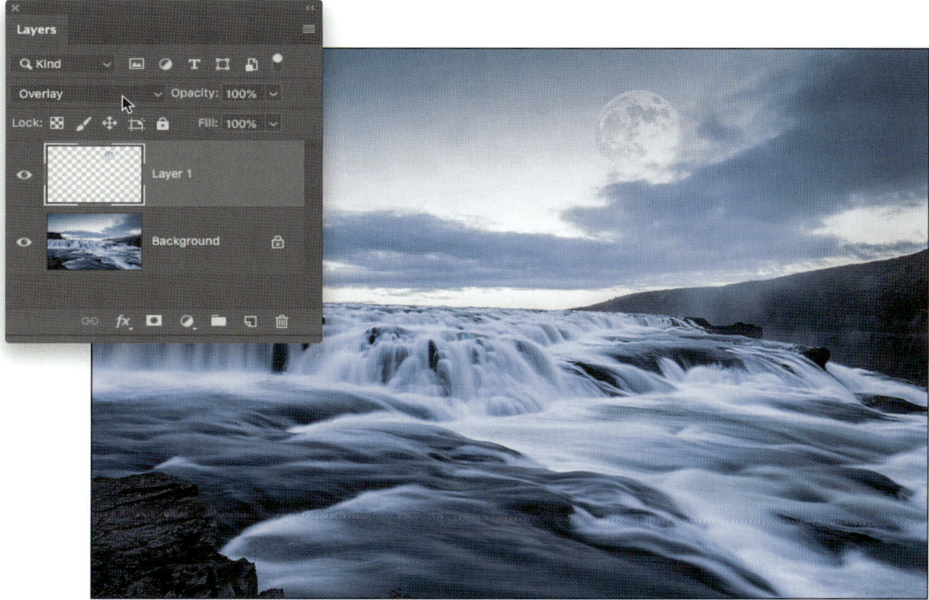

To add a detailed shot of the moon to your landscape image, start (of course) by taking a detailed shot of the moon. If the moon is full (or mostly full) and clearly visible in your shot, you'll shoot and expose for the landscape scene (on a tripod), and then shoot a second shot where you'll expose for the moon, not worrying about the exposure of the landscape at all. Then, you'll simply put the two images together in Photoshop. Well, even if you didn't do that, it's simple to put the images together. First, get the Elliptical Marquee tool **(M)** and click-and-drag a selection, nice and tight, around the moon. (*Tip:* Press-and-hold the Spacebar on your keyboard, while you're dragging out the selection to reposition it as you drag it out. It makes this part so much easier—you'll see why when you try it.) Now, press **Command-C (PC: Ctrl-C)** to Copy that selected moon, then switch to your landscape image and press **Command-V (PC: Ctrl-V)** to Paste the moon into your landscape image (it will appear on its own separate layer). Get the Move tool **(V)** and click-and-drag the moon where you want it to appear in your landscape. If you need to make it larger/smaller, press **Command-T (PC: Ctrl-T)**, then click-and-drag a corner point outward/inward to make it larger/smaller, and then press **Return (PC: Enter)** to lock in your resize. Now it's just a matter of making the moon blend in with the rest of the image by: (1) Changing the layer blend mode of the moon layer to either Overlay or Soft Light (but, you can scroll through the menu to see if any look better). And (2), lowering the Opacity a bit, so it doesn't stand out so much. That's all there is to it. Wanna know how I made part of it appear behind the clouds? I made a video for you, and you know where to find it. :)

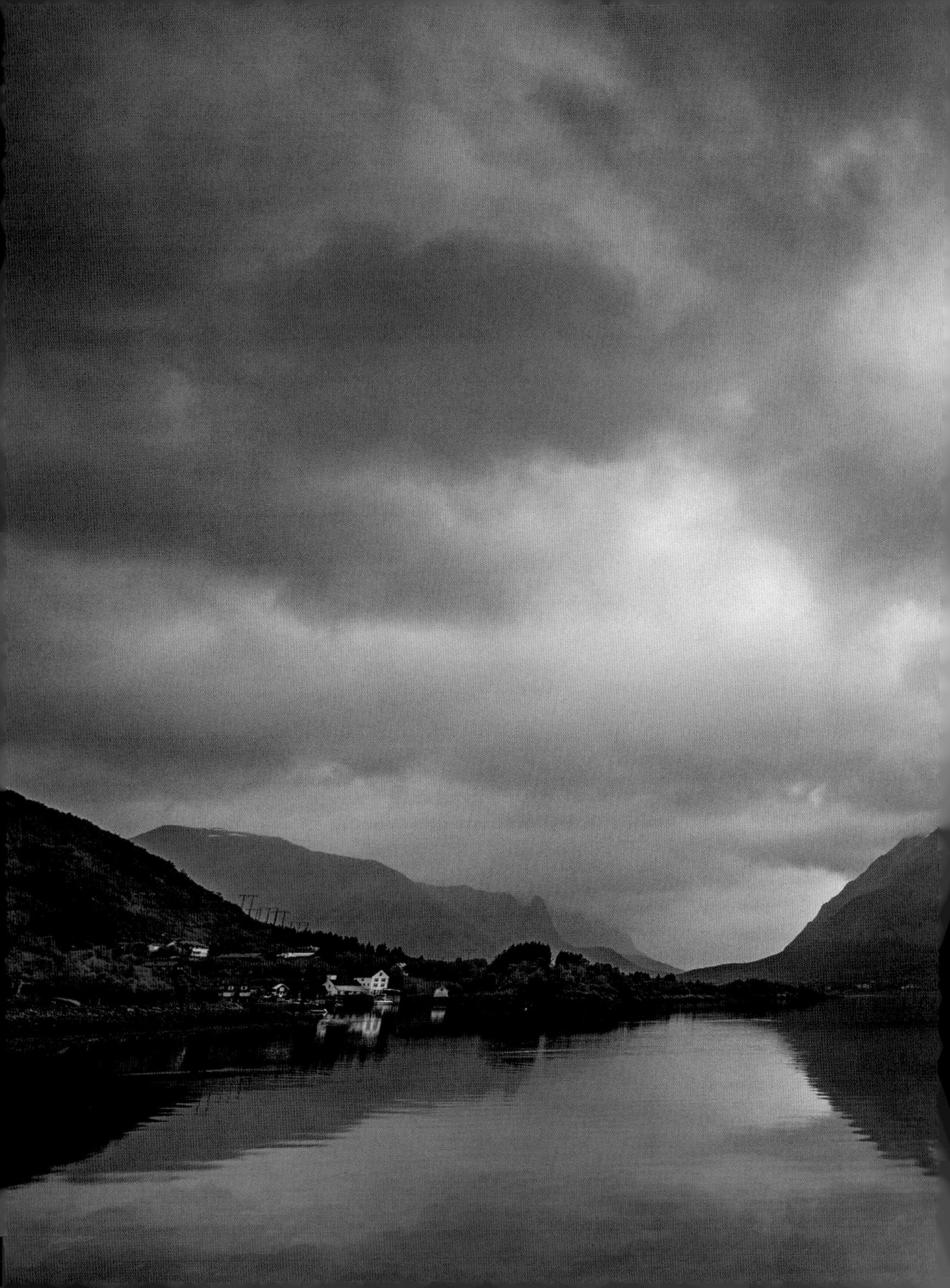

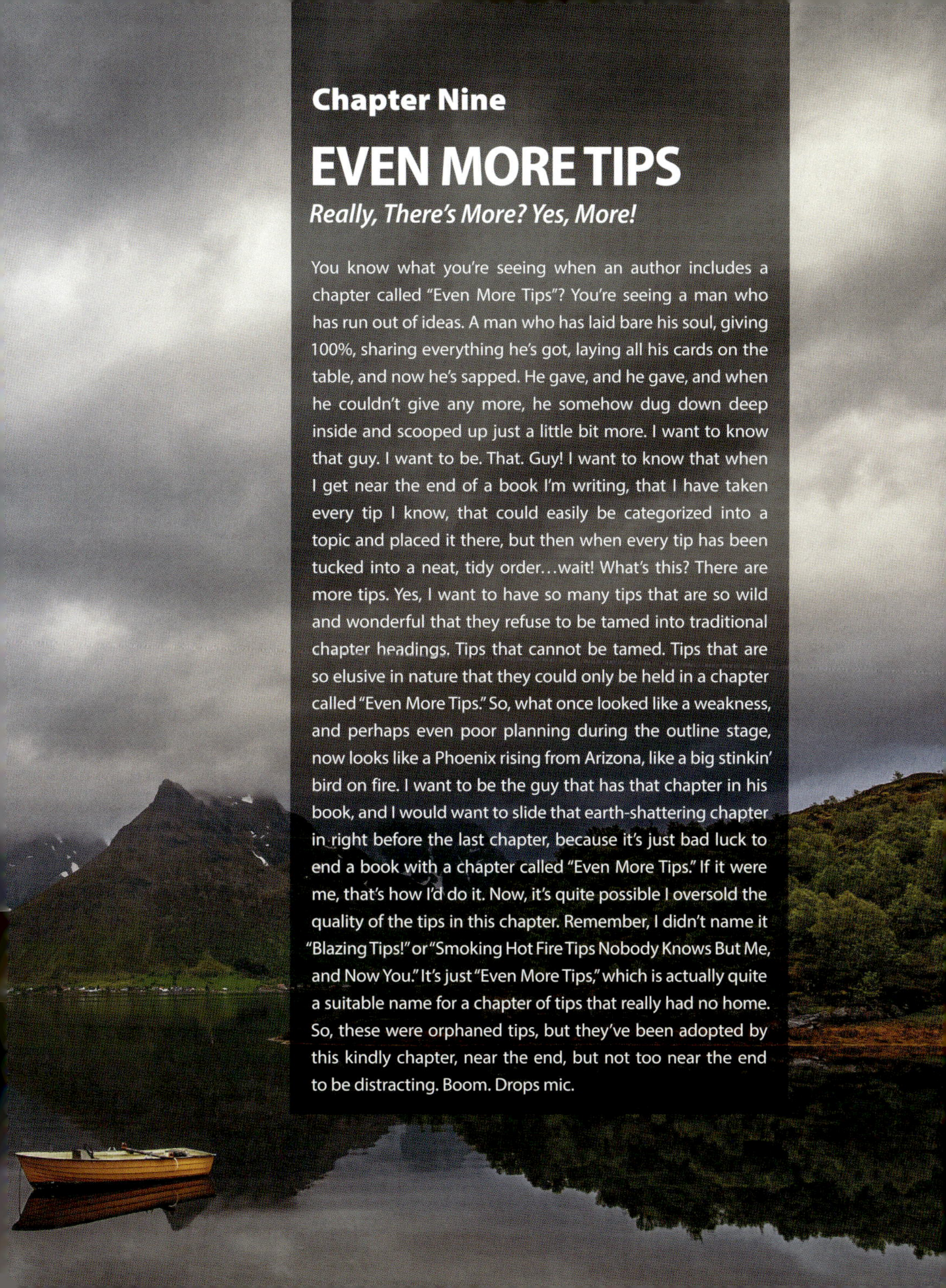

Chapter Nine

EVEN MORE TIPS

Really, There's More? Yes, More!

You know what you're seeing when an author includes a chapter called "Even More Tips"? You're seeing a man who has run out of ideas. A man who has laid bare his soul, giving 100%, sharing everything he's got, laying all his cards on the table, and now he's sapped. He gave, and he gave, and when he couldn't give any more, he somehow dug down deep inside and scooped up just a little bit more. I want to know that guy. I want to be. That. Guy! I want to know that when I get near the end of a book I'm writing, that I have taken every tip I know, that could easily be categorized into a topic and placed it there, but then when every tip has been tucked into a neat, tidy order…wait! What's this? There are more tips. Yes, I want to have so many tips that are so wild and wonderful that they refuse to be tamed into traditional chapter headings. Tips that cannot be tamed. Tips that are so elusive in nature that they could only be held in a chapter called "Even More Tips." So, what once looked like a weakness, and perhaps even poor planning during the outline stage, now looks like a Phoenix rising from Arizona, like a big stinkin' bird on fire. I want to be the guy that has that chapter in his book, and I would want to slide that earth-shattering chapter in right before the last chapter, because it's just bad luck to end a book with a chapter called "Even More Tips." If it were me, that's how I'd do it. Now, it's quite possible I oversold the quality of the tips in this chapter. Remember, I didn't name it "Blazing Tips!" or "Smoking Hot Fire Tips Nobody Knows But Me, and Now You." It's just "Even More Tips," which is actually quite a suitable name for a chapter of tips that really had no home. So, these were orphaned tips, but they've been adopted by this kindly chapter, near the end, but not too near the end to be distracting. Boom. Drops mic.

Rain Gear (and Why You Need It)

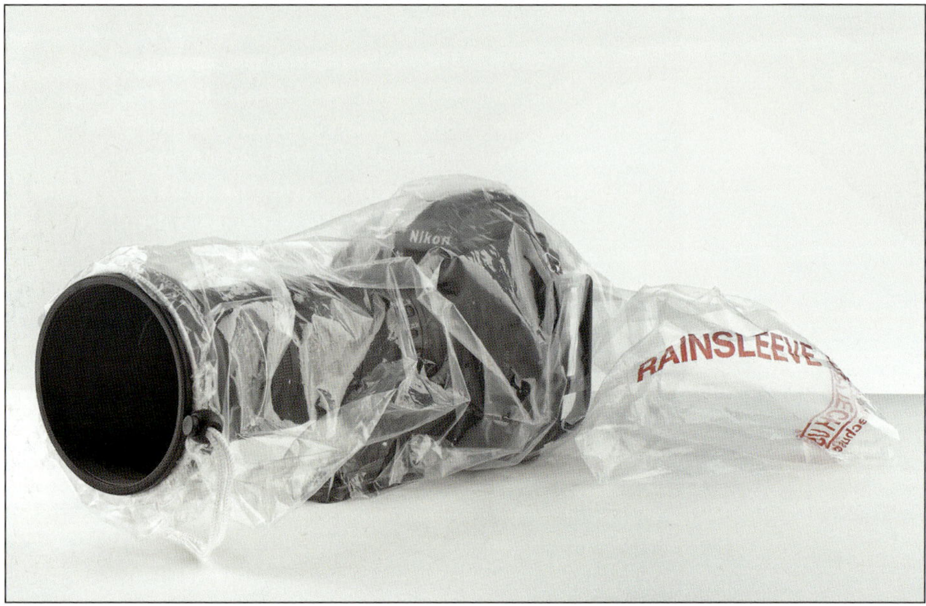

You're shooting outdoors—anything can happen. Especially when you're heading out to a dawn shoot when it's still pitch black outside—that rain can sneak up on ya. So, you're going want to have some rain covers with you, but also for those awesome opportunities right before a rain, or right after, where it might be sprinkling (or about to), but you want to be shooting. They make expensive high-end rain covers, but I think those are more for folks like sports photographers who will be shooting in the pouring rain for hours. Instead, get something small and lightweight that you can keep in your camera bag and pull out whenever you need it (the best rain gear is the one you will actually carry with you). The smallest and least expensive are the OP/Tech Rainsleeves. I think of these as emergency covers, and they kind of look like a plastic bag with a hole at both ends. But, if you get caught out in rain you weren't expecting, at least these will keep your gear dry, so you can shoot for a while longer. They're super-cheap (a set of two is just $7). However, a big step up from those quality-wise are the Think Tank Photo Emergency Rain Covers (don't let the name fool you—these are awesome and not just for emergencies). They fit easily in your camera bag, they're simple to use, quick to deploy, and they're an amazing deal for the money (around $35 at B&H). If you can spring for the $35, they are well worth it.

How to Dry Your Wet Gear

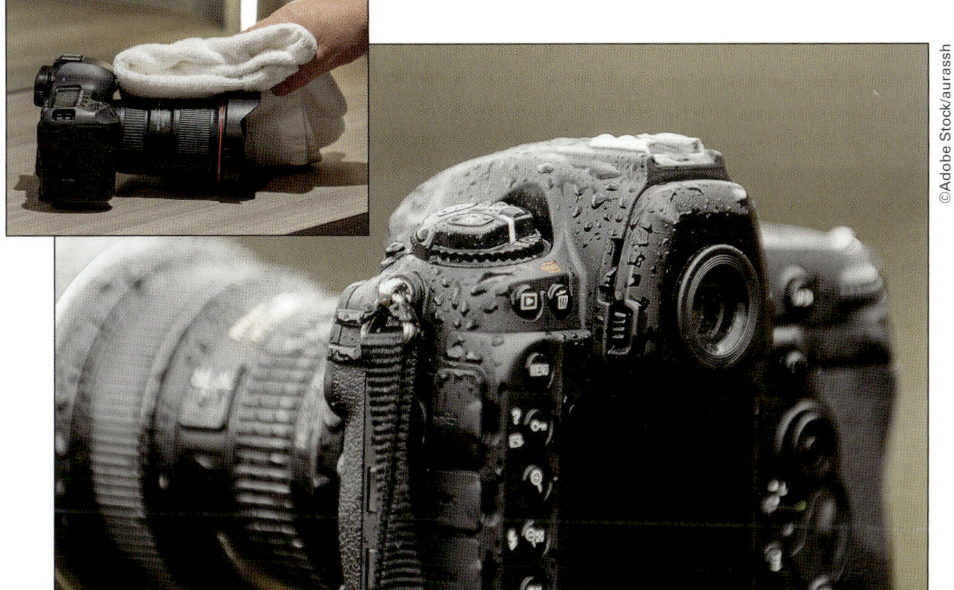

If you get caught out in the rain without rain gear (hey, it happens), you'll want to be able to dry your gear when you get back in your car or back to your hotel. Even if your gear is weather-sealed (many high-end DSLRs are sealed to keep rain out), you don't want to do this wrong and accidentally create a problem during the drying process. Just take a soft towel and pat your gear dry. Don't wipe it—you risk pushing water into your electronics—just pat it down.

Small Ponds or Puddles for Reflections

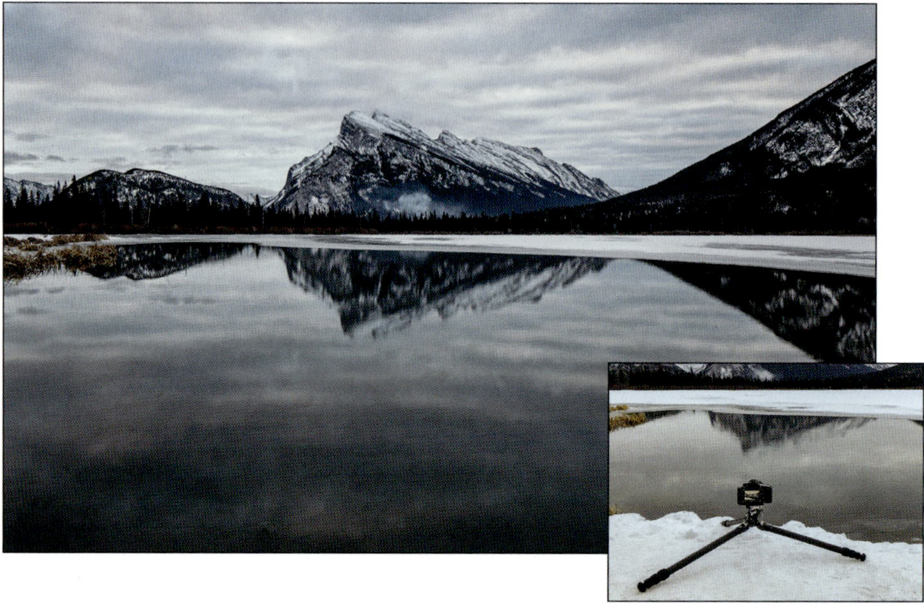

You don't need a big, epic lake to get great reflections—you only need a small pond or even a tiny puddle of water. The trick is to get your camera just a few inches above the puddle, so the reflection in the puddle becomes your entire foreground. This works better than you'd imagine, and you can get that mirror reflection right on the money. Before we dig into how to do this, I recommend doing a quick test with your phone's camera to see how well this is actually going to work. Just set your phone's camera to self-timer mode, press the shutter button, then put it down where it's just a few inches above the puddle, and let it take its shot. If the result looks pretty decent with your phone, imagine how great it will look with your DSLR or mirrorless? If it doesn't look good, at least you know that before you jump through any hoops to get the shot. To get down really low, you're going to need either a Platypod (see page 7), or something small, like a GorillaPod, or you'll need to set up your tripod really low. It's easy to do (with most tripods), but at the same time, it's a bit of a pain because you have to re-move your ballhead, then pull the center column out, and then reinsert it in the center of your tripod upside down from the bottom. Then, you reattach the ballhead to the upside down center column, and then attach your camera to the ballhead (yes, your camera will be upside down now). Lastly, lower your center column to where your up-side down camera is just a few inches above the puddle (see why I use a Platypod for this?). When you open the shot in Lightroom or Photoshop, of course it will be upside down, so you'll need to rotate the image 180° so it's right side up. In short, if you have a tripod with a center column, you've gotta really want that reflection shot.

Cloudy Days—Enjoying Nature's Softbox

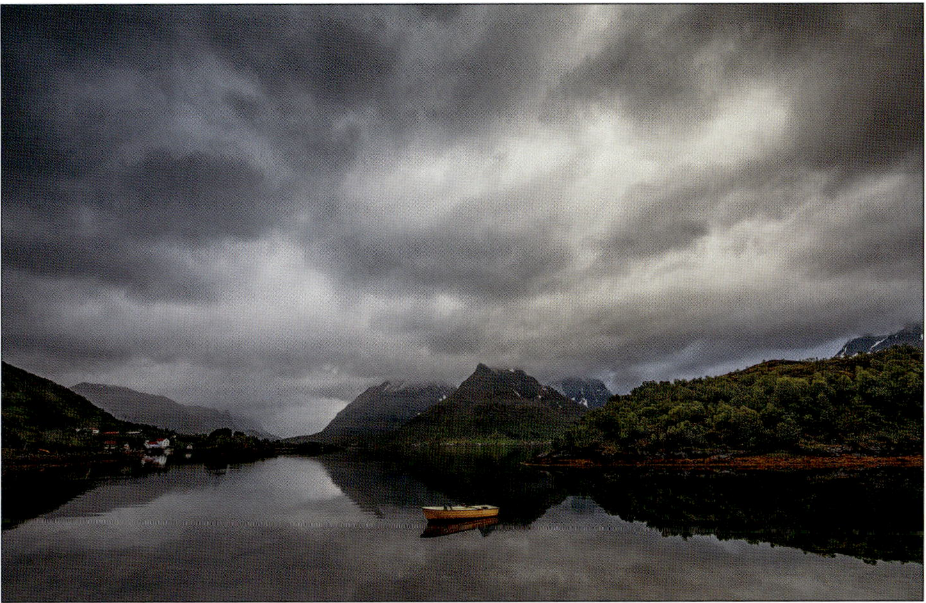

Bright, sunny days create harsh, nasty light, and that's why during the day we use that time for scouting locations, doing our post-processing, napping, shopping— pretty much anything other than shooting, unless (this is a big unless) it's a really cloudy or overcast day. If the sky is covered with clouds, that means the harsh sun is hidden behind those clouds, so the light is softer and more flattering for landscapes. I've heard a cloudy day referred to as "nature's softbox" because it softens and diffuses the light. Cloudy or overcast days are also a great time to shoot things that need a long exposure, like waterfalls and creeks, because some-times you can get away with not using an ND filter—the light is so low, you can just use a really high-numbered f-stop, like f/16 or f/22, for a long exposure that often stays open for a few seconds on a really cloudy day. Just something to keep in mind—clouds are our friends pretty much anytime.

Don't Shoot Black & White In-Camera

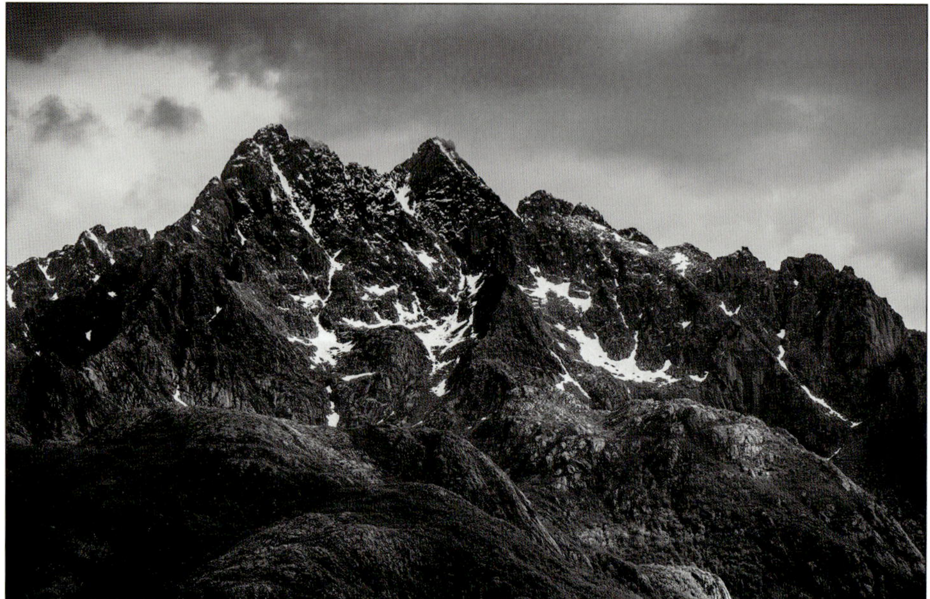

Some cameras have a built-in black-and-white setting, and I'm going to encourage you not to use it because it's going to limit your options later in post-processing. The best way to create a great black-and-white landscape image is to start with a great color landscape image. Having all that color data gives you a lot of things you can do in post-production, by boosting or subtracting various colors (imagine boosting or darkening a grassy field by moving the Greens slider or changing the darkness of the sky by dragging the Blues or Cyans slider). All that goes out the window if you shoot in black and white—you'll just greatly limit your post-processing options without gaining anything other than the ability see a black-and-white on the back of your camera. Keep your options open, and always shoot in color, even and especially when you know you're going to make it a black-and-white image later.

Putting People in Your Landscape

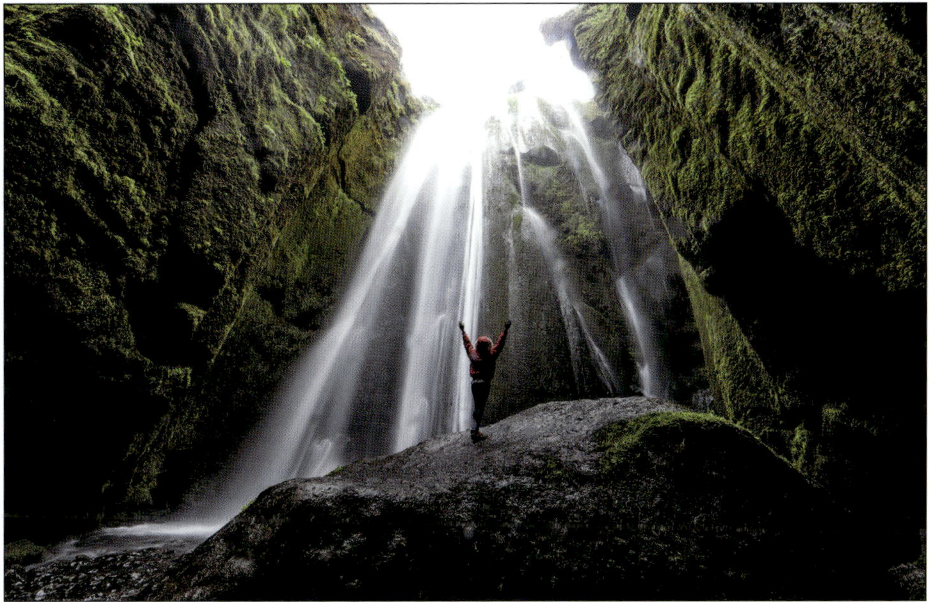

For so many years, "proper" landscape photos never or rarely included a person in the shot, but today it's very common to see a person, or people, in a landscape photo. There are very accomplished and quite popular landscape photographers on Instagram who have made having a person in their shot their "look," and it's becoming more and more popular every day. If done well, it can actually add a lot of visual interest, and a sense of scale, without taking away from the landscape itself. Some examples are a fisherman in a stream, someone walking alone on a beach, a hiker way up in the mountains, or a person in the front of a canoe looking out into a vast lake (or maybe someone standing alone on a dock looking out into a huge lake). It can be as simple as someone sitting cross-legged in the foreground looking out into the scene, or a group of people camping at night with their tents lit, or even a shot of another photographer out there, with their tripod, shooting the scene from a different angle. If you haven't thought of including people in your scene, maybe now is the time to give it a try.

Creating Mystery with Fog and Atmospheric Effects

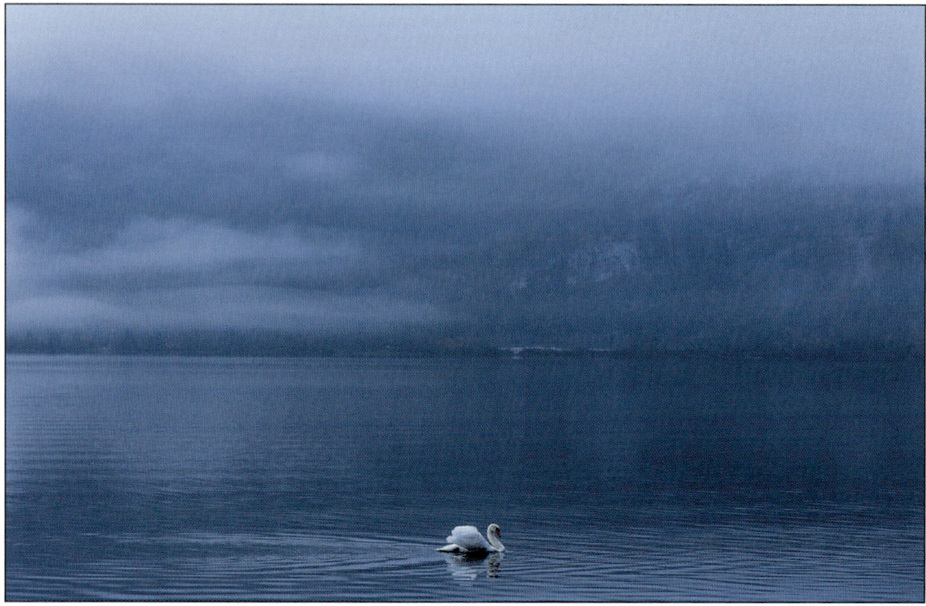

I'm a sucker for fog, and luckily I'm not alone. When I show a landscape photo with some clearly defined low-lying fog, or I'm up high, shooting down into a valley with a line of fog covering the land below, or a misty lake at dawn, it always draws a response from viewers. These atmospheric effects (as long as there's not too much) are real crowd-pleasers because they add drama and mystery to your shots. So, where and when are you most likely to find fog? In valleys or low-lying areas, early in the morning, or on days when the temperature falls below the dew point. It also can't be a windy day—the wind has to be pretty light for the fog to hang around. If it's cloudy the night before, your chances go up. When all those things come together, there's a good chance for fog. Of course, if you do get fog, you have a limited time to shoot it because once the sun comes up, the ground and air start to warm up and the fog burns off (it doesn't really burn off, but it goes away, so…it might as well). Anyway, it's tricky to know exactly when fog will happen (predicting the future is tricky), so your best bet is probably your local weather forecast. If you hear it's going to be a foggy morning the next day, that's not your cue to sleep in— that's your cue to get out there before the fog burns off. Drama and mystery await (and right after that, pancakes, so really, there's just no way to lose here).

De-fogging Your Lens

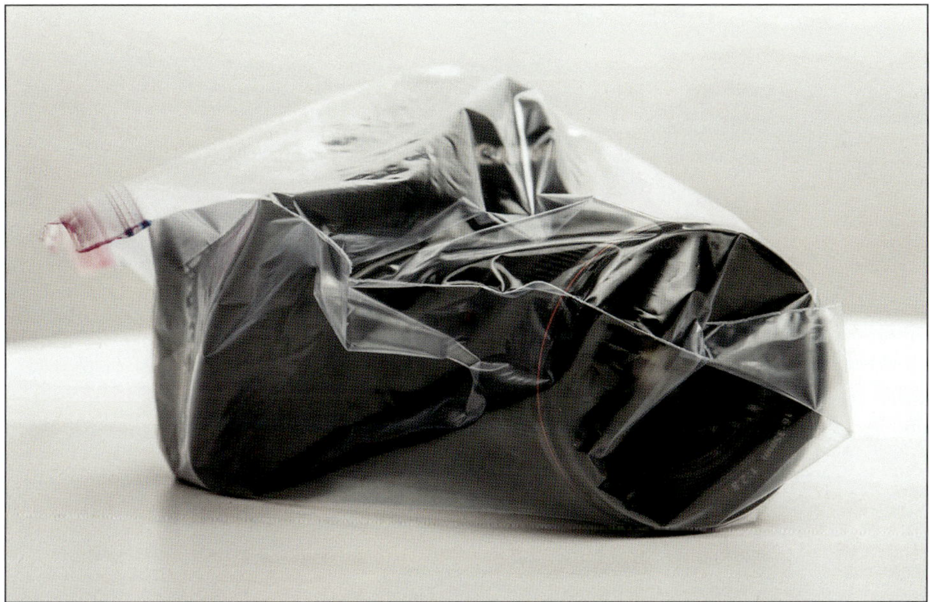

If your gear has been in your nice air-conditioned hotel room, and then goes in your nice air-conditioned car, there's a good chance that when you pull it out at your warm, sunny shooting location, your lens is going to be fogged up with condensation on the outside, or inside, and your shots are going to be just as foggy. It's that rapid change of temperature that causes the problem. This condensation will go away over time as your lens becomes acclimated to the current conditions, but it's going to take time (sometimes as much as 30 minutes). This is another reason why I tell folks to get to their shooting location earlier than they think they need to, especially for a dawn shoot. It's possible you'll need an extra 15 to 30 minutes for your lens to unfog (defog? unfogilate?). First, let's talk about what we can do to minimize our chances of this happening. One popular technique is to put your camera and lens inside a large, sealable plastic bag (like you'd use for storing food—you can find surprisingly large ones online), but before you seal it, try to get as much air out of the bag as possible. Then, put your camera into your camera bag and zip it up tight, which will help warm up your gear a bit. As you get closer to your shooting location, start making the car a bit warmer so your gear can start to acclimate to the warmer temperature. If you take your gear out and there is some condensation on your lens, don't wipe it off. Just let it go away naturally. Don't wipe it with your shirt (always a bad idea) or your microfiber cleaning cloth, or your lens will get smudged and smeared, and you'll just have to clean it all over again in a few seconds anyway. Instead, just "let it be" (sorry, Paul) and give it a few minutes to go away on its own.

The Secret to Getting an Amazing Sky

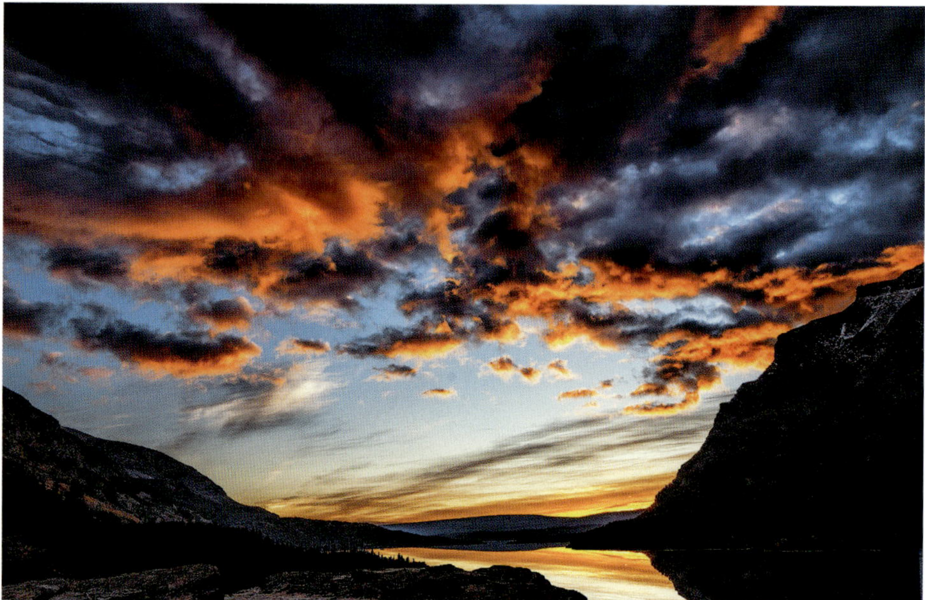

We've all had it happen. You've done everything right. You carefully scouted the location, got up early, got to the location, and you were in place with your gear set up to catch that amazing sunrise. Except, it didn't happen. You were fogged in, or rain clouds covered the sky, or it was a bald, cloudless sky and it wasn't exactly a "sunrise"—it just went from dark to bright. It's a busted shoot, and if it hasn't happened to you yet, it surely will. Nature is just too unpredictable, and the weather report that sounded ideal the night before, turned out to be way off (hey, it's hard predicting the future, even if it's just a few hours away). If it was a killer location, but Mother Nature didn't show up to do her thing, don't scratch it from your list and move on to the next shoot. Come back the next morning and try again, and if you get a bust that day, too, come back again the next day. The photographers who have that type of perseverance are the ones who come back with shots that make other photographers jealous. "Aw, man, you got so lucky! When I was there, the sky was awful!" You didn't get lucky. You just didn't give up. You worked it! You kept going back to that same great location again and again until you were there on the right morning. You mastered one of the hardest parts of landscape photography, and that's waiting for that perfect sky, that perfect morning, where it all just comes together. That's when truly magical landscape photos happen, and when it does, it's just glorious! You're not just getting great pictures, you're seeing God's best work on display. Think of it this way: how many days a month does an amazing sky happen? A handful. If you just go once, what are you chances? Low. Want to double your chances? Go again.

How to Get Detail in the Moon

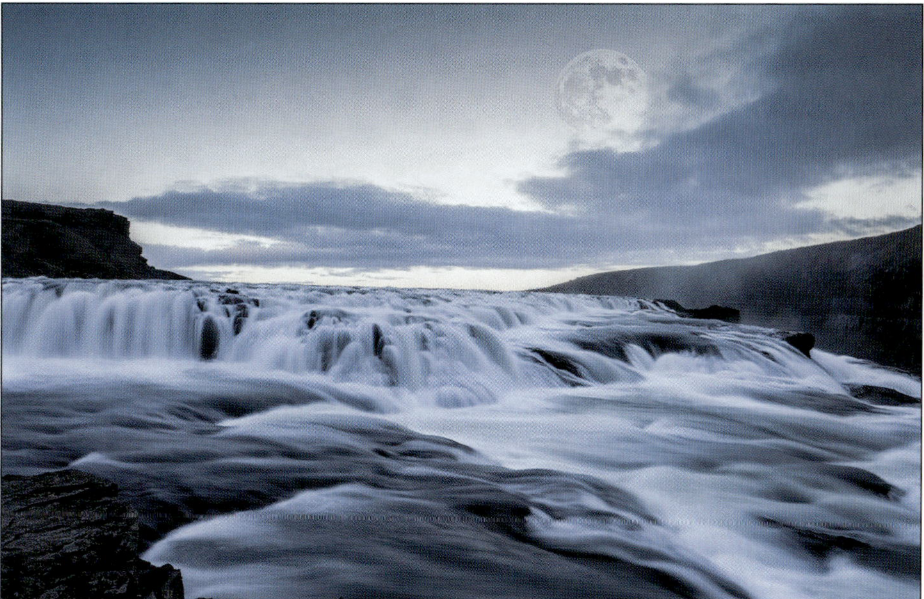

If you have a big, beautiful full moon over your landscape (lucky you), you're probably going to be really disappointed when you open your shot on your computer later only to find out that there's no detail in the moon at all. It's just a big white ball of light, kind of like a darker version of the sun. So how do you get a properly exposed shot of your landscape, and keep the detail in the moon? You take two shots: one exposed for the landscape, and then you change your settings (darkening your exposure by quite a bit) to expose for the moon, and then in Photoshop, in about 30 seconds, you put these two together into one image (it's so easy—see page 175 in the Post-Processing chapter). Now, you could simply try turning on your camera's exposure bracketing feature and set it to take a normal shot, one that's two stops darker (that's the one you'll use for the moon), and one that's two stops brighter (you'll probably throw that one away). But, since you just shot a bracketed exposure, couldn't you just combine them into an HDR to get the best of both worlds? Well, you can try, but I don't think you'll like the results nearly as much as doing the simple technique on page 175.

Longer-Lasting Batteries in Cold Weather

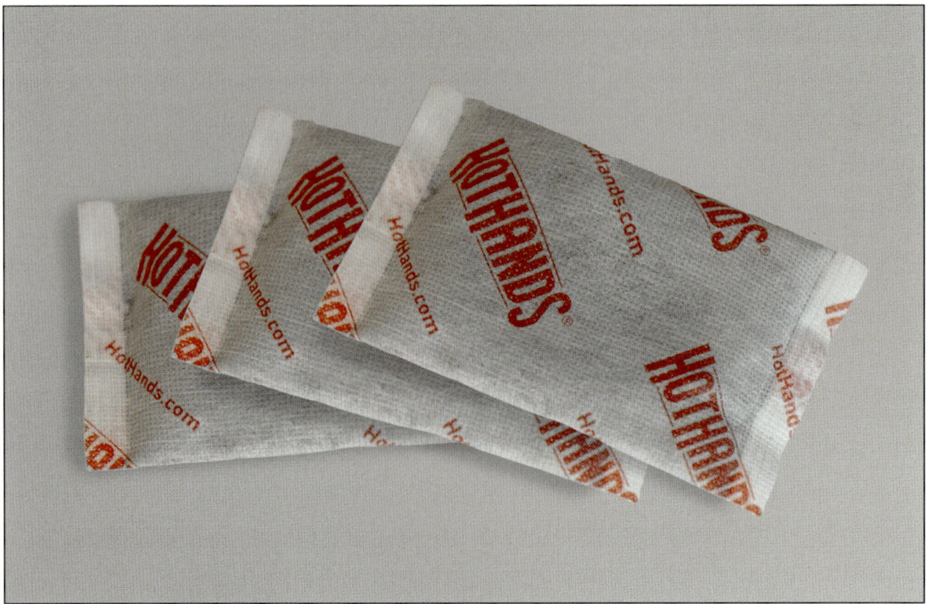

If you're shooting in cold weather, you are going to need lots of extra batteries because for a bunch of boring reasons, camera batteries die fast in the cold. That's why if you want your batteries to last longer when shooting at cold locations, you'll want to toss a hand warmer or two right alongside them. You can get the inexpensive packets or high-tech fancy rechargeable ones, and keep your batteries nice and toasty until you need to use them. It's either that, or tote a whole bunch of batteries out in the cold. Your call.

Creating Beams of Light in Forests

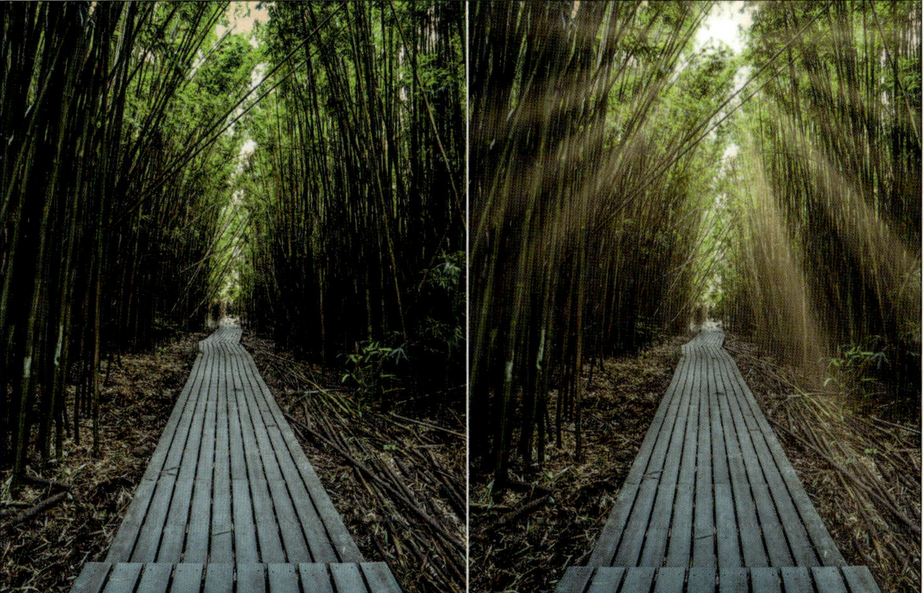

You might get lucky. You might be there, in the forest, on a particular day that's not too foggy, but foggy enough to create amazing beams of light streaming through the trees. Or, you can do what a number of landscape photographers that I know do and that's to add light beams after the fact in Photoshop. Or, easier yet, there's a plug-in for both Photoshop and Lightroom called "Luminar" and their Sun Rays (light beams) feature is pretty darn amazing, very powerful, and super-easy to use. (That's it in use above right.) If you want to do it all in-camera, there are still some tricks. One is to buy a few cans of aerosol spray smoke (the stuff they use on movie sets. It's not cheap, at around $12 a can, but it's easy to use and very portable). Right before you shoot, spray the area where light is coming in, and it creates the beams. It's the same thing when you're shooting in slot canyons. You don't see those light beams whatsoever unless you get another photographer there to toss handfuls of sand up into the air—that's when you see the beams. Otherwise, it's just bright light. If you really want to smoke it up so you get mega-beams, you can buy (or rent) a wireless fog machine (yes, they make those) and take it with you on location to create amazing beams of light on demand. So, you can get lucky, or you can kinda make your own luck (ahem).

Creating Sun Starbursts

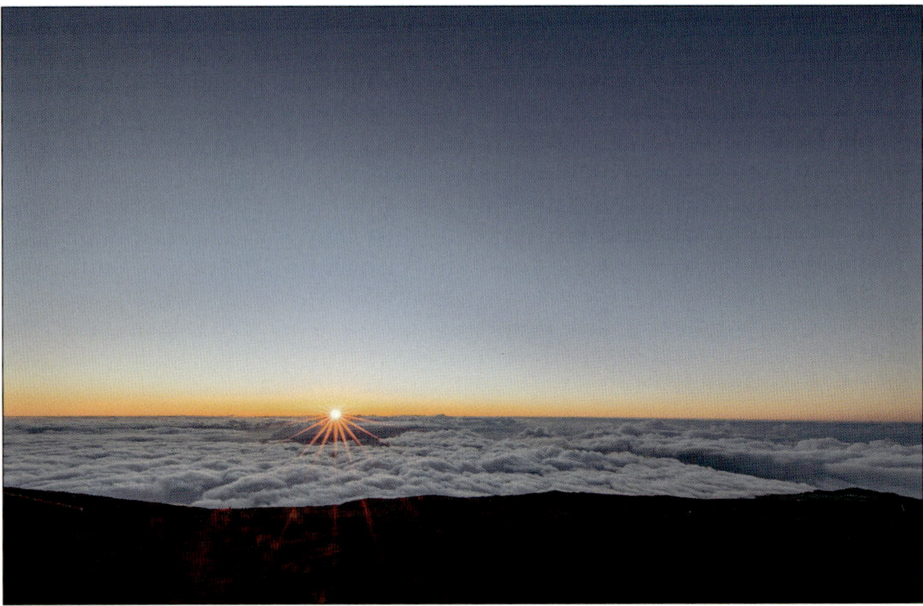

Usually, if the sun is in our shot, it's just a big glowing orb of brightness. But you've also seen shots where the sun is more contained and it has these wonderful well-defined rays coming off it like a starburst. What's the trick to getting those starbursts? It's two things: (1) You need to position the sun, so that it touches the edge of something—the side of a mountain, the edge of a tree, the tip of an arch, it just has to touch something. (2) Shoot the scene at f/22, and that will give you the starburst effect. That's it? Yup, that's it.

Increasing Your Depth of Field Through Focus-Stacking

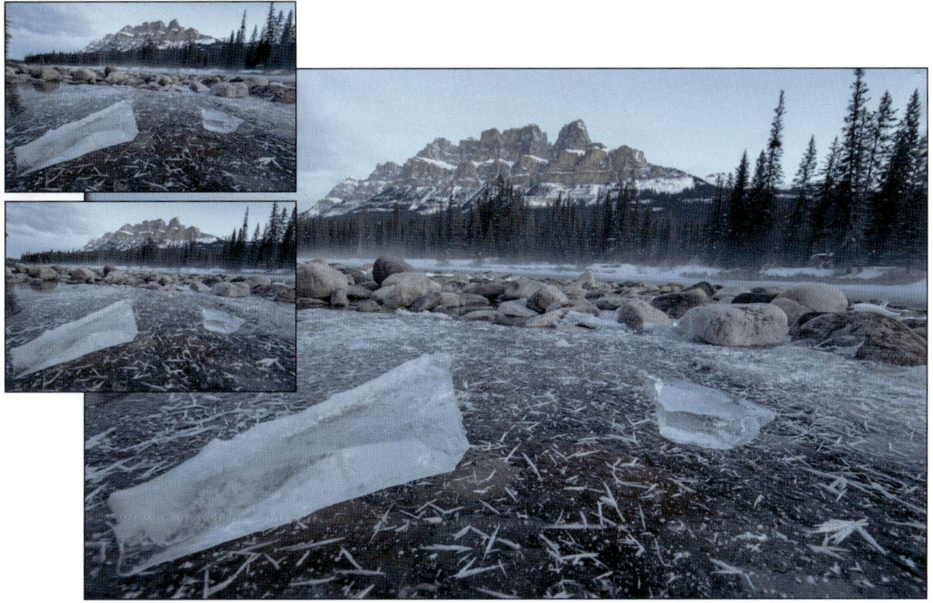

When you're constructing a landscape image with a strong foreground, how do you keep that foreground element (like maybe a rock, or a tree limb, or a wildflower) in sharp focus? Getting the stuff off in the distance, like a mountain or a large rock formation, is easy as it'll be taken care of by using an f-stop like f/11. But, how do you get that rock or wildflower right in front of you as sharp as the objects in the distance? You use what's called "focus stacking" to increase your depth of field. You're going to take multiple shots, focusing on different areas of your landscape, and then you'll combine them all into a single image in Photoshop (sounds complicated, but it's actually simple). First, know that no matter when you're shooting, you'll get the best results if you do this focus stacking technique on a tripod. In the first shot (top left), I started with my focus point on the chunk of ice in the foreground, and you can see the rows of rocks right behind it are soft and out of focus. The second shot (bottom left) is where I moved the focus point over the rocks, and now the chunks of ice up front are soft and out of focus. (Of course, you could continue with this concept and take a shot focused on the tree line, then one on the mountains behind them, too.) The third shot is after I took these two images into Photoshop and applied Auto-Blend Layers. This took the sharp parts from both photos and blended them into a new layer where the ice up front and the rocks are both in sharp focus. Then, I just flattened and saved this new image with expanded depth of field (I show you exactly how to post-process your focus stack back on page 166. It's easy, but I'm just running out of room on this page as you can see).

Avoiding Sensor Dust

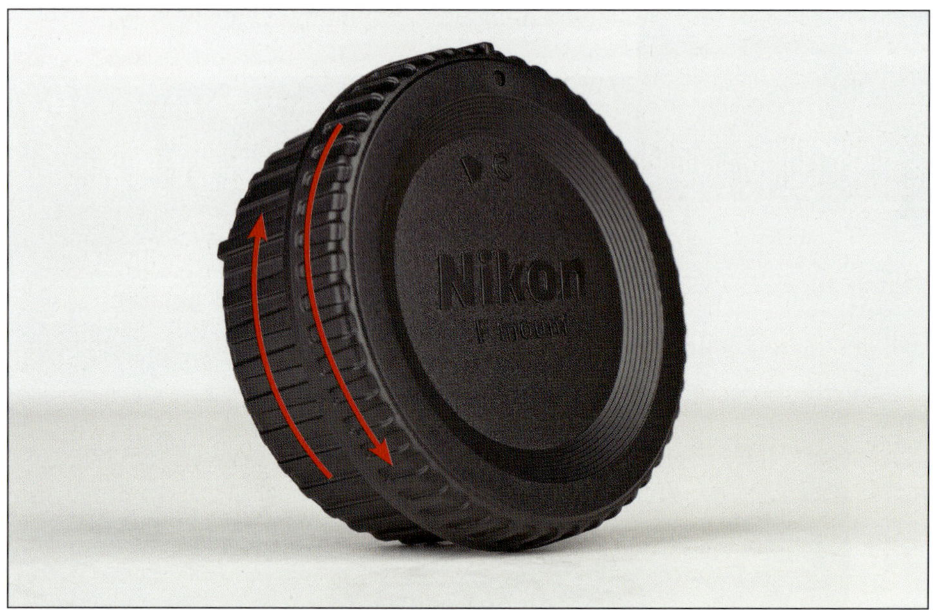

Sensor dust is the worst. What I hate most about it is, if you see it on one of your photos, it's not just on that one photo—it's on all your photos, in the same location on every photo—and its location will be wherever it's really a pain in the b$&# to remove in Photoshop. So, it's best just to try to avoid it altogether. One thing you can do to help prevent sensor dust happens when you first get on location and you're taking your lens out of your camera bag and attaching it to your camera. The five seconds it takes to attach your lens probably won't be when you're going to get dust and gunk in your camera. It's later, at the end of the shoot. Your lens cap and body cap have been sitting in your camera bag or pocket, just collecting junk in them for hours. You're now going to take those dusty caps and put them back on your lens and camera, and whatever has accumulated in them is about to pour into the lens and lens opening on your camera body. That's a recipe for sensor dust. Luckily, the fix is so easy: when you take the lens cap and body cap off your lens and camera, screw them into each other (as seen here). This creates a tight seal between the two and nothing can get in, which means you won't be pouring a bunch of dust and junk into your body or lens.

Changing Lenses On Location

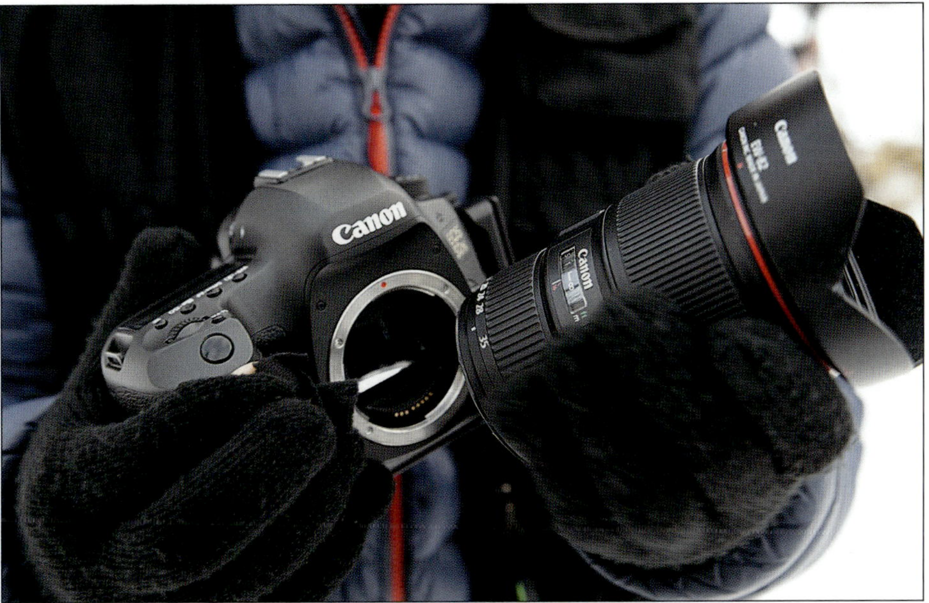

Here are a few tips to help you make the swap safely, without getting junk on your camera's sensor: (1) Turn your camera off before you change lenses. That way, the sensor isn't "charged" and won't be as likely to have dust or junk attach to it. (2) Anytime you're swapping lenses outdoors, to avoid dust falling into your body, do this quickly—the less time with your body cap off, the better. (3) Before you change lenses, take a few seconds to decide if you're in an environment where this makes sense. If it's sprinkling, dusty, or windy, with stuff blowing around, maybe head back to your car or somewhere indoors first. (4) Take the back cap off the lens you're swapping to, so it's ready to attach before you take your current lens off. (5) Turn your camera body downward, so the open hole is facing down when you're changing lenses and there's less chance of anything falling into your body opening (how I have it above is okay, but it's better facing down). Lastly, (6) this is one of those times where you need one more hand—you need one to hold the body, one to hold the lens you're about to attach, and a third to hold the lens you're taking off. Don't be tempted to stick the lens you just took off under your arm—that's a surefire recipe for dropping it. Since we're a hand short, here are a few safe ways to handle the swap: (a) After you remove your current lens, put both caps on, then set this lens somewhere safe for a moment. (b) Put this lens in an empty slot in your camera bag (maybe where the lens you just took out was). Or my favorite, (c) hand it to a friend. That way, they can put the caps on while you're attaching the other lens to your body (they become "the third hand," which would actually make a great name for a horror movie).

Your "Landscape Assistant" Phone App

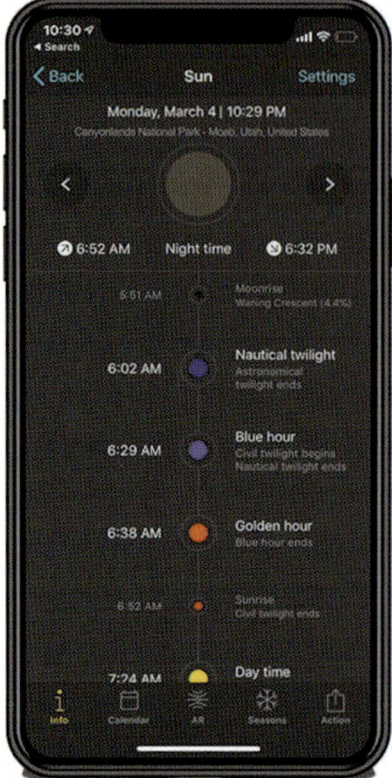
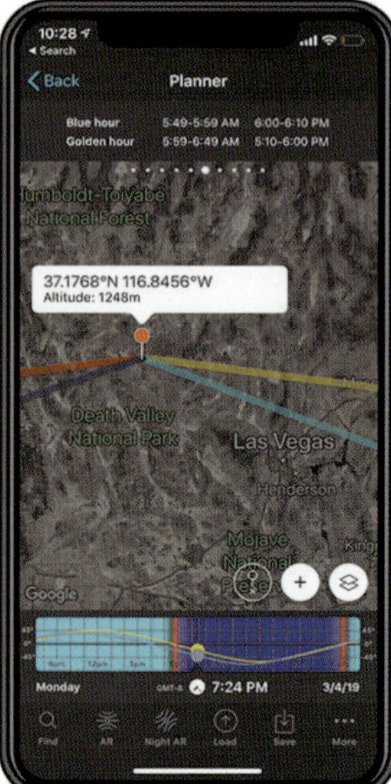
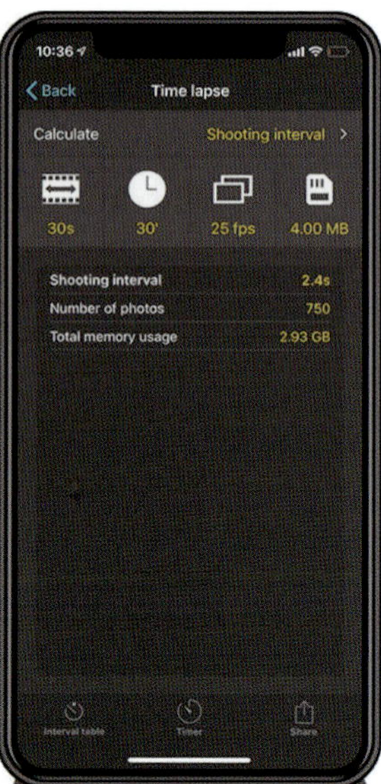

It's called PhotoPills, and it's a really popular app with landscape photographers because it goes way beyond letting you know when and exactly where the sun will rise and set on any given day—it also tells you when blue hour or golden hour will occur, it has a moon phases calendar, plus it has everything from a depth-of-field calculator, to a calculator for determining hyperfocal distance, to long exposure and time lapse calculations. It's an incredibly powerful little app for $9.99 in the App Store or the Google Play store (well, it was $9.99 the last time I checked, but like pricing on everything, it's subject to change). Anyway, if you're looking for a kick-butt, all-around app (did I mention it has 3D augmented reality, so you can hold the app up and see, for example, how the Milky Way would look over the scene you're aiming at. Incredibly helpful for your composition. See page 127 for more on this), spend the $10 and you'll have a landscape shooting assistant with you out in the field (and it doesn't need food or shelter, other than your pocket or purse).

Shooting Time-Lapse Photography

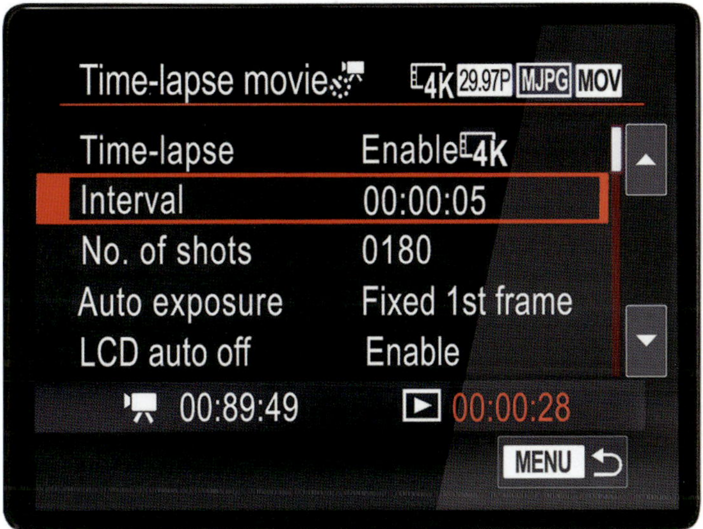

You're up before dawn, or maybe shooting an hour before sunset, and you'll be there for a half hour or more after sunset. Clouds are moving across the sky. You know what would be awesome? If you used your backup camera to shoot a time lapse of your sunrise or sunset. Many of today's cameras have this feature built-in (if they don't, there are shutter releases that have an intervalometer feature, like the Vello ShutterBoss II Timer Remote Switch, which I use). Here's what to do: You don't want any camera movement, so put your camera on a tripod, make sure it has a fresh battery in it, and a memory card with lots of space. Set your camera to aperture priority mode, choose an f/stop, like f/11, so you have nice depth throughout, and use a low ISO, like 100. Get your focus set using auto focus, then on your lens, switch off Auto focus, so it stays in Manual focus mode. Next, in your camera's menu, turn on Time-Lapse Movie (it's really a bunch of stills that, when put together, look like a movie. That's why it's called "time-lapse photography"). Set the interval that you want each image taken, like having it take one shot every 30 seconds, or every 5 seconds (your call). Then, choose how many total shots you want it to take (say you're shooting for 90 minutes, with a shot every 30 seconds. You'd set it at 180 shots). (*Note:* Finding out how many seconds you need between each shot for the scene you're shooting might take a few quick test shots.) Now, press the shutter button (or the start/stop button on your shutter release) to start your time lapse, and it will automatically stop when it reaches 180 shots (or whatever number you chose). I made a short video for you on how you can put your time lapse together in Lightroom (super-easy) that you can find on the book's companion webpage (mentioned in the book's introduction).

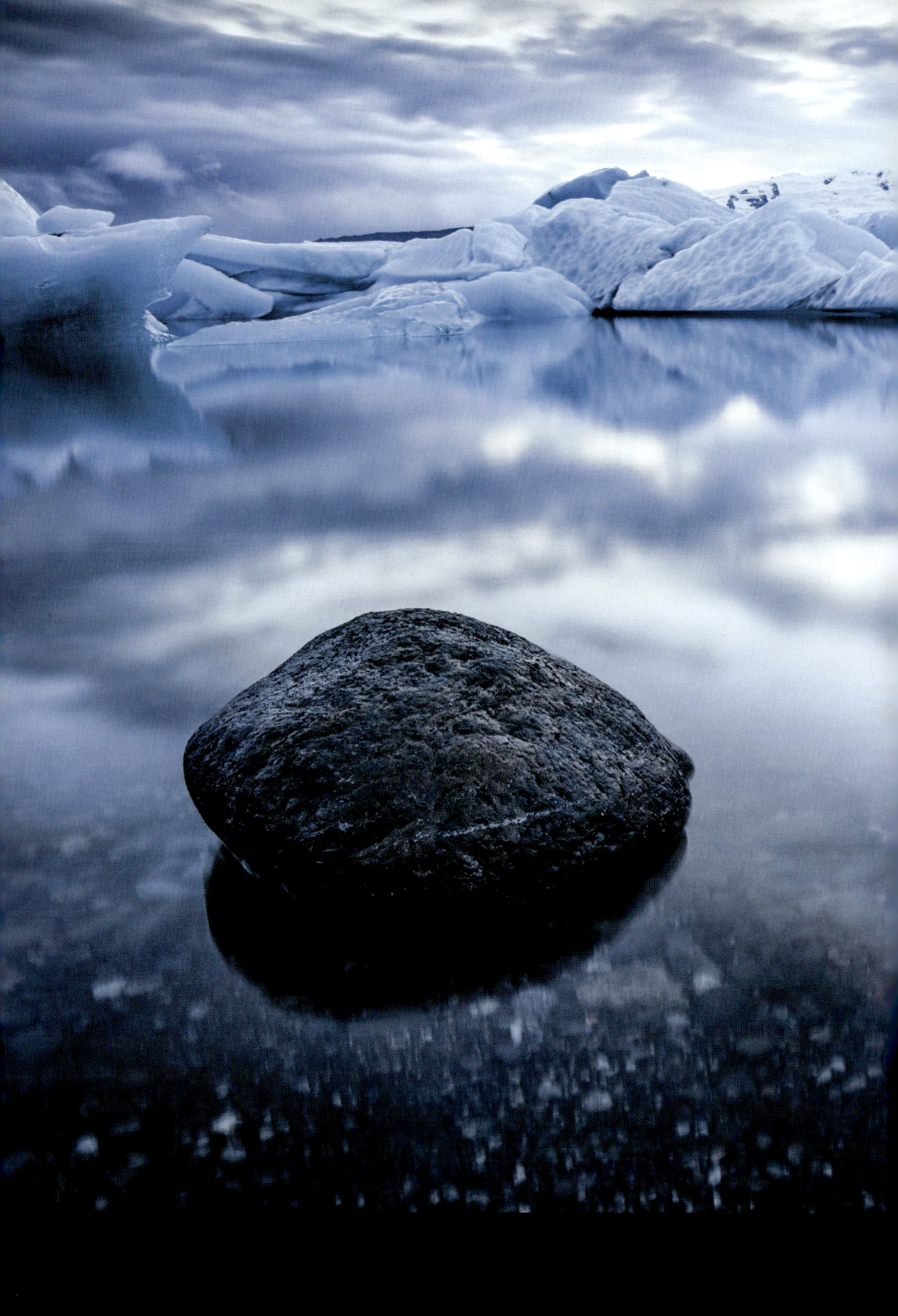

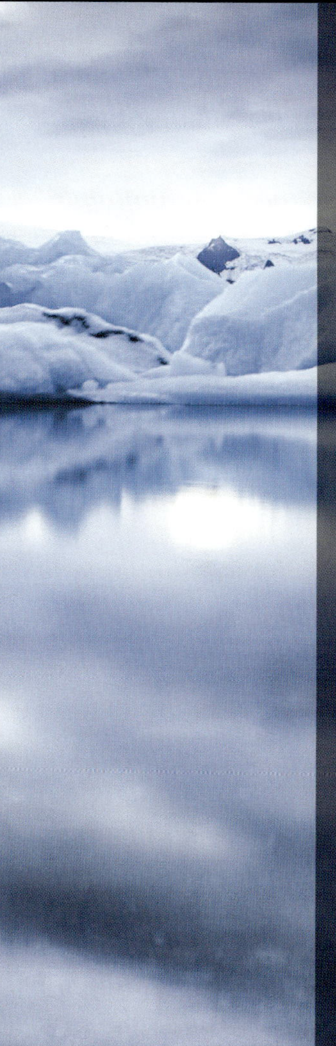

Chapter Ten

LANDSCAPE RECIPES

How to Cook Up Some Tasty Looks

I can't believe that you've come this far. I can't believe that it's Chapter 10, the final chapter in the book, and you've read all the chapter intros. Even the one about shooting the night sky and all—but you don't even care about that stuff, and yet you read the intro page. You know what that tells me? It tells me a lot about you. Five things, actually: (1) It tells me you don't conform to the crowd. You're a rebel. An outsider. I like that about you. (2) You don't bend to peer pressure from other landscape photographers who say things like, "I like the book, but I can't take those silly chapter intros…." Remember, people who call things "silly" are, by and large, not fun to hang out with. (3) You have a highly evolved taste in literature. You knew the meanings of many of the Latin phrases used throughout these intros, and yet you still went on to read my rough translations, many of which are…well…rough. I dig you. (4) You realized, about 2/3 of the way through the seventh chapter intro that these somewhat random, "stream-of-consciousness-style" intros are more than they seem. That there's another layer beneath them, and you peeled back that layer to uncover a spiritual connection between you and I that can never be broken. Very much like the relationship of a tree's root system to the vegetation that surrounds it and thrives because of it. Through these intros we have journeyed to a different place where we understand each other in a way, and on a level, others could not. We have transcended the boundary of what is real and what is an acronym used by General Pershing in the First World War. We have an unbreakable bond. An unspeakable union that dare not speak its name. We are young. Heartache to heartache, we stand. No promises. No demands. Love is a battlefield. And, (5) you're probably an alien and shoplifted this book.

You'll Need These Two for Most of These Recipes

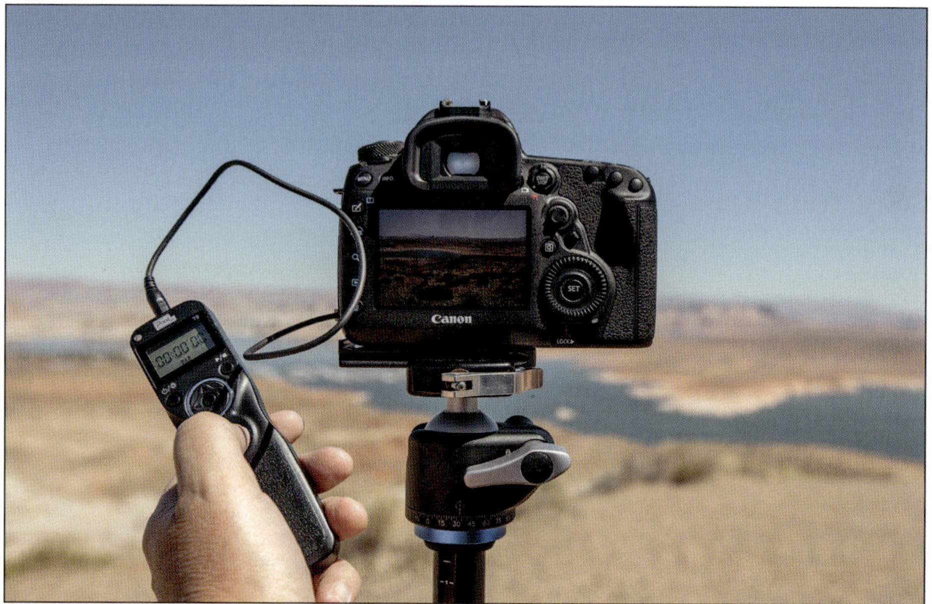

To keep you from having to read this over and over again, for most of the recipes in this chapter: The first step is to put your camera on a tripod and attach a cable release or use a wireless shutter release. I'm just going to write that once, here on this first page, and then it's just implied for the other recipes. Well, quite honestly, I didn't use a tripod for the daylight shot on page 207, or a couple of others I shot in daylight, so it's for *most* of the shots. For those that were taken in broad daylight, I knew I would have a really fast shutter speed with that much light, so I didn't pull out my tripod or Platypod like I did for the rest of the shots. Now, would the shots have been sharper if I had? You bet! Anyway, as you've learned throughout this book, a tripod and cable release for landscape photographers are as important as a stove and some cooking utensils are for a chef. You need both pretty much every time to nail the recipe. From here on out, I'll just give you the type of photo it is, and the recipe to get the look, without going into all that tripod and release stuff, 'cause like a good chef (which is one who cooks lots of comfort food or things smothered in sauce, by the way), you already know that stuff. Alright, preheat the oven, let's get cookin'.

Leading Lines Composition

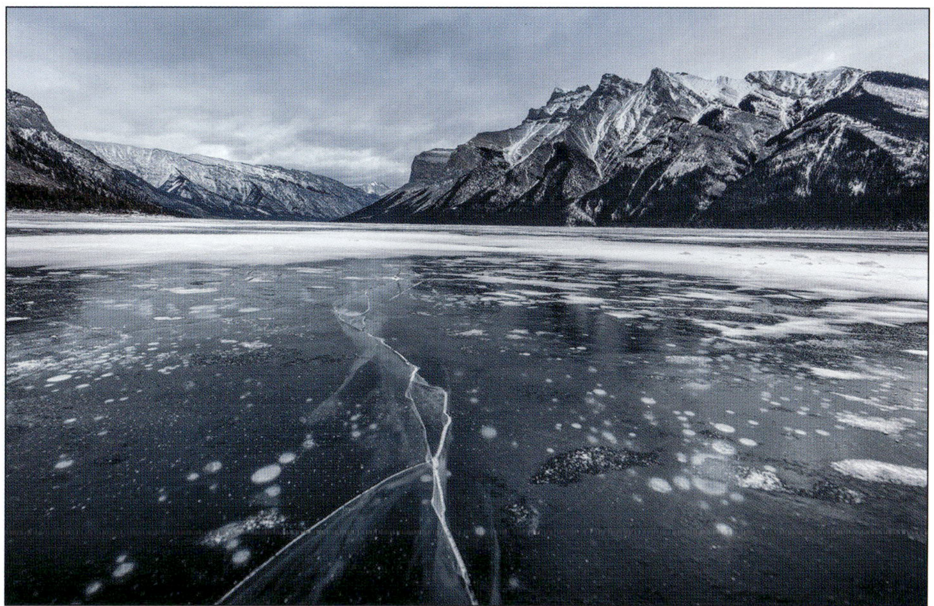

Characteristics of this type of shot: A clear, leading line in the ice leads the viewer's eye into the frame.

Ingredients: The leading lines are what's driving this shot. Finding something in the foreground that leads the viewer's eyes into the frame is what you're looking for. In this example, I walked around the lake looking for cracks in the ice that were aiming at the mountains in the background. I could find cracks leading in every direction out there, but the only ones you care about are the ones aiming in the direction you want to lead the viewer. Once I found that crack, I set my tripod down right behind it, and as low to the ground as possible, to make the most of that leading line. That "getting really low" part made the cracks in the ice much more prominent and made the leading line effect that much stronger. If I had my tripod at eye level, those cracks would be farther away and much more subtle. Also, because I was very low to the ground and had a close foreground element, I was able to use a very-wide-angle lens.

Location: Jasper National Park, Alberta, Canada.

Camera settings: Shot in aperture priority mode; 16–35mm lens at 16mm; ISO 100 at f/11; shutter speed: 1/4 of a second.

Mirror-Like Reflections

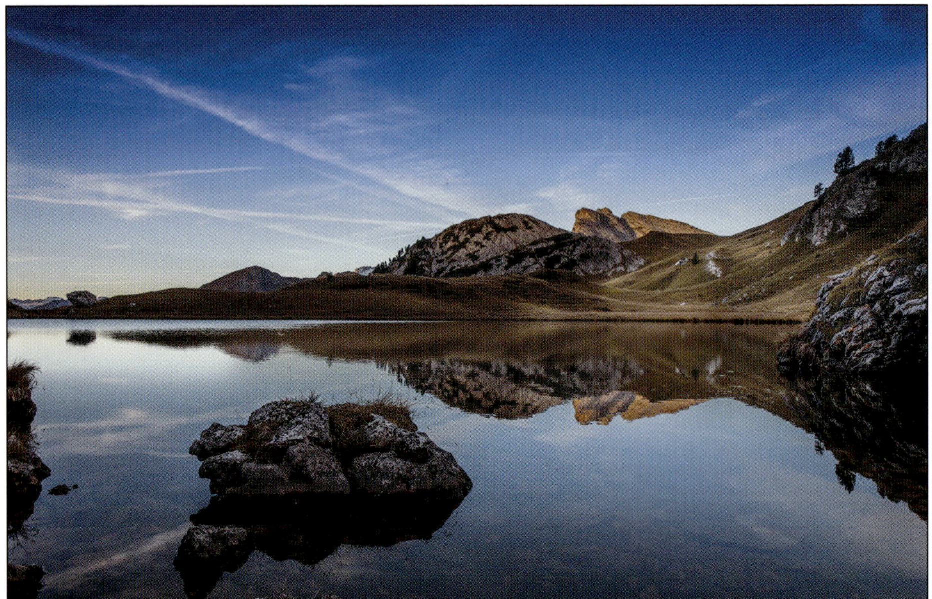

Characteristics of this type of shot: A glassy, mirror-like reflection of the scene.

Ingredients: To get that still, glassy water, you want to shoot first thing in the morning before the winds kick up. In most cases, an hour later and you're too late—the water gets choppy and the reflection mostly goes away. Because the water is still, you can see through to the rocks in the shallow water in the foreground. If you wanted to see more of those rocks underwater, you could put a polarizing filter on your lens, which cuts the reflections big time, but in this case, our goal was to see the reflection. Compositionally, the horizon line appears to be in the center, which is about my least favorite place for it to be, however, this image is cropped for height to fit the book layout—the actual full-size photo is deeper. Also, to get a lower shooting perspective, I lowered the tripod's legs (see Chapter 1 for more on tripods).

Location: Lake Valparola in the Dolomites mountains of northern Italy, on the road between the hamlet of La Villa and Falzarego Pass.

Camera settings: Shot in aperture priority mode; 24–70mm f/2.8 lens at 24mm; ISO 100 at f/8; shutter speed: 1/250 of a second. Why f/8 instead of my go-to aperture of f/11? I probably moved the dial by accident, but it was a lucky accident because f/8 is the next best choice to f/11, so no harm done.

Strong Foreground Elements

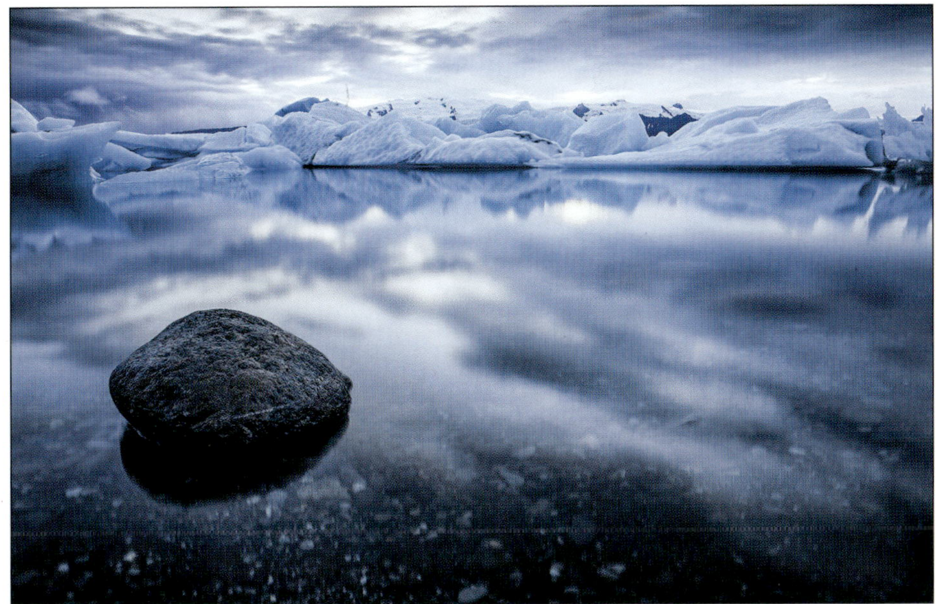

Characteristics of this type of shot: A strong foreground object that draws you into the rest of the image.

Ingredients: The rock in the foreground is there to add dimension and depth, and to lead the viewer's eye into the shot. It's the visual introduction to the shot. I walked along the banks until I could find something to put in the foreground—your eye is immediately drawn to the rock in the foreground—and then I had the lucky occurrence of the reflection in the water creating some leading lines to visually lead you from the rock and shore out to the iceberg. It's almost a big arrow in the water in front of the rock. I lowered the tripod quite a bit for a lower perspective.

Location: Jökulsárlón Glacier Lagoon, in southeastern Iceland about 50 minutes from the town of Höfn.

Camera settings: Shot in aperture priority mode; 24–70mm f/2.8 lens at 24mm; ISO 100 at f/22; shutter speed: 1/30 of a second. Why the f/22 f-stop? It was an experiment. The background is a row of snow-capped mountains and I was okay with trading a little sharpness, and maybe some lens diffraction, to get the foreground and background both in focus. In this case, it didn't really pay off. There's not enough separation between the ice and the mountains to really notice.

Dramatic Skies

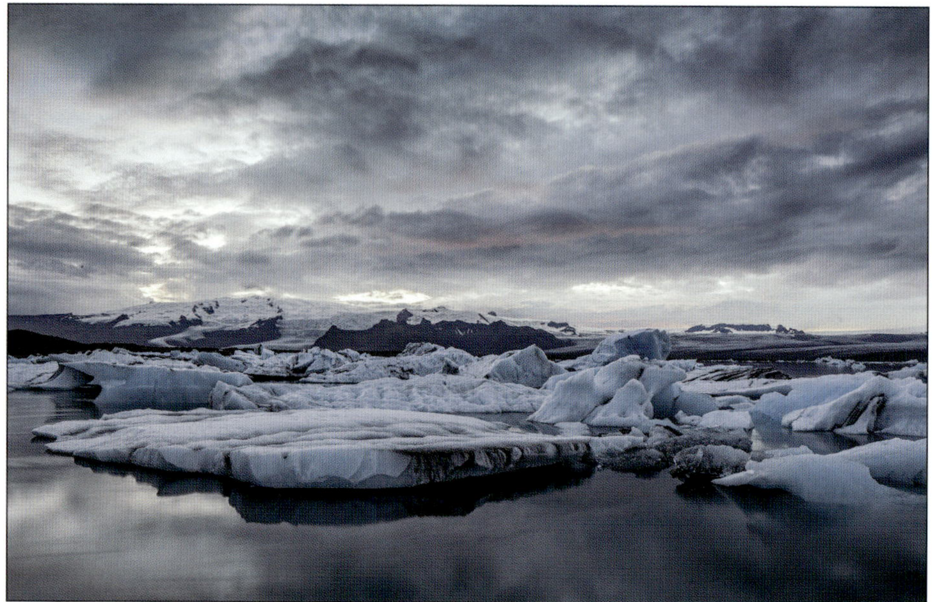

Characteristics of this type of shot: A dark, dramatic, cloudy sky.

Ingredients: You've heard me mention a few times how you can get some great shots right before or right after it rains, and you're seeing that type of sky here—after the storm. It was absolutely pouring rain for hours. Pouring so hard, in fact, that during an early dinner, my buddy and I had decided not to even leave the hotel for a sunset shoot since there would be no sunset. But, when he spotted a small break in the clouds, we took our chances (and a 50-minute drive), knowing that if it cleared even a bit, we'd at least have an interesting sky—and boy did we. It rained all the way to the site and stopped just before we arrived. When you have a great sky like this, you compose the shot to show less foreground and more sky. Shooting after sunset ensures nice, soft light, and the clouds mean you'll probably have a little color. I lowered my tripod and positioned my setup where some of the ice would be right in front of me as my foreground. The still water was a lucky break, but the fact that the rain cleared at all was, too.

Location: Jökulsárlón Glacier Lagoon, in southeastern Iceland about 50 minutes from the town of Höfn.

Camera settings: Shot in aperture priority mode; 24–70mm f/2.8 lens at 24mm; ISO 100 at f/9; shutter speed: 6 seconds.

Mountaintops

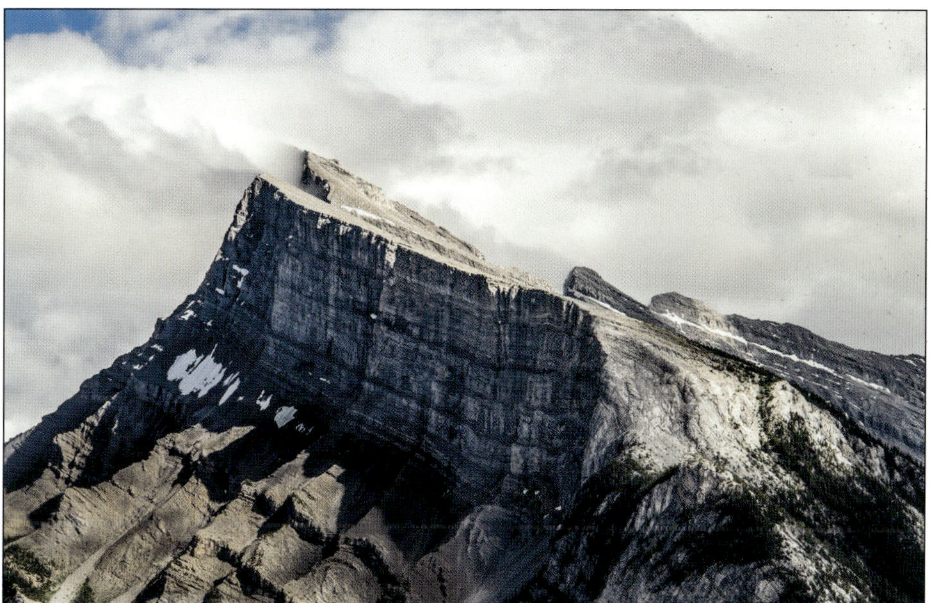

Characteristics of this type of shot: Tight detail of clouds on a mountaintop.

Ingredients: Since mountains are most often shot from the ground looking up, changing your perspective and shooting from up high like this gives people a different view. Then, getting in close like this shows another view they don't usually see, since most shots are taken from ground level, and the tops of the mountains are small and far away. Here, you're bringing them right up close and showing detail that they wouldn't normally see.

Location: Banff, Alberta, Canada.

Camera settings: Shot in aperture priority mode; 28–300mm f/3.5–5.6 lens at 150mm; ISO 200 at f/10; shutter speed: 1/640 of a second.

Waterfalls

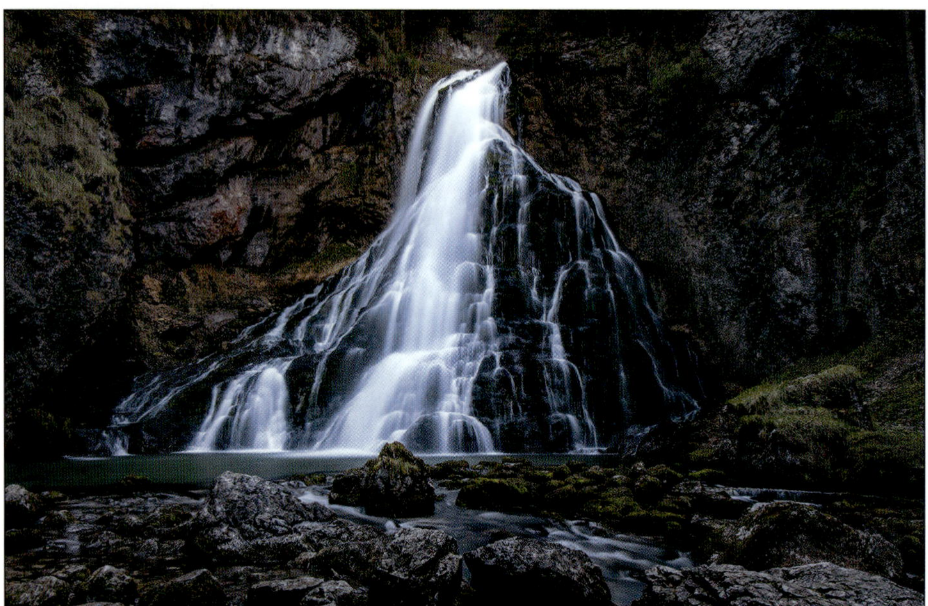

Characteristics of this type of shot: Soft, silky, flowing water of a waterfall.

Ingredients: When you see a waterfall with smooth, silky water shot with daylight, you know an ND filter was used, probably a single 10-stop filter or they stacked multiple ND filters (see Chapter 6 for more on using filters). Right overhead in this shot, it's a bright, sunny, cloudless day, but even if I wanted to show the sky, I would need a wider lens or I'd need to do a multi-level pano to take it all in (see Chapter 5 for more on panos). Here, I'm down low, on top of a rock, using a Platypod tripod replacement with the spikes extended to keep it anchored.

Location: Gollinger Wasserfall in Golling an der Salzach, Austria.

Camera settings: Shot in bulb mode; 24–105mm f/4 lens at 24mm; ISO 100 at f/8; shutter speed: 37 seconds (which is beyond the standard maximum number of seconds for regular modes, which is why I wound up shooting in bulb mode). I used a 10-stop ND filter to keep my shutter open for 37 seconds (which is longer than I probably needed by about 30 seconds). Once I got tired of waiting for 37 seconds for each shot, I switched to a 3-stop filter—that was much quicker, and the water looked just as silky. The length of time you wait for silky water at a waterfall or stream has diminishing returns after about 5 seconds.

Creeks with Silky Water

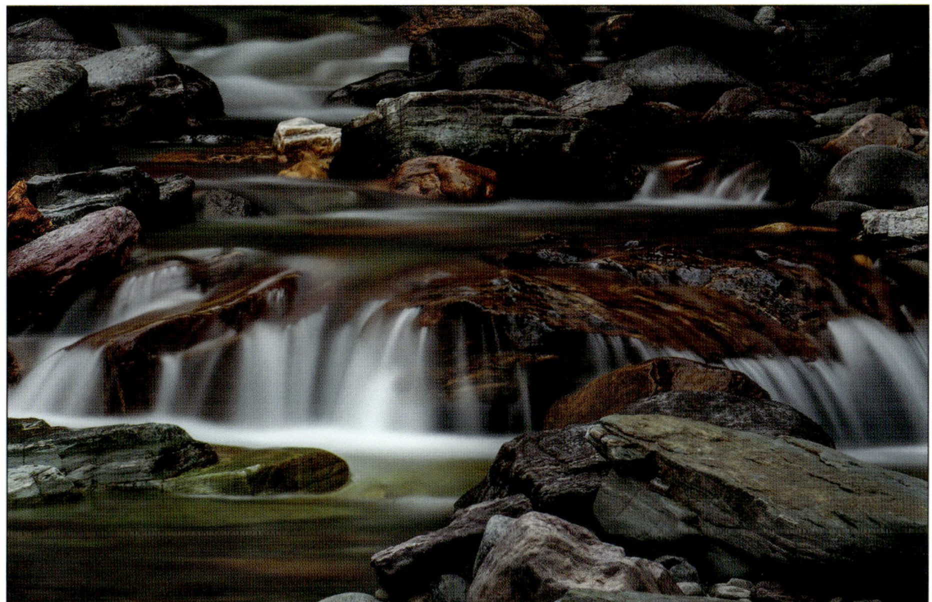

Characteristics of this type of shot: Creek with smooth, silky water.

Ingredients: It's harder to make a solid creek shot than you'd think, mostly because they're so messy. There are often all kinds of sticks and leaves and distracting stuff in the shot, so what I try to do is find an area of the stream where it's as clean as possible, and then I zoom in tight on that area (the scene I'm standing in front of is much larger than you see here—this is one small area). If there's a small stick or two I can remove easily in Photoshop, I'm fine with that, but starting with as clean a scene as possible is key. Also, this is a long exposure and, normally, to get the water this smooth and silky, you'd need an ND filter. But, it had been raining, with a dark gray sky overhead and a lot of tree cover and shade on top of that, so I could just use a high-numbered f-stop like f/22 to make the shutter stay open long enough to get that smooth water effect (in this case, the shutter was open 30 seconds, which is surprisingly long without using an ND filter).

Location: Glacier National Park, Montana, USA.

Camera settings: Shot in aperture priority mode; 70–200mm f/2.8 lens at 200mm; ISO 100 at f/22; shutter speed: 30 seconds.

Oceanside Sunrise

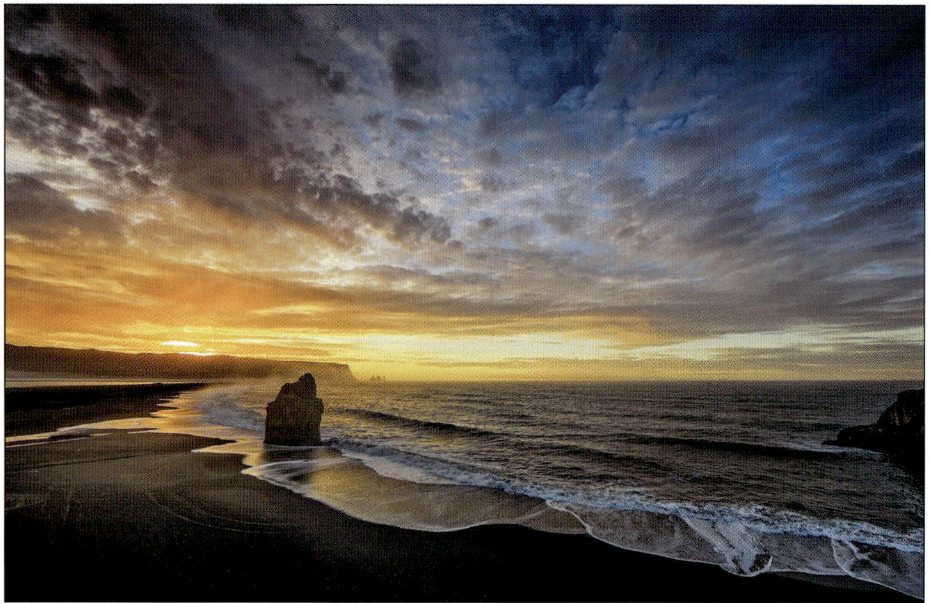

Characteristics of this type of shot: Wide, epic-style sunrise scene.

Ingredients: The biggest part of this shot was luck—being lucky enough to be there one morning when Mother Nature delivered an awesomely cloudy sky to catch all that morning light. Without those clouds (with a bald sky) it would be okay because the light would be soft, but you wouldn't have all that color, and that's what really makes the shot. Taken from an overlook up high, with an ultra-wide-angle lens.

Location: Reynisfjara Black Sand Beach, taken from the overlook at Dyrhólaey near the town of Vík, Iceland.

Camera settings: Shot in aperture priority mode; 14mm f/2.8 lens; ISO 100 at f/11; shutter speed: 1/30 of a second.

Daytime Landscape

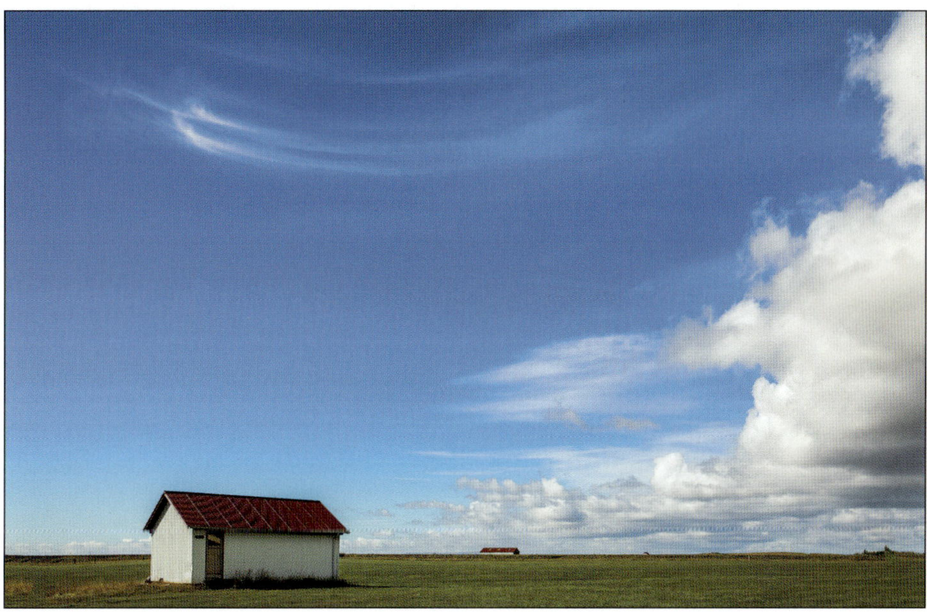

Characteristics of this type of shot: Daytime landscape where the sky is the focus of the shot.

Ingredients: Four things make this simple shot work: (1) It has wonderful balance. The shack on the left, with its strong simple shape and colors, balances wonderfully and diagonally with the clouds in the top right, and that sense of balance really gives the shot its cohesiveness. (2) Outside of the shack, the foreground is otherwise uninteresting. Minimizing the amount of it you see is the way to go compositionally, so the horizon line is very low in the shot, emphasizing the sky and those great clouds (though, the streak of clouds above the shack, to me, is more interesting than the large clouds on the right), and (3) the sheer simplicity of the shot makes it compelling. Lastly, (4) while we are shooting in direct sun, the light and shadows aren't harsh. In fact, you don't really see shadows at all—just on one side of the shack. It's hard to come by direct light that's not harsh and nasty, but this particular scene hid the harshness, which was a lucky bonus.

Location: Southern Iceland on the road between Gullfoss waterfall and Reykjavik.

Camera settings: Shot in aperture priority mode; handheld; 24–70mm f/2.8 lens at 30mm; ISO 100 at f/8; shutter speed: 1/800 of a second.

Long Exposure Water

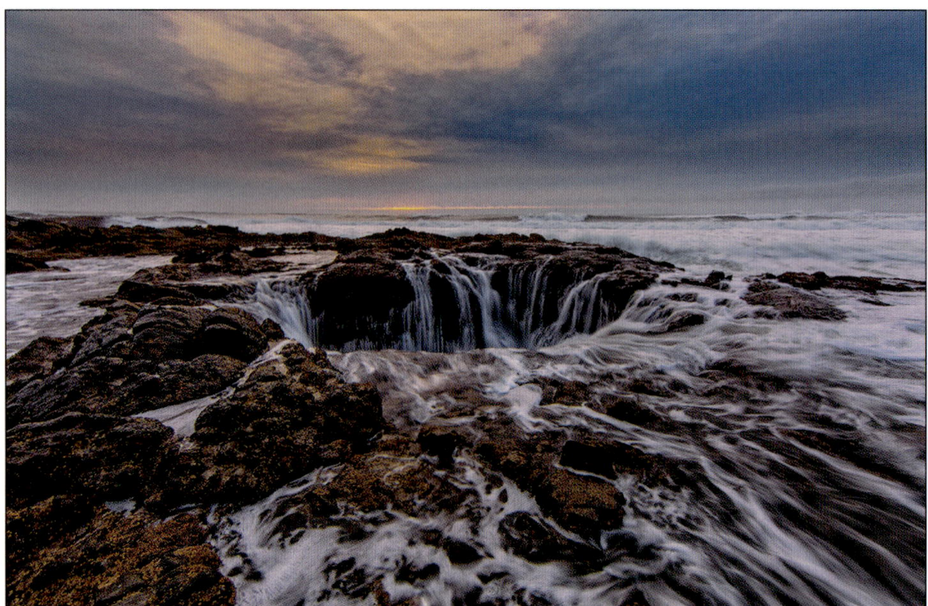

Characteristics of this type of shot: A sunset shot with smooth, silky water.

Ingredients: There's a lot of standing and waiting involved, and that's really all there is to a shot like this—waiting around until enough water reaches the hole so your long exposure of the water looks decent. The day I was there, I couldn't do a long enough exposure to get the seawater outside the well to be super silky—the water would rush in and right back out too quickly. So, the main ingredient, here, is patience. Unfortunately, there was a thick marine layer of hazy clouds, so the sun didn't so much "set" as it just kind of went away, leaving me with a not-so-awesome sky, so I concentrated on the composition of the well itself (note the high horizon line, which limits how much sky you see). I used the rocks in front of me as a foreground to draw the eye to the well. I'm standing on the rocks and my tripod legs are in the water. It wasn't long before a wave came up and totally drenched me and my gear. *Note:* This shot, and the one on the facing page, were both shot at the same location.

Location: Thor's Well, Yachats, Oregon, USA.

Camera settings: Shot in aperture priority mode; 14mm f/2.8 lens; ISO 100 at f/20; shutter speed: 1/4 of a second. I didn't have an ND filter with me, so I used f/20 to keep the shutter open longer. I could have gone to f/22 to keep it open a little longer, but the water was gone so fast it wouldn't have made much of a difference.

HDR Landscape

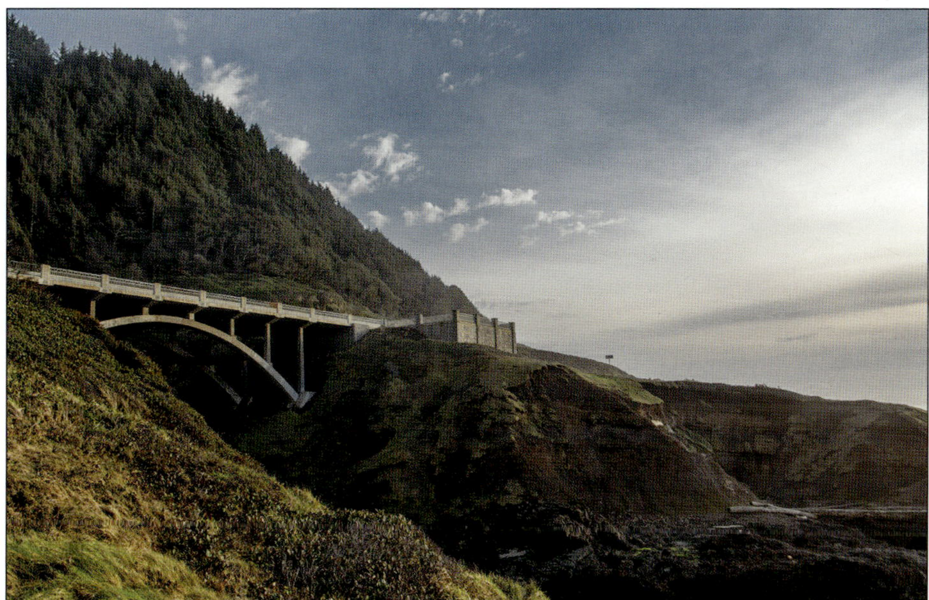

Characteristics of this type of shot: Added depth in shadow areas without noise.

Ingredients: When you combine bracketed photos into a single HDR image in Lightroom or Camera Raw, one of the biggest advantages (besides extra tonal range) is that you can open the shadow areas up much more than you normally would without introducing a bunch of noise (like under the bridge and in the rocks) and because of the expanded total range, you can push things a bit more when you edit the photo, and that gives the image a "look." This shot is taken from the same exact location as the shot on the previous page—Thor's Well. I just turned around and saw this scene when looking back to the road, so I took the shot.

Location: Thor's Well, Yachats, Oregon, USA, looking back toward Spouting Horn and the Oregon Coast Highway.

Camera settings: Shot in aperture priority mode; 28–300mm f/3.5–5.6 lens at 28mm; ISO 100 at f/6.3; shutter speed: 1/160 of a second. Why f/6.3? I clearly wasn't paying attention—ideally, I should have shot it at f/11.

Mountainscape with Layers

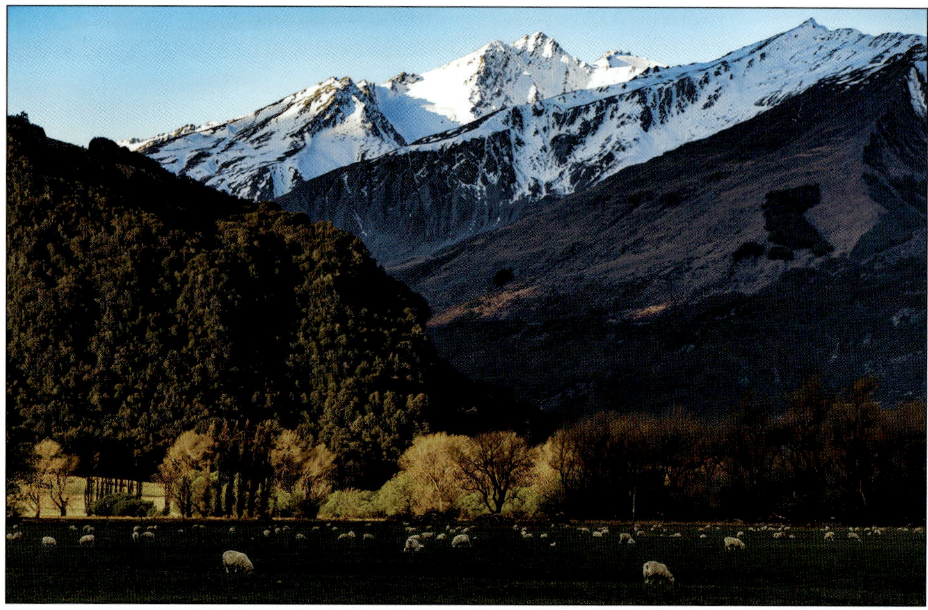

Characteristics of this type of shot: A mountain landscape with lots of depth.

Ingredients: There are two main compositional things going on here: (1) There was not a cloud in the sky, and in situations like this, we try to show as little of the boring thing (the sky) as possible. So, take a look at my composition. I framed the shot to show just enough sky to give a little bit of background for the mountains to sit in front of. (2) The other thing is creating that foreground-to-background depth. The foreground element is the sheep in the field, and then you have lots of interesting layers from there, with the tree line behind them, then a tree-covered hill, then some darker mountains to the right of those, then behind them, some snow-covered mountains, and finally the sky. Lots of depth and layers going on here, and luckily, all the colors work so nicely together (I'm totally cool with getting lucky at a shoot).

Location: On the road between Queenstown and Auckland, New Zealand.

Camera settings: Shot in aperture priority mode; 70–200mm f/2.8 lens at 145mm; ISO 200 at f/6.3; shutter speed: 1/125 of a second. Why f/6.3 and ISO 200? This was a handheld shot. We were driving, and I had my camera in hand. We pulled over and I hopped out for a sec to take the shot. At a higher f-stop, my shutter speed would have been too slow for me to hand-hold and get a sharp shot, which is also why I raised the ISO to 200—to help me get up to 1/125 of a second. The 145mm length was to get past the fence along the highway.

Simplicity

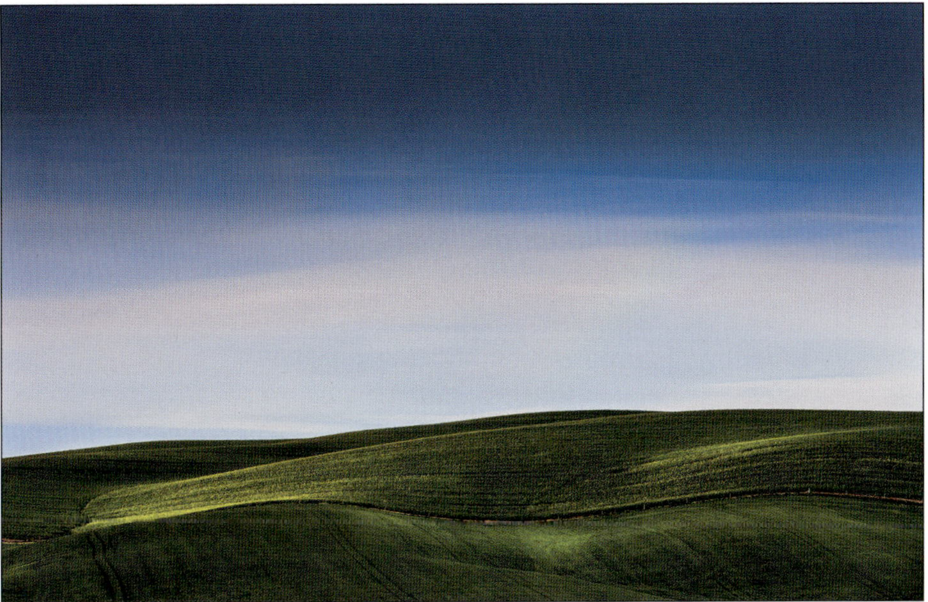

Characteristics of this type of shot: A clean, simple shot kissed by little pools of light.

Ingredients: My favorite landscape shots are usually the simplest ones—with very little going on in the shot—and this is a great example of that. I saw little spots of light hitting the top of these small hills, so we pulled the car over for me to get a shot of them. The sky had a nice gradation of color and was pretty enough that I let a lot of it show, and positioned the horizon line at the bottom 1/3 of the shot. That negative space from the sky leads your eye directly to the smooth, rolling shapes of the hills. In post-production, I painted over the light pools on the hills with Lightroom's Adjustment Brush set to +0.50 (half a stop) Exposure to bring them out even more. The great light comes from shooting late in the day (about an hour or so before sunset).

Location: On the road between Queenstown and Auckland, New Zealand.

Camera settings: Shot in aperture priority mode; 70–200mm f/2.8 lens at 168mm; ISO 400 at f/10; shutter speed: 1/640 of a second. I was hand-holding this shot, so I raised the ISO up high enough to let me shoot at a higher-numbered f-stop like f/10 to get everything in focus. The ISO was overkill—I didn't need to go nearly that high and, in fact, I'm not sure I really needed to raise it at all. I could have lowered the ISO to 200 easily, then lowered my f-stop to f/8 (you wouldn't really see a difference in sharpness between f/8 and f/10), and I would have gotten a cleaner shot (noise-wise).

Panoramic Images

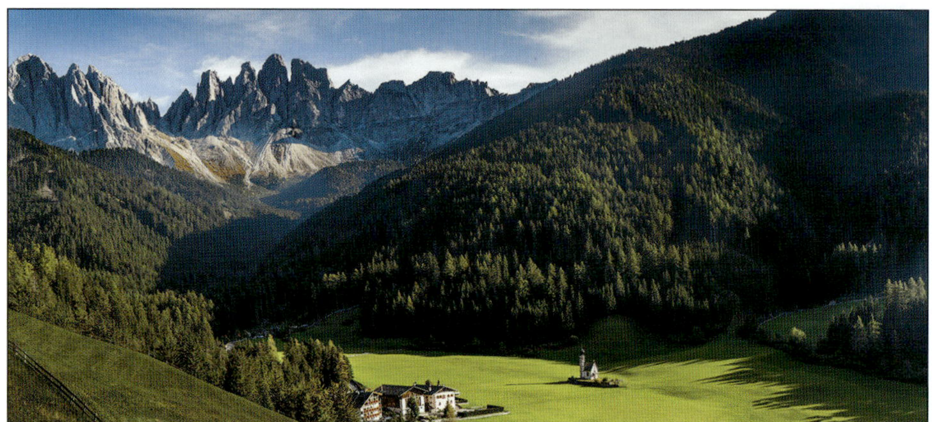

Characteristics of this type of shot: Panoramic image without tight cropping.

Ingredients: This shot is multiple frames combined into a single panoramic image in Lightroom, shot from up on a hill overlooking the scene. I shot the image at 70mm to limit the distortion you'd get from using a wider-angle lens, and I shot it with the camera vertical for the same reason—to limit distortion—but also to make sure I captured enough that I wouldn't have to crop off much of the foreground or the tops of the mountains. By shooting tall like that, I had extra room if I had to crop away gaps that happen during the stitching process. However, when the image was in Lightroom, I used the Boundary Warp feature to keep as much of the original image as possible (see Chapter 5 for more on panos).

Location: Val di Funes in the Dolomites mountains of northern Italy.

Camera Settings: Shot in aperture priority mode; 70–200mm f/2.8 lens at 70mm; ISO 100 at f/7.1; shutter speed: 1/250 of a second.

Low-Angle Wide

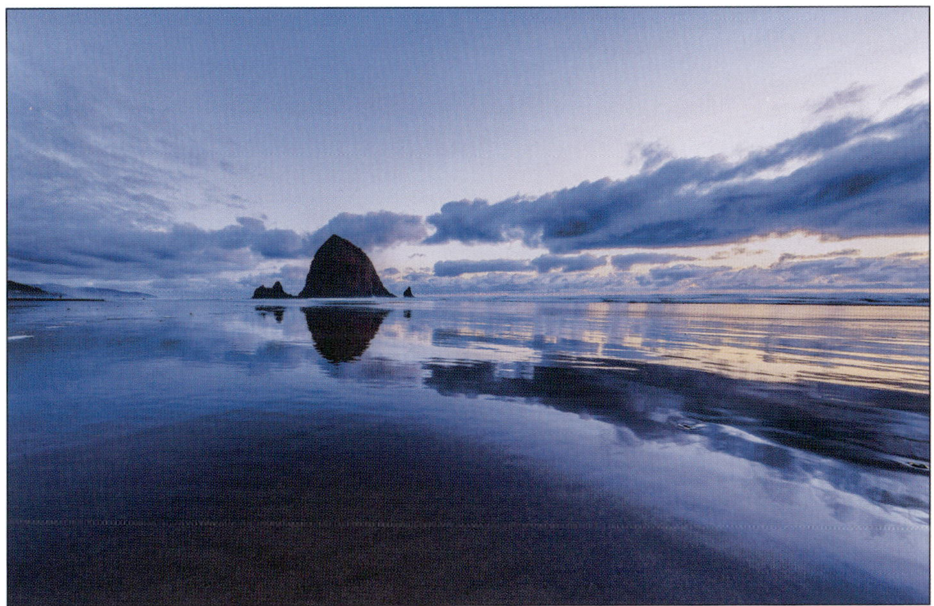

Characteristics of this type of shot: A sweeping oceanscape sunset with reflections, great color, and great clouds.

Ingredients: Shooting in beautiful light at sunset sets the stage. The reflections from the water on the beach are more visible, clear, and obvious by putting the tripod low to the ground. It didn't look like glass when we were standing there, but that low perspective really brought it out (I lowered all three legs all the way on my tripod. I did, though, have to pick it up and run from an unexpected wave from time to time). A super-wide-angle lens pushes the scene away from you and outward, and while it does move objects back away from you, it also creates the wide, sweeping "epicness" of the shot. The clouds really helped hold the color, and while the color was fairly nice in person, I tweaked the white balance using the Temp and Tint sliders in Lightroom (they're also in Camera Raw) to get the color you see here (those sliders are where I go to when I want to create an artistic white balance, rather than an accurate one. See Chapter 8 for more on creative white balance).

Location: Cannon Beach, Oregon, USA.

Camera Settings: Shot in aperture priority mode; 11–24mm f/2.8 super-wide-angle lens at 11mm; ISO 100 at f/11; shutter speed: 1.3 seconds.

Atmospheric Effects

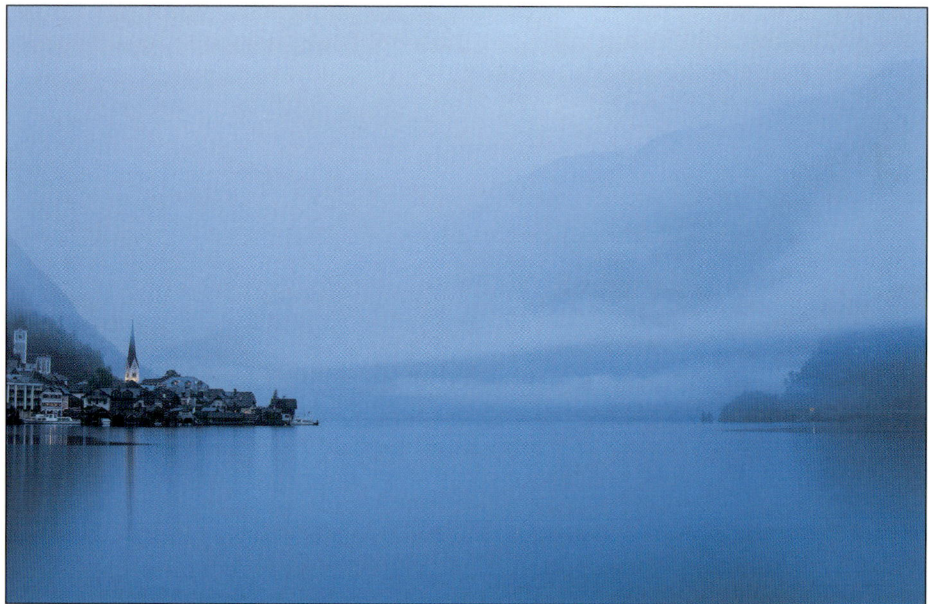

Characteristics of this type of shot: Low-lying fog adds a sense of mystery to the scene.

Ingredients: I have a number of shots of this exact same scene, taken at different times of day, but this shot, with the fog, is hands-down my favorite. Atmospheric effects like low-lying fog add a sense of mystery to your shot, but they also add a sense of calm, taking the harsh edge off the shot, and I love that. Plus, having layers of fogs helps as well, like we have here where you see very, well-defined low-lying clouds of fog just above the lake, but then you have another layer of fog mostly obscuring the mountain behind it. The best time to catch fog like this is in the early morning—in this case, before dawn (to learn when fog it most likely to occur, see Chapter 9). So, get up earlier than usual because as soon as the sun rises, that fog will start to burn off.

Location: Hallstatt, Austria.

Camera settings: Shot in aperture priority mode; 24–70mm f/2.8 lens at 24mm; ISO 100 at f/11; shutter speed: 1/60 of a second.

Canyon Slots

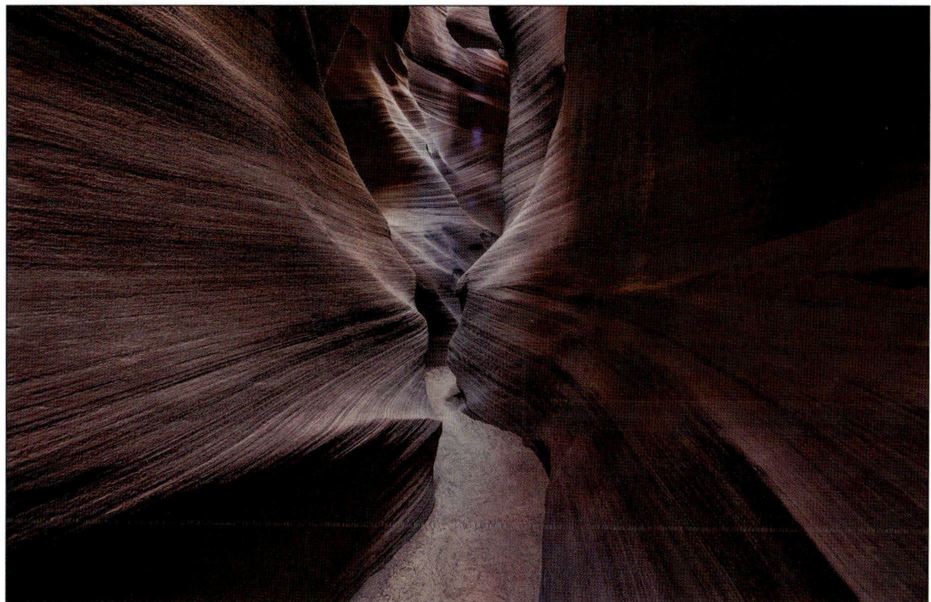

Characteristics of this type of shot: Smooth, colorful walls with interesting light and lots of sharp detail.

Location: Just outside Page, Arizona, USA. These are not the famous Upper and Lower Antelope Canyon slots, which are overrun by hundreds of tourists each day (whose main goal it seems is to walk in front of your long exposure). This is the much less traveled, more photographer-friendly Horseshoe Bend Slot Canyon (a.k.a. "Secret Slots").

Camera settings: Shot in aperture priority mode; 14mm f/2.8 lens; ISO 100 at f/10; shutter speed: 3.2 seconds.

Notes: After shooting the slots a number of times, the biggest composition tip I can give you is to try to include the ground in your shots. Otherwise, the viewer isn't sure what they're looking at, and it starts to look like a desktop pattern for your computer screen. The biggest challenge when shooting slot canyons out in Arizona is everybody wants to shoot slot canyons out in Arizona. Like I mentioned, there are so many photographers shooting all at once in the two best-known canyons that it's sometimes hard to find a spot to shoot, and people keep walking into your long exposure shot and bumping into you and your gear. Also, it's very dusty/sandy and photographers toss sand into the air to catch any visible light beams, so it's smart to put your camera in a rain sleeve to keep dust out of your electronics.

O

P

web resources
    500px.com, 48
    Google Images and Maps, 49
    Pinterest, 47
wet gear drying technique, 179
white balance
    adjusting, 143, 148–149
    camera setting for, 36
    creative use of, 149
    presets for, 83, 148
White Balance Selector tool, 148
white point, 150, 159
Whites slider, 143, 150
wide orientation
    composing landscapes in, 61
    low-angle shots with, 213
    shooting panos in, 87
wide-angle lenses, 42–43
    choosing for landscapes, 42
    night sky photography and, 135
    panos vs. shots taken with, 83
    ultra-wide-angle, 43, 135
window reflections, 13
windy conditions, 2–5
wireless remote, 9, 104

Z

zooming LCD screens, 37, 38

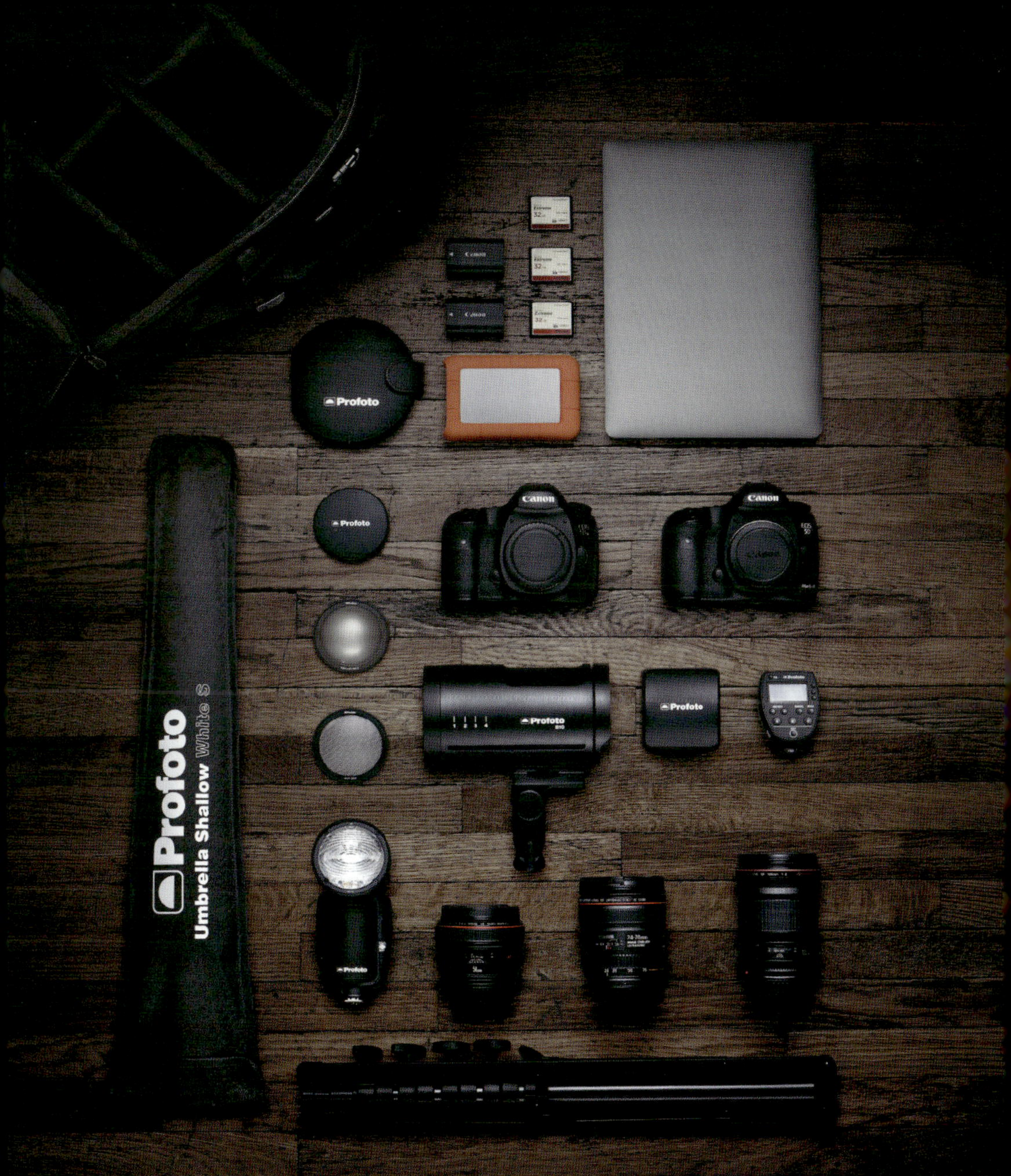

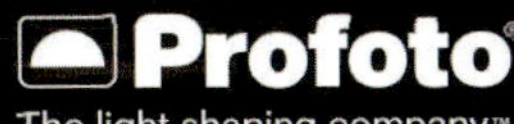

The power of small
Profoto B10

Can you spot our new light? It's in the middle just below the first
camera. So yes, the Profoto B10 is small, yet it's more powerful
than five speedlights and compatible with more than 120 light
shaping tools - so it delivers beautiful light. This is small without
compromise; and on-location - size matters.

Discover the B10 at profoto.com

Profoto®

The light shaping company™

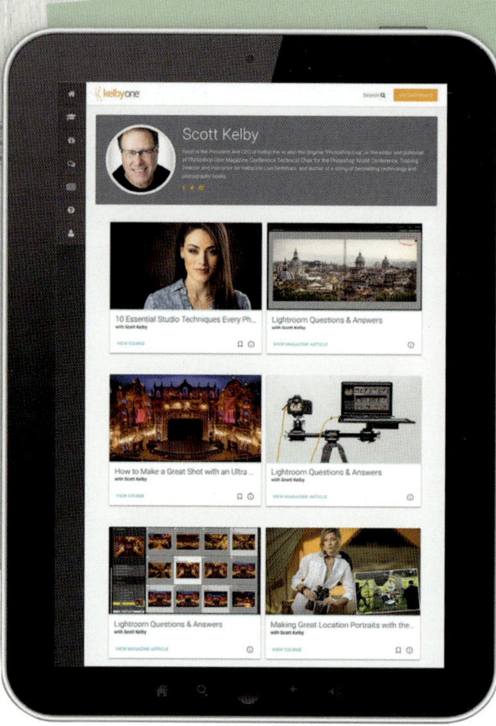

CONTINUE YOUR PHOTOGRAPHY TRAINING—ONLINE

with more courses
from Scott Kelby,
and other top instructors
in the industry

Why Become a KelbyOne Member?

Your annual membership gives you unlimited access to over 600 step-by-step full-length courses and over 10,000 topic-specific video lessons, wherever you are, whenever you want. We have exclusive classes and amazing instructors you won't find anywhere else and we release a new full-length online class almost every single week. Whatever your goals are, we have classes on every topic, and special tracks for beginner, intermediate and advanced users.

The Benefits of Membership

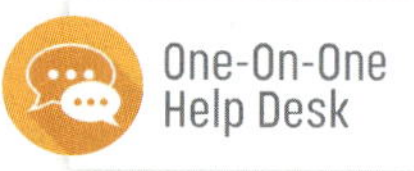
One-On-One Help Desk

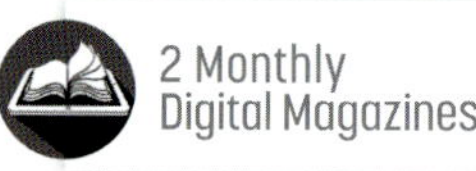
2 Monthly Digital Magazines

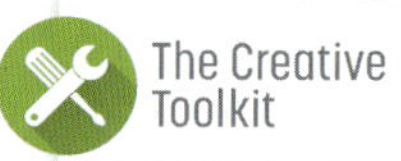
The Creative Toolkit

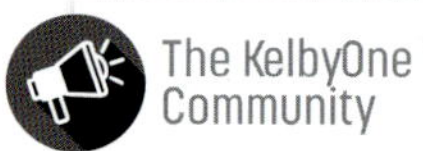
The KelbyOne Community

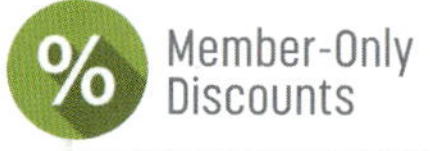
Member-Only Discounts

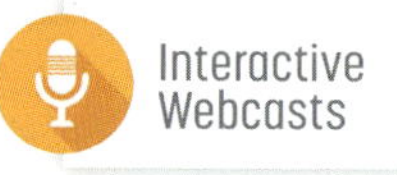
Interactive Webcasts

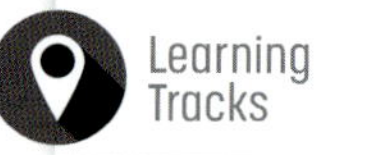
Learning Tracks

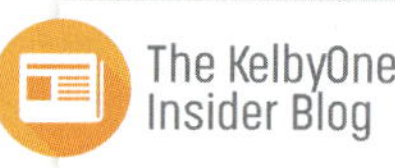
The KelbyOne Insider Blog

kelbyone | KELBYONE.COM | FACEBOOK.COM/KELBYONEONLINE | #KELBYONE